**Modernism
and Opera**

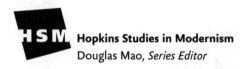

Hopkins Studies in Modernism
Douglas Mao, *Series Editor*

Modernism
and Opera

Edited by Richard Begam
and Matthew Wilson Smith

Johns Hopkins University Press
Baltimore

© 2016 Johns Hopkins University Press
All rights reserved. Published 2016
Printed in the United States of America on acid-free paper
9 8 7 6 5 4 3 2 1

Johns Hopkins University Press
2715 North Charles Street
Baltimore, Maryland 21218-4363
www.press.jhu.edu

Library of Congress Cataloging-in-Publication Data

Names: Begam, Richard, 1950- editor. | Smith, Matthew Wilson,
    editor.
Title: Modernism and opera / edited by Richard Begam and
    Matthew Wilson Smith.
Description: Baltimore : Johns Hopkins University Press, 2016. |
    Series: Hopkins studies in modernism | Includes bibliographical
    references and index.
Identifiers: LCCN 2015047645 | ISBN 9781421420622 (hardcover :
    alk. paper) | ISBN 9781421420639 (electronic) | ISBN 1421420627
    (hardcover : alk. paper) | ISBN 1421420635 (electronic)
Subjects: LCSH: Opera—20th century. | Modernism (Music)
Classification: LCC ML1705 .M63 2016 | DDC 782.109/04—dc23
    LC record available at http://lccn.loc.gov/2015047645

A catalog record for this book is available from the British Library.

*Special discounts are available for bulk purchases of this book. For
more information, please contact Special Sales at 410-516-6936 or
specialsales@press.jhu.edu.*

Johns Hopkins University Press uses environmentally friendly book
materials, including recycled text paper that is composed of at least
30 percent post-consumer waste, whenever possible.

In memory of our friend and fellow scholar
Daniel Albright
1945–2015

Contents

Acknowledgments

We would like to begin by thanking the contributors to this volume for their patience and good humor through all those proposals, drafts, revisions, further revisions, and editing deadlines. Their understanding and professionalism lightened our labors and reminded us of how fortunate we are to have such generous colleagues. We are also indebted to the anonymous reviewers of the manuscript who identified errors, made improving suggestions, and offered encouragement. At Johns Hopkins University Press, we wish especially to thank Douglas Mao, our series editor, whose attentive reading helped us further refine the manuscript, as well as Matt McAdam, acquisitions editor in Humanities and Literary Studies, Catherine Goldstead, senior editorial assistant, and freelancer Carrie Watterson, our splendid copy editor. We are also grateful to Michael Opest, Phillip Bandy, and Jessi Piggott who provided invaluable research and editorial assistance in the preparation of this volume. Finally, our most heartfelt thanks go to our wives, Christiaan Marie Hendrickson and Bernadette Meyler, who supported and sustained us as *Modernism and Opera* went from idea to book.

Earlier versions of chapters 1 and 7 appeared in *Modernist Cultures* 3.1 (2010), © Edinburgh University Press Limited, and are reproduced with permission of Edinburgh University Press Limited via PLSClear. Both essays were substantially revised for this book.

Modernism
and Opera

Introduction

Richard Begam and Matthew Wilson Smith

> But you, divine one, you resounding to the end.
> When attacked by the swarm of rejected maenads,
> gorgeous god, you drowned out their shrieks with order,
> the architecture of your song rose from the destroyers.
>
> Rilke, *The Sonnets to Orpheus*, 135

In opera, one always dies of the thing one loves. To love less than the impossible, less than that for which one cannot live, is not to love at all: the eternal return of this *Liebestod* is opera's Orphic mystery. Which is simply to say what every opera lover already knows—that opera is forever dying in hopes of being reborn, transformed.

The essayist Charles de Saint-Évremond was only one of the more eloquent in a long line of opera opponents when, around 1670, he dismissed the art as mere fancy and opined that "the fatigue" among opera spectators "is so universal, that everyone wishes himself out of the house."[1] Amid the Querelle des Bouffons—the "battle of the comic actors" that raged in 1750s Paris over the artistic merit of opera buffa—partisans cried murder on either side of the aisle, stirring resentments that had barely been extinguished before Gluck's *Iphigénie en Aulide* kindled another and yet fiercer conflagration. Skipping ahead to the beginnings of modernism, we may take Tolstoy as representative of a new guild of opera assassins when, after suffering through two acts of *Siegfried* in 1889, he complained, "I could stand no more of it, and escaped from the theatre with a feeling of repulsion which, even now, I cannot forget"—an evisceration of the work that forms the centerpiece of his aesthetics in *What Is Art?*[2] Tolstoy's sense of physical aversion is as integral to the operatic experience as is Nietzsche's shudder of nervous ecstasy, felt two decades earlier when he first heard the overtures to *Die*

Meistersinger and *Tristan und Isolde*: "Every fiber, every nerve in me twitches, and I have not had such a lasting feeling of reverie in a long time."[3] Nietzsche would later submit to opera's repetition compulsion and regurgitate his god "—*he has made music sick*—" while delivering an encomium to Bizet's tale of a corporal who destroys himself by murdering the gypsy he adores.[4]

Now if we agree that opera is, in Herbert Lindenberger's words, the "extravagant art," then its relation to modernism is vexed.[5] The flamboyance of the prima donna, the extraterrestrial bodies both vile and *wunderbar*, the blessed rage for ornament—every juicy trait captured by that adjective "operatic"—would appear to be the very antithesis of the cool formalism and streamlined geometry we so often associate with modernism. The operatic stage is a realm where function follows form more often than the other way around, and where avant-garde practices—twelve-tone composition, minimalist costuming, sets constructed entirely of light and shadow or else made shockingly au courant—tend to reify into mere gestures with peculiar rapidity. As quintessence of the theatrical, opera is "a prototype of precisely that which today is deeply shaken," according to Adorno in 1955, looking back on the previous eighty years or so of operatic innovation.[6] Modernist opera's bind, he concludes, is that "the genre cannot dispense with its appearance without surrendering itself, and yet it must want to do so."[7] In this sense, modernist opera shares a great deal with modernist fashion, another quasi-oxymoron in which modernism's tension between timeless myth and commodified ephemerality vibrates with peculiar force.

Admittedly, the idea of modernism as detached and abstracted—presided over by a God indifferently paring his fingernails—has been justifiably challenged in recent years. But even if we substantially qualify this view of the modern, for many it will seem incongruous to place the cerebral experimentalism of James Joyce or T. S. Eliot alongside the baroque theatricality of the musical stage. Then again, it's worth pointing out that both *Ulysses* and *The Waste Land* make repeated and revealing references to opera. Joyce's novel fairly bristles with quotations from Bellini, Bizet, Donizetti, Flotow, Lehar, Meyerbeer, Rossini, Verdi, and Wagner, and Molly Bloom—the novel's heroine and central focus—is herself a celebrated soprano. Critics have sometimes ignored Joyce's interest in opera, assuming it is nothing more than a foil to his modernism, a kind of musty Victorianism that serves to counterpoint his avant-gardism, yet the operatic material in *Ulysses* is integral to its plot and technique. Mozart's *Don Giovanni* and Flotow's *Martha* provide Joyce with crucial subtexts—subtexts that are inextricably linked to the novel's audaciously modernist "Sirens"—and Joyce's stream-of-consciousness technique is itself indebted to Édouard Dujardin's attempt (in *Les lauriers sont coupés*, 1887) to find a literary analogue to Wagner's use of leitmotif. Similarly, references in *The Waste Land* to Wagner's *Tristan und Isolde* may be dismissed as an overly lush Romanticism, meant to contrast with the sterility and desolation that otherwise dominate Eliot's modernist classic. But again, it should be remembered that the poem, with its vision of thwarted love, impotence, and wounds that unman, is a retelling not only of *Tristan und Isolde* but also—and perhaps more evocatively—of Wagner's *Parsifal*. In other words, opera does more than haunt these modernist masterpieces: it significantly and substantially determines their form and content.

The enthusiasm British modernists showed for opera is also richly attested to by the number of major writers—including E. M. Forster, W. H. Auden, Arnold Bennett, Robert Graves, and Stephen Spender—who penned libretti. Within an English context, this intersection of music and text is memorably represented by the collaboration of Edith Sitwell and William Walton on the musical recitation, *Façade*, which premiered in 1922, the same year *Ulysses* and *The Waste Land* were published. If we shift our focus to the Continent, the interest in collaborative work becomes even more remarkable. Obviously, the best-known example is the scandalous 1913 ballet, *Le sacre du printemps*, which featured music by Igor Stravinsky, sets by Nicholas Roerich, and choreography by Vaslav Nijinksy. This kind of cooperative artistic work was also evident in the 1917 ballet *Parade*, which brought together some of the greatest modernists of the period, including Erik Satie (music), Jean Cocteau (scenario), Pablo Picasso (set design), and Léonide Massine (choreography). Among the collaborative efforts in opera that followed are Oskar Kokoschka and Paul Hindemith's expressionist *Mörder, Hoffnung der Frauen* (1919), Jean Cocteau and Igor Stravinsky's neoclassical *Oedipus Rex* (1927), Bertolt Brecht and Kurt Weill's agitprop-influenced *Threepenny Opera* (1928) and *The Rise and Fall of the City of Mahagonny* (1931), and Guillaume Apollinaire and Francis Poulenc's surrealist *Les mamelles de Tirésias* (1947). This interest in working across the arts—indeed across the media of language, music, and visual representation—played a decisive role in the definition and development of modernism.

One of the larger assumptions behind this volume is that the intermediality that characterized so much of modernist praxis is most memorably realized in the synthetic genius of opera—in its ability to bring together the literary, dramatic, visual, and musical in a single aesthetic expression.[8] This impulse toward integrating—or at least coordinating—different artistic media, especially those that focus on words and music, is evident in the present collection in such pairings as Maurice Maeterlinck and Claude Debussy, Hugo Hofmannsthal and Richard Strauss, Georg Büchner and Alban Berg, Karel Čapek and Leoš Janáček, Gertrude Stein and Virgil Thomson, and Igor Stravinsky and W. H. Auden. At the same time, many of the chapters in this volume examine how artists, engaged by the problem of mimesis, challenged or redefined the limits of representation, whether by emphasizing consonances or dissonances among various artistic media. By studying the ways in which operatic theater of the past 120 years foregrounded collaboration across the arts, problematized formal integrity, and sought to transcend traditional modes of expression, we hope to understand more fully the aesthetic program that shaped both opera and modernism.

■ ■ ■

If opera is forever dying in the hope of being reborn, so too is modernism. As its etymology indicates (from the Latin *modo*, meaning "now"), modernism is committed to what is contemporary or happening in the moment, but the word's suffix temporally extends its root, suggesting a state of ongoing or continuous innovation, a sort of perpetual novelty that, like Wagnerian melody, never ends. The problem, of course, is in sustaining the newness of the new. For once modernism achieves the kind of stability necessary to give it definitional shape, once it acquires the weight of tradition and authority of a canon, it risks becoming just one more version of the status quo. Like Janáček's Emilia Marty or Wilde's Dorian Gray, modernism begins to resemble an anxious diva or dandy, forever worrying lest the mask of youthful vitality slip away, revealing that what lies beneath is that most unmodern of all things—the passé.

In recent years, the most influential effort to renew and revitalize modernism as a scholarly field has centered on the New Modernist Studies and its commitment to a more comprehensive canon, one that incorporates those elements of avant-garde and popular culture that, in the 1980s and 1990s, were often viewed as post- or antimodern. The program of the New Modernist Studies was most succinctly articulated by Douglas Mao and Rebecca Walkowitz in their well-known 2008 article of that title.[9] As Mao and Walkowitz put it, "Were one seeking a single word to sum up transformations in modernist literary scholarship over the past decade or two, one could do worse than light on *expansion*."[10] That expansion has moved along three axes. The temporal axis enlarged the historical scope of modernism beyond the "core period of about 1890-1945," reaching back to the middle of the nineteenth century and forward to the beginning of the present century.[11] The spatial axis extended the geographic reach of modernism to a genuinely international, indeed global, scale, no longer confining itself within the boundaries of a few national literatures, especially the Anglo-American tradition. Expansion along the vertical axis meant breaking down divisions, largely defined by Clement Greenberg and Theodor W. Adorno, between a "high" art associated with an austere formalism and a "low" art characterized by a "kitschy" sensationalism. Finally, we argue that the New Modernist Studies also developed along a fourth, horizontal axis, which we would add to Mao and Walkowitz's account.[12] In terms of subject matter, this axis encourages scholars to move *across the arts* in ways that, as we have seen, are especially congenial to a mixed-media form like opera.[13] In terms of approach, this axis involves precisely the kind of cross-disciplinary work that motivates this volume, work that not only brings together scholars from literature and music but that also utilizes research methods and protocols drawn from different disciplines.

With this last point in mind, we think it is also useful to contextualize the present work in terms of what has come to be known as the New Musicology. Interestingly, much of the New Musicology took its inspiration from changes that were already underway in literary studies. In what is often referred to as the article that launched the movement, "How We Got into Analysis, and How to Get Out," Joseph Kerman polemically draws a comparison between the formalism dominating musicology in 1980s and the earlier influence of New Criticism in literary studies: "One is reminded of the state of literary studies in the 1930s. Musical analysis has also reminded many observers of the New Criticism which arose at that time."[14] In "Adorno and the New Musicology," Rose Rosengard Subotnik similarly suggests that musicology look to literary studies as a guide, especially to developments in Marxism and poststructuralism: "At the fall 1990 Annual Meeting of the American Musicological Society, in Oakland, California, scholars of all leanings were hit by an unprecedent[ed]ly strong blast of the critical theory that had been altering the study of literature at American universities for two decades."[15] The New Musicologists (aside from Kerman and Subotnik, its best-known representatives include Carolyn Abbate, Lawrence Kramer, Susan McClary, and Gary Tomlinson) wanted not merely to reintroduce sociology to musical analysis but to introduce musical analysis to Continental theory. Figures such as Bakhtin, Derrida, Foucault, and Lacan—none of whom had been much of a presence in musicology before, say, 1990—became increasingly unavoidable.

As Subotnik suggests, New Musicology was to a certain degree simply catching up with movements that had already profoundly shaped literary studies. If there is a sense of belatedness to the movement, that sense is underscored by comparison with the New Modernist Studies, which takes the importance of critical theory more or less for granted while at times expressing impatience with the antiformalism of some recent sociologists of literature. One senses, with the decline of the shock of New Musicology and the advent of New Modernism, an abatement in the so-called theory wars. By the turn of the new century, after all, critical theory had become standard operating procedure in many departments across the humanities, shaping everything from scholarship to undergraduate teaching and even reaching into the sciences. In literary studies as in musicology, old battle lines between formalism and critical theory (to choose just one pair of names for the shifting and often ill-defined opposition) were coming to be seen not just as entrenched but as increasingly irrelevant, as the crucial fights were now being waged elsewhere, notably in deans' offices, where axes were falling on departmental budgets across the humanities. If there is a certain posttheoretical tenor to many of the chapters in this collection, the "post" should indicate not an exhaustion with theory—and some return to the good old business of just dealing with the (musical, linguistic) texts before us—but rather a sense that many of the insights of fin-de-XXe-siècle theory have been incorporated into our scholarly vocabulary.

Recalling Mao and Walkowitz's "axial" account of New Modernist Studies, we can trace a number of ways the chapters in this volume rechart the field. The interest in traversing the arts—the horizontal axis—is immediately evident in those chapters that examine the relation between score and libretto, which is to say between music and literature. Daniel Albright, for instance, argues that the impressionist Debussy finds his perfect vehicle in the symbolist Maeterlinck, revealing the kinds of transformations that occur when modernist opera straddles different movements as well as different arts. In using Adorno to examine Berg's musical adaptation of Büchner's drama, Bernadette Meyler explores how moving across artistic media also involves moving through time, producing a modernism that unfolds dialectically in relation to an antecedent tradition. Approaching modernism as a historical phenomenon is also crucial to Derek Katz's analysis of *The Makropulos Case* as both drama and opera. In 1922 Čapek's play seemed radically new, but its novelty had substantially faded by 1926 when Janáček adapted it to the operatic stage, resulting in two distinct conceptions of contemporaneity in Czech modernism. The movement of modernism from literature to music is further complicated in Cyrena N. Pondrom's account of *Four Saints in Three Acts*. Although Thomson worked closely with Stein on the opera, the minimalist and iterative structures that later characterized the contemporary opera of Philip Glass and John Adams are most evident in Stein's libretto, suggesting intriguing confluences between literature and music. The sense of the temporality of modernism is also evident in Herbert Lindenberger's account of Stravinsky's collaboration with W. H. Auden on *The Rake's Progress*. The neoclassicism that represents a point of arrival for Stravinsky—an evolution beyond an earlier phase of modernism—represents for Auden a point of departure.

What all of these cases illustrate is the extent to which modernism functions as a series of uneven temporalities in which movements as diverse as symbolism, impressionism, nationalism, minimalism, and neoclassicism crisscross each other, converging and diverging at various points, entering into conflict here and finding accommodation there. Such an approach—one that assumes a dynamic and ever-evolving modernism—is especially well suited to the broadened timeline of the New Modernist Studies (its temporal axis), and our historical purview therefore extends from the last third of the nineteenth century up to the twenty-first century. The volume's chronological organization into three sections (an emergent prewar modernism, a middle interwar modernism, and a late contemporary modernism) is meant to provide our study with conceptual structure and developmental coherence. Insofar as the operas we treat are in conversation with each other—and with parallel developments in theater, literature, and philosophy—we consider the historical approach we have taken both useful and justified. If Wagner "breaks the back of tonality" and provides a pushing-off point for much of modernist opera, it is important to situate him at the beginning of the volume. Debussy, Strauss, and Schoenberg all respond directly to Wagner; Berg's and Janáček's operas are inseparable from their historical situations; Thomson and Stein anticipated minimalist techniques that emerged after World War II; and the entire last section of the volume engages with issues related to aesthetic and institutional changes that took place in the second half of the twentieth century. At the same time, we recognize that there are chronological asymmetries and temporal disjunctions in our tripartite organization. Thus, although we have grouped together *Parsifal*, *Pel-*

léas et Mélisande, and *Bluebeard's Castle* as examples of opera from World War I and before, one could argue that Strauss stylistically shares more with Wagner than with Debussy or Bartók. *Wozzeck* (1925), *The Makropulos Case* (1926), *Moses und Aron* (1932), and *Four Saints in Three Acts* (1934) form a tidy interwar modernist grouping, yet the last act of Schoenberg's opera, in a gesture worthy of John Cage, abandons music altogether, while Stein and Thomson's minimalism arguably has more in common with Glass and Adams than with the operas of the 1920s and 1930s. Even the last section, devoted to late modernism, includes operas that are stylistically quite distinct. Stravinsky's pared-down neoclassicism stands in contrast to Britten's galliards and lavoltas, as does Messiaen's abstracted modernism in relation to Saariaho's textured lyricism. It is precisely this interplay of formal similitude and difference—evident within and across our three groupings—that enables these operas to achieve a set of loosely defined family resemblances within the matrix of a historically extended modernism.

Coverage is always a problem in any synoptic account of a large field, and inevitably omissions occur—as they have here—of both worthy composers and influential traditions. Within the limitations of Euromodernism, we have, however, sought to show that modernism produces points of intersection not only in time but also in space (the Mao-Walkowitz spatial axis). The German Wagner, who arguably stands as the father of modern opera, makes his presence felt almost everywhere, from France (Debussy and Messiaen), Hungary (Bartók) and Austria (Strauss, Schoenberg, and Berg) to Czechoslovakia (Janáček) and Finland (Saariaho). Belgian literature is translated into French music in *Pelléas et Mélisande,* the impact of Berg is registered in Prague in *The Makropulos Case,* Russia comes to England in *The Rake's Progress,* and Darmstadt modernism shapes French and Finnish music in *Saint François d'Assise* and *L'amour de loin.*

Where an earlier view of international modernism argued for its universalism by often overlooking or ignoring historical contexts, many of the chapters in this volume demonstrate how fully modernist opera engages with the topical and the political. The changing view of women in early modernism is the subject of two of the first three chapters. Matthew Wilson Smith examines Kundry, the principal female character of Wagner's *Parsifal,* in terms of an emerging psychoanalytic discourse on hysteria, while Klára Móricz investigates the transformation of women from symbols of redemptive power in the nineteenth century to demonic temptresses in the twentieth century. In a more explicitly political vein, Bryan Gilliam reads Strauss's

The Egyptian Helen and *Arabella* in terms of the collapse of the Austro-Hungarian Empire, Richard Begam examines Schoenberg's *Moses und Aron* as a response to the National Socialist attack on "degenerate art," and Irene Morra scrutinizes the difficulties that Britten encountered in *Gloriana* negotiating nationalist commitments and modernist aesthetics. Finally, if politics is of importance to Gilliam, Begam, and Morra, religion is the focus of Linda and Michael Hutcheon's engagement with Messiaen's *Saint François d'Assise*, which reveals how Catholic devotion finds expression in modernist form and technique.

We have contextualized some of the ways the New Modernist Studies and New Musicology have influenced our approach to opera, but of equal significance is recent scholarship, much of it revisionary, on modernism and theatricality. It is an overriding argument of this volume that taking opera seriously as a central aspect of modernism not only expands but also destabilizes our understanding of this elusive term. To better grasp how this destabilization functions and what it means, we must revisit the old question of modernism and theatricality.

■ ■ ■

The antipathy of many modern artists toward the theatrical is far more than just another instance of the well-worn antitheatrical prejudice famously charted by Jonas Barish; it is a tendency within, if not quite a criterion of, modernism itself, already visible in revolts against mid-nineteenth-century conventions of theatrical illusion as different as naturalism and symbolism. Indeed, as Martin Puchner has shown, modernism so often defined itself in opposition to the theater and theatricality that the very phrase "modernist theater" has at times come to seem nearly oxymoronic.[16] Yet what makes modernist antitheatricality especially slippery is the fact that the meaning of "theatricality" itself changed rapidly from the late nineteenth to the late twentieth century, yielding countergestures as diverse as Ibsen's unmasking of domestic masquerades and Pirandello's reintroduction of stage masks, Wagner's extinguishing the house lights at Bayreuth, and Brecht and Weill's use of agitprop placards in *The Rise and Fall of the City of Mahagonny*. Meanwhile, alongside these changes, certain age-old themes persisted: theatricality continued to be associated, as it has since Plato, with the inauthentic, the unserious, the vulgar, the feminine, degenerate, and queer. More troubling still is theater's dreadful dependence on the whims and conceits of a present audience: as anyone who has ever been involved in live performance knows, the theater artist relies upon a public not just for a work to be successful but for a work to be a work at all. In short, many modernists—playwrights such as Pirandello, Brecht, and Ionesco; composers such as Debussy, Berg, and Schoenberg—found in theatricality a form at once proximate and other, a form to be simultaneously drawn from, rejected, and reinvented. This persistence of modernist antitheatricality can be found across political, artistic, and national spectra, linking not only artists as different as Ibsen and Brecht but also theoreticians as opposed as Adorno and Greenberg.

Given their enormous influence as exemplars and interpreters of modernism, Adorno and Greenberg may be considered the principal theoretical architects of the modernist resistance to theater. Adorno's antitheatricality, fittingly inseparable from his championing of Berg and Beckett, can be found in its starkest form in his *In Search of Wagner* (written 1937–38, published 1952), with its fulsome attacks on Wagnerian gesture. The work borrows heavily from Nietzsche's fin-de-siècle assault on the theater (and Bayreuth above all) as "always only *beneath* art, always only something secondary, something made cruder, something twisted tendentiously, mendaciously, for the sake of the masses."[17] Like Nietzsche again, Adorno associates the theater and theatricality with mob mentality and manipulation, an association that shapes Adorno's myriad descriptions of mass-media audiences as gawkers and fetishists. It is this unyielding critique of mass culture —whether fascist or "pop"—together with the notion of theatricality as inimical to the modernist temperament, that binds together Adorno's aesthetic writings with those of Greenberg. In a characteristic passage of *Art and Culture* (1961), Greenberg writes that "a modernist work of art must try, in principle, to avoid dependence upon any order of experience not given in the most essentially construed nature of its medium. This means, among other things, renouncing illusion and explicitness. The arts are to achieve concreteness, 'purity,' by acting solely in terms of their separate and irreducible selves."[18]

The logic of Greenberg's aesthetics, whereby each art form strives to emancipate itself from the others in order to realize most fully what is peculiar and exclusive to it, is almost intrinsically hostile to a compound and collaborative art form such as the theater, to say nothing of the omnivorousness of opera. It is perhaps to be expected, then, that Greenberg's most influential student, Michael Fried, considers the theater antiartistic almost by definition; existing between art forms, the theater simply has no inherent qualities to be cultivated. When Fried concludes, in "Art and Objecthood" (1967), that the "success, even the survival, of the arts, has become increasingly to depend on their ability to defeat theatre," he speaks for a sort of cultural guardianship that came to define the institutions of Cold War modernism.[19] If Fried's essay represents a hardening, even a reification, of earlier modernist gestures, it also exemplifies a cultural attitude still not entirely past.

What might it mean, in the face of such positions, to speak of a truly *operatic modernism*, one that can neither be positioned with avant-garde performance (manifestos, actions, happenings, etc.) and thereby distinguished (as per Peter Bürger) from the stream of modernism nor condescended to as haute-bourgeois kitsch and thereby handed entirely over to sociological analysis and ideology critique? To answer this question, it might help to turn not to opera but to that foundational work of modern drama, Ibsen's *A Doll's House* (1879), and more specifically to the moment when Nora dances the tarantella—dances it to nervous chaos. According to Toril Moi, in her incisive analysis of the play, the dance is *both* an authentic expression of Nora *and* a theatrical objectification of her, without showing us which of the two possibilities we ought to choose:

> If we try, we find that either option entails a loss. Do we prefer a theatre of authenticity and sincerity? Do we believe that realism is such a theatre? Then we may be forgetting that even the most intense expressions of the body provide no certain way of telling authenticity from theatricality, truth from performance. Do we prefer a theatrical theatre, self-consciously performing and performative? If so, we may make ourselves deaf to the pain and distress of others by theatricalizing it. If I were asked whether I would call Nora's tarantella theatrical or absorbed, I would not quite know what to say. Both? Neither one nor the other?[20]

Moi locates Ibsen's modernism in precisely this undecidability, this "impossibility of either choosing or not choosing between theatricality and authenticity."[21] And it is in this same conflicted space that operatic modernism resides.

The space is a risky one, and not only in the sense that all art is potentially risky. The extravagant performance of one's own body entails the perennial danger of that most nightmarish of experiences: being laughed at. It's an ancient worry, one we find already expressed by old Cadmus in *The Bacchae*, as he hobbles out to dance in the Dionysian revels: "Won't folks say I ought to be ashamed, taking up dancing/ now that I'm so old, and putting ivy on my head?"[22] Among those who viewed modernism as an ascetic aesthetic cult, such shame was so unthinkable that even the risk-takers had to be exiled from the temple. It was not only Dionysus who must be dismissed; Cadmus too was suspect. The shamefulness of the theater, inseparable (as *The Bacchae* reminds us) from its destabilization of performances of gender and status—and inseparable as well from the theater artist's humiliating dependence upon that most fickle of masters, the public—this embarrassment is one that operas have played upon from *Parsifal* through *Four Saints in Three Acts*.

This desire to move beyond modernism's antitheatricality toward its rich vein of theatricality, and to do so without simply replacing one favored term with another, is shared by a number of recent scholars.[23] It is shared, too, by several authors in this volume. Daniel Albright, for example, discusses not only Debussy's debt to Maeterlinck's minimalist dramaturgy but also his (ambivalent) enthusiasm for Wagnerian Sturm und Drang, the "great nervous gasps, chromatic whirls in which the chroma varies from dark blue to black, the sound equivalent of van Gogh's *Starry Night*." Similarly, Herbert Lindenberger, who has previously written on the antitheatricality of much twentieth-century opera, here turns his attention to the vexed relation of Stravinsky and theatricality.[24] While fully conscious of the ways in which *The Rake's Progress* "asks its listeners to note the extreme artifice at the heart of the form," Lindenberger also notes that the work "is as overtly theatrical as any opera in the classic repertory." And Irene Morra, to take another instance, discusses the strong association of Elizabethanism with theatricality as well as the "celebration of theater as history and history as theater." From such chapters we discover that modernist opera may best be read not simply as theatrical or antitheatrical but as riven, often ostentatiously so, between the desire to estrange and the equally compelling desire to absorb and enchant. Rather than dubbing the former tendency modernist and the latter pre-, post-, or simply non-, we ought to learn to see in modernist opera precisely this vexation. In this way we might learn to find, too, a sort of authenticity that is not merely theatricality's antithesis.

If operatic modernism entails a kind of authenticity that is not theatricality's other, then what might it mean to speak of *modernist opera*? For when we choose to take both terms of "modernist opera" seriously, a different modernism emerges and a different opera too. In his enlightening essay "The Politics and Aesthetics of Operatic Modernism," Michael Steinberg argues that to view modernism's relation to history as one of mere rejection and wholesale reinvention is to miss the repetition within modernist differ-

ence. For Debussy, for Schoenberg, for Janáček, for Thomson, the injunc-
tion to "make it new" never meant to create ex nihilo but to rebuild (even if
from the ground up) largely with existing materials. "Modernism's drive for
freedom did not entail a disavowal of history so much as distance from the
reactionary aspects of history," Steinberg writes.[25] While the claim is perhaps too broadly stated, in that it would seem almost to rule out by definition what Jeffrey Herf has dubbed "reactionary modernism," Steinberg discovers in modernist *opera* in particular little alliance with fascism. Despite
Strauss's ambiguous relation to the Nazi regime, there are no Knut Hamsuns
or Filippo Marinettis in the world of modernist opera composers. While
many German opera composers fled (Schoenberg, Hindemith, Korngold),
many Italians went into something like internal exile (Pietro Mascagni, Fran-
cesco Cilea, Riccardo Zandonai), and few if any modernist opera composers
anywhere were determined collaborationists.[26]

The resistance to, or at least distance from, fascism is linked, in Steinberg's view, to modernist opera's basic cosmopolitanism. Modernist opera
was essentially "European, international, and emancipatory where its leading historical and political referents are German, nationalistic, and hege-
monic."[27] The crucial turn is the one from Wagner to Strauss, with the former seen as (in the main, and by the time of his death) nationalistic while
the latter is viewed as (again, in the main) postnationalist, with *Salome* and
Elektra allied in a mutual disinterest in nationalist mythmaking. In this respect Hans Pfitzner's *Palestrina*, with its call for a return to national and artistic "roots," stands as a paradigmatic antimodernist opera.

The chapters in this volume to some degree support and to some degree
complicate Steinberg's claim of the genre's postnationalism. Bryan Gilliam
argues that Strauss's *The Egyptian Helen* and *Arabella*—written in part as a
response to Wagner—gave expression to the idea of a unified Europe in
which East and West would come together in an allegorical marriage of na-
tions. Derek Katz, meanwhile, distinguishes between the modernism of
Karel Čapek's drama *The Makropulos Case*, which was inseparable from a
broader Czech movement of National Revival, and the modernism of Leoš
Janáček's opera version, which arose during a more cosmopolitan moment
of Czech modernism. The chapter adds some weight as well as some nuance
to Steinberg's internationalist thesis, as indeed does Linda and Michael
Hutcheon's consideration of both the internationalist and the distinctively
French elements of Olivier Messiaen's *St. François d'Assise*. Of all the works

considered in depth in this volume, only Benjamin Britten's *Gloriana* would seem to work against the grain of postnational modernism, and it is this peculiar quality of the opera that Irene Morra attends to here.

■ ■ ■

Part 1 of this volume, "World War I and Before: Crises of Gender and Theatricality," takes as its point of departure Richard Wagner, whose revolutions in composition and staging—famously described by him as *Zukunftsmusik*, or the "music of the future"—laid the foundation for what would become modernist opera, while inspiring composers like Debussy and Bartók.[28] Reflecting social and aesthetic transformations occurring at the end of the nineteenth and the beginning of the twentieth century, this section highlights changing ideas of gender and theatricality. Age-old associations among theatricality, hysteria, and "woman" have been central to the (mistaken) conception of modernism as detached, cerebral, and masculine. The chapters in this section problematize this conception by showing that ideas of the feminine and the theatrical were sharply contested sites in which an emerging modernism struggled with its own self-definition.

Matthew Wilson Smith's "Laughing at the Redeemer: Kundry and the Paradox of *Parsifal*" deals with the figure of the woman as a harbinger of modernism while relating her to Wagnerian innovations in staging. Smith notes that the period between the writing of the libretto (1877) and the premiere of the opera coincides with the medicalization of hysteria brought about by Jean-Martin Charcot's research at the Salpêtrière, which Sigmund Freud attended in the mid-1880s. Related to the opera's interest in hysteria and selfhood is a developing crisis of representation in the late nineteenth-century theater that pointed in two directions: toward a symbolism that subordinated matter to spirit and toward a naturalism that subordinated spirit to matter. Wagner's interest in creating an "invisible theater" (burying the orchestra beneath the stage, extinguishing house lighting, etc.) is connected to his desire to transcend materiality. But as Smith observes, the character of Kundry haunts the opera not only as woman but also as the specter of corporeal theatricality. She represents both a disruptive eroticism, which must be suppressed, and an incipient modernism that keeps breaking out of Wagner's nineteenth-century costume drama, expressing itself in that most transgressive of all forms—laughter.

Daniel Albright also deals with issues of theatricality and Wagnerianism in his chapter on Debussy's *Pelléas et Mélisande* (1902), often regarded as the first fully modernist opera. Debussy's source was the drama of the same title by the Belgian playwright, Maurice Maeterlinck, usually associated with the symbolist movement. Albright shows, however, that Maeterlinck brought a high degree of irony and self-consciousness to his stage productions. Indeed, many of his plays bear a striking resemblance to the work of that most antidramatic of twentieth-century dramatists, Samuel Beckett. What results is a theater that tends to cancel out its own theatricality—plays with plot designs and symbolic structures that deliberately undermine themselves. Debussy was also uncannily sympathetic to Maeterlinck's aesthetic, so that the "first" modernist opera in a certain sense looks like what we might imagine as the last: a Beckettian work of shadowy vignettes with half-formed characters uttering half-formed thoughts in timeless, placeless settings. Debussy finds the musical equivalent to this dramatic aesthetic in what Albright calls the *Verleitmotiv*, a leitmotif that effectively undoes itself. Albright concludes by showing—in ways that look back to Smith's chapter— the debt *Pelléas et Mélisande* owes to Wagner's *Parsifal*.

Klára Móricz rounds out this section with "Echoes of the Self: Cosmic Loneliness in Bartók's *Duke Bluebeard's Castle*," which analyzes the figure of the woman alongside a modernist sense of isolation and anomie in Béla Bartók's opera, composed in 1911 and staged in 1918. Comparing Bartók's work with Schubert's "Der Doppelgänger," Móricz shows how love—a redeeming force in nineteenth-century art—becomes in the twentieth century the means of the protagonist's mental destruction. In Bartók's opera, the failure of redemption through love is depicted as a wedding night that ends with the cosmic loneliness of the male protagonist. *Bluebeard* is only one in a long list of artworks that exemplify turn-of-the-century paranoia concerning women. What distinguishes the opera from other misogynistic works is that Bartók casts the male protagonist, and not the woman Judith, as living in harmony with nature. In *Bluebeard*, man's spirituality finds its nourishing environment within the secure enclosure of his castle, a world into which light cannot penetrate without shattering identity into painful and fragmentary memories. Self-knowledge in Schubert's "Doppelgänger" brings temporary relief, but in *Bluebeard* the revelation of the protagonist's soul, facilitated by Judith, renders the darkness of the castle more impenetrable and man's solitude more inescapable.

Part 2, "Interwar Modernism: Movement and Countermovement," traces modernist opera from the lush harmonics of Strauss's *The Egyptian Helen* and *Arabella* to the one of its sparest articulations in Stein and Thomson's *Four Saints in Three Acts* in the 1930s. If Wagner's *Zukunftsmusik* marks the

first shudderings of musical modernism, this section examines how in the
wake of World War I composers attempted to move beyond Wagner as
modernist opera sought to consolidate itself. Among the issues discussed
here are modernism's relation to history and tradition, the politics of nationalism and postnationalism, the philosophy and aesthetics of "degenerate
art," and an emergent musical minimalism that looks forward to post-World
War II opera. As this tally of issues shows, the interwar modernism of the
1920s and 1930s was far from unitary in either its preoccupations or its
techniques. Indeed, the composers under discussion in this section explored varied and conflicting modes of musical expression and dramatization, aligning themselves with movements as divergent as expressionism,
symbolism, naturalism, serialism, abstractionism, and minimalism. While
World War I was a catalyzing event and while Wagner was increasingly a point
of negative reference—especially for composers in the Austro-German world
—the modernism of this period was dynamic and ever shifting, as it struggled toward a sense of what it meant to be "new."

    As Bryan Gilliam shows in "The Great War and Its Aftermath: Strauss and
Hofmannsthal's 'Third-Way Modernism,'" World War I marked a turning
point for Straussian opera. *Die Frau ohne Schatten* (1918)—arguably Strauss
and Hofmannsthal's grandest creation—was conceived in peacetime, composed during war, and premiered just months after the Treaty of Versailles.
Vowing that future works would be stripped of their "Wagnerian musical
armor," Strauss developed a "third way" in modernism, a musical idiom that
rejected the metaphysics and idealism of Wagner but that retained its tonal
language—now leavened with irony and pastiche. But if the turn away from
Wagner was crucial to the development of a more modern opera, so too
was Austro-Germany's defeat in the Great War and the end of the Austro-
Hungarian Empire. The latter especially traumatized Hofmannsthal, who
wrote numerous essays envisioning a "United States of Europe" where East
and West would be reunited in Vienna. The vision of a postnational Europe
was the covert message of two operas Strauss and Hofmannsthal wrote in
the late 1920s: *The Egyptian Helen* (1928) and *Arabella* (1929/33). While both
operas focus on issues of love and marriage, the central characters represent countries (Greece and Troy, Austria and Croatia), and their possible
unions symbolize the resolution of conflict and the promise of peaceful
coexistence. Especially important is the positive focus on marriage in these
works, which represents a rejection of the romanticism of Wagnerian love.
In both *The Egyptian Helen* and *Arabella*, redemption comes not from a

Liebestod that overwhelms and annihilates but from the dedication and patience of two marriage partners working together.

Like Albright, Bernadette Meyler takes up the musical adaptation of a dramatic work, in this case Alban Berg's response to Georg Büchner's *Woyzeck*, in "Adorno's Shifting *Wozzeck*." Meyler's chapter discusses Berg's opera—and its effort to "rescue" or "salvage" (*retten*) Büchner's fragmentary work—in relation to the philosophies of history articulated by both Adorno and his fellow Frankfurt school critic, Walter Benjamin, another admirer of *Wozzeck*. In doing so, Meyler scrutinizes how Berg specifically conceived of his modernism in historical terms—that is, in relation to a past that is both retrieved and effaced. Much more than the works of his contemporaries Schoenberg and Webern, Berg's music seems to recall the language of the nineteenth century, but its modernity consists precisely in the quality of its relation to that earlier material, a relation neither of imitation nor of nostalgia. In the "posthumous court of appeals" of Berg's opera, doing justice to Büchner's tragedy entails ripping the work from its historical context while simultaneously introducing a moment of temporal disjunction into the twentieth-century modernist movement itself.

In chapter 6, Derek Katz contextualizes yet another operatic rewriting of a famous dramatic work, this time within the horizon of Czech modernism. "Many Modernisms, Two Makropulos Cases: Čapek, Janáček, and the Shifting Avant-Gardes of Interwar Prague" takes as its subject Leoš Janáček's 1926 opera *Věc Makropulos* (*The Makropulos Case*) and Karel Čapek's 1922 play of the same title. These two works represent telling instances of the ways in which an emergent nationalism and an emergent modernism were intertwined in Czech culture in the late nineteenth and early twentieth centuries. Čapek briefly benefitted from a cultural moment in which to be Czech—that is, to assert one's national identity—was a substantial component of being modern. In less than a decade, however, this moment would pass, as a younger generation matured, which took the completion of the National Revival for granted and aligned itself more with Soviet culture and international modernism than with a parochial nationalism. By examining Čapek and Janáček's versions of *The Makropulos Case* alongside each other, we see how Czech modernism—like so many other national modernisms—functioned as a series of currents and countercurrents, in which different schools and movements (nationalism, avant-gardism, Marxism) staked competing claims and contested disputed ground.

Like Katz's chapter, Richard Begam's "Schoenberg, Modernism, and De-

generacy" historically contextualizes modernism, interpreting Arnold Schoenberg's *Moses und Aron* (1932) as a response to the National Socialist polemic
against *entartete Musik*, or "degenerate music." As a matter of polemical
provocation, Schoenberg accepts the Nazi identification of modernism with
Judaism, treating the Decalogue's prohibition against graven images as the
beginning of an abstract aesthetic. But Schoenberg reverses the Nazi argument, contending that degeneracy in art—especially a degeneracy that promotes the "primitivism" and "atavism" the Nazis deplored—results not from
the rejection of mimesis but from its idolatrous worship, as the episode of
the golden calf so vividly illustrates. The principal conflict of the opera
centers on a debate between Moses and Aaron on the status of representation, but Schoenberg aligns himself with neither of his title characters.
Moses' commitment to abstraction is so uncompromising that it ultimately
leads to the end of music, as exemplified by Moses' use of *Sprechstimme* and
an unscored third act. However, while Aaron better understands the contingency of representation than does his brother, Schoenberg is equally critical
of Aaron's penchant for conjuring up images that that are dangerously incarnational. What Schoenberg seeks and his opera delivers is a compromise
between Moses' rigorous abstractionism and Aaron's seductive pictorialism.

In "Gertrude Stein, Minimalism, and Modern Opera," Cyrena N. Pondrom
takes an intermedial approach to Gertrude Stein and Virgil Thomson's *Four
Saints in Three Acts* (1934). Looking ahead to the next section of this book,
she considers Stein's impact not only on Thomson but also on post-1950s
musical minimalism, especially operas like Philip Glass and Robert Wilson's
Einstein on the Beach (1976) and John Adams's *Nixon in China* (1987). Focusing on formal features like repetition, hammering rhythms, phased language, and use of the vernacular, Pondrom documents the direct influence
Stein had on Thomson and later on John Cage, both of whom first encountered her work when they were students. Cage would in turn later influence
La Monte Young and Terry Riley, who, along with Steve Reich and Philip
Glass, helped pioneer American minimalism. In addition to her influence on
music, Stein also helped to shape the narrative construction of minimalist
opera, which often organizes itself more around a series of tableaux or images than around a sequence of events. Glass and Wilson have explicitly
acknowledged Stein's importance for their work, with Wilson expressing
his special appreciation of Stein's notion of plays as "landscapes" rather than
traditional, plot-driven stories.

Part 3, "Opera after World War II: Tensions of Institutional Modernism,"

examines how, in the second half of the twentieth century, modernist practices of musical composition and opera production became increasingly
standardized, subsidized, and institutionalized. Postwar modernism generated its own internal tensions, several of which are discussed in the four
concluding chapters. Herbert Lindenberger explores how Auden and Stravinsky responded to their situation as belated modernists in *The Rake's Progress*;
Irene Morra analyzes the conflict between British nationalism and British
modernism in Benjamin Britten's *Gloriana*; Linda and Michael Hutcheon discuss Olivier Messiaen's attempt to reinvent modernist aesthetics as a call to
recover religious orthodoxy in *Saint François d'Assise*; and Joy H. Calico examines Kaija Saariaho's recovery and transformation of tonality in *L'amour
de loin*. Belatedness, nationalism, orthodoxy, tonality: these are elements
not often associated with modernism, though hardly ever quite absent from
it. In the latter half of the twentieth century, as this section shows, they
return with a vengeance.

Like Pondrom, Herbert Lindenberger takes up the issue of a poet and
composer working across the arts in "Stravinsky, Auden, and the Midcentury Modernism of *The Rake's Progress*." Auden, a generation younger than
Stravinsky, first emerged as a poet in the wake of the radical innovations of
Pound and Eliot. Stravinsky, by contrast, was often regarded as one of the
founders of musical modernism, at least outside the German-speaking
world, and to maintain his avant-garde credentials he recreated himself several times during his long career. His neoclassical period, which culminates
in *The Rake's Progress* (1951), represents not only a single but also a central
stage in his own progress. By the time that Auden, together with his partner,
Chester Kallman, worked with Stravinsky on the opera, his style had assumed a new direction: although still employing traditional forms, it had
become more self-consciously literary and less politically committed. The
opera on which these two men collaborated so successfully occupies a
unique moment in the history of modernism, one in which two figures representing distinct phases in the development of their particular art forms
allow their aesthetic programs to coincide. Lindenberger's chapter shows
how Stravinsky and Auden both express themselves in the opera and helped
to define midcentury modernism and its commitments with their formalism, irony, and engagement with earlier styles.

In "*Gloriana* and the New Elizabethan Age," Irene Morra investigates another midcentury response to high modernism, Benjamin Britten's *Gloriana*
(1953), commissioned by the British Arts Council in honor of the corona-

tion of Elizabeth II. Conceived as a nationalist celebration, the opera's libretto was written by William Plomer, who adapted the story of Elizabeth and Essex from Lytton Strachey's novelistic history of that title. By the early 1950s Britten had earned a reputation not only as a modernist composer but also as a distinctly English composer, one who had helped rejuvenate the opera of his country and brought it to prominence in the twentieth century. This produced a set of mixed expectations, with some assuming that *Gloriana* would pay tribute to a nationalist narrative rooted in imperial models, while others anticipated a more modern treatment of the subject in keeping with the contemporary realities of postwar England. Such a clash of ideas is present in the opera itself, with its conflicting idealizations of nationalist sentiment and modern musical and literary culture. The opera is further complicated by the relationship between a libretto and a score that attempt at once to be self-consciously up to date and to conform to models of Englishness for which there was very little operatic precedent—and no future.

While Morra looks back to debates on nationalism and modernism in late nineteenth-century opera, Linda and Michael Hutcheon's "One Saint in Eight Tableaux: The Untimely Modernism of Olivier Messiaen's *Saint François d'Assise*" reconsiders many of the modernist themes and forms already encountered in this volume, including Debussy's impressionism, Schoenberg's atonality, Stravinsky's neoclassicism, and the ecclesiastical subject matter of Stein and Thomson. The first major musical influence on Messiaen was Claude Debussy, the father of French musical modernism, and although Messiaen was for a time part of the Darmstadt summer music school (1949-50), he would soon break from it and go his own way. A devout Catholic, Messiaen regarded birds as the greatest musicians, and out of this belief comes much of his most innovative work, including *St. François d'Assise* (1983). The opera represents, in religious terms, the modernist search for the means to suspend time within a temporal medium. As an opera composer, Messiaen had to deal with a narrative staged in time, but he worked to transcend it in ways that recall symbolist attempts to do the same. The eight tableaux that constitute the opera are relatively static as scenic and sonic "pictures," with a libretto that is repetitive both in actions and words. Such techniques of stasis recall Albright's comparison of the temporality of *Pelléas et Mélisande* with that of Beckett, as well as Pondrom's analysis of the protominimalism of *Four Saints in Three Acts*.

The last chapter of the volume brings us to the contemporary moment with Joy H. Calico's "Saariaho's *L'amour de loin*: Modernist Opera in the

Twenty-First Century." Directly inspired by Messiaen's *Saint François d'Assise* and bearing strong affinities to Debussy's *Pelléas et Mélisande*, *L'amour de loin* (2000) joins the beginning of the century to its end. Calico draws upon David Metzer's idea of late modernism in examining Saariaho, whose training in modernist composition included study with Paavo Heininen at the Sibelius Academy, Darmstadt summer courses, and time at Pierre Boulez's IRCAM in Paris in 1982, where she became interested in spectralism as an alternative to serialism.[29] For Metzer, spectralism is connected to the modernist interest in flux of sound, with its emphasis on timbre, and it is in these terms that Calico analyzes the opera. But if Saariaho's music is late modernist in its acoustic texturing and tonal coloring, it is also deliberately operatic in its commitment to emotional evocation and communication. Each of the three principal characters is associated with recurring musical features, and dramatic expressivity is achieved through harmonic and melodic devices that function in concert with a soundscape of ever-shifting timbres. Calico concludes with a brief discussion of Peter Sellars's production of *L'amour de loin*, which employed the same static staging that attracted Saariaho to *Saint François d'Assise* and persuaded her to bring her own brand of modernism to the operatic stage.

■ ■ ■

CLOV (*turning towards Hamm*): One hasn't the right to sing anymore?
HAMM: No.
CLOV: Then how can it end?
HAMM: You want it to end?
CLOV: I want to sing.
HAMM: I can't prevent you.
Beckett, *Endgame*, 72-73

The chapters in this volume survey approximately 120 years of opera, from Wagner's *Parsifal* (1882) to Saariaho's *L'amour de loin* (2000), viewing it in relation to various modes and manifestations of modernism. Yet as robust, as varied, and as innovative as the opera of this period has been, anxieties persist that the end is nigh. From the nineteenth century through the interwar period, opera played a far more central role in the social life of major European cities than it does today—and its fall from prominence was such that Richard Taruskin has gone so far as to declare that operatic culture was "effectively killed" by the 1930s.[30] Economic depression, dictatorship, and war all played their parts, of course, but why did opera (unlike, say, theater) not rebound? For Taruskin, the chief culprit was the talkies—"which were really singies, with or without songs." With the masses now discovering their divas at movie palaces, opera aficionados became an increasingly rare and preening breed. Opera continued to shuffle consumptively along, according to Taruskin, but it had lost its high notes. Dying once more, it fell into the arms of its last, lonely lovers.

To be again reborn? As the last section of this volume demonstrates, some of the richest works of the operatic repertoire emerged after the Second World War. By the 1970s, the United States, generally an importer rather than an exporter of new opera, was yielding a bumper crop. The renaissance began, fittingly, in the bicentennial year of 1976, with Philip Glass's *Einstein on the Beach*, to be followed by the other two-thirds of his Portrait Trilogy (*Satyagraha* [1979] and *Akhnaten* [1983]), as well as John Adams's duet of collaborations with the librettist Alice Goodman (*Nixon in China* [1987] and *The Death of Klinghoffer* [1991])—to say nothing of the rock-opera performances of Lori Anderson, Lou Reed, John Zorn, and Diamanda Galás, or the operatic musicals of Stephen Sondheim. As the twenty-first century advances, other formerly provincial zones continue to make themselves central. While Saariaho, for example, may live and work primarily in Paris, her native Finland has experienced an opera boom since the rejuvenation of the Savonlinna Opera Festival in 1967. The nation now boasts at least five prominent opera composers (Aulis Sallinen, Atso Almila, Ilkka Kuusisto, Kalevi Aho, and of course Saariaho herself) as well as numerous emerging talents (such as Kimmo Hakola, Olli Kortekangas, and Tuomas Kantelinen). Turning toward the East, we find new opera blossoming in China. The Chinese premiere of Zhou Long's *Madame White Snake* and the world premiere of Ye Xiaogang's *Song of Farewell* both occurred during the same week at the Beijing Music Festival in 2010, as did an avant-garde production of Handel's *Semele* directed by performance artist Zhang Huan. That year also saw the establishment of the Academy of Opera at Peking University, with the first Chinese Opera Festival following in 2011. Most recently, British opera has resurfaced in the shape of George Benjamin and Martin Crimp's extraordinary *Written on Skin* (2012). And alongside such national resurgences must be placed a more emphatically international one: the explosion of the digital simulcast as a potent medium of opera's global dispersion. The Metropolitan Opera's Live in HD series, which began in December 2006, had sold more than ten million tickets by April 2012, at which point it was beaming opera simulcasts to roughly 1,500 movie screens worldwide. These simulcasts—along with the yet larger market of CDs, DVDs, and streaming media productions—have produced an audience for opera that is more global than it has ever been. What opera has lost in cultural centrality, at least for parts of Europe, it seems to be gaining in breadth and hybridity.

As the following chapters show, the love duet between modernism and opera has been a dissonant as well as a harmonious affair. Will opera continue dying? Of course it will.

Notes

1. See Saint-Évremond.
2. Tolstoy 119.
3. Nietzsche, *Briefwechsel* 77. Letter dated October 28, 1868.
4. Nietzsche, *Birth of Tragedy* 164.
5. See Lindenberger, *Opera*.
6. Adorno 25.
7. Ibid. 27.
8. For a discussion of intermediality, see Wolf.
9. See Mao and Walkowitz, "The New Modernist Studies." Mao and Walkowitz offer an earlier account of the New Modernist Studies in their introduction to *Bad Modernisms*.
10. Ibid. 737.
11. Ibid. 738.
12. One sees evidence of this horizontal axis both in the journal *Modernism/modernity*, which has published numerous articles that are intermedial and interdisciplinary, and in the annual Modernist Studies Association conference. Indeed, this volume had its beginnings as a session at MSA entitled "Modernism and Opera."
13. For excellent examples of this kind of scholarship, see Albright's *Untwisting the Serpent, Panaesthetics,* and *Putting Modernism Together.*
14. Kerman himself acknowledges that the "analogy" with New Criticism "is not one that will survive much scrutiny," but he defends it on the grounds that it does "point to one of the constants in intellectual life as this applies to the arts: as intellectual stimulus, positivistic history is always at a disadvantage beside criticism" (319).
15. Subotnik 234-35. Stanley Rosen also evoked literary studies in describing, from a decidedly more detached perspective, the practitioners of the New Musicology who "deplore the pretended autonomy of traditional musicological studies and present an explicit program of bringing the subject into contact with social science, political history, gay studies, and feminism . . . to transform musicology into a field as up-to-date as recent literary criticism"; see "The New Musicology" in Rosen 255-56.

16. See Puchner, *Stage Fright.*
17. Nietzsche, *Case of Wagner* 182–83.
18. Greenberg 139.
19. Fried 139.
20. Moi 271–72.
21. Ibid. 272.
22. Euripides 9.
23. Recent scholarship in this direction is various and rich. See, for instance, Anderson; Miller; Preston; and Marcus.
24. See Lindenberger, "Anti-theatricality in Twentieth-Century Opera."
25. See Steinberg.
26. Ibid. 636.
27. Ibid. 631–32.
28. See Wagner.
29. IRCAM stands for Institut de Recherche et Coordination Acoustique/Musique.
30. Taruskin 548.

Bibliography

Adorno, Theodor W. "Bourgeois Opera." *Opera through Other Eyes.* Ed. David J. Levin Stanford: Stanford University Press, 1993. 25–43.

Albright, Daniel. *Panaesthetics: On the Unity and Diversity of the Arts.* New Haven: Yale University Press, 2014.

———. *Putting Modernism Together: Literature, Music and Painting, 1872-1927.* Baltimore: Johns Hopkins University Press, 2015.

———. *Untwisting the Serpent: Modernism in Music, Literature and the Other Arts.* Chicago: University of Chicago Press, 2000.

Anderson, Mark. *Kafka's Clothes: Ornament and Aestheticism in the Hapsburg Fin-de-Siècle.* Oxford: Oxford University Press, 1992.

Beckett, Samuel. *Endgame* and *Acts without Words.* New York: Grove Press, 1958.

Euripides. *The Bacchae.* Trans. Paul Woodruff. Cambridge: Hackett, 1999.

Fried, Michael. "Art and Objecthood." *Artforum* (June 1967): 116–48.

Gibson, Nigel, and Andrew Rubin, eds. *Adorno: A Critical Reader.* Oxford: Blackwell, 2002.

Greenberg, Clement. *Art and Culture.* Boston: Beacon Press, 1961

Kerman, Joseph. "How We Got into Analysis, and How to Get Out." *Critical Inquiry* 7.2 (1980): 311–31.

Lindenberger, Herbert. "Anti-theatricality in Twentieth-Century Opera." *Modern Drama* 44.3 (2011): 300–17.

———. *Opera: The Extravagant Art.* Ithaca: Cornell University Press, 1984.

Mao, Douglas, and Rebecca Walkowitz, eds. *Bad Modernisms.* Durham: Duke University Press, 2006.

——. "The New Modernist Studies." *PMLA* 123.3 (2008): 737–48.

Marcus, Sharon. "Salomé!! Sarah Bernhardt, Oscar Wilde, and the Drama of Celebrity." *PMLA* 126.4 (2011): 999–1021.

Miller, Monica L. *Slaves to Fashion: Black Dandyism and the Styling of Black Diasporic Identity*. Durham, NC: Duke University Press, 2009.

Moi, Toril. "'First and Foremost a Human Being': Idealism, Theatre, and Gender in *A Doll's House*." *Modern Drama* 49.3 (Fall 2006): 256–84.

Nietzsche, Friedrich. *The Birth of Tragedy* and *The Case of Wagner*. Trans. and ed. Walter Kaufmann. New York: Vintage, 1967.

——. *Briefwechsel mit Erwin Rohde*. Vol. 2. Leipzig: Insel-Verlag, 1903.

Preston, Carrie. *Modernism's Mythic Pose: Gender, Genre, Solo Performance*. Oxford: Oxford University Press, 2011.

Puchner, Martin. *Poetry of the Revolution: Marx, Manifestos, and the Avant-Gardes*. Princeton: Princeton University Press, 2006.

——. *Stage Fright: Modernism, Anti-theatricality and Drama*. Baltimore: Johns Hopkins University Press, 2002.

Rilke, Rainer Maria. *Duino Elegies* and *The Sonnets to Orpheus*. Trans. A. Poulin Jr. Boston: Houghton Mifflin, 1977.

Rosen, Stanley. *Critical Entertainments: Music Old and New*. Cambridge, MA: Harvard University Press, 2000.

Saint-Évremond, Charles de. "Saint-Évremond's Views on Opera." *Opera: A History in Documents*. Ed. Piero Weiss. Oxford: Oxford University Press, 2002. 51–59.

Steinberg, Michael. "The Politics and Aesthetics of Operatic Modernism." *Journal of Interdisciplinary History* 36.4 (Spring 2006): 629–48.

Subotnik, Rose. "Adorno and the New Musicology." *Adorno: A Critical Reader*. Ed. Nigel Gibson and Andrew Rubin. Oxford: Blackwell, 2002. 234–54.

Taruskin, Richard. *The Oxford History of Music*. Vol. 4. Oxford: Oxford University Press, 2005.

Tolstoy, Leo. *What Is Art?* Trans. Aylmer Maude. New York: Crowell, 1899.

Wagner, Richard. "Zukunftsmusik." *Judaism in Music and Other Essays*. Trans. William Ashton Ellis. Lincoln: University of Nebraska Press, 1995. 293–345.

Wolf, Werner. "Towards a Functional Analysis of Intermediality: The Case of Twentieth-Century Musicalized Fiction." *Cultural Functions of Intermedial Exploration*. Ed. Erik Hedling and Ulla-Britta Lagerroth. Amsterdam: Rodopi Press, 2002. 15–34.

1 World War I and Before

Crises of Gender and Theatricality

1 Laughing at the Redeemer
Kundry and the Paradox of *Parsifal*

Matthew Wilson Smith

> "People will say," [Wagner] remarks jokingly, "that if Amfortas had seen the vision of the Grail and heard the lament, he could have carried out the task of salvation as well as Parsifal!" "But just as a professional task," say I, "and if Parsifal had listened to Kundry, then she would have laughed, and then everything would have been all right, too!"—Lengthy discussion about this new miracle.
>
> Cosima Wagner (2:215/2:186)

Opera's Human Comedy

"I have big hips, and Covent Garden has a problem with them."[1] Thus Deborah Voigt, after receiving word of Covent Garden's decision to break her contract to perform the title role in *Ariadne auf Naxos* in March 2004. Director Christof Loy intended to update the Strauss opera in a manner that emphasized sleek forms and placed the protagonist in a little black dress, and Voigt's remarkable size destroyed the concept. There was a predictable outcry, with fury over the insult to the diva on one hand and defense of the director's prerogatives on the other. The debate, in fact, soon broke down along lines familiar to any historian of opera, with voice battling text, music battling mise-en-scène for supremacy. Yet if the conflict was an old one, then the solution was decidedly contemporary: a year later Voigt went in for gastric bypass surgery, lost a hundred pounds, and was rehired.

Voigt, of course, is not alone, as so many of our greatest singers are oddly proportioned for the roles they play. Jane Eaglen's Isolde has a large body and a crystalline voice; Placido Domingo's Parsifal is a husky senior voicing a lost child; Bryn Terfel's Wolfram is monumentally lyrical. There are beautiful dissonances in opera between ungainly frames and the agile sounds that emerge from them, between aging bodies and the young ones they play. And if a comedy occasionally emerges from such juxtapositions, then it is a very human one; most of us have soaring souls in awkward flesh. It is a wonderful subject for art, this valiant, humbling struggle of bodies and voices, but it was never a subject for Wagner's art. At least, not by intention. In practice, however, the new wine in the old cask and the canary in the big-boned cage are some of the central features of the Wagnerian stage. And this serious, delightful, profoundly moving human comedy is particularly germane to that music drama that resists it most strongly.

The profundity and the preposterousness of *Parsifal* are inseparable from each other. Indeed, they are the identical form, seen in different ways, and for at least some of us the experience of watching *Parsifal* can be an uneasy balance of rapture and bemusement, absorption and abstention. Thus can almost any Wagner opera become Wittgenstein's optical illusion: looked at one way a duck, another way a rabbit. This duck-rabbit doubleness, rising and falling abruptly between heaven and earth, is especially common to the work that is arguably Wagner's most Schopenhauerian, and therefore most precariously balanced between idealism and biology. Alongside much else that Wagner gained from that bleakest of philosophers, he gained an unintentional comedy of bodies and wills.

The Weight of Genius

There are two kinds of Wagner critics: those who care about Schopenhauer and those who don't. The former group tends toward a cultural conservativism of the high modernist sort.[2] Take for example Bryan Magee: "What has bred such confusion in much of the Wagner literature of recent generations, especially in the literature about *Parsifal*, is that Schopenhauer has remained a closed book to so many people who have chosen to write on the subject." For Magee, the problem is not simply one of ignorance but of a general decline of cultural values. Scholars' obsession with "politico-social programmes" has made them lose touch with "serious and deep concerns." Thus the short-shrifting of Schopenhauer becomes but one particularly egregious "example of attempts to explain the greater in terms of the less, art in terms of journalism, the subtle and sophisticated in terms of the crude, the insightful and revealing in terms of the imperceptive, and altogether the profound in terms of the superficial."[3]

And Magee is right to worry, if only because the latter group, the ones who don't spend much time writing about Schopenhauer, has become the larger of the two. Catherine Clément, Slavoj Žižek, Carolyn Abbate, Marc Weiner, David Levin—to name just a few recent critics—all mention Schopenhauer sparingly, if at all, in their work on Wagner.[4] And one takes their implied point: What more is there to say? After a century and a half of influence studies, beginning with Wagner's own writings about himself, Wagner's relationship to his philosophic mentor has perhaps become a tiresome topic of conversation, maybe even a false lead: what's *really* going on must surely be elsewhere.[5]

The lines, then, are clearly drawn. Or are they? Schopenhauer, after all, was not simply the philosophical inspiration of Wagner and of symbolism; he also developed a number of ideas (the existence of the unconscious, the relation of the unconscious to repression, the importance of the body generally and sexuality in particular) that would prove central to psychoanalysis.[6] To a degree never before seen in a philosopher, and rarely seen since, Schopenhauer was the thinker of the gross material body, of genitals and guts. More than many of the critics Magee excoriates, and certainly long before them, it was Schopenhauer who attempted to explain "the greater in terms of the less," "the sophisticated in terms of the crude," "the profound in terms of the superficial." Schopenhauer's whole philosophy of the will, indeed, might be understood as precisely this inversion carried out on a universal scale.

There is something almost paradoxical about Schopenhauer's thought, at once vertiginously abstract and as meaty as a bloody wound. On one hand, it would be hard to find a more thoroughly elusive, utterly intangible category than Schopenhauer's omnipresent "will," the single reality behind the veil of illusion that passes for the world. On the other hand, Schopenhauer's most important development of Kant is this: that he brought the body to bear on the mind, and thus on the world. While, for Kant, we have access to the world only through the lens of the transcendental categories, for Schopenhauer we are able to perceive the world immediately and directly only through our own bodies. It is through the body that we discover the will; as Schopenhauer writes, "My body and my will are one . . . or, My body is the *objectivity* of my will."[7] Without a body, the "purely knowing subject" might imagine the operations of the world to be merely causal and would have no access to the inner force beneath all phenomena. For it is only by analogy with the perception of our own bodies that we are able to discover the truth of the will in all things (2:125/1:103).[8]

Schopenhauer struggles throughout *The World as Will and Representation*

with a dissonant cultural condition by attempting to reconcile German idealism with the discoveries of nineteenth-century biology (most of all, with
the emergent biology of mind).[9] The philosophy that results from this effort
can read like unintentional comedy. In his chapter "On Genius," for instance,
Schopenhauer begins in a high-idealist vein that reflects his years of immer-
sion in Plato and Kant.[10] He defines genius as the "predominant capacity" for
the perception of "(Platonic) *Ideas*," the ability to "perceive a world different
from [that of the rest of humanity], since [the world] presents itself in his
mind more objectively, consequently more purely and distinctly" (3:430/
2:376). Just a few pages later, however, Schopenhauer's idealist account of
the abstract consciousness of genius turns suddenly, grotesquely corporeal.
For genius to be possible, we are told, "the cerebral system must be clearly
separated from the ganglionic by total isolation," "even a good stomach is a
condition on account of the special and close agreement with this part of
the brain," "the texture of the mass of the brain must be of extreme fineness
and perfection, and must consist in the purest, most clarified, delicate and
sensitive nerve-substance." Drawing on postmortem evidence of Byron's
brain, he tells us that "the qualitative proportion of white to grey matter . . .
has a decided influence" on genius, while, ruminating on Goethe's height,
he concludes that "a short stature and especially a short neck" are favorable
for genius, as "the blood reaches the brain with more energy" (3:449-
50/2:392-93). Thus is the German Romantic cult of the *Künstler* forced into
marriage with physiological determinism.

   Cultural change is such a complex process that it is difficult to assign a
single set of reasons for Schopenhauer's sudden emergence into popularity
in the 1850s, after decades of languishing in obscurity. Certainly, the collapse of the revolutionary movements of 1848-49, the consolidation of conservative power under Bismarck, and the upheavals of the Second Industrial
Revolution created a more fertile ground for Schopenhauer's relentless historical pessimism than existed in the far more hopeful days of the previous
three decades. In light of such sweeping transformations, Schopenhauer's
murder of the Romantic myth of Promethean man suddenly seemed sensi-
ble, even attractive, to a number of intellectuals and artists. His writings
have a Gothic sensibility not only in their singular gloominess but also in
their reversal, through extension, of Romantic idealism. If Kant's crowning
of subjective perception was treated as an elevation of the artist to semi-
divinity by so many Romantics, then Schopenhauer's relentless pursuit of

Kantian logic ended up in a frigid landscape littered with body parts and haunted by a single, insatiable ghost. Perhaps most disturbingly of all, Schopenhauer swept aside that centerpiece of bourgeois virtue and that backbone of modern masculinity: willpower. In the face of the Schopenhauerian will, such concepts as willpower and free will come to be seen as so much flotsam atop a great sea, and consciousness itself is shown to be "the mere surface of our mind, and of this, as of the globe, we do not know the interior, but only the crust" (3:149/2:136).

It is a commonplace that Wagner was never the same after reading Schopenhauer in October 1854.[11] Critics who discuss Wagner's transformation generally focus on three or four themes: his turn away from the relative optimism of, say, *The Artwork of the Future* or *Siegfried's Death*; his embrace of an ideal of renunciation and the annihilation of the will to live; the central ethical importance he would give to compassion (*Mitleid*) for all living things; and, finally, the increasing centrality of music in the construction of the music dramas. All of these changes in his ethics and aesthetics were inspired, or at least reinforced, by Schopenhauer's writings, a debt Wagner was the first to acknowledge. Largely unexplored, however—and unacknowledged by Wagner because almost certainly unconscious—is a less thematic and more formal transformation. This transformation may be described as a paradox in Wagner's work: increasing attention to the material body uncomfortably coupled with an increasing disembodiment of the stage. What Wagner's most Schopenhauerian music dramas (*Tristan and Isolde, The Twilight of the Gods, Parsifal*) recall is the philosopher's juxtaposition of vile bodies to the most intangible abstractions of consciousness.

This transformation marks not merely the introduction of a new idea or technique in Wagner's work but a whole new discourse of selfhood. More than this, the discourse it inaugurates will become central to the development of theatrical modernism, taken up and transformed by Strindberg and thereafter by Wedekind and the artists of the expressionist stage. But to return to the moment of transition, we find this new discourse entering Wagner's writings soon after his discovery of Schopenhauer. Having written to Liszt six months earlier announcing his discovery of the philosopher who has "entered my lonely life like a gift from heaven," Wagner writes again in June 1855 (6:298/323). The letter opens with a paean to Liszt's artistry and to the miraculous powers of creativity in general. The terms are textbook *Künstlerkult*.

Allow me, best of men, to begin by expressing my amazement at your *immense creativity*! So you are planning a Dante Symphony? And you hope to show it to me, already completed, this autumn? Do not take it amiss if I sound amazed at this marvel. When I look back on your activities during recent years, you strike me as being quite superhuman [*ganz übermenschlich*]! There must indeed be something quite unique about it. But it is entirely natural that we should find pleasure only in creative work, indeed only in that way can we make life at all tolerable: only when we create do we become what we really are. (7:203/343)

The letter continues as a celebration of Liszt's genius—indeed, a hymn to the power of creativity itself—until the beginning of the second paragraph, where Wagner suddenly begins to voice his qualms.

And so—a "Divina Comedia"? It is certainly a most splendid idea, and I am already looking forward to enjoying your music. But I must discuss certain details of it with you. That the "Inferno" and "Purgatorio" will be a success I do not doubt for a moment: but I have some misgivings about the "Paradiso," and you yourself confirm these misgivings when you tell me that you are planning to include choruses in the work. In the Ninth Symphony (as a work of art), it is the last movement with its chorus which is without any doubt the weakest section, it is important only from the point of view of the history of art since it reveals to us, in its very naïve way, the embarrassment felt by the real tone-poet who (after Hell and Purgatory) does not know how finally to represent Paradise. (7:203/343)

Wagner's reservations here are a long way from his essays of the previous decade, essays such as "Beethoven's Choral Symphony at Dresden 1846," in which he rhapsodizes about the last movement above all else ("we clasp the whole world to our breast; shouts and laughter fill the air, like thunder from the clouds, the roaring of the sea; whose everlasting tides and healing shocks lend life to the earth, and keep life sweet for the *joy* of man to whom God gave the earth as home of *happiness*," and so on [2:64/7:255]). In the intervening decade—and here we must particularly recall the failed Dresden revolution of 1849—much of Wagner's joy had been shattered. For Wagner in 1856, the trouble with the fourth movement of the Ninth lies not in the limitations of Beethoven's imagination but rather in the impossibility of convincingly representing paradise at all. Over the course of the second paragraph of his letter, therefore, Wagner attempts to transplant Dante's paradise in the soil of Schopenhauer. He imagines "sinking into rapt contemplation of Beatrice, [in order that] I might cast aside my entire personality, devoid of will" (7:204/343). Arguing that Dante's vision can only be appreciated now as a historical artifact, he nevertheless expresses the "wish that I could have lost my private consciousness, and hence *consciousness in general* [das Bewusstsein], in that refining fire" (7:205/344).

The revision is radical: it is not, as for Dante or for Liszt, sin that must be burned away but simply consciousness itself. The juxtaposition of Wagner's two highlighted phrases—"amazement at your *immense creativity*" and "wish that I could have lost . . . *consciousness in general*"—neatly epitomizes Wagner's crisis. In the former phrase, he is gazing up at the peaks of the artist-gods, while in the latter he plummets into the abyss of Thanatos. What they have in common is vertigo.

At this point in the letter, Wagner is still expressing his death drive in idealist terms, as a crisis of abstract consciousness. While the influence of Schopenhauer can already be seen in the desire to annihilate the will, the more thoroughgoing influence of the philosopher comes in the third paragraph of the letter, when Wagner suddenly abandons his idealist vocabulary in favor of an instrumentally materialist one. Human organs, writes Wagner,

> are created to meet various needs, and one of these organs is his intellect, i.e. the organ for comprehending whatever is external to it, with the aim of using such objects to satisfy life's needs, according to its strength and ability. A *normal* man is therefore one in whom this organ—which is directed outwards and whose function is to perceive things, just as the stomach's function is to digest food—is equipped with sufficient ability to satisfy a need that is external to it, and—for the *normal* person—this need is exactly the same as the most common beast, namely the instinct to eat and to reproduce; for this will to live, which is the actual metaphysical basis of all existence, demands solely to live, i.e. to eat and reproduce itself perpetually. (7:206/344-45)

At a stroke, Wagner reduces the whole panoply of mental functions to mere appetite and places the mind on the level of the gut. And while this bleak materialism holds true for "*normal*" people, with geniuses the light shines no brighter. "So we also find (albeit rarely, of course) *abnormal* individuals in whom the cognitive organ, i.e. the brain, has evolved beyond the ordinary and adequate level of development found in the rest of humanity, just as nature, after all, often creates monsters in which *one* organ is much more developed than any other. Such a *monstrosity* [*Eine solche* Monstruosität]—if it reaches its highest level of development—is *genius*, which essentially rests on no more than an abnormally fertile and capacious brain" (7:206-07/345).

The artist-genius, "übermenschlich," at the beginning of Wagner's letter, degenerates into a "*Monstruosität*" by the end. And not grandly monstrous in a manner that might recall Milton's Satan but merely a freak of nature, a big-brained baby. An object that speaks more of pity than of awe.

The Paradox of *Parsifal*

For all its attention to the pains of the physical body, *Parsifal*, like the Festival Theatre it was intended to consecrate, strains toward the incorporeal. The Festspielhaus, after all, was designed in large part to eliminate the sight of unwanted bodies, and its three most significant innovations are all connected to this project of dematerialization. According to Wagner's "Bayreuth" essay (1873), the decision to bury the orchestra beneath the stage stemmed from the need that his new theater make "invisible the technical source of its music"—more specifically, that it conceal the bodies of the musicians (9:336/5:333). Further, the decisions to eliminate box seating and to extinguish the house lights arose from Wagner's desire to neutralize the audience's eyesight "by the rapt subversion of the whole sensorium," which "can be done only by leading [the eye] away from any sight of bodies lying in between" it and the stage (9:336/5:333).

In no other modern drama is *Mitleid* so central and so corporeal as in *Parsifal*. For this reason, the usual translation of the oft-repeated *durch Mitleid wissend* as "knowing through pity" is insufficient; more accurate would be the more literal "knowing through shared suffering" or "knowing through compassion" (with "compassion" taken to its etymological roots). In *Parsifal*, suffering is passed like a virus across the stage, and its mark is the wound. Two wounds prefigure the action of the drama: the evil sorcerer Klingsor's self-castration and Klingsor's wounding of the Grail King Amfortas. These wounds, passed from Klingsor to Amfortas, pass again to Parsifal, first as a flesh wound, later as a deep penetration. The flesh wound comes at the end of act 1, when Parsifal witnesses Amfortas lying in his litter, his wound "bursting out afresh": "Parsifal, on hearing Amfortas' last cry of agony, clutches his heart and remains in that position for some time" (10:345). Parsifal's compassion for Amfortas means that he catches Amfortas's wound—not by means of a spear but by means of the eye, not in the thigh but in the heart. The wound returns again as a much deeper cut in act 2, when Parsifal is in the moment of consummating his oedipal union with the maternal seductress Kundry:

Amfortas!—

Die Wunde!—die Wunde!—

Sie brennt in meinem Herzen.— (10:358)

Here, the experience of the burning wound of Amfortas—or, one might more accurately say, the wound of Klingsor-Amfortas-Parsifal—becomes the catalyst of Parsifal's sexual renunciation and ascension to sanctity. The wound, vaginal in form and grammatically feminine (Parsifal's cry literally reads: "Amfortas!—/The wound!—the wound!—/She burns in my heart.—"), travels from one male host to another. As it travels it mutates, turning from literal castration (removal of the genitals) to quasi-castration (a wound to the side that renders impotent) to symbolic castration (an invisible wound "straight to the heart" that recalls these previous wounds and likewise cuts off sexual passion). This motion from the somatic to the symbolic underlies the work as a whole.

More broadly, both the Festspielhaus and *Parsifal* reflect many aspects of Wagner's post-Schopenhauerian aesthetics. Whereas Wagner had, in his Zurich writings (1849–57), argued that music should serve drama, he sharply revised that view in the decades following his turn to Schopenhauer. The *Beethoven* essay of 1870 may serve as a mark of this transformation in its maturity. He insists there on the subordination of all three-dimensional arts to the supreme art of music, which is uniquely capable of expressing the universal. Music's superiority to plastic arts is particularly seen in its avoidance of mere gesture. Whereas a three-dimensional art form "fixes gesture [*Gebärde*] with respect to space, but leaves its motion to be supplied by our reflective thought, music speaks out gesture's inmost essence in a language so direct that, once we are saturated with the music, our eyesight is positively incapacitated for intensive observation of the gesture, so that finally we understand it without our really seeing it" (9:76–77/5:76). Music, then, does more than obviate physical gesture. It does what gesture cannot: it takes us directly to the heart of that which gesture more clumsily attempts to capture. Blinding our vision of the body, music shows us the body in its innermost form.

A distinction needs to be drawn here between Wagner's turn away from physical gesture in his late works, especially *Parsifal*, and his broader commitment to theatricality. The distinction is necessitated by the fact that the terms "gesture" and "theatricality" have become deeply intertwined within the critical lineage running from Nietzsche through Adorno. As Martin Puchner writes in *Stage Fright*, "Nietzsche and Adorno agree that Wagner's art suffers from being too gestural and that his fixation on gestures, even and especially in music, is an effect of both his theatricality and his excessive reliance on vulgar mimesis. . . . Gesture becomes a shorthand for the mimetic actor lingering at the heart of the theatre and, due to the general slippage between anti-mimesis and anti-theatricality, for the theatrical effects the theatre imposes on the other arts."[12] Particularly in Adorno's use of the term, "gesture" generally refers to a reified mimetic expression, with the leitmotif seen as the heart of Wagner's regressively allegorical technique. This is so even for motifs that are meant to represent abstract themes (such as Fate or Grace), the names of which become allegorical emblems and so operate gesturally: "Allegorical rigidity has infected the motiv like a disease. The gesture becomes frozen as a picture of what it expresses."[13] Adorno is thus able to preserve the term "gesture" even for—in the case of thematic leitmotifs, *especially* for—aspects of music drama quite removed from the embodied action of the stage.

For our purposes, the trouble with this approach is that it elides important distinctions between stage gestures and the broader category of mimesis. While this elision serves Nietzsche's and Adorno's larger attacks on theatricality (understood as mimesis in extremis), it obscures a significant transformation in Wagner's aesthetics. Simply put, Wagner's theatrical practice in his early music dramas places music largely in the service of stage action, often making physical gesture the driving force of the total effect.[14] In Carolyn Abbate's account, the transformation begins with *Tristan and Isolde*, which "introduced mirror effects that led to a radical separation of voice from body."[15] The voice, Abbate argues, enters the orchestra, which becomes a sort of gramophone avant la lettre; the onstage bodies, by extension, are overshadowed by the orchestral creature that sings beneath them. While the *Ring* marks a half step back from the extremity of the disembodiment of voice in *Tristan*, one might argue that the end of *The Twilight of the Gods* and the entirety of *Parsifal* push the experiment forward once more. Abbate's argument is complemented by that of Carl Dahlhaus in a 1969 lecture on Wagner's use of gesture, in which he identifies a transition in Wagner's work from "outer drama" (centering on physical gesture) to "inner drama" (centering on states of consciousness). Though he sees intimations of the turn in *Tristan*, he ultimately places the moment of transition with the Beethoven essay of 1870.[16] Regardless of the precise date, what is clear from both Abbate and Dahlhaus is that Wagner's theory and practice turn against corporeal gesture in the latter half of the nineteenth century, and do so especially in his most Schopenhauerian works.

Of all Wagner's works, only *Tristan* and *The Twilight of the Gods* are comparable to *Parsifal* in their emphasis on music over theatrical action, yet these two works ultimately rely more on physical gesture than does Wagner's final opera. (Take, for example, the finales of each opera: Isolde's love-death, Brünnhilde's leap into the flames.) Moreover, *Parsifal*'s music tends even more strongly toward the symphonic than does the music of either of these earlier works, and it offers a degree of harmonic complexity without equal in Wagner's oeuvre. The harmonic complexity of *Parsifal*'s score is significantly detached not only from the action of the drama but from action itself. Reflecting the concern of the work as a whole with meditative, ritualistic consciousness, the score of *Parsifal* is substantially unrelated to the physical business of the stage. Consider for example the prelude to act 1, which begins with a somewhat arrhythmic phrase played on reeds and strings, an amorphous theme made more mysterious when joined by A♭ chords. The theme bursts forth for a moment like some hothouse orchid, then just as suddenly dies, before returning again transposed into C minor, altered now by chromaticism, and dying away twice more. While identified by Wagner as a theme of "Liebe," the love it suggests is no physical gesture of intimacy—is not kissing, hugging, nor (like the *Liebestod*) explosive orgasm followed by collapse—but rather, like Parsifal's wound, a disembodied symbol into which the body has been transmuted.[17]

Wagner was concerned, in fact, that his *Parsifal* preludes not be confused with gestic music of any sort. On October 31, 1878, Cosima seems to have made just such an error and was corrected. "He plays the prelude to me . . . ," she writes. "It begins like the lament of an extinguished star, after which one discerns, like gestures [*wie Gebärden*], Parsifal's arduous wanderings and Kundry's pleas for salvation." Wagner seems to have corrected her on this point, as Cosima adds the following in the margin: "That is to say, not the lament, but the sounds of extinction, out of which lamenting emerges.—'My preludes must be elemental [*elementarisch*], not dramatic like the *Leonore* Overtures, for that makes the drama superfluous.'" Reading Cosima's entry, Wagner seems to have been at pains to stress that it is not any dramatic gesture (whether of lament, wandering, or pleading) that the prelude expresses but rather something "elemental." Wagner's new attitude toward gesture is not a rejection of mimesis so much as a shift from the imitation of the body by means of musical motifs to an imitation of that which underlies the body, that immaterial reality of which the body is (like drama itself) a superfluity. Significantly, Cosima notes of the prelude that "none of this could be sung—only the 'elemental' quality can be felt here, as R. does indeed emphasize."[18] Unlike, say, the role of Isolde, which stretches the vocal capabilities of the human body beyond what seemed the limits of possibility, much of *Parsifal* is meant not to expand the vocal range but to exceed it and thus further humble the body before dematerialized music.[19]

Parsifal's obsession with the body, a body rendered at once grossly material and profoundly mysterious, reminds us that the work's premiere was roughly contemporaneous with the development of psychiatry. More precisely, the period between Wagner's libretto (1877) and the premiere of *Parsifal* (1882) coincided with the modern medicalization of hysteria. As Elaine Showalter recalls, the modern diagnosis of hysteria largely developed out of Jean-Martin Charcot's quasi-theatrical stagings of hysterical subjects at the Salpêtrière in the 1870s and 1880s, stagings that made a particularly profound impression on Freud, who studied at the Salpêtrière in 1885 and 1886.[20] This connection of hysteria with theatricality was one that Nietzsche had in mind when he accused Wagner of hysterical stagecraft in *The Case of Wagner* (1888). "Wagner's art is sick. The problems he presents on the stage—all of them problems of hysterics—the convulsive nature of his affects, his overexcited sensibility, his taste that required ever stronger spices, his insatiability which he dressed up as principles, not least of all the choice of his heroes and heroines—consider them as physiological types (a pathological gallery)!—all of this taken together represents a profile of sickness that permits no further doubt. *Wagner est une névrose*."[21] Nietzsche, of course, knew the potent implications of this charge. Hysteria, after all, was not seen simply as a histrionic disease; it was more specifically a disease of women and Jews.[22] The repressed, Nietzsche suggests, returns in the very form of the Wagnerian *Gesamtkunstwerk*. With Nietzsche as a guide, we might say that the *Gesamtkunstwerk* is a hysterical discourse that displaces its own troubles of bodies and wills onto hysterical characters such as Kundry.

The *Gesamtkunstwerk*, like any totalizing project, relies on a necessary Other, a figure or figures who must be present in order to be excluded. "Given Wagner's commitment to the *Gesamtkunstwerk*, to a program of seamless aesthetic totalization," argues David Levin in his essay on *The Mastersingers of Nuremberg*, "the Jew functions as the structural guarantor of that totality by representing, within the work, that which does not be-

long, which must be exorcised. We might think of Jews, then, as the 'I don't'
that guarantees a series of polygamous unions: the reconciliation of language and nature in a non-Jewish artwork of the future; the union of the arts
in the *Gesamtkunstwerk*; or, more concretely, the union of Walther and Eva,
which is, of course, repeatedly (if only temporarily) marred by what must
nonetheless be seen as its guarantor."[23] While there has been some critical
debate about how strongly to read the Jewishness of Wagner's Beckmesser,
Kundry is a more straightforward case, explicitly identified with the Wandering Jew in the text of *Parsifal* as well as in other writings of Wagner.[24] In
her Jewishness—though not only in her Jewishness—Kundry represents the
Other upon which the *Gesamtkunstwerk* relies, the Other whose purpose it
is to *not belong*. Moreover, since the form of the *Gesamtkunstwerk* is late
Wagnerian—that is, is particularly shaped by the late Wagnerian project of
the extinction of corporeal gesture—Kundry's otherness is particularly centered upon her embodied theatricality.

Kundry is a great caldron into which all the necessary exclusions of the
late Wagnerian *Gesamtkunstwerk* are thrown. Having taken many forms
throughout time, Kundry functions as a Wagnerian totality in negative, assuming and incorporating all the marginalized and rejected elements of
Bayreuth into a pseudo-organic whole. Her "special form of neurosis," like
that of "woman" generally according to Luce Irigaray's reading of Freud, is
therefore "to 'mimic' a work of art, to be *a bad (copy of a) work of art*," "a
counterfeit or parody of an artist process."[25] When we first encounter Kundry, she is a wild woman, the very antithesis of the liturgical *Gesamtkunstwerk*. "*Kundry bursts in, almost staggering; wild clothes tied high; a snakeskin
belt hanging low; loose locks of black, fluttering hair; dark brownish-red com-
plexion; piercing black eyes, sometimes wildly blazing, but more often glassy and
as rigid as death*" (10:326). From the outset, Wagner clearly marks Kundry—
with her fixed and glassy eyes, her loose hair, her wild laughter, her sudden
exhaustions, her screaming, and her manic contortions—as a hysteric,
which further emphasizes her singular position as woman and Jew on an
otherwise male, gentile stage. As act 1 continues, the Grail Knights refer to
Kundry as a "heathen" and a "sorceress," "burdened with a curse" (10:329).
In act 2, Klingsor calls her a "nameless creature," "first sorceress," "Rose of
Hades," "Herodias," and "Gundryggia" (a wild huntress of Nordic myth;
10:345–46). Her identities proliferate still further, as she plays the roles of
lover and mother while attempting to seduce Parsifal and reveals herself, in
the opera's climax, as the Wandering Jew, eternally cursed for laughing at

Christ. Wagner's decision to make the Wandering Jew a woman of course goes against tradition, and it may seem odd until placed in the context of Kundry's overall dramatic function, which is to serve as the receptacle of all that which the opera must ultimately exclude. Through Kundry, Wagner is able to unify the eternal femme fatale (itself combining deadly seductress and deadly mother) and the eternal Jew in a single hysterical figure; he is able, too, to stage the rejection, the shattering, and the redemption of this creature, whose last words are "dienen, dienen" (to serve, to serve) before she falls silent and dies. The apotheosis of *Parsifal*, with its unification of Spear and Grail, celebrates an androgynous totality that is a mise en abyme of the *Gesamtkunstwerk* itself.[26] But redemptive androgyny is here a discourse that occurs exclusively between men and between gentiles; "woman" and "Jew" must be broken and redeemed, and finally die, in order to be preserved in the higher synthesis of Monsalvat.

Kundry's bodiliness—and therefore her threat to the obsessively sublimated Grail community—is in large part manifested through her hysteria. Certainly her manic gestures throughout the first act ("*Kundry rushes in, almost reeling*"; "*She throws herself on the ground*"; "*She trembles violently; her arms drop powerlessly*"; etc.) keep our attention on Kundry as fleshly creature, half human and half "wild animal" (10:329). Noting that "hysterics force us to pay attention to their bodies," Mary Ann Smart shows that Wagner's music tightly shadows Kundry's movements in act 1.[27] When she fetches water in act 1, for instance, the music captures her physicality (fig. 1.1). The sequentially ascending four-note motif (fig. 1.2) captures Kundry's agitated movements. After four repetitions, Wagner increases the intensity by shortening the phrase to its final gesture and repeats that twice before the climactic chord (fig. 1.3).

Of the fourth measure of the six-measure section, Smart writes that "we might imagine Kundry turning and rushing back toward Parsifal; the pivot of this gestural arch is marked by an iteration of Kundry's motif, hurtling downward and coming to rest as she reaches her goal."[28] By musically echoing her bodily gestures in this way, Wagner goes against the grain of his late style, making the music, in at least these instances, subservient to physical action. By act 3, however, Kundry's metamorphosis from shrieking hysteric to silent supplicant is mirrored in the almost complete silencing, too, of her bodily presence in the music. Recalling act 1, Kundry goes to fetch water again in act 3, but now the action produces a very different orchestral response.

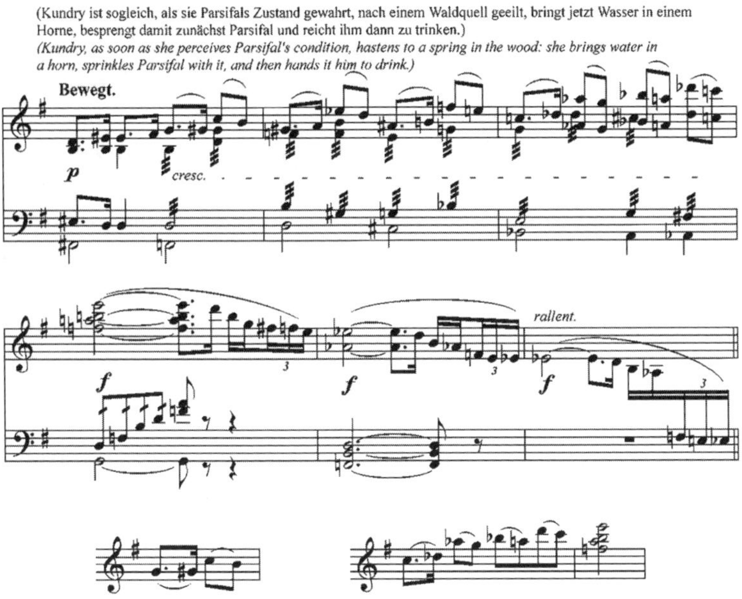

(Kundry ist sogleich, als sie Parsifals Zustand gewahrt, nach einem Waldquell geeilt, bringt jetzt Wasser in einem
Horne, besprengt damit zunächst Parsifal und reicht ihm dann zu trinken.)
*(Kundry, as soon as she perceives Parsifal's condition, hastens to a spring in the wood: she brings water in
a horn, sprinkles Parsifal with it, and then hands it him to drink.)*

Figures 1.1-1.3. The orchestra initially mirrors Kundry's gestures

The only remaining traces of bodily mimesis are the repeated cello tattoos that
punctuate the early part of this scene, suggesting fluttering breath or a weak
heartbeat. Once Kundry exits for the water, a gentle rising line is initiated by
clarinet and continued by the oboe, and as Gurnemanz comments on Kundry's
transformation, wondering if this is the effect of Good Friday, we hear hints of
both the motive of Amfortas's suffering and the Grail motive, the first time in the
opera that Kundry has been associated with any of these crucial musical symbols
of meaning and redemption.[29]

Kundry's journey, from a performance that emphasizes her body to a performance that transmutes her body into an abstraction, repeats the wound's
journey from corporeal to symbolic form. It is a process that is iterated time
and again over the course of the opera; ultimately, it is the journey of the
Grail quest itself—a prize that, as Gurnemanz tells us, cannot be attained by
any earthly route. [30]

The curious thing about Kundry's hysteria—about, more precisely, the
hysteria that afflicts the whole Grail community and is displaced onto
Kundry—is that it at once focuses attention on the body and renders the

body radically mysterious. As Elisabeth Bronfen argues in her study of Kundry, hysteria is a diagnosis that "eludes any precise nosology" and has thus "proven itself a useful screen for the diagnostic fantasies of the doctors faced with their own impotence and helplessness while confronting this medical enigma."[31] Hysteria serves, then, as an emblem of the problem of the body and the will first wrestled with by Schopenhauer. Performing hysteria—whether on- or offstage—at once foregrounds the performer's body and radically destabilizes it, raising the question of who the true actor is: the visible person or the invisible mystery lurking beneath. On one hand, it is this question that *Parsifal* aims to answer by means of the wholesale substitution of symbols for bodies. On the other hand, Wagner, reflecting Charcot's own practice at Salpêtrière, attempts to address the hysteria of his stage by means of hypnosis and electricity.[32]

Hypnosis and electricity are unified in the curtain-closing culmination of *Parsifal*, the moment when Parsifal holds up the electrically illuminated Grail. George Davidson, a member of the Bayreuth Patrons' Association and another observer of the original production of *Parsifal*, describes the effect:

> I don't think it will take anything away from the experience of future audience members if I tell how the wonderful illumination of the Grail is accomplished. When the boy, who carries the shrine of the Grail ahead of King Amfortas, has placed it on the tabernacle in the middle of the rotunda, an invisible wire connection is established that runs between a small Siemens electrical bulb inside the red chalice and a motor [i.e., a battery] inside the tabernacle. This connection is established by a man who has been placed next to the motor and who is also hidden behind the tabernacle. In this way, the previously dark chalice suddenly glows in a red light, while Amfortas in the first and Parsifal in the last act kneel to pray in front of the uncovered Grail. This incandescence continues when both take the goblet into their hands, raise it slowly, and gently sway it in all directions. The effect remains a wondrous one, even if the means by which it is accomplished are known.[33]

Wagner was making use of novel stage technology for this illusion; it was only a year previous that London's Savoy had been the first theater to be lit by electricity. If there is any truth to Nietzsche's charge that Wagner was a master hypnotist, then this surely is one of the Master's grandest effects, intended to enthrall both the Grail community and the Bayreuth audience— intended, indeed, to make the former an idealization of the latter. The moment is Wagnerian theatricality at its grandest, and it is, significantly, an electrified, hypnotizing symbol rather than an actor's body that is the focus of the last stage image of Wagner's career. The moment completes the transfiguration from corporeal theatricality, still present in acts 1 and 2 in the gestures of Kundry, to more fully dematerialized theatricality. The music that plays above it, dominated by the quiet strains of the Faith and Grail motifs, is as far as possible from the explicitly hysterical, musically accompanied shriek of Kundry's laugh.

What would Kundry be without her laugh? It is not quite the only laughter we hear in *Parsifal* (Gurnemanz laughs at Parsifal's misunderstandings; Parsifal marches on Klingsor with rosy-cheeked laughter; the Flowermaidens laugh as they seduce), but Kundry's dominates the drama as does no other. It is integral to her character and is so from the outset. Cosima records that Wagner told her the following on February 16, 1877: "I have made a note: Kundry can only laugh and scream, she does not know true laughter." And seven months later, on September 27, as again recorded by Cosima: "I also have some accents for Mademoiselle Condrie, I already have her laughter, for instance." Curious, here, that Cosima, in transcribing Wagner's words, should (mis)spell the witch's name this time with the first two letters of her own name: is it only a French jest, or is it a sign of a more significant desire? If Kundry's false, screaming laughter is one of her first "accents" to emerge, then it seems to arise together with its antithesis, the sighing smile of servility. Wagner's comment on the laugh of "Condrie" is immediately followed, in Cosima's account, by another exchange. " 'You and I will go on living in human memory,' he exclaims. 'You for sure,' I exclaim with a laugh."[34] Thus does Cosima's laugh replace Condrie's, and one woman's blasphemous cackle gives way to another's worshipful trill.

Kundry's laughter marks her as a hysteric and a femme fatale, and it is central to her character for another reason as well: because Wagnerian theatricality calls it forth. In an opera distinguished by its lack of such connections, Kundry's laughter binds music closely with gesture. In act 1, her slander of Parsifal's mother—"die Törin! [*Sie lacht*]"—is caught in the musical phrase that captures her first laughter of the opera (fig. 1.4). Already we find the sudden drop (here from E♭ to F) that will come to characterize Kundry's laugh throughout the work. In this first instance of her laugh, however, the descending seventh actually represents not the laugh itself but her spoken mockery ("die Törin!"). Her laughter, by contrast, is represented in the vocal line by five beats of rest and is presumably meant to be either pantomimed or improvised (though often, in performance, the stage direction is simply

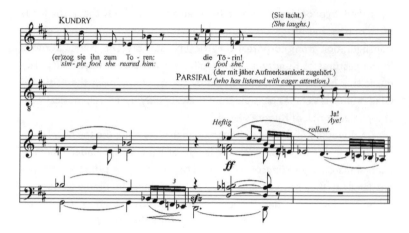

Figure 1.4. The orchestra laughs for Kundry

ignored). The transition from speech ("die Törin!") to laughter (*Sie lacht*), meanwhile, is marked by a transition from vocal to orchestral scoring. Thus, in this first instance of her laughter, it is not Kundry who laughs but the orchestra that laughs for her. As might be expected in the light of the *Beethoven* essay, music gives us Kundry's bodily gestures in their innermost form.

It is not until act 2, when she recalls her original blasphemy, that her laughter begins to return from its orchestral sublimation. Now it enters the vocal line with tremendous force and does so in a fashion that unifies vocal and orchestral lines. "Ich sah Ihn—Ihn—und—lachte . . ." (I saw Him—Him —and—laughed . . .), she sings, making the last word howl. Kundry's huge drop of an octave and a seventh ("lach-te") recalls the drop of a seventh in the example from act 1, but the line is now, for the first time in the opera, unambiguously one of vocalized laughter. While, in the earlier instance, her laughter was expressed through the orchestra alone, here her laughter is rooted in her body through her voice. Moreover, in what may be the most precipitous vocal descent in all Wagner, he very nearly delineates the singer's range in the space of two beats. Finally, he brings Kundry's voice together with the orchestral line, unifying voice and orchestra on high B, before having the voice plummet unaccompanied into the depths. Kundry's laughter now returns us, forcefully, to the corporeality that defines her and brings that corporeality into union with the orchestra (fig. 1.5).

Figure 1.5. Kundry's laughter returns from its orchestral sublimation

This is the outrageously gestural Kundry who erupts, taking the orchestra with her, at the end of act 2. Examples could be multiplied, but consider the return of her laughter some minutes later in the scene. The sudden drop that characterizes Kundry's laughter has now become a descending, partly arpeggiated line ("Ich verlachte, lachte, lachte, ha-ha!"), but one that once more unifies voice and orchestra, in their unison descents from E to G, from F to A#, and from G# to C#, and in their parallel ascent from G to B ("ha-ha!"). Here the orchestra no longer embodies the "real" drama of which

Figure 1.6. Kundry's laughter once more reunifies music and drama

the staged bodies are but shadows; instead, we find voice and orchestra, text and music, drama and will brought into something close to a single expression without subordination. It is this final passage of Kundry's laughter that reintroduces the vocal body most strongly into *Parsifal*, that brings Wagner furthest away from the Schopenhauerian aesthetics of the *Beethoven* essay, and that returns Wagner most forcefully to the sister arts theories of his Zurich period. These passages embody Kundry's aesthetic (and more than aesthetic) threat to Wagner's newly Schopenhauerian conception of the *Gesamtkunstwerk*. It is no accident that these most threatening vocal gestures immediately precede Parsifal's rejection of Kundry in favor of the Grail and the shattering of her power over the Grail Knights and the opera as a whole (fig. 1.6).

While the main thrust of *Parsifal* is toward the translation of bodies into symbols, a demand partly expressed through the dominance of thematic over gestural motifs throughout the work, the emphatically corporeal motif of Kundry's laugh poses an increasing threat to the first two acts.[35] Ultimately, Kundry's laugh not only threatens Wagner's larger aesthetic project but is also produced by it. It is produced by it precisely because that project's obsession with the body and the body's extinction tends toward the ludicrous. Ironically, no one has understood the comedy that arises from a disjunction between consciousness and the body better than Schopenhauer. It is Schopenhauer, in the end, who provides some of the sharpest insights into the threatening necessity of Kundry's laugh.

The Ludicrous Remainder

We return to Schopenhauer not because he grasps some eternal truth of humor but because his theory best captures the ludicrousness of the same totalizing discourse that gave it birth and that helped to form Wagner's late *Gesamtkunstwerke*: "The ludicrous [*das Lächerilich*] is always the paradoxical, and thus unexpected, subsumption of an object under a concept that is in other respects heterogeneous to it. Accordingly," Schopenhauer writes, "the phenomenon of laughter always signifies the sudden apprehension of an incongruity between such a concept and the real object thought through it, and hence what is abstract and what is perceptive. The greater and more unexpected this incongruity in the apprehension of the person laughing, the more violent will be his laughter" (3:99/2:91). In the light of Schopenhauer's theory of laughter, his entire corpus may be seen as a particularly long-winded example of the ludicrous. *The World as Will and Representation* offers the reader all-encompassing abstractions (chiefly the "will" itself) apprehensible only through sensuous particularities. Time and again, Schopenhauer's central claim that we must judge the world according to the analogy of our own bodies leads him, as it does Wagner, to incongruous juxtapositions of abstract concepts and sensuous objects of perception.

Schopenhauer's theory of laughter has particular resonance for the study of the late-nineteenth-century theater because it was during this period that the relationship between the abstract and the perceptual became particularly fraught. The developing crisis of representation that would come to define modernism was felt with peculiar vigor on the late-nineteenth-century stage, a medium far more beholden to sensuous material representation (bodies, props, costumes, sets, lighting, stage architecture, etc.) than is the written word. The two most influential avant-garde movements of the fin-de-siècle stage, symbolism and naturalism, exemplify two very different responses to this crisis. Symbolist theater would attempt to avoid the increasingly ridiculous juxtaposition of the perceptive and the abstract by entirely subordinating the former to the latter—a movement for which *Parsifal* and *La revue wagnerienne* would prove especially influential. Naturalist theater, by contrast, would attempt to solve the same crisis by going in precisely the opposite direction, subordinating the abstract to the perceptive such that concrete particulars of environment and heredity, rather than immaterial symbols, would determine stage action. While symbolism and naturalism were locked in mortal combat at the threshold of the twentieth century, each captured an element of that increasingly ludicrous concatenation of idealist and materialist discourses called the modern bourgeois subject. The two movements were, as Adorno would later remark of mass culture and the avant-garde, "the torn halves of an integral freedom, to which, however, they do not add up."[36]

It is likely that in none of the fin-de-siècle arts was the distance between the abstract and the perceptive so great as in the theater, a condition to which Schopenhauer's discussion of the ludicrous at least partly testifies. Over the course of his argument, Schopenhauer provides eighteen comic examples, drawn from sources ranging from poetry to oral tales to newspaper reports, to prove his case. Tellingly, almost half the examples—eight in total—are drawn from the theater. The theatrical anecdotes, by and large, draw attention to the unintentionally comic slippages created by live performance. Consider, for example, the following three examples Schopenhauer uses to illustrate his theory of laughter:

> [1] The audience at a theatre in Paris once asked for the Marseillaise to be played, and as this was not done, they began shrieking and howling, so that in the end a police commissioner in uniform came on to the stage, and explained that for anything to be done in the theatre other than what appeared on the play-bill was not allowed. A voice then shouted: *"Et vous, Monsieur, êtes-vous aussi sur l'affiche?"* [And you, sir, are you on the playbill?], a hit that raised universal laughter. (3:101/2:93)

> [2] After [the actor Unzelmann] had been strictly forbidden to improvise at all in the Berlin theatre, he had to appear on the stage on horseback. Just as he came on the stage, the horse dunged, and at this the audience was moved to laughter, but they laughed much more when Unzelmann said to the horse: "What are you doing? don't you know that we are forbidden to improvise?" (3:102/2:93)

> [3] There is the case of the laughter into which Garrick burst in the middle of playing a tragedy, because a butcher, standing in front of the pit, had put his wig for a while on his large dog, so as to wipe the sweat from his own head. The dog

was supported by his fore-feet on the pit railings, and was looking towards the stage. (3:107/2:97)

While Schopenhauer uses such anecdotes to argue for his general theory of humor, he also suggests, without quite meaning to, that the theater is a space that particularly lends itself to the ludicrous. It does so because of the many opportunities it offers for accident and thus for the sudden, unintentional interruption of the particular into a general concept alien to it (a police announcement seen as a part of the playbill, a defecating horse seen as an improvisational actor, a bewigged dog seen as a spectator). In European theater, the unique capacity for live performance to produce such disorienting juxtapositions has stood metonymically for a broader crisis of representation at least since *Hamlet*, and perhaps even as far back as *The Bacchae*, but never before was this capacity explored so relentlessly as it was on the modernist stage. Schopenhauer's theory succeeds, in other words, less as a general theory of humor than as a presentiment of the theater of the absurd.

At the root of such absurdity is the problem of the body, and indeed all laughter for Schopenhauer is a kind of revolt of flesh against reason: "It is the concepts of thinking that are so often opposed to the satisfaction of our immediate desires, since, as the medium of the past, of the future, and of what is serious, they act as the vehicle of our fears, our regrets, and all our cares. It must therefore be delightful for us to see this strict, untiring, and most troublesome governess, our facility of reason, for once convicted of inadequacy. Therefore on this account the mien or appearance of laughter is very closely related to that of joy" (3:108/2:98). Predating Freud's *Jokes and Their Relation to the Unconscious* by more than half a century, Schopenhauer describes laughter here as a cruel delight taken by the bodily perceptions in the humiliation of their "troublesome governess," reason. Though he does not use the word in this passage, the essence of laughter becomes, in his account, a sort of schadenfreude. The irony is that schadenfreude is precisely the emotion that Schopenhauer elsewhere most forcefully rejects. Calling it "the worst trait in human nature," Schopenhauer writes in *Parerga and Paralipomena* that "*Schadenfreude* is diabolical and its mockery is the laughter of hell" (6:229-30).[37] Schopenhauer's disgust with schadenfreude is no idiosyncrasy but follows of necessity from his ethics as a whole, since schadenfreude marks the very antithesis of *Mitleid*. As with Schopenhauer, so with late Wagner. Indeed, it is *Parsifal's* message of *Mitleid* (in the person of Parsifal) and rejection of schadenfreude (in the person of Kundry) that is perhaps that work's most obviously Schopenhauerian aspect.

If Schopenhauer's grand metaphysical project often produces precisely the laughter it attempts to exclude, and does so for reasons accounted for by the theory of laughter his work itself offers, then much the same can be said of Wagner's own totalizing creation. *Parsifal* may be sublime and ridiculous by turns, but it can admit laughter only in order ultimately to banish it. The ridiculousness of *Parsifal* is created by precisely the extreme juxtaposition that we find in *The World as Will and Representation*: the collision of the most idealist conception of consciousness with the most materialist conception of the body. It is a juxtaposition exacerbated by *Parsifal* in performance, since theatrical performance, with its often ungainly bodies, imperfect voices, and awkward mechanics, always threatens to widen the divide between conceptual and perceived reality. The stronger the aspiration toward idealist totality, the sharper the threat of that totality's becoming suddenly, unexpectedly undone by the intrusion of alien corporeality. While a defecating horse might amuse audiences at a Berlin theater ("don't you know that we are forbidden to improvise?"), at Bayreuth it would be an outrage. One can easily imagine the audience response: either fury or a desperate attempt to ignore the intrusion or—what else?—laughter. It is this profound sense of dissatisfaction with theatricality that provoked Wagner's famous remark to Cosima about wanting to create an "invisible theatre."[38] Though the joke is frequently cited, often unmentioned is the fact that it was occasioned by Wagner's frustration with the performance of *Parsifal* in particular—and especially with the performance of Kundry. "[Wagner] comes to his *Parsifal* and says: 'Oh, I hate the thought of all those costumes and grease paint! When I think that characters like Kundry will have to be dressed up, those dreadful artists' balls immediately spring to mind. Having created the invisible orchestra, I now feel like inventing the invisible theatre!'" (2:181/2:154).

Parsifal, in its attempt to move dramatic representation away from bodies and actions and toward a direct expression of eternal symbols, pursues a thoroughgoing subsumption of concrete perception to abstracted representations. Such a strategy of high seriousness, ironically, replicates precisely the dynamic at the root of laughter, and so, like Schopenhauer, Wagner risks becoming risible through sheer profundity. Kundry stands for the necessary exclusions of *Parsifal* by virtue not only of her gender and her race but also of her laughter, which is (unlike that of, say, Siegfried, Brünnhilde, or Gurnemanz) essentially anti-Wagnerian. Not quite speech, not exactly an act, Kundry's laughter is nevertheless a speech act, one that condemned her at the moment of its utterance to tortured exile. The moment she laughed at her redeemer is the moment that transformed her to the allegorical form of eternal femme fatale and Wandering Jew. Her moments of laughter in *Parsifal* are but further iterations in her age-long recycling of that primary speech act, iterations that will end only with her conversion from cruel laughter to high seriousness, and from allegory to symbol, a conversion marked by her silent servitude and followed shortly by her death.

Kundry, in short, haunts *Parsifal* not only as woman and Jew but also as the specter of corporeal theatricality. Indeed, the combined threats of her femininity, her Jewishness, her corporeality, and her theatricality are inseparable from one another, are in fact mutually reinforced through nineteenth-century discourses that constructed "woman" and "Jew" as distinctly bodily and mimetic types. Through the hysterical gestures that draw attention to her body, through the mimetic relationship between her gestures and the music, through her laughter that brings together music, voice, and gesture, Kundry operates as the antitype to *Parsifal*'s drive toward dematerialization. She is the unintentional but inevitable ridiculous at the heart of the Schopenhauerian-Wagnerian sublime. Though antitype, however, she is never allowed to become antidote. Instead, the cure that is offered in *Parsifal* for the crisis of corporeality is always and everywhere sublimation forced to neurotic extremes. The Grail-Spear becomes, in other words, a paradoxical object, simultaneously a product of sublimation and of repression: an obsessive and symptomatic sublimity.[39]

With remarkable if not fully self-recognized insight, what Wagner shows us toward the end of *Parsifal* is nothing less than an addiction to symbols, an addiction that threatens, if left unsated, to turn blood brothers into fratricides. Before Parsifal returns to the Grail Temple at the end of the opera, Amfortas refuses to perform his office as Grail King, provoking his own order of Knights to turn on him. "*The Knights press nearer to Amfortas*," demanding that he "Uncover the Grail!/Serve now your office!/Your father commands you:/You must! you must!" and Amfortas reacts by rushing about in "mad despair," screaming, laughing, tearing open his clothes. It is a scene usually directed with foreboding, as the compassionate order, deprived of its symbol, becomes suddenly brutal. Thus does the hysteria, formerly displaced onto Kundry, come home to the Grail Knights, in their mob-like desperation for symbolic relief, and it centers even more strongly upon their king, whose insane death drive seems the only alternative to supernatural succor. Kundry's laugh, too, returns, in Amfortas's hysterical "Ha!" marked by a single quarter-note ejaculation. Further, Amfortas's laugh is linked, like Kundry's, to the exposure of his body, suddenly revealed as he tears open his clothes. We hear the return of the unredeemed Kundry, too, in the "*lebhaft*" (animated) orchestral line beneath Amfortas's "No!/No more!/Ha!" This orchestral line recalls Kundry's motif from the example given above from act 1, most obviously in the rhythmically identical descending lines shaped as a duplet plus a triplet (notated in sixteenth notes in act 1 and in eighth notes here) ending chromatically in both passages (fig. 1.7). For a moment—but only for a moment—the virus of the wound reverts back to its corporeal origin, and the old, bad Kundry risks returning in the shape of the Grail King himself.

Laughing at the Redeemer

The modernist debate over the theatricality of opera has occasionally been framed as one between two camps, with Wagner and Stravinsky standing as advocates of theatricality on one hand and Nietzsche and Adorno opposing it on the other.[40] Yet the dichotomy, eliding the highly ambiguous and fluid positions of each of these figures, obscures as much as it reveals. While our understanding of all of these figures is compromised by the opposition, our understanding of Wagner suffers the most. Nietzsche's caricature of Wagner as actor-showman-hypnotist is so evocatively expressed, and captures so much of the truth, that it has become difficult ever since to recall the sheer complexity of Wagner's position on theatricality. Ironically, the late Wagner, with his sharp rejection of spectacle and gesture and his insistence on the internalization of music, actually comes uncomfortably close to Adorno. One possible response to this discomforting proximity would be to argue, as Puchner does, that Wagner's late rejection of theatricality is essentially a feint.[41] While Puchner's response is largely correct when applied to many of Wagner's only superficially antitheatrical elements (such as the character of Mime, with its displacement of "bad" mimesis onto anti-Semitic stereotype), there are still genuine transformations in Wagner's views on theatricality when it comes to his more distinctly Schopenhauerian works. These transformations are particularly linked to the role of the performing body, which is subjugated to the increasingly symphonic voice arising from the "mystic gulf" beneath the stage. Kundry is the mark of the performing body, a body that haunts the opera that is its exorcism.

Figure 1.7. Symbol addiction and the hysterical order

Parsifal marks the extreme of Wagner's effort to close the gap between idealized and real performance, and to do so by excluding the body, so far as possible, from theatrical performance. The opera as a whole is a liturgy in celebration not so much of Christ as of the *Gesamtkunstwerk*, and more particularly of the *Gesamtkunstwerk* now understood in a particularly Schopenhauerian fashion.[42] The totality that *Parsifal* at once celebrates and attempts to achieve, in other words, is based upon the thoroughgoing translation of drama to music, of the visual to the aural, of the body to the symbol. Unsurprisingly, Wagner intended to have done with music drama after *Parsifal* and looked forward to devoting himself instead to the composition of symphonies. The remnant of corporeal theatricality still occupies the stage, however, in the character of Kundry, whose redemption, silence, and death are Wagner's ritual sacrifice. Kundry's laughter not only draws attention to her body and reminds us of her hysteria; it also points to the unavoidable ludicrousness of Wagner's project of idealist totality. In a period when fissures between idealism and corporeality were destabilizing modernist subjectivity even at the moment of its formation, Kundry's laughter threatens to turn against the redemptive project of the Festival Theatre itself.

It was Wagner's wish that *Parsifal* never be performed anywhere except at Bayreuth and to be performed in precisely the same manner, fixed forever like a ritual or a movie reel. Despite Wagner's wishes, however, his "stage-consecration festival play" has now been performed in places far from its birth, in stagings of which he never would have dreamed, and it has been revivified by both transgressions. Theatricality, with its inevitable slippages between text and performance, is often most strongly felt in those works that struggle most fervently against it. While Wagner's redemptive vision now seems impossible at best and apocalyptic at worst, Kundry's fleshly laughter at the redeemer continues to be reborn.

Notes

1. Dyer. For more on the controversy, see also Tommasini, "Should the Fat Lady Diet Before She Sings?"; and Tommasini, "With Surgery, Soprano Sheds a Brünnhilde Body."

2. Not all critics who take an interest in the relations between Wagner and Schopenhauer tend toward the culturally conservative, however. Exceptions include Lydia Goehr, Paul Lawrence Rose, and James Treadwell.

3. Magee, *Tristan Chord* 278, 279.

4. Clément's *Opera: The Undoing of Women*, Abbate's *Unsung Voices*, Levin's *Richard Wagner, Fritz Lang, and the Nibelungen*, and Žižek's "The Wound Is Healed" offer some of the most provocative insights of the past quarter century into Wagner particularly and opera generally, and none contains a reference to Schopenhauer. Similarly, Weiner's important *Richard Wagner and the Anti-Semitic Imagination* contains just three references to Schopenhauer (despite his influential anti-Semitism) over the course of roughly four hundred pages. While the diminution of Schopenhauer's importance among Wagner scholars may be at least partly attributable to simple Scho-

penhauer fatigue, the same cannot be said for his neglect among theater scholars. Despite Schopenhauer's enormous influence on the development of the modernist stage, his omission from theater history is almost total. Oscar Brockett's *History of the Theatre* (8th ed.), John Russell Brown's *Oxford Illustrated History of the Theatre*, and Christopher Innes's *Avant Garde Theatre*, all works of impressive scope and depth, omit the philosopher. J. L. Styan's three-volume *Modern Drama in Theory and Practice* mentions Schopenhauer just once, in a subclause on Wagner's indebtedness to "Schopenhauer and German metaphysics" (2:5). Nor is Schopenhauer to be found in more focused studies (such as Frantisek Deak's otherwise excellent *Symbolist Theatre*) of theatrical movements where his influence was particularly central. Even setting Wagner aside, Schopenhauer's importance for such central figures of the modern stage as Turgenev, Nietzsche, Zola, Strindberg, Wedekind, O'Neill, and Beckett has been largely forgotten.

5. There is another implied reason behind much of the scholarly silence, which is that Schopenhauer's complete dismissal of Hegel in particular and historicism in general puts him beyond the pale of much contemporary literary theory. Added to this was his excoriation by the late Nietzsche and Adorno, and his almost complete neglect by Heidegger and Levinas.

6. Schopenhauer's anticipation of Freudian theory was occasionally acknowledged by Freud himself, for example, "What [Schopenhauer] says [in *The World as Will and Representation*] about the struggle against acceptance of a painful part of reality fits my conception of repression so completely that I am again indebted for having made a discovery to not being a wide reader" ("On the History of the Psycho-Analytic Movement," *Collected Papers* 4:355).

7. Schopenhauer, *Sämtliche Werke* 2:122. English modified from Schopenhauer, *World as Will and Representation* 1:102-03.

8. When citing German-language primary sources, I have included the volume and page number of the German text, followed by a slash, followed by the volume and page number of the translation. In cases where I provide my own translation, I have referenced the German source alone. Unless otherwise noted, all excerpts from Wagner's prose writings are taken from the *Gesammelte Schriften*. For the sake of accuracy and readability, I have occasionally modified W. Ashton Ellis's translations of Wagner's prose writings.

9. The fascination with the brains of "geniuses" was relatively common among European intellectuals in the nineteenth century, with the skulls and brains of Kant, Schiller, Byron, and Schopenhauer, among many others, studied, debated, and held up as evidence for the physiological roots of intellectual superiority. Indeed, the first biography of Schopenhauer, published in 1862, featured a portrait of his skull alongside those of illustrious figures such as Kant, Schiller, Talleyrand, and Napoleon. The brains of Heinrich von Kleist and Friedrich Hölderlin were also examined, the latter for evidence of insanity (Hagner 206). By the late nineteenth century, "brain-clubs,"

in which distinguished men bequeathed their brains to science, were founded in Munich, Paris, Stockholm, Philadelphia, Moscow, and Berlin (215). Two excellent studies of nineteenth-century developments in the biology of mind are Hagner and also Young, *Mind, Brain, and Adaptation in the Nineteenth Century*. The relationship between such developments and Romantic idealist conceptions of consciousness, however, is a subject that merits further study.

10. Schopenhauer, *World as Will and Representation* vol. 2, ch. 31.

11. In his letters and autobiography, Wagner emphasized the "vast importance" of Schopenhauer for his development as a thinker and artist (see, e.g., *Selected Letters* 323, 338; *My Life* 508). The overwhelming majority of critics have agreed with this self-assessment. Magee of course emphasizes the centrality of Schopenhauer to Wagner's later work (see esp. *Philosophy of Schopenhauer* ch. 17; *Tristan Chord* chs. 8-11), as do Barry Millington and Stewart Spencer (Wagner, *Selected Letters* 163) and Michael Tanner (Tanner, *Wagner* 100). Ernest Newman is somewhat more nuanced in his verdict, arguing that "Schopenhauer merely reinforced [Wagner's] emotions and intuitions with reasons and arguments. That, and that alone, was Schopenhauer's 'influence' upon him: but it was the most powerful thing of the kind that his mind had ever known and was ever afterwards to know" (2:431).

12. Puchner 34-35.

13. Adorno, *In Search of Wagner* 46.

14. Several of these musical imitations of physical gestures are traced in Reeser.

15. Abbate, "Immortal Voices, Mortal Forms" 296.

16. Dahlhaus.

17. Wagner, *Sämtliche Schriften* 12:347.

18. C. Wagner 2:214-215/2:186.

19. As Ryan Minor has demonstrated, the journey that the Grail Knights undergo over the course of the music drama parallels this process of dematerialization in disturbing fashion. The chorus of Knights, he argues, devolves "from autonomous participant to powerless observer" as it joins the invisible treble choir at the work's conclusion (36).

20. Showalter, *Female Malady* 147-48.

21. Nietzsche 6:3:16. In his essay "The Sufferings and Greatness of Richard Wagner" (1933), Thomas Mann renders a similar verdict on *Parsifal*, which he describes as "one advanced and offensive degenerate after another," though a work largely redeemed by the "sanctifying, mythologizing power" of its music (336-37).

22. For the construction of hysteria as a specifically female and Jewish disease, see, e.g., Showalter, *Female Malady*; and Showalter, "Hysteria, Feminism, and Gender"; as well as Gilman.

23. Levin, "Reading Beckmesser Reading" 131.

24. On the Jewishness of Beckmesser, see Millington; Rose 112; Weiner 66-72; Borchmeyer; Dennis.

25. Irigaray 125.

26. The "grand united artwork," Wagner writes in *Religion and Art*, is a unity of "the masculine principle" of "the poet's work" (i.e., the text) and "the feminine" principle of "music" (10:167/6:165). The most important study of Wagner's interest in androgyny is Nattiez.

27. Smart 196.

28. Ibid. 197.

29. Ibid. 198.

30. It is worth noting, too, that religious mysticism (especially that of Jansenists and Eastern Jews) was often associated, in late-nineteenth century studies, with hysteria (Gilman 367-79). In this regard, *Parsifal*'s lavish veneer of Roman Catholic mysticism may again raise the threat of hysteria (and indeed Nietzsche's attacks on *Parsifal* for its hysteria are linked to his attacks on it for its pseudo-Catholicism). If so, then the Jew may serve in the opera as a way of displacing the hysteria called forth by the opera's embrace of mystical rapture.

31. Bronfen 149.

32. The reflection is clearly unintended, since Wagner seems to have been unaware of Charcot's experiments. But this is not to say that the coincidence of Wagner and Charcot's parallel stagings of hysteria, hypnotism, and electricity are accidental. Both drew on broader nineteenth-century discourses of electricity and hypnotism. For more on the development of these discourses, see Asdendorf; Lenoir; McCarren 748-74.

33. Davidson, n.p.

34. C. Wagner 1:1031/1:978, 1:1073/1:984.

35. In this way, *Parsifal* essentially duplicates Freud's own gendering of sublimation as work from which women are largely excluded, repression and hysteria being more congenial to women. See especially Irigaray's critique of Freud on this point (123-27).

36. Adorno, "Correspondence with Benjamin" 66.

37. It should be noted that Wagner read the *Parerga and Paralipomena* as well as *The World as Will and Representation* (Newman 2:431).

38. As William Kinderman notes, the vexed antitheatricality of *Parsifal* can also be found in the character of Klingsor, who, with the dazzling illusions of his *Zauberschloss*, "most resembles an opera director" (227).

39. I am particularly influenced here by Doane's critique of the Freudian opposition between sublimation and repression (249-67).

40. This dichotomy is well expressed in Puchner (39).

41. "We should not understand [the depiction of Mime's deceptive theatricality], or any of Wagner's other doubts [about theatricality], as a revocation of his total theatricalization of the work of art. Mime does not prove that Wagner envisions an essentially nonmimetic and nontheatrical art. What he shows instead is Wagner's

anxiety about false mimesis and false theatricality, an anxiety that is deeply rooted precisely because Wagner's entire conception of the work of art is based on such theatrical and mimetic gestures. Wagner and the audience can safely laugh about the dilemma in which Mime is caught without having to acknowledge that perhaps a similar kind of theatrical mimesis, theatrical gestures, and gestural music lies at the heart of Wagner's entire oeuvre" (Puchner 51).

42. For more on *Parsifal* as a liturgy in celebration of the *Gesamtkunstwerk*, see my *Total Work of Art* ch. 2.

Bibliography

Abbate, Carolyn. "Immortal Voices, Mortal Forms." *Analytical Strategies and Musical Interpretation: Essays on Nineteenth-and Twentieth-Century Music*. Ed. Craig Ayrey and Mark Everist. Cambridge: Cambridge University Press, 1996. 288-300.

———. *Unsung Voices*. Princeton, NJ: Princeton University Press, 1991.

Adorno, Theodor. "Correspondence with Benjamin." Trans. Harry Zohn. In *New Left Review* 81 (1973): 55-80.

———. *In Search of Wagner*. Trans. Rodney Livingstone. New York: Verso, 1991.

Asdendorf, Christoph. *Batteries of Life: On the History of Things and Their Perception in Modernity*. Berkley: University of California Press, 1993.

Borchmeyer, Dieter. "The Question of Anti-Semitism." *The Wagner Handbook*. Ed. Ulrich Müller and Peter Wapnewski. Trans. Stewart Spencer. Cambridge, MA: Harvard University Press, 1992. 166-85.

Brockett, Oscar. *History of the Theatre*. 8th ed. Boston: Allyn and Bacon, 1999.

Bronfen, Elisabeth. "Kundry's Laughter." *Richard Wagner*. Spec. issue of *New German Critique* 69 (Autumn 1996): 147-61. <http://www.jstor.org/stable/488612>.

Brown, John Russell. *Oxford Illustrated History of the Theatre*. New York: Oxford University Press, 1995.

Clément, Catherine. *Opera: The Undoing of Women*. Trans. Betsy Wing. Minneapolis: University of Minnesota Press, 1988.

Dahlhaus, Carl. *Die Bedeutung des Gestischen in Wagners Musikdramen*. Munich: R. Oldenbourg, 1970.

Davidson, George. *Bayreuther Briefe: Augenblicksbilder aus den Tagen der Patronatsaufführnungen des "Parsifal."* Leipzig: n.p., 1882.

Deak, Frantisek. *Symbolist Theatre*. Baltimore: Johns Hopkins University Press, 1993.

Dennis, David. "'The Most German of All German Operas': *Die Meistersinger* through the Lens of the Third Reich." *Wagner's Meistersinger: Performance, History, Representation*. Ed. Nicholas Vazsonyi. Rochester, NY: University of Rochester Press, 2002. 98-119.

Doane, Mary Ann. *Femmes Fatales: Feminism, Film Theory, Psychoanalysis*. London: Routledge, 1991.

Dyer, Richard. "In Opera, Size Matters." *Boston Globe* 28 Mar. 2004.

Freud, Sigmund. *Collected Papers.* Vol. 4. Trans. Joan Riviere. New York: Basic Books, 1959.

———. "On the History of the Psycho-Analytic Movement." *Collected Papers.* Vol. 1. Trans. Joan Riviere. New York: Basic Books, 1959.

Gilman, Sander. "The Image of the Hysteric." *Hysteria beyond Freud.* Ed. Sander Gilman et al. Berkeley: University of California Press, 1993. 345-452.

Hagner, Michael. "Skulls, Brains, and Memorial Culture: On Cerebral Biographies of Scientists in the Nineteenth Century." *Science in Context* 16.1-2 (2003): 195-218.

Innes, Christopher. *Avant Garde Theatre 1892-1992.* London: Routledge, 1993.

Irigaray, Luce. *Speculum of the Other Woman.* Trans. Gillian C. Gill. Ithaca, NY: Cornell University Press, 1985.

Kinderman, William. *Wagner's "Parsifal."* Oxford: Oxford University Press, 2013.

Lenoir, Timothy. "Models and Instruments in the Development of Electrophysiology, 1845-1912." *Historical Studies in the Physical Sciences* 17.1 (1986): 1-54.

Levin, David J. "Reading Beckmesser Reading: Antisemitism and Aesthetic Practice in *The Mastersingers of Nuremberg.*" *New German Critique* 69 (Autumn 1996): 127-46.

———. *Richard Wagner, Fritz Lang, and the Nibelungen: The Dramaturgy of Disavowal.* Princeton: Princeton University Press, 1998.

Magee, Bryan. *Philosophy of Schopenhauer.* Oxford: Clarendon Press, 1983.

———. *The Tristan Chord: Wagner and Philosophy.* New York: Henry Holt, 2000.

Mann, Thomas. "Sufferings and Greatness of Richard Wagner." *Essays of Three Decades.* Trans. H. T. Lowe-Porter. London: Secker and Warburg, 1947. 307-52.

McCarren, Felicia. "The 'Symptomatic Act' circa 1900: Hysteria, Hypnosis, Electricity, Dance." *Critical Inquiry* 21.4 (Summer 1995): 748-74.

Millington, Barry. "Nuremberg Trial: Is There Anti-Semitism in *Die Meistersinger?*" *Cambridge Opera Journal* 3.3 (1991): 247-60.

Minor, Ryan. "Wagner's Last Chorus: Consecrating Space and Spectatorship in Parsifal." *Cambridge Opera Journal* 17.1 (2005): 1-36.

Nattiez, Jean-Jacques. *Wagner Androgyne.* Trans. Stewart Spencer. Princeton: Princeton University Press, 1993.

Newman, Ernest. *The Life of Richard Wagner.* 2 vols. New York: Knopf, 1946.

Nietzsche, Friedrich. *The Birth of Tragedy* and *The Case of Wagner.* Trans. Walter Kaufmann. New York: Random House, 1967.

Puchner, Martin. *Stage Fright: Modernism, Anti-theatricality, and Drama.* Baltimore: Johns Hopkins University Press, 2002.

Reeser, H. E. "Audible Staging: Gesture and Movement in the Music of Richard Wagner." *Essays on Drama and Theatre: Liber amicorum Benjamin Hunningher.* Ed. Benjamin Hunninger. Amsterdam: Moussault's Uitgeverij bv Antwerpen, 1973. 140-44.

Rose, Paul Lawrence. *Wagner: Race and Revolution*. New Haven: Yale University Press, 1992.

Schopenhauer, Arthur. *Sämtliche Werke*. 7 vols. Ed. Arthur Hübscher. Wiesbaden: Eberhard Brockhaus, 1946-50.

——. *The World as Will and Representation*. 2 vols. Trans. E. F. J. Payne. New York: Dover, 1966.

Showalter, Elaine. *The Female Malady: Women, Madness, and English Culture*. London: Virago, 1985.

——. "Hysteria, Feminism, and Gender." *Hysteria beyond Freud*. Ed. Sander Gilman et al. Berkeley: University of California Press, 1993. 286-344.

Smart, Mary Ann, *Mimomania: Music and Gesture in Nineteenth-Century Opera*. Berkeley: California University Press, 2004.

Smith, Matthew Wilson. *The Total Work of Art: From Bayreuth to Cyberspace*. New York: Routledge, 2007.

Styan, J. L. *Modern Drama in Theory and Practice*. 3 vols. Cambridge: Cambridge University Press, 1981.

Tanner, Michael. *Wagner*. Princeton: Princeton University Press, 1996.

Tommasini, Anthony. "Should the Fat Lady Diet before She Sings?" *New York Times* 14 Nov. 2004

——. "With Surgery, Soprano Sheds a Brünnhilde Body." *New York Times* 27 Mar. 2005.

Wagner, Cosima. *Die Tagebücher*. 4 vols. Munich: R. Piper, 1982.

——. *Diaries*. 2 vols. Trans. Geoffrey Skelton. New York: Harcourt Brace Jovanovich, 1977, 1980.

Wagner, Richard. *Gesammelte Schriften und Dichtungen*. 10 vols. Leipzig: C. S. W. Siegel, 1907.

——. *My Life*. Authorized translation. New York: Dodd, Mead, 1911.

——. *Prose Works*. 8 vols. Trans. W. Ashton Ellis. London: Keagan Paul, Trench, Trübner, 1895-96.

——. *Sämtliche Schriften und Dichtungen*. Ed. Hans von Wolzogen and Richard Sternfeld. Leipzig: Breitkopf & Härtel, 1911.

——. *Selected Letters*. Trans. and ed. Stewart Spencer and Barry Millington. New York: W. W. Norton, 1988.

Weiner, Marc. *Richard Wagner and the Anti-Semitic Imagination*. Lincoln: University of Nebraska Press, 1995.

Young, Robert M. *Mind, Brain, and Adaptation in the Nineteenth Century: Cerebral Localization and Its Biological Context from Gall to Ferrier*. Oxford: Clarendon, 1970.

Žižek, Slavoj. "The Wound Is Healed." *Opera through Other Eyes*. Ed. David J. Levin. Stanford: Stanford University Press, 1994.

Maeterlinck, Debussy,
and Modernism

Daniel Albright

Maeterlinck's Subtractions

Pelléas and Mélisande talk intently about the fountain that no longer restores the sight of the blind. He notes that Mélisande's hair is so long that it has fallen into the water; he warns her not to keep tossing her wedding ring high in the air, because it might fall into the water. But Mélisande cries "Oh!"

PELLÉAS: It fell!
MÉLISANDE: It fell in the water!
PELLÉAS: Where is it? Where is it?
MÉLISANDE: I didn't see it go down.
PELLÉAS: I see it shining!
MÉLISANDE: My ring?
PELLÉAS: Yes, yes; down there . . .
MÉLISANDE: Oh! Oh!
   IT'S SO FAR FROM US!
   NO, NO, THAT'S NOT IT . . . THAT'S NOT IT.
   IT'S LOST . . . LOST . . .
   Nothing left but a big circle of water.[1]

But during this scene the singers aren't sitting on the edge of a fountain: they're talking to each other quietly in a luxurious high-ceilinged room, wearing expensive, more-or-less modern clothes. They seem to be improvising an operatic scene to amuse themselves—they are too well bred, too reticent to talk directly about their affection for one another, so they make up a pseudo-medieval play world in which they can obliquely describe their emotional landscape. Pelléas and Mélisande are simply names of characters in a role-playing game—a sort of Dungeons and Dragons for the listlessly rich, but almost completely improvised. When two people engage in this sort of feigning-together, one party proposes an event, then the second party either agrees ("It fell"; "It fell in the water!"), thereby affirming the event's existence, or corrects ("I see it shining!"; "That's not it"), thereby retracting the proposed event and substituting a new one.

I'm describing here the 1987 Lyons production, in which the director, Pierre Strosser, found a brilliant solution to a problem that had long vexed Maurice Maeterlinck himself: the inadequacy of human actors.[2] Maeterlinck liked to write marionette plays, and noted, in a preface to a volume of plays including *Pelléas et Mélisande*, that he did not intend to write for ordinary actors:

> Isn't it evident that the Macbeth or the Hamlet we see on the stage bears no resemblance to the Macbeth or the Hamlet we read in the book? . . .
>
> In my dreams I remember Hamlet's death. One evening I opened the door to the poem's usurper. The actor was illustrious. He entered. It took only one glance to show me that he wasn't Hamlet. Not for one instant, as far as I was concerned. For three hours I saw him stomp around in a lie. . . . [H]e was trying in vain to interest me in a life that wasn't his own and that his very presence had made a sham.[3]

But if Hamlet were sitting with Laertes on a sofa, talking through a pretend fencing match, then Maeterlinck would not have to worry about the actor's inadequacy to the role: the actor would be, in effect, reading a book out loud from memory and inviting the audience to read along with him. If he shouted, if he sobbed, the audience would see it not as enacting a role but as illustrating it, giving voice-color, voice-shape, to some fleeting personage nowhere in the playhouse, nowhere in the world. The communal experience of the theater and the intimacy of reading are almost perfectly integrated in Strosser's production.

Maeterlinck is a modernist in that his plays concern characters on the threshold of nonentity, losing the power of speech, dwelling in a self-discrediting theatrical space. Despite his love for extravagant special effects, Maeterlinck is a minimalist:

ARKËL: How are you?

MÉLISANDE: Fine, fine. Why are you asking me that? I've never been better. It seems to me, however, that I know something.

ARKËL: What are you saying? I don't understand you.

MÉLISANDE: I no longer understand all that I'm saying, you see. I don't know what I say. I don't know what I know. I'm no longer saying what I want to say. ARKËL: But you are, you are.[4]

CLOV: I use the words you taught me. If they don't mean anything any more, teach me others. . . . Then one day, suddenly, it ends, it changes, I don't understand, it dies, or it's me, I don't understand that either. I ask the words that remain—sleeping, waking, morning, evening. They have nothing to say.[5]

These echoey, nearly contentless exchanges—speech that keeps calling itself into question—tatters of language fluttering or flagging on the stage— show how Maeterlinck opens some of the paths on which Beckett was to go further. Sometimes Maeterlinck's anticipations of Beckett are striking. In his gripping play *Intérieur* (published 1894; first performed 1895), written soon after *Pelléas et Mélisande* (1892; 1893), the Old Man and the Stranger are standing outside a house, staring through a window at a happy domestic scene in which a family is putting the baby to sleep—the spectators know that the family in a moment will receive news of the death of a young daughter of the house. The two men at the window note that the family members have ceased all movement so as not to make any noise—a skein of silk drops amid the hush—everyone is looking at the baby:

THE STRANGER: They don't know that others are looking at them.
THE OLD MAN: Someone is looking at us, too.[6]

This moment has something of the shiver of the famous speech in *Waiting for Godot* (1953) when Vladimir says, as Estragon dozes, "He'll know nothing. . . . At me too someone is looking, of me too someone is saying, He is sleeping, he knows nothing, let him sleep on."[7] There is a sudden sense of dilation of the reference frame, in which looking and being looked at, knowing and not knowing, are absorbed into some rhythm beyond all horizons.

The oxymoron-riddle, the leaving off at the far verges of language, the sense of a rickety theater inset within the larger, still more rickety theater of the earth itself—these are modernist themes but also themes that Maeterlinck learned from Shakespeare. I am not what I am. The rest is silence, O O O O. We are such stuff as dreams are made on. Nothing, nothing, nothing, nothing, nothing. Maeterlinck's best-known works are dramas with such severe restrictions of language and incident that it is easy to forget that he was a both a versatile playwright and a man of learning and intellectual curiosity—he read Schopenhauer, Emerson, and Darwin with care, translated Novalis's *Fragments* and Ford's *'Tis Pity She's a Whore* into French, and took Marcus Aurelius as his hero. We remember his fairy-tale plays—abstractions and evacuations of the normal theater of his age—but Maeterlinck also wrote a worthy satirical drama (*Le miracle de Saint Antoine* [1904], in which St. Anthony of Padua visits a bourgeois household holding a wake and resurrects the matriarch from her coffin, to the consternation of most of the family, who would prefer her dead) and a topical play about the Great War (*Le bourgmestre de Stilmonde* [1918], in which the mayor of an newly invaded Belgian town has to decide whether to offer his own life in place of the life of his old servant, wrongly accused of shooting a German officer).

Maeterlinck learned from the symbolist theater of his time, especially from the works of Villiers de l'Isle-Adam, but he learned more from Shakespeare. Maeterlinck's first play, *La princesse Maleine* (1889) is a bizarre combination of motifs from *King Lear*, *Macbeth*, *Othello*, and other plays. It is, for a Maeterlinck play, unusually eventful: The princess escapes from a locked tower and disguises herself as a servant in order to be near her beloved, the son of a weak and dithery king; but she learns that her beloved is now engaged to be married to the daughter of an evil queen, who has seduced the prince's father, the weak king. The play ends in general havoc, as the evil queen and the weak king strangle Princess Maleine and the prince stabs the evil queen to death, then kills himself with the same dagger. It is as if Lady Macbeth whispers hateful counsel to King Lear, and then, transforming herself into a female Iago, manages to destroy the life of a green and guileless Othello.

Maeterlinck returned to Shakespeare in a still more overt, but more spare and intent manner, in *Joyzelle* (1903). This is, in effect, *The Tempest*, stripped of all characters except Prospero, Miranda, Ferdinand, and Ariel, with the difference that Prospero's child is now a son and the test of fitness to marry is now given to a woman, Joyzelle, newly arrived on the island. Prospero (named Merlin in this play) plots with his familiar, Arielle (a female spirit), devising various schemes to ensure that Joyzelle's love for his son is unconditional, absolute; in the most interesting twist, Merlin makes Joyzelle think that he himself is trying to seduce her, so that father and son seem rivals. This is as close as fin-de-siècle theater can approach to the modality of Tom Stoppard's *Rosencrantz and Guildenstern Are Dead* (1966).

Maeterlinck lived a long life and spent a great deal of time pondering Shakespeare. He was profoundly suspicious of Shakespeare's taste for the grandiose—for all the bloody blameful blades that bravely broach those boiling bloody breasts. *Othello* in particular struck Maeterlinck as over-wrought, excessive. As he says in his essay "Le tragique quotidien" (from *Le trésor des humbles*, 1896):

> I admire Othello, but it doesn't seem to me that he lives the distinguished daily life of a Hamlet, who has time to live just because he doesn't act. Othello is ad-mirably jealous. But isn't it maybe an old error to think that it's in moments when we're possessed by such a passion, and of other equally violent passions, that we truly live? I've come to believe that an old man sitting in his armchair, standing by under a lamp, listening without knowing it to all the eternal laws that reign around his home, interpreting without understanding what is in the silence of the doors and windows . . . I've come to believe that this motionless old man lived, in reality, a life more profound, more human, more universal, that the lover who strangles his mistress.[8]

Maeterlinck never wrote a play in which a man sits in a chair and does noth-ing at all—no playwright did until (perhaps) Samuel Beckett's *Nacht und Träume* (1982; 1983). But Maeterlinck was nevertheless engaged in a theater of *kenosis*, emptying: behind his plays there is often a conventional melo-dramatic plot, such as a love triangle, but Maeterlinck systematically dis-mantles most of the intrigue, either by moving it offstage or by omitting large pieces of it. This taste for eventlessness would spread widely through the modernist age: Gertrude Stein's theater, such as the opera *Four Saints in Three Acts* (1927-28; 1934), displays actors who stand still or noodle around the stage speaking almost contentless dialogue—indeed Stein thought that all successful plays were plays in which "nothing was happening. . . . [A]fter all *Hamlet* Shakespeare's most interesting play has really nothing happening except that they live and die. . . . [A]n interesting thing is when there is noth-ing happening. I said that the moon excited dogs because it did nothing, lights coming and going do not excite them."[9] Maeterlinck too was more interested in what he could subtract than what he could add, more inter-ested in what he could paralyze than what he could set in motion.

Possibly Maeterlinck reached his limit in the domain of subtraction and paralysis quite early in his career when, in 1890-91, he wrote *Les aveugles* and *Les sept princesses*. *Les aveugles* concerns a group of blind men and women lost in a forest—their guide, a priest, seems to have abandoned them, and they debate what to do; at last they find the priest, dead, and it begins to snow. *Les sept princesses* is an eerier play: arriving on a warship sailing through a narrow canal, a prince enters a castle to see his grandparents (the king and queen) and his cousins, the seven princesses; but he can see the girls only vaguely, from a distance, on the other side of a locked door, as if through a misted window or a mirror. At one point the queen remarks that the hall appears as though it is full of shadows. The prince calls them white shadows; he peers intently, but he can't make out whether he's seeing their hair or another shadow. The queen knocks on the window to try to awaken the sleepers, softly, because they are ill and mustn't be disturbed; but they remain imperturbable, blank. The king tells the prince about a corridor that goes under the princesses' cell: he makes his difficult way, pushes up the flagstone, enters—six of the princesses begin to stir, but the seventh, Ursula, the one he loves, cannot be awakened, is not asleep, though the hysterical queen keeps crying that the servants must wake her. The play seems to concern the inaccessibility of the imagination's treasures —"Nothing that we love over-much/Is ponderable to our touch," as Yeats puts it.[10] But it also seems to concern the playwright's difficulty in putting on stage a nothing-thing, an emotionally charged stasis. Like *Intérieur*, *Les sept princesses* is a dumb show framed by an interpretive dialogue; but unlike *Intérieur*, *Les sept princesses* gives the audience something between a *tableau vivant* and a *tableau mort*, a tantalizing glimpse at a gesture so restrained that it scarcely constitutes itself as a gesture at all. In Beckett's prose piece "Imagination Dead Imagine" (1965), a man and a woman are folded together, two white images in a white rotunda, almost completely still except for an "infinitesimal shudder instantaneously suppressed." Something of this liveliness of dead imagination is anticipated in *Les sept princesses*.

Le Hasard et la Nécessité

Maeterlinck's predilection for an abstract theater affected the design of his fables. Because he had little interest in subplots, his plays can be quite linear: when he took some elements of a play by Paul Heyse to create his *Marie-Magdeleine* (1910), he simplified the plot to the point where he called Heyse's original incomparably richer than his own; and we've already seen how he seized one minor theme in *The Tempest* to make *Joyzelle*. However, the linear design of a Maeterlinck play usually has yawning gaps: the catastrophe is often at once inexorable and improbable, unmotivated. In *Pelléas et Mélisande*, Golaud is a gigantic, powerful, desperately jealous man, but he's a floundering Othello, without glory, without even a handkerchief. In the course of the play this noble prince gets lost in a forest and is injured after being thrown from his startled horse—he seems as inept as Lewis Carroll's White Knight. He tries to gather evidence of Mélisande's infidelity by bribing his little son to spy, but the son reports nothing more sinister than that Pelléas and Mélisande keep staring steadily at the light. Golaud will finally kill Pelléas, but Mélisande dies too, even though she has suffered only the smallest of wounds. In Maeterlinck's plays, you die not so much because a train of events culminates in your dying but because you have an air of death about you. At one point the Doctor tells Pelléas that he has the grave and friendly look of someone who won't live long; elsewhere, Mélisande tells Golaud that she feels that she won't live for a long time; and early in the play Pelléas reads a letter urging him to visit quickly his friend Marcellus, who knows the exact day when he's going to die. Things you ought to know you don't know, such as (in Mélisande's case) who you are and where you come from; things you ought not to know you do know, such as the day of your death. Causality works sideways—synchronically, not diachronically: at the exact moment when Mélisande's wedding ring plops into the fountain, Golaud's horse starts and topples onto Golaud. The design of the plot is linear, but the line is zigzag and full of holes.

Maeterlinck understood this quite well. In his important essay "L'évolution du mystère" (from *Le temple enseveli*, 1902), Maeterlinck speaks of rereading two or three of his plays and noticing how fate worked in them:

> The wellspring of these little dramas was terror of the unknown that surrounds us. People trusted in powers enormous, invisible, and fatal, whose intentions no one could guess, but that the soul of the drama imagined as spiteful, attentive to all our actions, hostile to smiles, to life, to peace, to love. Maybe these powers were at bottom just, but just only in rage, and they exercised their justice in a manner so subterranean, so tortuous, so slow, so remote, that their punishments —for they never gave rewards—took on the appearance of arbitrary and inexplicable acts of destiny. In a word, it was the idea of the Christian God combined with the idea of the fatality of the ancients, thrust back into nature's impenetrable night, and, from there, taking pleasure in studying, thwarting, disconcerting, darkening the plans and the happiness of men.[11]

Maeterlinck seems almost amused by the blackness of his own dramatic imagination, but he took the notion of fatality seriously, and indeed most of his writing on drama can be seen as a long meditation on the theme of fate. He thought that all great drama depends on a sense of fatedness—a sense of some implacable process that generates the plot and ennobles the struggles of those who succumb to it. Dramatists, he believed, made use of several kinds of fatalities—one is the fatality of passion itself:

> But in order for a passion to be truly fatal in a conscious soul . . . it requires the intervention of a God, or of some other infinite and irresistible force. Therefore Wagner had recourse to the philter in *Tristan und Isolde*, Shakespeare to the witches in *Macbeth*. . . . We find that we've gone in a circle, back to the very heart of what the ancients called necessity. This circling-back is more or less admissible in a drama set in archaic or legendary times, when every sort of poetical fantasy is permitted; but in a drama that would like to press closer to the truth of the present day, it would be necessary to find another sort of intervention, that would appear to us truly irresistible, in order to dress up the crimes of a Macbeth . . . with the excuse of fatal compulsion, and so to impart to them the dark grandeur, the dark nobility that they don't have in themselves.[12]

You see Maeterlinck's problem. He hungers to present in the theater contemporary problems, contemporary science, the whole intellectual/social milieu of his age. But he also thinks that a good play requires some iron slab looming in the background, secretly moving to the foreground, dropping when ripeness is all. Macbeth is just a commonplace murderer unless his act has some black aureole playing around it. So Maeterlinck is almost always willing to sacrifice contemporaneity in order to regain the fatedness available only in legend.

Maeterlinck never succeeded in his quest to find some contemporary equivalent of predestination. He looked with great interest at Ibsen's experiment in finding a modern fate surrogate:

> Thus Ibsen, in quest of a new and so to speak scientific form of fatality, placed in the middle of his best dramas the veiled, grandiose, tyrannical figure of Heredity. But at bottom, in his works, it is not the scientific mystery of heredity that stirs in us certain human fears, deeper than our animal fears. . . . No; what excites a terror of a different kind from the terror of imminent but natural danger, is the obscure idea of a justice that heredity manifests—the bold affirmation that the sins of the father fall on the children.[13]

Maeterlinck is thinking of Ibsen plays such as *Ghosts* (1881-82), in which the legacy of the vile Captain Alving is the hereditary syphilis that destroys the mind of his son. But, as Susan Sontag points out, it's dangerous to take illness as a metaphor for anything at all, let alone for the patient working of justice; the spirochete is a contrived and artificial nemesis, compared to (say) the Furies of the *Oresteia*. Maeterlinck, therefore, thought that Ibsen, like all other contemporary dramatists, had failed to find new and credible Parcae: "We can affirm that the poet who would find today, in the material sciences, in the unknown that surrounds us, or in our own heart, the equivalent of the fatality of the ancients, that is to say a predestining force as irresistible, as universally acknowledged, would for certain write a masterpiece."[14] Maeterlinck believes that he needs Fate in his dramas to provide a teleology, an importance, even in some sense a sanctity to the deeds of his characters; but he has little confidence in any Fate that makes larger claims than the simple statement, You are often unhappy and you are certainly going to die. One reason for the celebrated wispiness of Maeterlinck's plays is that destiny, design, is asserted but asserted in bad faith, amid a regression into fairy tale. When Arkël says, in *Pelléas et Mélisande*, that we see only the back side of fate, it sounds as if someone or something sees the front side; but in fact Maeterlinck has the gravest doubts about the existence of an obverse.

There is probably no better description for the role of fate in Maeterlinck's plays than the random inevitable. He returns to this theme in one of his last books, a collection of aphorisms: "inexplicable errors of nature or of a universe where all is predetermined."[15] He was obsessed with the notion that the history of the universe was preengraved in unalterable bronze but that this general inexorability was the result of errors, blotches, random thrusts. He tended to look at human life under the aspect of eternity, as if time were an unrolled filmstrip in which everything was visible at the same time:

> In the eternal present that is the sole reality of time, you would be perfectly able to see yourself die before you were born. . . .
>
> What does it matter what happens to me, since everything that happens to me was already there before I was born?[16]

All time has, in a sense, already happened; as Eliot says, the future is a faded song. But there is no true continuity in the great story, for events come to pass through blind spasms. Beneath the utter determinedness of events there lies sheer indeterminacy. Maeterlinck wasn't entirely comfortable with Darwin's theory of natural selection by means of random variation, but he was willing to accept it as a sort of provisional truth.[17] And Maeterlinck's plays are gardens full of odd sports.

The architecture of Maeterlinck's castles reifies fate's own architecture.

His plays are full of underground tunnels, occult connections between distant things, like the corridor in *Les sept princesses* that bypasses the locked
door. Opening doors and gates requires a great deal of effort, if it is possible
at all: *Pelléas et Mélisande* begins with a scene, omitted in Debussy's opera,
in which the servants struggle with all their strength to push open the castle's great portal. Doors threaten in other ways too: Mélisande tears her
dress when it snags on a door. Maeterlinck tends to understand fate as an
endless series of closings-off, intermitted by painful accessions to your future life.

Not only is your path hemmed in and full of obstacles, but the ground
beneath your feet is at any moment likely to give way. Often the castle is
constructed precariously over some dank grotto: in *Pelléas et Mélisande*, Golaud and Pelléas grope their way down a slippery subterranean path, full of
the smell of death, and try not to fall into the stagnant water below. The first
play that Maeterlinck wrote after *Pelléas et Mélisande* was *Alladine et Palomides* (1894), in which he develops at length the theme of the grotto beneath the castle—indeed the castle of this play is Maeterlinck's most elaborate architectural fantasy. Alladine's pet lamb falls in the castle moat and is
swept away; later the desperate Alladine and Palomides find themselves in
the castle's dark foundation space and embrace in desperate wonder. The
lovers imagine that they are in a heaven of roses and smiling jewels, surrounded by water so blue that it seems a distillate of sky. But when the
sunlight at last streams in, they see that the grotto is actually all fungus and
rock and rot; the decomposed body of the lamb is there, too. This refocusing of the theater's eye from love's delirium to death's squalor is one of
Maeterlinck's simplest but most effective presentations of fate's undergirding, fate's stamina.

The castle is perched over an abyss, but it also incorporates the abyss, so
to speak, into the design of the superstructure:

ALLADINE: I can't help being uneasy when I come back to the palace. . . . It is so
     big and I'm so little, and I still get lost in it. . . . And then all those windows on
     the sea. . . . You can't count them. . . . And corridors that keep turning for no
     reason; and others that don't turn and lose themselves between the walls. . . .
     And halls where I dare not go in. . . .
PALOMIDES: We'll go everywhere. . . .
ALLADINE: You could say that I wasn't made to live in it, or that it wasn't built for
     me. . . . Once, I wandered off. . . . I pushed open thirty doors before finding

daylight. . . . And I couldn't get out; the last door opened on a pool. . . . And
vaults that are cold all summer long; and galleries that fold back endlessly on
themselves. . . . There are staircases that lead nowhere and terraces from
which you can't see anything.[18]

Where did Maeterlinck find the inspiration for this extraordinary castle?
The *Carceri d'invenzione* (1750) engraved by Piranesi—phantasmagorical
prisons seemingly designed for lunatics by lunatics—are one possibility. Another possibility lies in apiculture, for Maeterlinck was a remarkably keen
student of bees and wrote an erudite account of the dynamics of the hive
(*La vie des abeilles* [1901]), based on his own curious experiments in bee
navigational systems and on the best science of his time. Note, for example,
his account of how bees begin hive construction: "At last, when she has
worked the substance until it appears to have the desired dimensions and
consistency, she applies it to the high point of the dome, thus putting in
position the first stone or rather the keystone of the vault of the new city,
for we have here an upside-down city that descends from the sky and
doesn't arise from the earth's breast in the way that a human city does."[19]
As far as Maeterlinck is concerned, a beehive is a miracle of complex architectural thrift, just as bee society is a miracle of unanimous intent cooperative to
the good of the whole. But Maeterlinck makes no claim to understand all its
internal workings and is deeply puzzled by the telepathic coordination of all
the individual drones, workers, and queens; here fate works perfectly but
incomprehensibly. In human society fate is not only incomprehensible but
scattered, distracted, haphazard, just a name for the usual misery of things;
a drama, any drama, is a poor thing next to the annual mystery play of the
hive. Still, the palace of *Alladine et Palomides* looks more like a hive than like
a normal palace: if not completely upside down, it contains many inverted
elements, and the galleries folded back on themselves, confusingly symmetrical, are like the hexagonal cells of the honeycomb.

Maeterlinck's absurd palace spatializes the way that fate works in time:
full of dead ends, sudden useless illuminations, vain repetitions—the repli-
cated galleries are like the sideslips in the plot, such as the horse that rears
at the instant that Mélisande's ring drops in the fountain. The elaboration of
the delicate pathos of the lost has a fin-de-siècle tint, but the sheer miscon-
structedness of the stage set (virtual or actual) and of the fable feels modernist. The atmosphere is refined, sober, eerily empty—Maeterlinck's king-
doms are nearly depopulated, except for the royal family and the occasional

blind or sleeping beggar; but there is an odd Looney Tunes aspect to the plays, in that the scenario consists of one damned thing after another, until the Acme safe, long suspended in air, squashes the characters flat.

Maybe Maeterlinck's most telling dramatization of fate can be found in one of his oddest projects, *Les fiançailles* (1922). This is a sequel to his most successful play (in terms of box office), *L'oiseau bleu* (1908), a probable factor in his winning the Nobel Prize in 1911. I'm not sure that I've ever read a play that I dislike more than *L'oiseau bleu*—but its very repulsiveness fascinates me. It's a childish, sentimental, heavy-handed *féerie* à la Perrault in which two impoverished children discover that their skimpy little cottage isn't so bad after all, after the Fairy takes them on a tour of a panpsychic world full of talking dogs, talking trees, talking bread, talking sugar, talking light, and other special tickles so cartoonish that they may have influenced some of the early creators of animated cartoons. I suspect that when, in *Lolita* (1955), Vladimir Nabokov damns the evil playwright Clare Quilty by calling him a new Maeterlinck, he had this play in mind—Nabokov also said in a 1970 interview that "Beckett is the author of lovely novellas and wretched plays in the Maeterlinck tradition."[20] And I also suspect that when Auden, in *The Sea and the Mirror* (1944) describes a fiasco of a play in which everything conceivable goes wrong, "even the huge stuffed bird of happiness," he is thinking of Maeterlinck's Blue Bird of Happiness.[21]

In *Les fiançailles*, Tyltyl, the boy protagonist of *L'oiseau bleu*, has passed puberty with flying colors, and the Fairy asks him to ponder possible brides from among the girls of his acquaintance. We need not trouble with further summary of the plot, except to note that there is a character named Destiny, the enemy of Light: "*Here a trapdoor opens, in the middle of the stage; and there slowly rises, like a tower, a gigantic form twice as high as a man. It is square, enormous, imposing, crushing, and gives the impression of a granite mass and of a blind and inflexible power. You can't see its face. It is dressed in grayish rigid draperies like a mountain ridge.*"[22] But Destiny shrinks: by the middle of the play Destiny is stumbling, limping; by the end (when Tyltyl's unborn children are trying to pick their proper mother), Destiny is no bigger than a small child and lisps like a baby when he talks. At the end of the play, Light comments that necessity in human affairs comes not from fate but from a kind of general racial will: "It's not destiny, as human beings say, but the will of those who know all and never die."[23] Just as the motions of bees are guided not by fate's decree but by an instinct arising from the pressure of all bee-kind being brought to bear on the performance of individual bees, so human Destiny recasts itself: it is no longer some exterior godhead, monumental and implacable, but a sort of collective plastic force that issues from the abiding presences of the dead, the living, the unborn. *Les fiançailles* is a cutesy-pie, uningratiating piece of work, but it suggests that, as Maeterlinck grew older and more determined to be cheerful, he made his peace, to some degree, with his old enemy, fate: fate's self-discrediting is now explicit, and if the alternative to Destiny is still unconvincing, at least Maeterlinck propounds it only in the course of an obviously contrived and preposterous fable.

Maeterlinck is usually regarded as a symbolist, but those who would identify him as such should ponder *L'oiseau bleu* and its sodden array of truly clunky symbols, from the Blue Bird of Happiness on down. He was often remarkably maladept at handling overt symbols and was disinclined to regard symbols as particularly important or useful literary devices. In "L'évolution du mystère," Maeterlinck declares that the poet should be honest—should not attribute the wretchedness of human life to causes (God, hereditary, and so forth) in which he doesn't personally believe: "Otherwise, he will see in hell, in God's wrath, in decrees written in bronze, only an ostentatious show of symbols that won't satisfy him any more. It's time for poets to recognize this: the symbol is sufficient to represent provisionally an accepted truth or a truth that we as yet can't or won't confront; but when the moment comes when we want to see truth itself, it's good for the symbol to disappear."[24] Not only do Maeterlinck's plot designs work to undesign themselves, but his symbols work to unsymbol themselves. Few writers offer such a spectacle of continual discomfort with the tools of their craft.

Blank Souls

In the great plays of the 1890s, Maeterlinck's plots are both overdetermined and underdetermined—overdetermined in that murder or enervation or some other doom is felt at every moment; underdetermined in that the doom isn't the culmination of some causal chain but an arbitrary infliction. (This is another way of stating the principle of the random-inexorable.) The characters are also overdetermined and underdetermined: overdetermined in that they are marionettes with carved faces and traditional roles (the jealous husband, the ingénue, the wise grandfather); underdetermined in that the characters are far more incoherent, unpredictable, and chance driven than their masks would suggest. The masks are deceptive, for Maeterlinck is far more concerned with some substrate of human being far beneath character traits or personality types. You think that Maeterlinck cares about the puppet's face; but his real interest is wood.

In *Pelléas et Mélisande*, the heroine often seems a figure of helpless pathos, a child forlorn in a world of adult sexual complexities, a fairy whose thin wings tremble in vain. However, it is perfectly possible for an actress to play the role in much cannier, more self-consciously histrionic way. After she confesses her love to Pelléas, her enraptured lover exclaims that her voice is like a breath over the springtime sea, that she speaks with an angel's candor; but a slightly darker thought strikes him:

> PELLÉAS: You aren't deceiving me?—You aren't lying just a little, to make me smile?
>
> MÉLISANDE: No; I never lie; I only lie to your brother.[25]

This line can be read in a hushed voice, as another proof of angelic candor; or it can be read slightly rushed, overeager in the fashion of a seductress, smiling at her lover but smiling more to herself. Mélisande is always a kind of doll: when her hair falls Rapunzel-like from the tower, Pelléas ties it to a branch of a willow; later, Golaud seizes her by her hair and madly swings her from right to left, from left to right—in both cases she seems more a plaything than a person. But in her perfectly submissive state she is nevertheless exercising power: both Golaud and Pelléas are in some sense lost in the toils of her hair. It's complicated, the question of who is the snarer, who the ensnared.

The play's main theme is love, but for Maeterlinck love is everything and nothing. His canon is a long and intense investigation of love from every possible angle, but love is a passion bizarrely detachable from those who suffer it. In *Aglavaine et Sélysette* (1896)—a play that like *Pelléas et Mélisande* concerns a love triangle, though in this case involving two women and a man—the title characters discuss the differing qualities of their love for Méléandre. Sélysette is a reticent lover, hiding the depth of her affection:

> SÉLYSETTE: It seems to me that I'd like for him to love me though I didn't exist. . . . And then I hid, I hid. . . . I'd like to hide everything. . . . It isn't his fault. . . . And that's why I was happy when he kissed me while shrugging his shoulders and shaking his head. . . . Much happier than when he kissed me while admiring me. . . . But that's not how you're supposed to love, I guess? . . .
>
> AGLAVAINE: No one knows how you're supposed to love . . . some love this way and others that way; and love does this, or love does that; and it's always just

right because it's love. . . . You look at love in the bottom of your being, like a
vulture or a strange eagle in a cage. . . . The cage belongs to you, but the bird
doesn't belong to anybody . . . you look at him anxiously, you warm him, you
feed him, but you don't know what he's going to do, if he's going to fly away,
or hurt himself against the bars, or sing. . . . There's nothing in the world that's
so far away from us as our love, my poor Sélysette. . . . You just have to wait,
and learn to understand. . . .[26]

We are almost in a pagan world where the passion to kiss, or to kill, is utterly
extrinsic to the person who feels it—where love is credited to Aphrodite,
belligerence to Ares, not to the motions of our own soul. In a Maeterlinck
play, love may be all-consuming, but it's always a visitor, not a native. There
is a part of you that love leaves untouched, an absolute calm far below the
tumult of the upper regions.

At around the time of *Aglavaine et Sélysette*, Maeterlinck wrote the essay
"La morale mystique" (1896), which elaborates considerably on this theme:

What would happen, for example, if our soul suddenly became visible and she
had to move forward into the midst of a gathering of her sisters, stripped of her
veils, but laden with her most secret thoughts and dragging behind her the most
mysterious acts of her life—acts that nothing could explain? What would make
her blush? What would she want to hide? Would she start to throw, like a modest
women, the long mantle of her hair over the numberless sins of the flesh? She did
not know them, and these sins have never reached her. They were committed a
thousand leagues from her throne; and even the Sodomite's soul would pass in
the midst of the throng without suspecting anything, and bearing in her eyes a
child's transparent smile. She hasn't intervened, she spent her life close to the
light, and this is the only life she will remember. . . .

Is there a mysterious morality that reigns in regions more distant than those
of our thoughts? Is there a central star that we don't see—a star around which
our most secret desires are merely powerless planets? Does there exist, at the
center of our being, a transparent tree whose ephemeral flowers and leaves are
all our actions and all our virtues?[27]

Maeterlinck thought that many great plays of the past were lacking in soul—
he even considered Racine's *Phèdre*, though a work of the greatest psychological acuity, talky and soulless.[28] Maeterlinck intended his plays to be, above
all, intimate—stage presentations of that precious wraith the human soul. But
if the actions and virtues and feelings of the personages are all pretty much

irrelevant to their souls, then Maeterlinck has in effect predismissed the entire apparatus of the theater even before the curtain rises for act 1.

This is perhaps the most modernist aspect of Maeterlinck: the abiding sense that, despite agony and bloodshed and birth and death, nothing at all is really happening. It's all a sort of melodramatic claptrap that dimly bodies forth that luminous blank, the soul, a remote tenderness that remains immune to love, hate, talk, deed. The characters are in some sense serious, but they can't take seriously any event, even any predicate attributed to themselves. You are not what you do, no matter how violent the deed. Rage, sorrow, loving, kindness, naïveté, whorishness, intelligence, lethargy, genius, obtuseness—these traits stamp us as determinate beings, but finally they all belong to the outer husk. Beneath the husk we're all exactly alike.

Oscar Wilde once wrote, "It is a humiliating confession, but we are all of us made out of the same stuff. In Falstaff there is something of Hamlet, in Hamlet there is not a little of Falstaff. The fat knight has his moods of melancholy, and the young prince his moments of coarse humour. Where we differ from each other is purely in accidentals: in dress, manner, tone of voice, religious opinions, personal appearance, tricks of habit, and the like."[29] In a late essay, published in 1936, Maeterlinck repeats, with more circumstantial detail, the idea that the heroes of Shakespeare are more or less idle variants of the same person:

> Coriolanus is the Hamlet of the South, a Hamlet pulled up two or three notches, no longer walking with muffled step in the dangerous silence, in the suspect darkness, in the muted decorum of Elsinore, but gesticulating in the sun, under the blinding light of the Forum; exuberant, hot-blooded, scornful, vociferous, always indignant, always full of rage, let loose against the crowd's stupidity and bad smell, and against the base intrigues of its leaders. At bottom the same man, the same soul, the same character, in a different milieu, in different circumstances, under different skies, and wearing different clothes. Coriolanus already bursts out in Hamlet, for example in the scenes with Polonius, with Ophelia, with the actors, just as all of Hamlet's sadness shows through in the Coriolanus of the final scenes with Volumnia and the silent Virgilia.
>
> But Coriolanus is also Macbeth, just as Macbeth is a Hamlet who dares to act because he is split in two: his will is exteriorized in the figure of his wife. At bottom, Macbeth is an irresolute man, a man of feeling beneath his iron armor, who dared to commit only after long meditation, and too late, the very act that Coriolanus ventured immediately, and too soon.

But above all, Coriolanus is King Lear. A Lear as yet swollen with the furious blood of youth. Transport Coriolanus, grown old, to the black castles and somber heath of Scotland, let his parricidal daughters Regan and Goneril make him flail, and he will speak or rather howl like Lear; just as Lear, at the age of thirty among the Romans and Volscians, would have uttered Coriolanus's cries of horror and rage. They are interchangeable because they are, though differing in their adventures and their locales, three brothers from the same stock, three clusters of grapes on the same vine, three aspects, three trial versions of the same individual, because they are always and everywhere, at their core, at their soul, at their essential *I*, at their axis of vitality, Shakespeare in person, that is to say the same man of genius, the same universal poet dipped in a gray, or red, or black bath, the creator in his multiform and inexhaustible appearance, who draws out of himself everything, the superman a thousand times man, proud, capricious, eloquent, contradictory, hermaphrodite, who carried in himself, as we all do, numberless beings.[30]

It is part of old romantic bardolatry, this notion of Maeterlinck's that Shakespeare was an androgynous chameleon in whom the whole human race was latent. But there is another notion a little less familiar, that Shakespeare's protagonists are also chameleons who will effortlessly metamorphose into one another if placed in different circumstances, dipped into a different vat of dye stuff. Northrop Frye argues, in *Fools of Time* (1967), that Shakespeare's plays are to some extent fragments of a single overplay that literary criticism could hope to reconstruct; and Maeterlinck is working along similar lines. Lady Macbeth turns out to be not an independent character but a psychological contingency, a projection of her husband's will; the boundaries between one character and another, one play and another, are fluid, transshifting. There is a single impredicable soul at the heart of Shakespeare's tragedies: Shakespeare's own.

There is a single soul at the heart of Maeterlinck's plays, too. Golaud's soul is interchangeable with Mélisande's, since Golaud finally has nothing to do with his jealousy, just as Mélisande has nothing to do with her pathos. All souls are equally fragile, equally ethereal. When the dying Mélisande asks to hold her baby, we usually see the baby in the form of an immobile something that might be a doll or a bundle of rags; and this uninflected thing might be her soul or the soul of any of the characters in the play. Maybe the moment when Maeterlinck comes closest to confessing the eerie interchangeability of his personages occurs in *Joyzelle*, when Merlin's son, speaking to Joyzelle, remembers a time when "all my thoughts surrounded your thoughts, as a transparent water surrounds a clearer water."[31] The difference between any two of Maeterlinck's characters, then, is the difference between transparent water and clear water.

Pelléas et Mélisande

I would now like to turn to Claude-Achille Debussy's *Pelléas et Mélisande*, written mostly from 1892 to 1896, though not performed until 1902. Debussy was uncannily sympathetic to Maeterlinck's aesthetic—in fact, in the entire history of Western opera I know of no case where a composer was better equipped to handle the special difficulties of a challenging text, with the possible exception of Alban Berg's response to Georg Büchner's *Woyzeck*. Even before Maeterlinck wrote *Pelléas et Mélisande*, Debussy was (so to speak) in search of that very text, as we know from a transcription of a conversation of 1890 between Debussy and his old teacher, Ernest Guiraud:

> DEBUSSY: I don't imitate. Other dramatic form to my way of thinking: music where the word leaves off. Music for inexpressible. It must come out of shadow. Be discreet.
>
> GUIRAUD: But then, where's your poet?
>
> DEBUSSY: The poet of things half said. Two linked dreams: there's the ideal. No country, no date. No scenery to make. No pressure on the musician who perfects. Music insolently predominates in the lyric theatre. They sing too much. Musical dressing-up too heavy. Sing when it's worth the trouble. Monochrome. Grisaille. No musical developments for the sake of "developing." Mistakes! A prolonged development doesn't stick with the words, can't stick. I dream of short poems: mobile scenes. Fuck the 3 unities [of time, of place, and of action]![32]

Pelléas et Mélisande fits this recipe so exactly that it's as if Debussy had commissioned it: a play of disjointed umbral vignettes, in which half-formed characters half-speak half thoughts in nowhere, nowhen.

After Debussy got permission from Maeterlinck to write the opera—he was surprised by the playwright's deference to him—he confronted the extraordinary difficulties of writing something like a speech opera, in which the speakers are indistinct or unreal presences and the plot is attenuated to near nonexistence.

Debussy's solution to the problem of the plot is to return to the aesthetic of the early opera: that is, to stick to the most local phenomena and to ignore most matters of continuity and large-scale form. Claudio Monteverdi wrote in 1627 to Alessandro Striggio that musical expression should be concentrated "on the word and not on the meaning of the sentence" (sopra alla parola et non sopra al senso de la clausula), and Debussy is equally determined to register minute responses to the text.[33] As he wrote in 1909 to Edwin Evans:

> Maybe it's better for music to try to render by simple means—a chord? a curve?—the successive states of the atmosphere, of the soul, better for music to adjust itself to everything that happens, without painfully forcing itself to follow a pre-existing and *always arbitrary* symphonic plot-line, which will necessarily tempt you to sacrifice the plot-line of the emotions; but you'll have succeeded in making a beautiful symphonic development . . . ! Once again, that has no place in lyric drama; moreover, it's too cheap a way of evading a difficulty. That's why there's no "guiding thread" in *Pelléas*, and why the characters in the opera don't submit to the slavery of the *Leitmotiv*, as a blind man is slave to his poodle or his clarinet![34]

A leitmotif, as the name suggests, leads and moves: its recurrent forms, altered, recolored, reworked in light of the changing dramatic situation, provide an Ariadne's thread through the opera's labyrinth. But Debussy craves a musical rhetoric discontinuous and uninstructive, in which the labyrinth is left labyrinthine, unsolved. He wants to impose no arbitrary form on the near formlessness—the random-inexorable—of Maeterlinck's play. Debussy tries to provide the single perfect chord, or a curve a few bars long, to make a musical dream double for a single instant of Maeterlinck's word-dream; as for large form, he is content to let the music sag into whatever sort of odd form that the play can provide.

The comment to Evans is part of a general attack on the Wagnerian leitmotif:

> What saws, these leitmotive! What eternal catapults! The *Ring of the Nibelung*, in which there are pages of staggering force, is a set of mechanical tricks. They even disfigure my beloved *Tristan*, and I grieve to feel myself severed from it.[35]

> The drama by M. Zola and M. Bruneau [*The Hurricane*] is noted for its numerous symbols, and I admit I don't understand this excessive need for symbols. They seem to have forgotten that the most beautiful thing is still the music. Naturally, the symbol summons forth the leitmotiv; and there it is, the music is still obliged to encumber itself with little obstinate phrases that insist on being heard in spite

of everything. In sum, to claim that such a succession of chords will represent such a feeling, or such a phrase some sort of personage—this is a rather unexpected anthropometrical game.[36]

Ah! my lord! How insupportable these folks wearing helmets and animal skins become by the fourth evening [*Götterdämmerung*] . . . Think of it, they never appear without being accompanied by their damned leitmotiv; there are even some of them who sing it! It's like the cute madness of someone who, as he hands you his visiting card, lyrically declaims what's printed on it![37]

Debussy's dislike of the leitmotif is twofold: first, the set of all its evolutions provides a form of musical continuity clumsily superimposed on the text, and probably irrelevant to it; second, as soon as you fasten a name to the musical theme, it becomes a gross and glaring form of musical commentary on the personages—as if Hunding, when he stalks around his hut in *Die Walküre*, bears on his chest a neon sign that keeps flashing the name HUNDING. The first objection pertains to the plot, the second to characterization. Debussy is following Maeterlinck's way of deconstructing, dissolving the personages, and a name plate works against what he is trying to accomplish. Pierre Boulez has it almost right when he comments on Debussy's nonleitmotif, "It's instead a matter of arabesques tied to the characters themselves, without variation other than decorative, effortlessly integrated into the general context."[38] But the liaison between the arabesque-like themes and the characters may be a little weaker than Boulez suggests. In some sense Debussy's themes are *Verleitmotive*, misleading motives. Just as Maeterlinck is uncomfortable with a vocabulary of symbols, Debussy is somewhat antisymbolic, too: he may well have thought that he is desymbolizing *Pelléas et Mélisande* by liberating his musical themes from names, from any intelligible semantics beyond glints and hints derived from Maeterlinck's evanescent rhetoric of feeling. Anthropometry was a sort of whole-body phrenology, in which measurements of body parts were used to define ratios that presumably gave insight into character and temperament; Debussy seems to be mocking the leitmotif system as a game that constructs icons of men and women, symbolic character shapes, through musico-mathematical procedures.

The personages in *Pelléas et Mélisande* are vanishing creatures on the brink of dissolution, half-formed beings that toy with the notion of being characters in an opera. And their musical symbols are pseudo-motives that fail to constitute themselves properly, fall into signlessness.

We've already looked in some detail at Maeterlinck's strategies for at-
tenuating and disindividuating—even in a sense abrogating—the characters
in his plays. Debussy, who could have known almost nothing of Maeterlinck's theories of the drama beyond what he could infer from the plays
themselves, was quite aware of the strange nullity of Pelléas, Mélisande, and
the rest of the crew and tried to supply his own nullities to match. As he
wrote to Chausson (probably at the beginning of 1894): "I've spent some
days in pursuit of this 'nothing' from which she (Mélisande) is made. . . .
Now it's Arkël who torments me. That one, he's from beyond the grave, and
he has the impartial and prophetic tenderness of those who are going to
vanish soon, and I have to say all that with do, re, mi, fa, sol, la, ti, do!! [sic]
What a job?"[39] Mélisande is nothing, and Arkël is a sort of ectoplasm thin-
ning into the void. Yet, as Roger Nichols and Richard Langham Smith have
pointed out, Debussy himself labels a four-measure passage at the beginning of act 1, scene 3, the *thème initial de Mélisande*, a theme that undergoes
many vicissitudes in the course of the opera. So we have here a curious
musical entity that both is and is not a leitmotif (fig. 2.1).[40] The little six-note
phrase in the middle stave of the first measure is indeed one of the opera's
most salient features. It's worth noting that Debussy isn't alone in labeling
it the Mélisande theme (or one of them): Paul Dukas, one of Debussy's keen-
est and most admiring critics, hears it the same way. In the play *Ariane et
Barbe-bleue* (1899), Maeterlinck amuses himself by assigning to Bluebeard's
first five wives—a spectral coven—the names of characters in his previous
plays: one of them is Mélisande. In Dukas's lucid, luminous opera *Ariane et
Barbe-bleue* (1907), as Sélysette announces to Ariane the name Mélisande,
Debussy's *thème initial* provides a charming *carte de visite*.

There are two themes heard with astonishing frequency in Debussy's
Pelléas et Mélisande: one is the *thème initial de Mélisande*, but I think that the
key to the opera's motivic structure lies in the other theme (fig. 2.2). This is
the opera's very beginning, prefacing the scene where Golaud, lost in the
forest, discovers Mélisande, lost in the forest; the theme I mean is the one
in measures 5 and 6. It has been sometimes labeled as the Golaud theme,
because it offers a striking contrast with the Mélisande theme (also conspicuous in this prelude) and because it sometimes sounds a bit stern and,
when played by horns, hunter-like; but—for reasons that will become
evident—I'll refer to it as the "Golaud" theme, in quotation marks. Here, in
its first appearance, it is harmonically tricky: the first chord might be construed as a half-diminished chord, but I think it would be better to describe

Figure 2.1. Debussy, *Pelléas et Mélisande*: *thème initial de Mélisande*

the theme as an alternation of two chords each derived from the whole-tone scale. Later in the opera, Golaud and Pelléas will grope their blind way down a subterranean path, accompanied by an up-and-down movement of a whole-tone scale, perhaps the purest expression in Western music of the directionlessness, the disorientation, the sheer absence of any possible tonic that the whole-tone scale (like any symmetrical division of the octave) entails. And right here at the beginning we have an alternation of a whole-tone chords, at once resolute sounding and completely aimless, introducing us to a tone domain that lacks a guiding thread, a sense of forward motion, a sense of fate—or, to say it better, that provides only a fake fatality in music, comparable to the fake fatality of Maeterlinck's text.

In the following measures we hear Golaud again, and then, sweetly, expressively, Mélisande, in a slightly different shape from what Debussy would label (at the beginning of scene 3) the *thème initial de Mélisande* (fig. 2.3).

Figure 2.2. Debussy, *Pelléas et Mélisande*: "Golaud" theme, first appearance

Now the "Golaud" theme is more normally formed, harmonically speaking:
a dominant chord in G minor (maybe a little unusual, in that G minor is the
tonic), alternating with an A-major chord (if a thirteenth chord can ever be
considered normal). The music seems to be refocusing, moving to a better-
adjusted space, a space you're less likely to get lost in. Then, for the first
time, the Mélisande theme appears, in a manner that is equivocal—neither
particularly disorienting nor particularly well oriented. The harmony isn't
overly challenging: you can hear the often-repeated accompaniment figure
as a slightly warped B♭ major⁷ arpeggio, undergirding a melody that counter-
asserts itself in B♭ minor. But I don't hear it in quite that way, and Debussy
(by writing the melody with a C♯ instead of a D♭) doesn't spell the notes in
a way that invites that interpretation. It might be better to think of the Mélisande theme, in this guise, as a pentatonic melody—if played on a piano,
the melody would be all black notes—with a whole-tone accompaniment:
as if both of the main themes need to be stated first in harmonic forms at
an angle to tonality.[41] But I think it's also important to note that the melody
and the accompaniment alike are entirely part of the whole-tone scale, except for the single melodic note C♯. According to either analysis, it's the C♯
that sticks out, since it is the one note that isn't in the whole-tone scale of
the accompaniment (if you're listening on this axis) or that deviates most

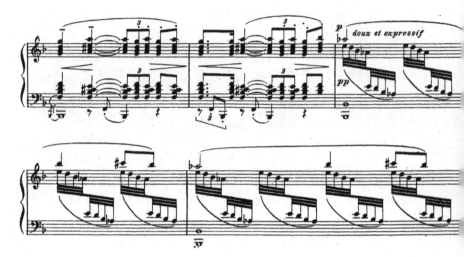

Figure 2.3. Debussy, *Pelléas et Mélisande*: "Golaud" and Mélisande

strongly from B♭ major (if you're listening on that axis). The theme is perfectly susceptible to far more orthodox harmonic forms, forms that leave
the topmost note in a less glaring position: for example, the still-sweeter
version from the beginning of scene 3 (qtd. in figure 2.1) works as a compact
melody supported by a B⁹ chord.

The persistence of these two themes (Mélisande and "Golaud") through
the opera, especially in the opening acts, is astonishing, unprecedented,
and without a successor. Debussy weaves many other threads through his
tapestry, some dark, some golden, such as the lovely, down-skipping theme
at the beginning of act 2—he lavishes a wealth of thematic material on the
opera—but the acoustic environment is created largely by the two main
themes.

There is another major work by Debussy that is similarly built up from
two themes—and from two themes bearing a striking similarity to these
two themes: *Sirènes*, the third of the *Nocturnes*. Debussy composed this
piece while working on *Pelléas et Mélisande*, and it was first performed in
1901, a year before the opera. Figure 2.4 shows the main theme. This is
Maurice Ravel's reduction for two pianos: in the original version, the sirens'
song (the theme that begins in the third measure here, *très expressif*) is sung
by a wordless female chorus. Like the "Golaud" theme, the sirens' theme
consists of two notes separated by a major second: indeed the whole of
Sirènes might be considered the apotheosis of the major second, since so

Figure 2.4. Debussy, *Sirènes*: sirens' song

much of the music is constructed around that interval. The E♯ makes for an intense sonority, since it's a tritone away from B, and B major is both the tonic and the chord that accompanies the theme, here in its first appearance; if you could reduce the opening flute solo in the *Prélude à L'après-midi d'un faune* to two adjacent notes, it might sound a bit like this. And like the "Golaud" theme, the rhythm of the sirens' song is complicated, with its ligatures connecting an eighth note to the first beat of an eighth-note triplet: the rhythm isn't urgent in the "Golaud" manner, but it is equally arresting, in a more languid way.

I think of *Sirènes* as even more oceanically alive than *La mer*. At the beginning the horns seem to make great bird cries of desire—the sirens of antiquity were not mermaids but women on top and birds on the bottom—but a particular kind of desire, endless and insatiable, for Odysseus's ship is never going to come to their rock. The music seems to have no particular sense of beginning or end: it doesn't drive toward a cadence but elaborates the big waves with little waves, underpulses, in the way that the surge of surf on a beach falls into long rhythms of tide and medium rhythms of regular wave fall and short rhythms of little splashes at the end of the regular wave fall. In the libretto that Debussy wrote for a projected opera on Poe's "The Fall of the House of Usher," Roderick Usher hears or imagines a lost bird—"*Ses ailes battent comme si c'était la respiration du temps*" (The bird's wings beat as if it were the respiration of time)[42]—and Debussy's rhythm in pieces like *Sirènes*, pulse without ictus, is the sound of time's breathing.

There is one other important theme besides the song itself (fig. 2.5). The chromatic figure marked *expressif* feels Asiatic, seductive, odalisque: it sounds

Figure 2.5. Debussy, *Sirènes*: snake-charming

like the music of sexual display, as if the sirens are wriggling their bodies as they sing.

Sirènes, we see, is constructed from two themes, one that is simply a complex dance across a major second and another that is melodically intense. This is a simplified version of the recipe of *Pelléas et Mélisande* itself, for the opera is constructed from the theme that is a complex dance across a major second and another theme that is melodically intense, though in a chaster manner than that of *Sirènes*.

Insofar as the "Golaud" theme is another casting of the theme of the sirens' song, it seems more appropriate to Mélisande than to Golaud. The demure, white, angelic Mélisande is properly represented by the *thème initial de Mélisande*; but, as we've seen, there is another way of regarding Mélisande, as a far more sexually alert being—and that version of Mélisande can be conceived along the lines of the sirens of the *Nocturnes*: the liquid Mélisande, the Mélisande of the fountain in the forest and the fountain of the blind and the grotto by the sea, the elusive Mélisande. Mélisande is Mélusine.

Maeterlinck's women are often, in one form or another, undines or naiads, images drawn on water that somehow rise into some semblance of human life. In one of Debussy's most beautiful songs, *La grotte* (1904), he sets a line by Tristan L'Hermite concerning reflections of flowers that seem like "les songes de l'eau qui sommeille."[43] Mélisande herself is a sort of dream of the sleeping water, in the pool where, as L'Hermite puts it, Narcissus died long ago.

In *L'oiseau bleu*, a play that works as a sort of bowdlerized child's anthology of all of his favorite themes, Maeterlinck invents, as a companion to little Tyltyl, a character named Water, dressed in a costume of dripping bluish gauze, with seaweed in her hair: she enters through the water tap and, as she becomes more fully personified, becomes disturbed that she cannot leave through the same aperture. Soon afterward the Fairy tells Water that it would be nice if she didn't keep flowing all over the place; later, Tyltyl tells his crybaby sister Mytyl that she shouldn't weep all the time, in the way that Water does. And Water is indeed a complaining sort: at one point she groans that she has never known the least happiness. However, Water is, in her quiet, tender way, a vocal sort: saying farewell, she gives some advice to the children, though her enemy Fire makes snide comments:

> WATER: Love the Fountains well, listen to the Streams. . . . I will always be there . . .
> FIRE: She's flooded everything!
> WATER: When you sit down, in the evening, by the edge of the Springs . . . you can find more than one here, in the forest—try to understand what they're trying to tell you—I can't, any more—I'm choked with tears and I can't speak. . . . Remember me when you see the jug . . . you'll also find me in the pitcher, the watering-can, in the tank and in the tap.[44]

It is striking how much Mélisande there is in all this: Mélisande enters the play through a forest fountain, almost without history, as if she had just recently turned into a human being; and she resists Golaud's attempts to carry her off into the human world, as if she would prefer to deliquesce back into nonentity. "Ne me touchez pas, ou je me jette à l'eau" (Don't touch me, or I'll throw myself in the water), she warns her future husband.[45] But, like Water, she seems already a little too big and dense to return through the tap. In this opening scene, and elsewhere, she melts into tears without much provocation. Her voice is fluent and attractive, watery: "Ta voix! Elle est plus fraîche et plus franche que l'eau" (Your voice! It's fresher and more open than water), Pelléas tells her.[46] But like the voice of a brook, her voice is not always very intelligible: "Je ne comprends non plus tout ce que je dis" (I no longer understand all I'm saying), she says as she dies, and it's not likely that others understand her riddling words very well, either.[47]

The "Golaud" motive—I'd prefer to call it the motive of water, along the lines of its cousin in *Sirènes*—is watery, *informe*, not just because of its un-steady sloshing between two chords but for other reasons as well. The heaving of the sailors in act 1, scene 3 is closely related to it (fig. 2.6). Here the contraltos go back and forth across a major second, in dotted rhythm, just as in the "Golaud" motive, in many of its forms. Sea spray often tends,

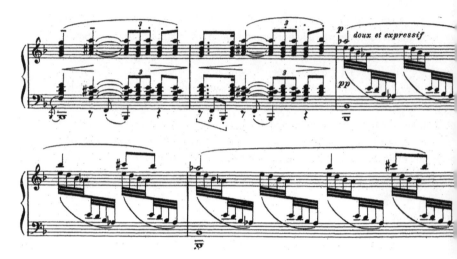

Figure 2.6. Debussy, *Pelléas et Mélisande*: sailors

in Debussy's imagination, to gather around such melodic phrases. In Debussy's best-known essay, "L'entretien avec M. Croche," from *Monsieur Croche
antidilettante*, he writes, "You must seek discipline in liberty and not in the
formulas of a worn-out philosophy, good only for the weak. Don't listen to
the counsels of anybody, except that of the wind that in passing tells us the
history of the world."[48] I'm not sure that Debussy has a particular musical
trope that represents the counsel of the wind, though there are a few places
where I could look; but I think that water has a distinct tendency to speak
in a language of irregular motions across a major second.

But the "Golaud" motive occasionally contracts, fascinatingly, from a
major second to a minor second, as in the interlude just before the beginning of act 1, scene 2 (fig. 2.7). Here the chords oscillate between B major[7]
and A minor. Such alternation between chords themselves a major second
apart is common in the harmonization of this theme, but the minor-second
melodic form is not so usual. In the later acts we sometimes hear other os-
cillations across a minor second (fig. 2.8). Golaud, distraught, tries to hide
his emotion from his son as he encourages the boy to spy on Pelléas and
Mélisande, so he invents a wolf to explain why he seems shaken. The imaginary wolf makes this faint ululation in the depths of the orchestra. In retro-
spect from today, it sounds like an almost erased allusion to the wolf theme
in Prokofiev's *Peter and the Wolf* (1936).

Figure 2.7. Debussy, *Pelléas et Mélisande*: "Golaud" motive in its minor-second form

Figure 2.8. Debussy, *Pelléas et Mélisande*: wolf

This sort of slow black trill is part of the normal operatic rhetoric of uneasiness. There is a similar moment in a later opera, Igor Stravinsky's *The Flood* (1962): a horn indulges in a nearly rhythmless vagrancy between adjacent semitones, B and C, as the Serpent comes to tempt Eve (fig. 2.9). Stravinsky describes his music as follows: "The Tarnhelm music for two muted horns is likely to be my first and last attempt to compose a belly dance."[49] It is the merest sketch of a belly dance, a dance for the skeleton of a belly dancer. That Stravinsky associates this little bit of music—scarcely more than an ornament—with Wagner's Tarnhelm is of interest. Now the Tarnhelm motive—the motive of Alberich's shape-shifting or invisible-making helmet in *Der Ring des Nibelungen*—appears initially as a G♯-minor chord that transforms itself into an E-minor chord, recedes back to G minor, tries out E minor once again, and then rises to a B chord, not marked as either minor or major (fig. 2.10). It is a harmonic riddle that poses the question, How many triads contain the note B?—B is the one stable element as the motive creeps up and contracts and creeps up again. (Similarly Alberich is always Alberich, whether in the form of dragon or toad—he is going no-

Figure 2.9. Stravinsky, *The Flood*: temptation of Eve

Figure 2.10. Wagner, *Das Rheingold*: Tarnhelm

where, just as the motive is going nowhere.) Stravinsky has oversimplified the Tarnhelm into the emptiest possible oscillation of two notes separated by a minor second, with a slight reinforcement (from the second horn) of the upward creep at the end of Wagner's motive.

The "Golaud" motive also operates as a kind of Tarnhelm and indeed may have been partly inspired by Wagner's invisibility music. It is a pure isolate of instability. Golaud is of course a weak, deeply unstable man, full of bad imaginings about his wife, full of murderous frustration, and driven mad, like Othello, by the general uninterpretability of human conduct. Mélisande trickles through Golaud's hands, through Pelléas's hands, like water. Arkël, according to Debussy, is a voice from beyond the grave. One important character, Pelléas's sick father, never appears and doesn't even have a name. These wraiths are almost too translucent to cast a shadow; they are given a good deal of beautiful and touching music, but their nobodiness is given expression by the "Golaud" theme.

Instability is also a property of the castle itself, built over a chasm of whole tones, indefinite musical spaces. The scene where the castle makes itself most psychically present is the scene in the underground grotto, but there are other moments where the castle looms forth, forbidding, tenebrous:

> GOLAUD: Can't you get used to the life we lead here?
> Is it too sad here?
> It's true that this castle is very old and very dark . . .
> It's very cold and very deep.
> And all who dwell here are already old.[50]

The brief passage in figure 2.11 is one of the glories of the score: in the lowest stave, the English horn quietly, insistently traces a four-note figure that becomes a kind of soft clock, a drift of sand through an hourglass, as if the castle's stones were making a faint sound of crumbling. Neither Maeterlinck nor Debussy push any further in the direction of the castle's falling into ruin, but at the climax of Debussy's fragmentary opera *La chute de la maison Usher* (on which Debussy worked from about 1908) there is a moment that seems an extrapolation of the castle of Allemonde into a state of full collapse. Debussy himself considered that his Usher project had nothing to do with *Pelléas et Mélisande*; as he told an interviewer in 1910, "I'm happy . . . not only because the atmosphere of secrecy, the sentiments, the tensions, the emotions found in Poe's stories have never been translated into music, but also because you can't find any contrast more absolute than that between Poe and Maeterlinck."[51] But I think that Debussy is wrong in distinguishing so strongly between Poe and Maeterlinck. A set designer for the scene where Pelléas and Golaud grope along the walls of the grotto beneath the castle might profit from studying Poe's account of Roderick Usher's painting:

> If ever mortal painted an idea, that mortal was Roderick Usher. For me at least— in the circumstances then surrounding me—there arose out of the pure abstractions which the hypochondriac contrived to throw upon his canvass, an intensity of intolerable awe, no shadow of which felt I ever yet in the contemplation of the certainly glowing yet too concrete reveries of Fuseli.

Figure 2.11. Debussy, *Pelléas et Mélisande*: castle

One of the phantasmagoric conceptions of my friend, partaking not so rigidly of the spirit of abstraction, may be shadowed forth, although feebly, in words. A small picture presented the interior of an immensely long and rectangular vault or tunnel, with low walls, smooth, white, and without interruption or device. Certain accessory points of the design served well to convey the idea that this excavation lay at an exceeding depth below the surface of the earth. No outlet was observed in any portion of its vast extent, and no torch, or other artificial source of light was discernible; yet a flood of intense rays rolled throughout, and bathed the whole in a ghastly and inappropriate splendor.[52]

Figure 2.12. Debussy, *La chute de la maison Usher*: crack

Maeterlinck's claustrophobias and agoraphobias are quieter than Poe's, less overwrought but no less intense.

In *La chute de la maison Usher*, the Friend reads aloud to Roderick Usher the story of how the knight Ulrich encounters an evil hermit who turns into a fire-tongued dragon: Ulrich rushes to seize a shining bronze shield hanging on the wall. In the reconstruction of the opera by Juan Allende-Blin, printed in figure 2.12, there is a maniacally repeated four-note figure that falls through major sevenths and minor seconds, from B to C to B to C.[53] It is as if the gentle structural instabilities in Arkël's very old, dark, cold, deep castle in *Pelléas et Mélisande* had zigzagged wide open—Usher's house is falling apart before our ears. The last act of *Pelléas et Mélisande* is simply a long tapering-off, as the Doctor gives up and Golaud weeps and Mélisande unsubstantiates herself. But among the unrealized potentialities of Maeterlinck's vagrant impossible plot is a louder ending, an implosion in which the vacuum at the play's heart would take aggressive shape. In *La chute de la maison Usher*, Debussy toys with the bang that is on the far side of all of Maeterlinck's whimpers.

The collapse of a building is a theme more resonant in opera than it is in prose fiction. Debussy was a keen student of early French opera and even composed an *Hommage à Rameau* (the second of the *Images pour piano*, 1904-05). A remarkable number of seventeenth- and eighteenth-century French operas (by Lully, Charpentier, Gluck) end with a scene in which a huffy witch (Armide, Médée) exits on a flying chariot while her magic palace falls into ruin. Debussy has no use for dragon-drawn witches, but he is deeply attracted to the idea of a building falling asunder. His older colleagues were similarly attracted: Camille Saint-Saëns's *Samson et Dalila* (1877) ends with Samson's pulling down onto his head the Temple of Dagon, and the second act of *Parsifal* (1882) ends with nightmare ferocity as Klingsor's magic castle undoes itself—you can hear in Wagner's music how the earthquake first topples the small stones at the top and then upheaves big slabs of wall.

As it happened, the composition of *Pelléas et Mélisande* was intimately bound up with *Parsifal*. On October 2, 1893, the exasperated Debussy wrote to Chausson that he was tearing up certain passages of his new opera:

> I was in too much a hurry to cry victory for *Pelléas et Mélisande*, for, after a sleepless night, the sort of night that brings good counsel, I've had to admit that I wasn't yet there at all! This part looked like a duet by Mr. So-and-so—it doesn't matter who—and above all the phantom of old Klingsor, alias R. Wagner, appeared at the curve of a measure. And so I've torn it all up, and started afresh in search of a little chemistry of more personal phrases, and have tried to be as much Pelléas as Mélisande.[54]

There is a sense in which Debussy's opera is about magic; but there is another sense in which it is about exorcism, the dispelling of Wagner's magic to make room for his own. Klingsor's castle has to fall down once and for all before Arkël's castle—another rickety structure—can be built.

Debussy is haunted not only by the remarkable music that Wagner wrote for Klingsor—great nervous gasps, chromatic whirls in which the chroma varies from dark blue to black, the sound equivalent of van Gogh's *Starry Night*—but also by the dramatic figure of Klingsor himself:

The most beautiful character in *Parsifal* belongs to Klingsor (former knight of the Grail, shoved out of the door of the Holy Place for his too singular opinions concerning chastity). He is a marvel of rancorous hatred; he knows what men are worth and weighs the solidity of their vows of chastity in the scales of his contempt. You could easily argue that this twisted magician, this old recidivist, is not only the only "human" personage, but the unique "moral" personage in this drama where the falsest moral and religious ideas are proclaimed; the young Parsifal is the heroic and nitwit knight of those ideas.[55]

Klingsor's too singular opinion on chastity is that it is a good idea to castrate himself to be immune from sexual temptation—Wagner even toyed with the idea of scoring the role for a male soprano, if Domenico Mustafa, a castrato in the Vatican choir, could be made available to sing it. Wagner's two greatest villains, Alberich and Klingsor, both renounce love to gain power: Klingsor manages to ruin Amfortas, the king of the knights of the Grail, by compelling the witch Kundry to seduce him. For Debussy, Klingsor is a hero of impotent despair. Debussy was far from sexually impotent, but he drove two of the women in his life to threats of suicide (his first wife actually shot herself), and I think that he may have seen himself as a sort of Klingsor, snide, spiteful, tormented and tormenting, a seducer who practiced his music-magic in a calculating, somewhat hollow manner.

Debussy, at least in certain moods, thought that his music was about emptiness: as he wrote to Pierre Louÿs on March 27, 1898, "The three *Nocturnes* are continuations of my felt life, and have been full of hope, then full of despair, and finally full of the void!"[56] Each of the three *Nocturnes* trails off into nothingness: the sirens first seduce and then turn their backs. As J. Alfred Prufrock says, "I do not think that they will sing to me." If Debussy had completed his opera on the fall of the house of Usher, it would have been his finest presentation of the vacuum at the heart of things. Maybe in its unfinishedness it is a still more impressive *rien*. Maeterlinck thought that the ultimate truth of human life is that it is full of sound and fury, signifying nothing. But neither Maeterlinck nor Debussy was particularly expert in fury; an old man sitting vacantly in a vacant room or a faint song heard from somewhere in a tower can adequately signify nothing, too.

Notes

1. Debussy, *Pelléas et Mélisande* 2.1.11-12 mm. 1-2. References to the score will be to act, scene, and rehearsal number, followed by measure when necessary. This and all subsequent translations are my own.

2. A DVD version of the production, originally recorded for television, is available. See Strosser.

3. Maeterlinck, *Pelléas et Mélisande* 7, 10. This and all subsequent translation of Maeterlinck are my own.

4. Debussy, *Pelléas et Mélisande* 5.1.5 m. 6-6 m. 7.

5. Beckett, *Endgame* 44, 81.

6. Maeterlinck, *Intérieur* 108.

7. Beckett, *Waiting for Godot* 104-05.

8. Maeterlinck, *Le trésor des humbles* 182-84, 187.

9. Stein 292.

10. In "Towards Break of Day" lines 17-18. See Yeats 208.

11. Maeterlinck, *Le temple enseveli* 112-13.

12. Ibid. 128-29.

13. Ibid. 158-59.

14. Ibid. 126.

15. Maeterlinck, *L'autre monde* 43.

16. Ibid. 96.

17. See his *La vie des abeilles* 273.

18. Maeterlinck, *Alladine et Palomides* 18-19.

19. Maeterlinck, *La vie des abeilles* 130.

20. Nabokov 172.

21. Auden 340.

22. Maeterlinck, *Les fiançailles* 36.

23. Ibid. 177.

24. Maeterlinck, *Le temple enseveli* 131.

25. Debussy, *Pelléas et Mélisande* 4.3.45 mm. 4-7.

26. Maeterlinck, *Aglavaine et Sélysette* 72.

27. Maeterlinck, *Le trésor des humbles* 68-69, 74.

28. Ibid. 33.

29. Wilde 1075-76.

30. Maeterlinck, *Avant le grand silence* 29-34.

31. Maeterlinck, *Joyzelle* 91.

32. Hoéré 28-29.

33. See my *Modernism and Music* 38, 33n.

34. Nichols and Smith 184-85.

35. To Guiraud in September 1890. See Hoéré 33; also cited Nichols and Smith, 193.

36. Comments from *La revue blanche* 15 May 1901. Debussy, *Monsieur Croche et autres écrits* 41-42.

37. In *Giles Blas*, 1 June 1903. See Debussy, *Monsieur Croche et autres écrits*, 180.

38. Boulez 134.

39. See Debussy's "Deux lettres de Debussy à Ernest Chausson," in *La Revue musicale* 7:7 (1 May 1926), 183-84. Cited in Nichols and Smith 34-35.

40. Nichols and Smith 144.

41. This is also how Nichols and Smith hear it (91).

42. Debussy, *La chute de la Maison Usher* 29.

43. Debussy, "La Grotte" 133.

44. Maeterlinck, *L'oiseau bleu* 246.

45. Debussy, *Pelléas et Mélisande* 9.

46. Ibid. 337.

47. Ibid. 372.

48. Debussy, *Monsieur Croche et autres écrits* 52.

49. Stravinsky 75.

50. Debussy, *Pelléas et Mélisande* 2.3.24.

51. Debussy, *Monsieur Croche et autres écrits* 310.

52. Poe 98.

53. Debussy, *La chute de la Maison Usher* 40. In the reconstruction by Robert Orledge, the effect is much less striking. See Debussy, *Le Roi Lear* 73-74.

54. Debussy, *Lettres 1884-1918* 55.

55. Debussy, *Gil Blas* 6 April 1903. In *Monsieur Croche et autres écrits* 143-44.

56. Debussy, *Lettres 1884-1918* 90.

Bibliography

Albright, Daniel. *Modernism and Music: An Anthology of Sources*. Chicago: University of Chicago Press, 2004.

Auden, Wystan Hugh. *Collected Poems*. Ed. Edward Mendelson. New York: Random House, 1976.

Beckett, Samuel. *Endgame*. New York: Grove Press, 1958.

———. *Waiting for Godot*. New York: Grove Press, 1954.

Borges, Jorge Luis. *El Aleph*. Buenos Aires: Losada, 1952.

Boulez, Pierre. *Points de repère*. Vol. 2, *Regards sur autrui*. Ed. Jean-Jacques Nattiez and Sophie Galaise. Collection Musique/passé/present. Paris: Bourgois, 2005.

Debussy, Claude. *La chute de la Maison Usher*. Transcription of voice and piano by Juan Allende-Blin. Paris: Société des Éditions Jobert, 1979.

———. *Claude Debussy: Lettres 1884-1918*. Ed. François Lesure. Paris: Hermann, 1980.

———. *Monsieur Croche et autres écrits*. Ed. François Lesure. Paris: Gallimard, 1987.

———. "La Grotte" (1904). *Songs of Claude Debussy*. Ed. James R. Briscoe. Milwaukee: Hal Leonard, 1993. 2:131-33.

———. *Pelléas et Mélisande*. 1902. New York: International Music, 1962.

———. *Le Roi Lear; Le diable dans le beffroi; La chute de la Maison Usher*. Series 6. Vol. 3. Ed. Robert Orledge. Paris: Durand, 2006.

Hoéré, A. "Entretiens inédits d'Ernest Guiraud et de Claude Debussy notés par Maurice Emmanuel (1889-1890)." *Inédits sur Claude Debussy*. Paris: Les Publications techniques, galerie Charpentier, 1942.

Maeterlinck, Maurice. *Aglavaine et Sélysette*. Paris: Société du Mercure de France, 1899.

———. *Alladine et Palomides, Intérieur, et La mort de Tintagiles: Trois petits drames pour marionnettes*. Brussels: Collection du Reveil, 1894.

———. *L'autre monde, ou Le cadran stellaire*. New York: Éditions de la Maison Française, 1942.

———. *Avant le grand silence*. Paris: Bibliothèque-Charpentier, 1934.

———. *Les fiançailles: Féerie en cinq actes et onze tableaux*. Paris: Fasquelles, 1922.

———. *Intérieur*. 1895. *Pelléas et Mélisande* et *Intérieur*. New York: Holt, 1945.

———. *Joyzelle*. Paris: Librairie Charpentier et Fasquelle, 1903.

———. *L'oiseau bleu*. Paris: Librairie Charpentier et Fasquelle, 1912.

———. *Pelléas et Mélisande: Alladine et Palomides*. New York: Dodd, Mead, 1896.

———. *Le temple enseveli*. Paris: Bibliothèque-Charpentier, 1908.

———. *Le trésor des humbles*. Paris: Société du Mercure de France, 1904.

———. *La vie des abeilles*. Paris, Bibliothèque-Charpentier, 1905.

Nabokov, Vladimir. *Strong Opinions*. New York: McGraw-Hill, 1973.

Nichols, Roger, and Richard Langham Smith. *Claude Debussy: Pelléas et Mélisande*. Cambridge: Cambridge University Press, 1989.

Poe, Edgar Allan. *The Fall of the House of Usher and Other Writings*. New York: Penguin, 1986.

Stein, Gertrude. *Everybody's Autobiography*. Cambridge: Exact Change, 1993.

Stravinsky, Igor. *Dialogues*. Berkeley: University of California Press, 1982.

Strosser, Pierre, dir. *Pelléas et Mélisande*. By Claude Debussy. DVD. Region 1. French with English subtitles. Image Entertainment, 2002.

Wilde, Oscar. "The Decay of Lying" (1889). *Complete Works*. Glasgow: Harper Collins, 2003. 1071-92.

Yeats, William Butler. *The Collected Poems of W. B. Yeats*. London: Macmillan, 1933.

3 Echoes of the Self
Cosmic Loneliness in Bartók's *Duke Bluebeard's Castle*

Klára Móricz

Duke Bluebeard's Castle, Béla Bartók's only opera, ends on an irreversibly dark note. Bluebeard's bride Judith slowly disappears behind the seventh door of his castle to join Bluebeard's previous wives, whom he married, in the libretto's symbolist wording, in the "morning, noon, and evening" of his life in an effort to break free of loneliness. Like them, Judith also failed to redeem him. Having reached the "night" of his life, Bluebeard resigns himself to spending his remaining time alone, closed in the darkness of the castle, the symbol of his soul. Bluebeard's last words, which Bartók added to the original libretto by Béla Balázs (1884-1949), indicate that he comprehends that with Judith his last hope disappears: "And it will be night evermore, night . . . night. . . ."[1] His tale told, Bluebeard vanishes from view without the mediation of a falling curtain, his figure dissolving in the slowly spreading darkness. Given the story's mythological resonances, the opera's ending is inevitable—the Prince of Darkness finally unites with his natural element. Yet the human side of the story, the tragic, final separation of the potential lovers who retreat into their separate worlds unredeemed, fatally wounded, and disillusioned, leaves the listener in a state of despair. Seen from this perspective, Bartók's *Bluebeard* is a paradigmatic portrayal of the modernist condition of loneliness, isolation, and alienation caused by the loss of faith in the redeeming power of human relations.

Like Claude Debussy's *Pelléas et Mélisande* (1902), Richard Strauss's *Salome* (1905), and later Alban Berg's *Wozzeck* (1925) and *Lulu* (1928-35), Bartók's *Bluebeard* (1911) is a *Literaturoper*, an opera that uses an existing literary text as its libretto. Balázs, a Hungarian symbolist writer, published his "mystery play" in 1910 and dedicated it to Bartók and Zoltán Kodály (1882-1967). Intended for his erudite friend Kodály, the play instead caught the interest of Bartók, who generally paid little attention to literature.[2] He had no high opinion of Balázs's literary talent and was attracted to the play not for its literary value but for its subject matter.[3] He was also intrigued by Balázs's attempt to recreate on the stage "the language and rhymes of old Hungarian Székely folk ballads," the music of which had fascinated Bartók since he had first encountered them in 1904.[4] Balázs's subject resonated strongly with the young composer, who was still recuperating from having been rejected by violinist Stefi Geyer. His 1908 Violin Concerto was conceived as a fare-well to Geyer; he sent her the score with Balázs's sentimental lines:

> My heart is bleeding, my soul is ill
> I walked among humans
> I loved with torment, with flame-love
> in vain, in vain
>
> No two stars are as far apart
> As two human souls.[5]

Bartók's sudden marriage to his piano student Márta Ziegler in 1909 does not seem to have soothed his wound: the young wife received the dedica-tion of *Bluebeard*, an opera about the impossibility of real love between man and woman, as a reward for her staunch support during this difficult period of Bartók's life.[6] The opera, into which Bartók poured his personal disap-pointment, created professional frustrations. The first disappointment came when the juries of the two competitions to which Bartók submitted the piece rejected it as "unperformable."[7] Later, Bartók himself admitted that the plot was rather slim for a conventional stage production, for, as he put it ironically, it "offers only the spiritual conflict between two individuals and the music does nothing more than depict this conflict in abstract sim-plicity. Nothing else happens on stage."[8] Irony aside, Bartók's focus on deep psychology and his complete lack of interest in theatrical illusion kept his opera—a genre commonly associated, as Richard Begam and Matthew Wil-son Smith write in the introduction to this volume, with the inauthentic, the insincere, and the vulgar—in the realm of authenticity and modernism.

The only surviving thematic sketch for *Duke Bluebeard's Castle* is in a black notebook that Bartók purchased for taking down folk music but used instead for compositional sketches between 1907 and 1922.[9] The first sketch in the notebook is the theme of the Violin Concerto dedicated to Geyer. A theme from *Bluebeard* (which in the final version of the opera Bartók assigns to the English horn and clarinet as they provide a lyrical extension of Bluebeard's stark statement, "My castle does not glitter"[10]) follows the continuity draft of the third of Bartók's *Four Dirges*, a series of short piano pieces composed around the same time as the opera and considered to be its stylistic forerunner.[11]

In the present chapter, I argue that the physical proximity of these two sketches suggests interpretative possibilities for *Bluebeard* that point far beyond the chronological and stylistic proximity between opera and piano piece. With its insistent hollow fifths in the low register, ringing pedal tones, and characteristic diminished fourths in the left hand, Bartók's *Third Dirge* bears a striking resemblance to Schubert's "Der Doppelgänger" (1828), a setting of a poem by Heinrich Heine. Heine's "Doppelgänger" is an early poetic expression of dissociation or out-of-body experience that would haunt artists to the end of the century and beyond as a metaphor for existential loneliness. Although dressed in lush orchestral garb, *Bluebeard* preserves some of the dark colors, hollow sounds, and, most crucially, the existential despair expressed in Schubert's "Der Doppelgänger," the Romantic prototype for Bartók's *Third Dirge*. Comparing *Bluebeard* to "Doppelgänger" via the *Third Dirge* thus highlights the existential question posed in Bartók's opera.

Another, more frequently noted nineteenth-century precursor of *Bluebeard* is Wagner's *Lohengrin*, an opera about the forbidden question, or about man's desire to be loved unconditionally and woman's failure to trust love without asking for assurances. Reading the polarized representation of gender relations in *Bluebeard* as inspired by Wagner and at the same time resisting Wagner's redemptive resolution helps specify the source of Bartók's existential anxiety. These comparisons not only show Bartók's debt to nineteenth-century Romantic paradigms but also reveal the modernist transformation of woman from Wagner's redeeming female into Bartók's paradigmatic fin-de-siècle femme fatale. Instead of saving man through self-sacrifice, this new woman reinforces man's existential loneliness, compelling him to look for redemption not in love but in a utopian folk community. Bartók thus translates Romantic feelings of loneliness, isolation, and longing for redemption through love into modernist notions of the self and its longing for community. The use of folk music, in this context, points beyond what in Igor Stravinsky's music is commonly designated as neonationalism, the creative combination of folk music and modernist idiom in which the supposed authenticity of folk music lends legitimacy to the modernist idiom. As I show, in Bartók's art the Romantic notion of finding a community through the folk turns into yet another alienating strategy, separating artists from their real social community and thus making their isolation more complete.

Figure 3.1. Schubert, "Der Doppelgänger"

"Doppelgänger" is one of Schubert's darkest songs—it portrays the self in its most fragile, most fragmented state. The protagonist's proposed serenade in front of his lover's abandoned house turns into the nightmare of a mental breakdown as he recognizes his own distorted double in the gesticulating figure that apes the outward gestures of his lovesick condition. Heine's poem is not a traditional love-turned-bitter story: love, or the lack of it,

serves here as a symptom of self-absorption that transforms the only remaining feeling, self-pity, into self-hatred and self-irony. Schubert's music
reacts sensitively to all of the minute details of Heine's psychological drama
(fig. 3.1). He captures obsession with a ceaselessly repeated four-bar motive.
The motive itself consists of two descending minor seconds, separated by a
diminished fourth. The shape of the melodic line bears a strong resem-

blance to the BACH cipher (the German spelling of Bach's name in music as B♭-A-C-B♮), used frequently as a reference to Johann Sebastian Bach. The four notes of the "Doppelgänger" ostinato can be symmetrically arranged between two F#s an octave apart, a note that Schubert uses as a continuous, compulsive pedal that provides the song with its existential core, its "self" trapped in neurotic obsessions. One suspects that because of the oppressive presence of this note, the possibility of escape from the nightmarish double can be gleaned only at moments when the menacing F# is absent or when C appears in the bass as a predominant that prepares B major, dominant of E minor, a key promised but never reached in the song.[12]

Bartók's *Third Dirge* is an abstract fantasy on Schubert's obsessive "Doppelgänger" motive (fig. 3.2). Bartók uses three variations of Schubert's motif: the first, presented in parallel octaves and fifths in the left hand, is the version Schubert uses only once, in the piano postlude of his song (cf. mm. 56–59 in fig 3.1 and mm. 1–2 in fig 3.2). Here Schubert expands the last interval into a major second, thus giving a harmonic context to C that previously appeared as a functionally foreign note in the given tonal context. Fragments and permutations of Schubert's main motive also occur in Bartók's score.[13] We hear Schubert's original motive four times: twice in the right hand, both starting from the piece's tonal center, A♭/G# (mm. 10, 12); and twice in the left hand, played in augmented form in *stretto* from D (m. 13) and B♭ (m. 14).

Parallels between Schubert's late song and Bartók's short piano piece go further than the similarities of their main motives. Both pieces evoke a sense of emptiness and obsession not only by the recurrence of similarly shaped motives, but also by frequent open fifths and long, gravitational pedal tones (F# in Schubert and B—the tonic of Schubert's song—in Bartók's *Dirge*). Both pieces contrast this static material with a gradual increase in dynamics and textural density that create an arch-like form with an emotional climax in the middle, followed by a return to the static and quiet material of the first part (the same arch governs *Bluebeard*'s structure). Schubert's song rises from *pp* to *fff* and then moves back to *ppp*, whereas in Bartók's *Dirge* the dynamics increases from *p* to *ff*, which then quiets down to *pp*. The violence of Schubert's *fortissimos* liberates the voice and allows the accompaniment to drift from its obsessive path: abandoning its previous circular motion, the bass finally rises chromatically, until it reaches an impasse of a tonic-dominant pendulum in D# minor (mm. 43–50 in fig. 3.1). Instead of a chromatic ascent, the right hand in Bartók's *Dirge* rises along an octatonic (tone-semitone) scale, which also reaches a stalemate as it stalls

Figure 3.2. Bartók, *Third Dirge*, op. 9a (1909-10)

on repeated Eb-E dyads (mm. 16-19 in fig. 3.2). Schubert supports the melodic climax on G in measure 41 by increased harmonic density and the introduction of a German-sixth chord on C. Bartók's climax manifests itself in
the expansion of range between the two hands, reaching more than five
octaves on alternating C-major/minor chords in measure 18. Melodic liberation, expressed in Schubert's song by the voice's final effort to rise above
the restricting F# to G and its ability to sing real melodies in D# minor as

opposed to recitative lines circling around F#, finds its parallel in Bartók's postclimactic *dolce* and *dolcissimo* phrases that, through the arpeggiated dominant-seventh chords in the right hand (E^7, C^7, A^7, and $B\flat^7$ in mm. 21–26), open up unfulfilled tonal possibilities. These chords and their tonal implications are just as strange in the musical language of Bartók's *Dirge* as the oddly sweet ornamental melisma in measures 54–55 that Schubert assigns to the closing line of the poem ("so many nights, in olden times") in the otherwise bare-bones style of the "Doppelgänger." Both gestures sound artificial and signal a sudden turn to olden times with styles that stand outside the main expressive vocabulary of the pieces. More significantly, both backward-looking gestures are immediately contradicted by contrasting musical utterances: by the return of the motto in Schubert's "Doppelgänger" (mm. 56–59) and by the presence of scattered notes from the main motive in the left hand at the end of Bartók's *Dirge* (C–B . . . D#–Cx).[14]

Despite these striking similarities, Bartók's and Schubert's laments about human loneliness end on a different tone. At the end of the *Dirge*, Bartók brings back the first chord, in its original register and hollow spacing. The piece moves in a full circle and closes where it began—breakout is denied by the frustrating stalling on the climactic $E\flat$–E, and by the artificiality of the dominant sevenths. In the last measures of "Der Doppelgänger," Schubert replaces the tonic B minor with its parallel major, signaling a possible escape to different regions. Schubert's concluding B major is anticipated in crucial points of his song. At the end it is prepared by a C-major chord (m. 59) that, functioning as a potential Neapolitan, turns B major into the dominant of E minor.[15] In this context, C acts as a strong opponent to the obsessive F#. That escape from F# is ultimately denied is not surprising if we consider that the frightening figure in the poem is identical with the protagonist—separation from him would be possible only through a fatal truncation of the personality. Schubert suggests the unity of the two figures by placing the contrasting C and F# as the sole accompaniment to the word *Doppelgänger* in measure 44: the overlap of these two notes indicates the inherent contradiction between contrast and sameness in the double identity of the protagonist.

On a much larger scale, *Bluebeard* has the same dramatic trajectory as the *Third Dirge*, while its fundamental dramatic and structural device, the contrast between C and F#, recalls "Doppelgänger."[16] Bartók casts Bluebeard's dark castle in F# minor. The first, skeletal melodic line, played in unison by the low strings, starts and ends on F# (fig. 3.3). Bartók modeled the tune on old-style Hungarian folk songs to match Balázs's archaic introductory prologue, which the poet devised in imitation of Hungarian folk bards who are believed to have preserved ancient pagan customs. As the curtain rises, the bard who introduced the opera disappears, and the audience faces a completely dark stage. Although the stage remains dark until the silhouettes of Bluebeard and Judith appear in the brilliant light of the open door at the top of the stairs (at rehearsal 2), the outlines of the cold, cave-like hall with its seven closed doors slowly become visible despite the darkness. In the stage directions, Bartók does not specify the source of this preliminary light that grants the audience its first vision, but the sudden intrusion of nervous melodic figures in the woodwinds, centered on C major above the strings' F# pedal (4 before rehearsal 1), forecasts the light that Judith will bring into the castle.[17] Indeed, a few measures later a variation of the same motive marks the appearance of Bluebeard and Judith in the "blinding white square" of the door. We hear the motive again (4 after rehearsal 4) as Bluebeard, now at the bottom of the stairs, looks up at Judith, whose words ("I'm coming I'm coming, Bluebeard"[18]) show determination but whose stopping in the middle of her descent indicates hesitancy. A distorted version of the motive appears as the castle responds with a sigh to Judith's aggressive banging on its first door (2 after rehearsal 25). The motive is thus clearly associated with Judith, both as a bringer of light and as an aggressive intruder.

In *Bluebeard* Judith fulfills her promise of light by making Bluebeard open the closed doors of his castle, gradually revealing the hidden crevices of his soul. The doors open one by one, exposing Bluebeard's complex personality: first his manly attributes—his cruelty (torture chamber) and his bravery (armory)—then his riches (treasury) and his gentleness (garden). Although not indicated in the text, the light emanating from the doors of his underground dungeon gradually gets brighter as Bluebeard shows chambers closer and closer to ground level. The culmination of this process is the opening of the fifth door, which reveals Bluebeard's realm—open space with a vast horizon (fig. 3.4). Bartók marks this moment of maximum light with a triple *forte* C-major chord that provides the perfect contrast to the beginning's *pianissimo* F# minor. Not only are F# and C polar opposites on the circle of fifths, the minor and major keys also spell the conventional oppositions of negative and positive, dark and bright, closed and open.

Although Judith craved light, here she shrinks back from the brightness radiating from the fifth door. As if suddenly changing perspectives with Bluebeard, who proudly identifies now with C major, she shields her eyes with her hands, quietly opposing his C-major invitation to admire the vast-

A kékszakállú herceg vára
                                                                Béla Bartók, Op. 11.

Prolog

Dies begab sich einst.
Ihr müßt nicht wissen wann, auch nicht den Ort,
da es geschah, Topographie und Jahreszahl.
„Aha", sagt ihr (und es klingt recht fatal) „eine
Legende!"Und fragt– denn es ist nützlich, das vor-
her zu wissen– was in Wahrheit sie bedeute.
Liebe Leute, ich muß euch sagen: die Wahrheit
ist ein Rauch und ist ein Echo nur von eines Seufzers Hauch.

Ihr seht mich an. Ich sehe euch. Ganz offen steht
der Vorhang unserer Augenlider. Ihr sucht die Bühne?
Ja, wo ist die aufgeschlagen? In dir? In mir? Am
rost'gen Pol der Zeit? O liebe Freunde, laßt es dabei
bewenden, beginnt nicht mit Fragen, die nie und
nimmer enden.

Ein Flickwerk ist das Leben. Und was auf Erden
blüht und Frucht wird, ernten Kriege. Aber, liebe
Leute, das ist nicht,woran wir sterben. Woran wir
denn zugrunde gehn? Die Antwort hängt im Strauch,
zerfetzt, befleckt, und ist das Echo nur von eines
Seufzers Hauch.

                                        (Der Vorhang geht auf)

Prológus

Haj regő rejtem
Hová, hová rejtsem
Hol volt, hol nem: kint-e vagy bent?
Régi rege, haj mit jelent,
Urak, asszonyságok?

Im, szólal az ének.
Ti néztek, én nézlek.
Szemünk pillás függönye fent:
Hol a színpad: kint-e vagy bent,
Urak, asszonyságok?

Keserves és boldog
Nevezetes dolgok,
Az világ kint haddal tele,
De nem abba halunk bele,
Urak, asszonyságok.

Nézzük egymást, nézzük,
Regénket regéljük.
Ki tudhatja honnan hozzuk?
Hallgatjuk és csodálkozzuk,
Urak, asszonyságok.

(A függöny szétválik a háta mögött)

Musik beginnt. Das Spiel hebt an. Hat es euch
Zene szól, a láng ég, Kezdődjön a játék.

gefallen– dann am Ende spart nicht mit Dank und regt die
Hände. Jetzt schließt den Vorhang eurer Augenlider.
Szemem   pillás   függönye   fent.
majd   ha   lement,   Urak,

Auftaucht das alte Haus. Muß ich es nennen? Ihr werdet's
tief in euch erkennen. Ihr wißt den Ort und wißt den
Namen auch: das Echo nur von eines Seufzers Hauch.
Tapsoljatok
asszonyságok.
Régi vár, régi már Az mese, ki róla jár, Tik is hallgassátok.

Mächtige, runde, gotische Halle. Links führt eine steile Treppe zu einer kleinen eisernen Türe. Rechts der Stiege befinden sich in der Mauer
sieben große Türen: vier noch gegenüber der Rampe, zwei bereits ganz rechts. Sonst weder Fenster. noch Dekoration. Die Halle gleicht einer finstern, düstern, leeren Felsenhöhle. Beim Heben des Vorhanges ist die Szene finster.
Hatalmas kerek gótikus csarnok. Balra merredek lépcső vezet fel egy kis vasajtóhoz. A lépcsőtől jobbra hét nagy ajtó van a falban; négy még szemben,
kettő már egész jobboldalt. Különben nem ablak, se disz. A csarnok üres sötét, rideg, sziklabarlanghoz hasonlatos. Mikor a függöny szétválik, teljes
sötétség van a színpadon.

Figure 3.3. First two pages of Bartók's *Duke Bluebeard's Castle* (piano reduction)

ness of his vistas with stunned, expressionless black-key pentatonic phrases. Judith's gesture of protecting herself from the brilliance of the light connects her to the mythological Semele who, doubting her lover's divine nature, demands that Zeus appear to her in his full glory but, since no mortal can bear the sight of a god, is burned to ashes by the flame ignited by Zeus's lightning rays.

In *Bluebeard* light threatens not the woman but the man, as C represents not only the polar opposite of darkness (F#) but also a disintegrating power capable of destroying the spiritual integrity of man's soul. Because light enables vision and thus potentially leads to knowledge, it can be related to the biblical forbidden fruit that Eve desires and tempts man to taste. The biblical

Figure 3.4. The fifth door in Bartók's *Duke Bluebeard's Castle*

Eve's curiosity and cunning persuasion of man to act against God's command are reflected in Bartók's Judith, whose curiosity is no less a motivating
force behind her actions than is her love. Her insistence on disclosing man's
secrets posits a dangerous temptation for Bluebeard, who almost loses his
soul in the forced process of self-revelation. Darkness and light, F# and C

thus exchange places as loci of negative and positive forces: F#, the sign of obsession in Schubert's "Doppelgänger," becomes a sign of wholeness in *Bluebeard*, while C, commonly associated with purity in Romantic music and offered as a potential escape in Schubert's song, appears as a corruptive force in Bartók's opera. As in "Doppelgänger" and the *Third Dirge*, in *Bluebeard* the clear vision brought by the climax reveals an emotional impasse that predicts an ending that reiterates the conflict posited at the beginning of the piece. The difference between the metaphorical significance of F# and C in *Bluebeard* and "Doppelgänger" shows a dramatic shift in worldview and signals a changed perspective on the possibility of redemption.

This reversal of perspectives becomes even more prominent if we consider the music's historical associations with Judith's figure. The impending doom is already embedded in the first motive connected with her (fig. 3.5a). While the motive's snake-like curling melodic line refers back to Eve, its rhythmic and melodic shape recalls Salome's impatient, hysterical demand for the head of John the Baptist in Strauss's *Salome*, an opera Bartók greatly admired (fig. 3.5b).[19] As Judith's name indicates, she is related to the biblical Salome who, like the biblical Judith, had her male opponent decapitated.[20] Unlike Salome, Judith is motivated by patriotic feelings: she seduces and kills Holofernes, the commander of the Assyrian army, to save her city from invasion.

Bartók's references go back even earlier than Strauss. The parallel thirds of Judith's motive evoke the leitmotif for the cursed ring in Wagner's *Ring* cycle (fig. 3.5c). This ring, which Alberich forged from the natural gold that lay hidden at the bottom of the Rhine, brings into play a number of negative associations: man's destruction of nature, his thirst for power, his greed, and his willingness to give up his most human qualities—the ability to love and the desire to be loved. Whoever comes into contact with the ring in Wagner's tetralogy is corrupted by it. In Wagner's mythology the ring is the symbol of the original sin, which can be erased only by Brünnhilde's self-sacrifice at the end of the cycle. Wagner's epic ends with redemption, with the return to the natural state of things, in which the ring loses its destructive power and becomes part of nature again. Although biblical in its basic conception, Wagner's *Ring* changes the biblical gendering of sin and redemption: instead of Eve instigating the original sin, in the *Ring* it is the greedy and sexually frustrated Alberich who unleashes corruption; instead of Jesus bringing salvation, it is Brünnhilde's sacrifice that restores the natural order of the world.[21]

Figure 3.5. (a) Motif of Judith's intrusion in *Bluebeard*, (b) Salome's motif in Strauss's *Salome*, (c) motif of the ring in Wagner's *Ring*

It is not Wagner's mythological *Ring*, however, that has the most reso-nance in Bartók's *Bluebeard* but his *Lohengrin*. In fact, it might have been Wagner, and not Schubert, who provided Bartók with the model of present-ing the polar opposites of good and evil by using the opposing keys of F# minor and C major.[22] In *Lohengrin*, F# minor is the key of Ortrud, the evil sorceress and wife of Frederick whom Elsa's mysterious bridegroom, the knight Lohengrin, removes from power. Ortrud's realm is the night and darkness, which Wagner depicts at the beginning of the second act by tim-pani tremolos and a treacherously curling unison melody in the low regis-ters of the cellos and bassoons. Wagner modeled Ortrud's musical land-scape on Carl Maria von Weber's depiction of the midnight scene in the Wolf Glen in *Der Freischütz* (1821), where the unfortunate hunter Max and his evil tempter Kaspar forge magic bullets. Weber contrasts the F# minor of dark forest music with the purity of C major, a key that stands for Max's saintly bride, Agathe, who saves him from Satan with the help of a hermit. Weber juxtaposes the evil F#-minor music and the pure C major in the overture, in which the melody of Agatha's aria serves as the triumphant contrasting theme that overcomes the threat of the dark forest music as well as Max's agitated theme.

Although Judith's relation to the mythological Semele, the biblical Eve, the man-killing Judith and Salome, and the curious Elsa mark her as a dan-gerous, negative character, her C-major key also associates her with the purity of Agatha and Elsa, successful and failed redeemers of operatic men. Wagner's contrast of F# minor and C major in *Lohengrin* is not as explicit as Weber's in *Freischütz*. Unlike Agatha, Elsa does not triumph at the end. To take revenge, Ortrud, like the mythological Hera in Semele's story, makes Elsa question the identity of her husband-to-be. Wagner's lesson is clear: no

less than blind and unconditional trust is expected from a woman who as-
pires for a noble husband. Elsa cannot pass the test Wagner regularly sets
up for his redeeming female protagonists who are willing to sacrifice themselves for the salvation of men. As Wagner formulates it at the conclusion
of part 1 of *Opera and Drama*, a woman can achieve

> full individuality only at the moment of surrendering herself. She is like the *ondine*
> who floats about aimlessly in the waves of her native element, without a soul,
> until she finally receives one through the love of a man. The look of innocence in
> the woman's eyes is the infinitely clear mirror in which the man can only recognize
> the general capacity for love, until he is able to recognize in it his own image: when
> he has done so, then too is the woman's polymorphous capacity for love condensed
> into a pressing need to love this man with the full ecstasy of surrender.[23]

The triumph of the feminine principle, which Goethe immortalizes at
the end of *Faust* by the invocation of *das Ewig-Weibliche*, or "eternal feminine," still dominates the outcome of Wagner's operas: the cursed Dutchman is saved by Senta's sacrifice in *The Flying Dutchman*, Tannhäuser is redeemed by Elisabeth's pure love in *Tannhäuser*, and the entire world is saved
by Brünnhilde's self-immolation in the *Ring*. In her immense desire to be
united with Siegfried, the wise Brünnhilde gains great power. But her strength,
like that of many self-sacrificing women, is turned into self-annihilation, the
total dissolution of her own will that is reduced to a will to serve the man
she loves. Ironically, in Wagner's view salvation through the love of a woman
can come only at the price of the destruction of the woman's self. As he writes
in *Opera and Drama*, "*To bear* gladly that which is received, this is *the deed* of
the woman,—and to accomplish such deeds it requires only that she be exactly what she is; there is no question of 'wanting,' for she can want only one
thing: *to be a woman!* Thus woman is for man the infallible measure of nature, for she is most perfect when she does not transgress the sphere of
beautiful instinct, the sphere which holds her in thrall by virtue of the one
thing that brings her joy, the necessity of love."[24]

This Romantic-bourgeois view of the feminine persisted until the turn of
the century. Staying at home while men braved the perils of the outside
world, women were supposed to be the guardians of men's soul. In his
Sesame and Lilies (1865), John Ruskin contrasts the function of men and
women: "The man's power is active, progressive, defensive. He is eminently
the doer, the creator, the discoverer, the defender. His intellect is for speculation and invention." In contrast, women were not suited for invention or

creation, only for "modesty of service." They should "be enduringly, incorruptibly good; instinctively, infallibly wise—wise, not for self-development, but for self-renunciation."[25]

Already in Wagner's writings there is a lurking fear that women may not always want to be limited to this selfless role. What if they want to "transgress the sphere of beautiful instinct"? Liberated women seem to have posed a serious threat to the bourgeois order of female submission. As Bram Dijkstra has demonstrated in his *Idols of Perversity: Fantasies of Feminine Evil in Fin-de-Siècle Culture*, turn-of-the-century culture waged a virulent war on women, suspected of "dragging man into a grim trough of perversion."[26] In this misogynist atmosphere, the image of the biblical Judith, previously the icon of patriotic heroism, was turned into a paragon of female perversion. Depicted as a lascivious, oversexed female predator, she was reconceived as a woman determined not only to squeeze pleasure out of Holofernes but also to take revenge on him for it. In this new interpretation, the decapitation of Holofernes is less a patriotic deed than a metaphorical act of castration, indicated by the frequent depictions of lascivious Judiths with a weapon in their hands.[27] As Carl Leafstedt has argued, these images were partially inspired by Christian Friedrich Hebbel's 1840 *Judith*, a play that presented a psychologically complicated heroine who is perversely attracted to her male antagonist. Hebbel's drama sexualized the Old Testament story just as Oscar Wilde later sexualized the New Testament tale of Salome. Hebbel's drama must have made an impression on Balázs, a Hebbel scholar himself, and might have inspired him to give the name Judith to his female protagonist in *Bluebeard*.[28]

Judith is just one of the many women whom turn-of-the-century artists have transformed into femmes fatales: the biblical Salome, Delilah, and Judith are among the best-known women whose mere existence posed a danger to men. Supposedly they all lusted after men, but they were also eager to destroy the object of their desire. Dijkstra argues that decapitation, the act of severing the head, seat of the brain, from the body, was seen as "the supreme act of the male's physical submission to woman's predatory desire."[29] In art these dangerous women replaced the self-sacrificing heroines of Wagner's operas. With the disappearance of female self-sacrifice, the possibility of redemption through love has also vanished.

Bartók's Judith must be read in the context of this fin-de-siècle anxiety about women. The change of perspective on women left a decisive mark on the old story of Bluebeard, which in Balázs and Bartók's version became a combination of myths, biblical associations, legends, fairy tales, folk ballads, and personal resentments. The biggest change in the tale is that the woman-killer Bluebeard of old legends is transformed into the potential victim of the man-killer Judith. Unlike Semele or Elsa, she does not need the temptation of jealous rivals to motivate her inquiry into Bluebeard's identity and thus undermine his integrity. She does not perish like Semele and is not forgiven like Elsa. Her punishment is to be banished to the realm of memory and thus be denied physical presence in the man's life. At the end of the opera, man's greatest temptation, the physical beauty of woman, dissolves into a mere mental image.

Bluebeard's parting words describing Judith's physical beauty ("You are beautiful, a hundred times beautiful, you were the most beautiful woman"[30]) are still addressed to the real Judith, but the past tense of the farewell has already expanded the physical distance between the protagonists. Blue-beard's farewell is underlined by treacherously curving parallel thirds in the strings (fig. 3.6, rehearsal 135). Because of their association with Wagner's cursed ring, these thirds warn of the deceptiveness and ephemeral nature of female beauty. The music that depicts Judith's slow retreat is stylistically the closest to Bartók's *Third Dirge*. At rehearsal 136 long pedals (here main-tained at the harsh dissonance of B♭–A), gradual increase and collapse of dy-namics, rising melodic line in the upper parts, the gravitational force of F in the trumpet and trombone, and the gradual expansion of gestures from falling minor-second sighs to a forceful perfect-fifth scream at the climax all point to the *Third Dirge*. As an additional connective link, Bartók inserts a transposed BACH cipher (G♭–F–A♭–G, 4 before rehearsal 138), a variant of the "Doppelgän-ger" motive, into the organ part that, reinforced by the English horn, for four measures provides the only sonority we hear. He might have intended the gesture as a little insider joke that associates the sound of the instrument with its greatest master, Johann Sebastian Bach. Because of its strong reli-gious overtones, the organ lends a ritualistic aspect to the moment when the castle closes its doors again and darkness regains its power. The only other time in the opera Bartók uses the organ is the scene's ritualistic coun-terpart, the opening of the fifth door, the moment when the castle achieves maximum light and openness.

The ending returns to the music of the beginning. We hear the skeletal F# tune again (at rehearsal 138), combined now with the nervous motives originally associated with Judith. Since they accompany Bluebeard's last lines, one can interpret their integration into the castle music as Judith's

Figure 3.6. End of Bartók's *Duke Bluebeard's Castle*

retreat into Bluebeard's memory. Alone again on stage, Bluebeard slowly withdraws into himself, into his dark castle that draws a protective shell around his ego. Only his vocal line indicates that the experience has left him scarred. Instead of the perfect fourths of pentatonic scales, his home terrain, he sings distorted fourths—first a diminished fourth (E#–A), then two

tritones (G–C# and F#–C), ending, significantly, on C. As the orchestra gradually zeros in on C#, the echo of Bluebeard's final C gets disguised as the lower note of Judith's nervous thirds that rigidify into chords before they yield to the ominous concluding C# in the bass. What hope can a low-register C bring when its promise is promptly contradicted by the text about the ensuing

eternal night ("And it will be night evermore, night . . . night. . . ."[31])? Emma
Gruber's German translation, which Bartók approved, lends further musical
resonance to Bluebeard's renunciation of love: "Nacht bleibt es nun ewig,
immer, ewig, immer. . . ." The repetition of *ewig* recalls the love duet of
music history's most famous lovers, Wagner's Tristan and Isolde ("So star-
ben wir, um ungetrennt, ewig, einig ohne End"[32]), transformed here into its
negative opposite. With this transformation Goethe's eternal feminine
(*Ewig-Weibliche*), men's assigned redeemer, disappears, leaving the eternally
unredeemable lonely man, commemorated in the nostalgic farewell of the
last song in Gustav Mahler's *Lied von der Erde* (1908–09), which ends with
sixty-four bars of repeated long notes on the word *ewig*.

Bartók's *Bluebeard* does not foreclose redemption altogether—but it
searches for it in an idealized human community, the "folk," rather than in
romantic love. Casting off Goethe's eternal feminine that draws men upward into higher realms ("Das Ewig-weibliche zieht uns hinan") as unfeasi-
ble for modern man because it was too deeply rooted in a religious worldview, the atheist Bartók looks in the opposite direction: not to heaven but
to earth, to nature and its culturally constructed human representative, the
peasant. What distinguishes *Bluebeard* from other similarly misogynistic
works at the turn of the century is that Bartók casts the male protagonist
Bluebeard, and not the woman Judith, as living in harmony with nature. And
that is why the binaries of male-female, dark-light, and pure-corrupt find
their musical equivalent in the opposing style of folk music (Bluebeard's
realm) and an assortment of other musical styles (Judith's realm). Bartók
presents the purest, ideal form of folk style in the strings' introductory melody at the beginning of the opera (fig. 3.3). Like old-style Hungarian folk
songs, it is pentatonic and consists of four gradually descending lines.[33] In
this simplified form, it sounds more like a prototype of folk song than a real
song, as Judit Frigyesi has put it, the "'melodic essence' of an old-style pentatonic folk song."[34] Bluebeard's first notes reinforce his ownership of F#
and of pentatonicism, whereas Judith's first words, sung on an arpeggiated
augmented chord, immediately posit her as an alien element in Bluebeard's
castle. Their musical styles do not remain completely separate during their
conflicted encounter. As Frigyesi has shown, their constant wanderings between musical styles sensitively register their changing emotional warmth
and coldness, symbolizing "the opposition between the belief that love can
bring happiness and the awareness that complete happiness is not possible."[35] At the fifth door, Bluebeard, feeling himself on the threshold of emo-

tional fulfillment, leaves his ascetic pentatonic utterances and approaches Judith with waltz-like figures ("Come, come, I'm waiting for your kiss"[36]). Judith responds to the marvel of Bluebeard's vast realm with reducing her music to short pentatonic phrases ("Your country is beautiful and enormous"[37]). Yet, despite the occasional overlapping of their musical styles in the course of the opera, the contrast set up at the beginning remains decisive.

In its presentation of gender conflict, Bartók's *Bluebeard* is a paradigmatically modernist work, its pessimistic outlook on human relations a product of fin-de-siècle disillusionment and anxiety. In the opera, man's spirituality can find its nourishing environment only inside the protective boundaries of his castle. Light cannot penetrate this world without breaking up the wholeness of the soul into fragmentary, painful memories. Self-knowledge in Schubert's "Doppelgänger" brings relief, even if it is only temporary. In *Bluebeard* the revelation of the content of the protagonist's soul, facilitated by Judith, makes the darkness of the castle even more impenetrable and permanent—man's loneliness even more absolute.

What is the role of folk music in this context? It seems strange to evoke folk music, which in the Romantic imagination represented the ideal, utopian community of the nation, as the home of the lonely soul, the isolated individual who cannot relate even to one other person, let alone a community. This combination of modernist disillusionment with the redemptive power of human relations and the utopian belief in the possibility of community represented by the "folk" is just one of the many contradictions inherent in Hungarian modernism. But in the case of *Bluebeard*, this strange combination also points to the autobiographical nature of Bartók's opera. Bartók's discovery of folk music provided him with a protective shield behind which he withdrew whenever he felt attacked by critics and rejected by the audience.[38] For him folk music functioned not as an entry into a community but as a means of isolation from his immediate urban circle. Despite the nationalist resonance of Bartók's turn to the peasants, his embrace of folk music did not initially make him a national hero. On the contrary. The gentry in Hungary despised peasants and their music and cherished instead urban Gypsy music as a musical emblem of national identity. Bartók's integration of the music of the peasants into art music was part of an active war against this Romantic national identity, and as such it made him an outcast. Instead of creating community around him, his mission to collect, preserve, and elevate peasant music into high culture made him even more isolated. Bluebeard represents not only man unredeemable by woman but also the artist who, searching for the "pure sources" of art in folk culture, finds himself alone, without an audience, as the real community rejects his music, while the folk community he has conceived as ideal exists only in his imagination.

Notes

1. "És mindég is éjjel lesz már . . . éjjel . . . éjjel. . . ." In his 1911 revision Balázs added the line "és mindig is éjjel lesz már" to the end, to which Bartók attached the twofold repetition of the last word, "éjjel . . . éjjel." See Vikárius, "Bartók's Opera" 32, 45–46.

2. Kroó 60.

3. Szegedy-Maszák 246.

4. As Balázs puts it in an annotated edition of the text, "I created this ballad of mine in the language and rhythms of old Hungarian Székely folk ballads. In character these folk ballads closely resemble old Scottish folk ballads, but they are, perhaps, more acerbic, simpler, their melodic quality more mysterious, more naïve, and more songlike. Thus, there is no 'literature' or rhetoric within them: they are constructed from dark, weighty, uncarved blocks of words. In this manner I wrote my Hungarian language *Bluebeard* ballad, and Bartók's music also conforms to this" (qtd. in Leafstedt 202; and Vikárius, "Sources of Béla Bartók's Opera" 111). About the folk resonances in Balázs's text, see Vikárius, "Sources of Béla Bartók's Opera."

5. Qtd. and trans. in Leafstedt 19.

6. According to Kodály, Bartók had no respect for the formalities of marriage. One day he brought Márta to his mother and said, "Here is my wife, she'll be living here from now on." He married Márta officially only because her father insisted on legalizing their relationship. See Kodály 211.

7. The first competition was sponsored by the Lipótvárosi Kaszinó, one of Budapest's coffee houses, the second by the music publisher Rózsavölgyi. It was this second jury that judged Bartók's opera "unsuitable for stage performance." For details of the competitions, see Leafstedt 144–53.

8. Bartók, "A Fából faragott királyfi" 777.

9. Bartók, *Black Pocket-Book.*

10. "Nem tündököl az én váram" (7 before rehearsal 20).

11. Vikárius, "Bartók's Opera" 5.

12. The note is absent only during the second vocal climax (m. 41) and in three measures during the music's sudden but short-lived move to D# minor (mm. 48, 50–51).

13. Bartók gradually reduces the motive to its basic elements (Fx–B): in the left hand of mm. 3–4 the second G# obscures the motive's diminished fourth; in m. 4, in the right hand, the diminished fourth (A#–[D]) is missing altogether from the motive.

After the climax in mm. 17-19, only the motive's first two notes, the descending seconds, remain.

14. As a final parallel: the gradual melodic ascent that assisted the voice's efforts to reach its climax in Schubert's song is balanced by the final descending gesture in the vocal part. Similarly, the chromatic rise in the right hand of Bartók's piano piece is followed by descending gestures that lead back to the initial B.

15. Whenever C appears in the bass, it suggests E minor as a potential escape route. In three out of four appearances, C serves as a strong predominant to B, either as a French or German sixth chord or as a Neapolitan (see mm. 32-33, 41-42, 59 in fig. 3.1).

16. About C and F# as polar opposites in *Bluebeard*, see Lendvai, especially chapter 2, "A Kékszakállú herceg vára" [Duke Bluebeard's castle] 65-112.

17. Lendvai describes the motive as representing the first light emanating from Bluebeard's torch (70), but the motive appears before Bluebeard.

18. "Megyek, megyek, Kékszakállú."

19. About Eve's association with the snake, see Higgins. In a letter to Emma Gruber (24 December 1905) Bartók writes, "I have vowed never to mention the Master [Strauss] in Budapest unless the opinion of the general public changes. My vow, however, does not prohibit expressing in writing the absolutely overwhelming effect 'Salome' made on me. Last week I started to study the piano reduction—and I was unable to put the work aside before playing it completely through. . . . At last, a new opera has been produced after Wagner! . . . What a great idea it was to choose a text exactly like this!" (qtd. in Vikárius, "Sources of Béla Bartók's Opera" 122). For more about Strauss's influence on Bartók, see Vikárius, *Modell és inspiráció.*

20. About the biblical associations of the name Judith, see Leafstedt, esp. ch. 7 ("The Significance of a Name"), 185-99.

21. In a speech on 29 Mar. 1935, Arnold Schoenberg identified "Erlösung durch Liebe" (salvation by love) as one of the three main components of Wagner's philosophy: "You were no true Wagnerian if you did not believe in his philosophy, in the ideas of *Erlösung durch Liebe,* salvation by love; you were not a true Wagnerian if you did not believe in *Deutschtum,* or in Teutonism; and you could not be a true Wagnerian without being a follower of his anti-Semitic essay, *Das Judentum in der Musik,* 'Judaism in Music'" (Schoenberg 503).

22. The polarity of C and F# also plays an important role in Debussy's *Pelléas and Mélisande.* In the climactic love scene of act 4, scene 4, F# is associated with Pelléas's passion and C with Mélisande's purity. Her deliberately understated declaration of love occurs on C and she reaches Pelléas's passionate F# only at the end of the scene.

23. Qtd. and trans. in Grey 134.

24. Ibid. 137.

25. "Now their separate characters are briefly these: The man's power is active, progressive, defensive. He is eminently the doer, the creator, the discoverer, the

defender. His intellect is for speculation and invention; his energy for adventure, for war, and for conquest, wherever war is just, wherever conquest necessary. But the woman's power is for rule, not for battle,—and her intellect is not for invention or creation, but for sweet ordering, arrangement, and decision. She sees the qualities of things, their claims, and their places. Her great function is Praise: she enters into no contest, but infallibly judges the crown of contest. By her office, and place, she is protected from all danger and temptation. The man, in his rough work in open world, must encounter all peril and trial: to him, therefore, must be the failure, the offense, the inevitable error: often he must be wounded, or subdued; often misled; and always hardened. But he guards the woman from all this; within his house, as ruled by her, unless she herself has sought it, need enter no danger, no temptation, no cause of error or offense. This is the true nature of home—it is the place of Peace; the shelter, not only from all injury, but from all terror, doubt, and division" (Ruskin, *Sesame and Lilies* 77-78). Parts of this passage are quoted in Dijkstra, 13.

    26. Ibid. vii.

    27. Ibid. 376-79. About the fin-de-siècle conception of the biblical Judith and Salome, see Sine. About interpretations of Salome, see Kramer.

    28. Leafstedt 185-99.

    29. Dijskra 375.

    30. "Szép vagy, szép vagy, százszor szép vagy. Te voltál a legszebb asszony!"

    31. "És mindég is éjjel lesz már, éjjel, éjjel."

    32. "Thus we might die undivided, one forever without end."

    33. Debussy also starts *Pelléas* with pentatonic lines imitating folk music, which he contrasts immediately with whole-tone sonorities.

    34. Frigyesi 253.

    35. Ibid. 243.

    36. "Gyere, gyere, csókra várlak."

    37. "Szép és nagy a te országod."

    38. Feeling disappointed in his professional perspectives in the United States, he wrote to his concert manager, "As a composer I am being boycotted, therefore in such capacity I am as far as possible withdrawing, and shall pursue activities only in the sphere of music-folklore" (qtd. in Tallián 220).

Bibliography

Bartók, Béla. *Black Pocket-Book: Sketches 1907-1922*. Facsimile edition of the manuscript. Ed. László Kalmár with commentary by László Somfai. Budapest: Editio Musica Budapest, 1987.

———. "'A Fából faragott királyfi'—a M. Kir. Operaház bemutatójához—II: A zeneszerző a darabjáról" [The wooden prince—to the premiere at the Hungarian Royal Opera—II: The composer about his piece]. *Magyar Színpad* 20.105 (12 May 1917): 2.

Rpt. in Béla Bartók, *Bartók Béla összegyűjtött írásai* [The collected writings of Béla Bartók]. Ed. András Szőlőssy. Budapest: Zeneműkiadó vállalat, 1966. 777.

Dijkstra, Bram. *Idols of Perversity: Fantasies of Feminine Evil in Fin-de-Siècle Culture.* New York: Oxford University Press, 1986.

Frigyesi, Judit. *Béla Bartók and Turn-of-the-Century Budapest.* Berkeley: University of California Press, 1998.

Grey, Thomas S. *Wagner's Musical Prose: Texts and Contexts.* Cambridge: Cambridge University Press, 1995.

Higgins, Jean M. "The Myth of Eve: The Temptress." *Journal of the American Academy of Religion* 44.4 (Dec. 1976): 639–47.

Kodály, Zoltán. Közélet, vallomások, zeneélet, Kodály Zoltán hátrahagyott írásai [Public life, confessions, musical life, unpublished writings of Zoltán Kodály]. Ed. Lajos Vargyas. Budapest: Szépirodalmi könyvkiadó, 1989.

Kramer, Lawrence. "Culture and Musical Hermeneutics: The Salome Complex." *Cambridge Opera Journal* 2.3 (Nov. 1990): 269–94.

Kroó, György. *A Guide to Bartók.* Budapest: Corvina Press, 1971.

Leafstedt, Carl. *Inside "Bluebeard's Castle": Music and Drama in Béla Bartók's Opera.* New York: Oxford University Press, 1999.

Lendvai, Ernő. *Bartók dramaturgiája: Színpadi művek és a Cantata profana* [Bartók's dramaturgy: Stage works and the Cantata profana]. Budapest: Akkord, 1993.

Ruskin, John. *Sesame and Lilies.* New Haven: Yale University Press, 2002.

Schoenberg, Arnold. "Two Speeches on the Jewish Situation." *Style and Idea: Selected Writings of Arnold Schoenberg.* Edited by Leonard Stein. Trans. Leo Black. Berkeley: University of California Press, 1975. 501–04.

Sine, Nadine. "Cases of Mistaken Identity: Salome and Judith at the Turn of the Century." *German Studies Review* 11.1 (Feb. 1988): 9–29.

Szegedy-Maszák, Mihály. "Bartók and Literature." *Hungarian Studies* 15.2 (2001): 245–54.

Tallián, Tibor. *Béla Bartók: The Man and His Work.* Budapest: Corvina, 1981.

Vikárius, László. "Bartók's Opera." *Duke Bluebeard's Castle, op. 11, Facsimile of the Autograph Draft.* By Béla Bartók. Ed. László Vikárius. Budapest: Balassi Kiadó, 2006.

———. *Modell és inspiráció Bartók zenei gondolkodásában: A hatás jelenségének értelmezéséhez* [Model and inspiration in Bartók's musical thinking: Toward the interpretation of the phenomenon of influence]. Pécs: Ars Longa Jelenkor Kiadó, 1999.

———. "The Sources of Béla Bartók's Opera *Duke Bluebeard's Castle* (1911): The Fascinations of Balladry." *Glasbeno gledališče: Večeraj, danes, jutri; 100-letnica rojstva skladatelja Danila Švare, 17. slovenski glasbeni dnevi April 9–12, 2002, Ljubljana, Slovenia* [Musical theater: Yesterday, today, tomorrow; The 100th anniversary of the birth of composer Danilo Švara, 17th slovenian musical days]. Ed. Primož Kuret. Ljubljana: Festival Ljubljana, 2003.

II Interwar Modernism
Movement and Countermovement

4 The Great War and Its Aftermath
Strauss and Hofmannsthal's "Third-Way Modernism"

Bryan Gilliam

In the 1960s, the classic approach to teaching twentieth-century music was drawn along the lines of two modernisms, one German and one French. The German model centered on Schoenberg and was rooted in Wagner and Brahms, while the French model centered on Stravinsky and was rooted in Debussy. This dialectic between harmonic innovation and innovations in rhythm and (perhaps) color was directly fueled by Theodor Adorno's essay *The Philosophy of New Music* (1948; English translation, 1973), which saw Stravinsky's atavistic and primitivist innovations as dishonest, even reactionary.[1] In this period of high modernism, harmony trumped rhythm, and the dominant narrative became the path toward atonality, with many accounts culminating (as did Donald Jay Grout's *History of Western Music* [1960]), with Schoenberg's student, Anton Webern. Of these two approaches, American academics favored the German model in which a Schoenbergian modernism led directly to such avant-garde contemporaries as Pierre Boulez and Milton Babbitt.

In American high modernism, style and ideology were hopelessly intertwined in a modernist dialogue that prized technical progress above all else. It was basically a note-driven discourse about the tendency of the materials (*Tendenz des Materials*), insulated from modernist discussions in arts and literature, which drew from criticism, aesthetics, and other disciplines. The so-called New Musicology of the 1980s was a direct response to this situation. At the same time, musicologists such as Kim Kowalke and Stephen Hinton were arguing that there was, indeed, a second German way, and they quite correctly reminded their readers that the Schoenberg (of the time of *Pierrot lunaire* [1912]) was not nearly as fresh and modern as were his works in the 1920s. A younger generation of composers had emerged after World War I: Kurt Weill, Paul Hindemith, and Ernst Krenek, among others. They were interested in music and technology, and they composed—when they wished—in quirky, ironic tonalities or none at all and were fascinated by American popular music, jazz, and dance.[2]

What role did Strauss, who lived until 1949 and composed throughout the Weimar period, play in this post-World War I narrative? Although Strauss's modernism is sometimes confined to *Salome* (1905) and *Elektra* (1908)—two milestones along the path to Schoenberg's atonality—Strauss always thought of himself as a modernist. Indeed, at the end of his life, he lamented that few understood his modern attitude, especially in opera:

> Why doesn't anyone see what is new [modern] in my works, how, in [these works], the individual becomes visible as only in Beethoven—this already begins in the third act of *Guntram* (the rejection of the collective), *Heldenleben, Don Quixote, Domestica*—and in *Feuersnot* the intentional tone of mockery, of irony, the protest against the run-of-the-mill libretto, the uniquely new, is obvious. Thus, the humorous satire of Wagnerian speech, as a result of Kunrad's speech (which should not be cut) this entire little non-opera came into being. The confession of *Intermezzo*, of *Capriccio*, is precisely what differentiates my dramatic works from the typical operas, masses, variations in direct succession to Beethoven, Berlioz, [and] the followers of Liszt. Music of the 20th century! The Greek-German.[3]

There are two key terms that might require some explanation for those not versed in the Wagnerian debates, especially the debates that followed after his death. The first, "the rejection of the collective," is part of Strauss's worldview that modern music (including Schoenberg) should get beyond Wagnerian metaphysics, beyond redemption (by the collective), be they Meistersingers or Knights of the Grail. He had concluded early on that in a modern world the subject and the object would remain separate. The second key term, to which I will return later, is the Griechische-Germane, suggesting Germany's roots were not in Christianity but in Greek culture. Neither the rejection of collective redemption nor the embrace of Greek myth is to be found in Wagnerism, which became conservative in Munich and Bayreuth.[4]

Adorno recognized in Strauss's unique modern attitude the protean composer's desire to undermine a transcendent and metaphysical worldview, even as the latter used Wagner's own technical and musical apparatus of a massive orchestra, chromatic harmonies, a system of leitmotifs, and the like. More significantly, Strauss created characters who rejected the collective (unlike Walther von Stolzing and Parsifal),[5] and he cared nothing about redemption.[6] But in an essay entitled "Richard Strauss at Sixty," written in 1924, Adorno registers his disappointment with Strauss's musical atheism, seeing in the older man a great but self-satisfied and soulless composer.[7]

What the twenty-one-year-old Adorno might not have perceived in 1924 was that Schoenberg's atonal modernism retained a post-Wagnerian metaphysics; to the end Schoenberg associated music with a mystical, redemptive, transcendent space. How confusing it must have been in the period of materialistic high modernism to deal with a composer such as Schoenberg, who eschewed tonality yet embraced romantic idealism (Kant, Schopenhauer), and Strauss, who eschewed such idealism and embraced a tonal language.[8] This apparent paradox is an integral part of what might be called third-way modernism, a modernism based on aesthetic content—Strauss's rejection of nineteenth-century German idealism—not merely musical innovation. The music of Adorno's favorite nineteenth-century composers could not work through this crisis of the modern age, a crisis that had grown out of the schism between subject (what he called the *psychologisches "Ich"*) and object (Strauss's "collective"), and that earlier composers had sought to resolve through older "authentic" forms, whether it was Mendelssohn's "shivering classicism," Schumann's "block sonata repetitions," or Bruckner's "congregationless chorales."[9] According to Adorno, Wagner tried and failed to resolve this crisis with the impotent wave of a magician's wand, but what unnerved the young critic was that Strauss seemed not to care at all. Read in this context (a context missing from American Strauss scholarship), Ernst Bloch's remark that Strauss possessed a "brilliant hollowness" is hardly a shocking indictment.[10]

The Prewar Operas

An aspect of Strauss's third way (later abetted by Hofmannsthal) was finding the profound in the seemingly ordinary and everyday aspects of modern life, especially in bourgeois marriage. As Leon Botstein observes, "In *The Egyptian Helen* [*Die ägyptische Helena*, 1928] the mythological and historical are rendered ordinary, in contrast to Wagner. . . . In the mundane, ordinary, and intimate there was sufficient ambiguity and poignancy for serious art."[11] Adorno himself was among the first to proclaim how the institution of marriage had been given "bad press" by Wagner.[12] Wotan/Wagner (the "bourgeois terrorist") contemptuously consigns Hunding ("the primordial husband") to the underworld with a mere wave of his hand: "Geh' hin,

Knecht! Kniee vor Fricka." (Be off, slave! Kneel before Fricka [the goddess of marriage].) For Wagner there was no place for lasting marriage in a world where metaphysical love broke all boundaries. In his essay "The Social Character," Adorno points to the void between the sexual and the ascetic, two opposite poles that can be reconciled only through death.[13] Parsifal, Tristan, Tannhäuser, Siegmund, Siegfried, Lohengrin, the Dutchman—none can marry or (in Lohengrin's case) stay married. Those who are betrothed—such as Wotan and Fricka, King Mark and Isolde, Siegfried and Gutrune—live in a state of what we would now call marital dysfunction. Outside of the domestic contract, Wagner offers the promise of highest bliss, an alternative world to a bourgeois audience suffering from the routine and ennui of family life.[14]

Adorno, who was one of greatest experts on Strauss in the twentieth century, saw it coming. He viewed *Guntram* (1894), Strauss's first opera, not as Wagnerian imitation but as the rejection of the collective and Wagnerian metaphysics. He also understood that the purpose of Strauss's *Feuersnot* (1901) is to rail against the current Wagner philistines who had run Wagner out of town decades earlier. *Salome*, likewise, was intended as a lampoon of *Parsifal* with a redeemer not redeemed but beheaded. It is not the harmonies of the work that make it modern but its mockery of John the Baptist "as a clown."[15]

Salome was a great hit after it premiered on December 9, 1905, and shortly thereafter it gained international stature. On October 21, 1905, Strauss saw the actress Gertrude Eysoldt (the original spoken Salome) playing Hofmannsthal's Elektra at the same theater under the direction of Max Reinhardt. Against his better judgment—which was always to compose contrasting, adjacent works—he saw the opportunity for further advantage in setting another femme fatale to music. *Salome* had, after all, met with great financial success, and Strauss now expressed his desire to set Hofmannsthal's play to music.[16] The composer changed his mind, however, saying that *Elektra* could be put on hold, and it took much of the spring of 1906 before he returned to the opera.[17] By the time Strauss had finished, his tragic vein was depleted, as was his interest in Nietzschean and Freudian ego assertion. In 1963, Ernst Krause, an East German and a brilliant Strauss commentator with a Marxian slant, called these works "abysses." *Salome* was old-fashioned and decadent—representative of a Secessionist, false modernism—and the title character's final monologue was a horrifying regurgitation of Wagnerian *Liebestod*.[18]

The protean Strauss, worn out by the strident twin tragedies, wanted to distance himself from a movement he perceived to be waning in the new century and happily engaged himself with Hofmannsthal in a new project called *Der Rosenkavalier*.[19] The Goethean Strauss joyfully reinvented himself, seeking a new avenue that turned away from the narcissistic and toward the social. Although the libretto bears an intentional resemblance to Da Ponte's *Marriage of Figaro*, it conflates a far wider range of sources, including Beaumarchais, Molière, Hogarth, and even parts of Wagner's *Meistersinger*. What had inspired Strauss, the lover of contrasts and juxtapositions, was the conflation of comic elements with those of genuine profundity. In order to realize such a wide range of emotions, Strauss developed a musical language more complex and challenging than *Salome*'s chromaticism or *Elektra*'s dissonance, for what Strauss sought in *Der Rosenkavalier* was a critical layering of musical styles (Mozart, Johann Strauss, Verdi, and others).[20]

Taking a step well beyond the old-fashioned, decadent, fin-de-siècle *Salome*, Strauss realized that the musical language for the new century would be stylistically diverse, a language that reflected the modernist preoccupation (not unlike that of T. S. Eliot or James Joyce) with the dilemma of history, one that arguably foreshadowed the dissolution of the ideology of style in the later twentieth century and the early twenty-first. Through the lens of *Rosenkavalier*, with its mannered anachronisms, we may see a composer who keenly recognized the disunities of modern life and believed that such incongruities should not be masked by a unified musical style. We find as much, if not more, stylistic variety in *Ariadne auf Naxos* (1912), an opera within a play written at the precipice of war and revised—in the midst of European conflict—as a musical prologue followed by an opera (1916). The work simultaneously features opera seria and commedia dell'arte.

The Postwar Period

The economic and political collapse that followed the conflict of World War I caused sweeping change throughout modern Europe but especially among the defeated Axis powers. Germany, beyond paying draconian reparations, not only lost lands to France, Belgium, Poland, Denmark, and Czechoslovakia, but also colonies in Africa, while the Austro-Hungarian Empire was divided east from west and its main constituent parts, driven by ethnic nationalism, produced various sovereign states: Hungary, Poland, Czechoslovakia, Romania, parts of northern Italy, and a confederation of Slovenian entities that became Yugoslavia.

Massive social, political, and economic changes were occurring all over Austria and Germany, as the two countries' respective republics were established in haste. There were important literary and musical ramifications to this historical cataclysm as manifested in the collaboration of Strauss and Hofmannsthal, which had already lasted thirteen years by 1919 and continued up to the poet's death in 1929. But their collaboration experienced a temporary interruption at the end of the war. Their most recent opera, *The Woman without a Shadow* (*Die Frau ohne Schatten*), was conceived before the war, composed during the conflict, and premiered only after the armistice in October 1919.

The premiere was intended to celebrate Strauss's move from Berlin to the codirectorship of the Vienna State Opera. The endeavor had exhausted both composer and poet, who agreed that it would be their "last romantic opera" and that any future work would be more modern, less metaphysical, and stripped of its "Wagnerian musical armor."[21] Strauss's solution (his next "reinvention") would be a light *Zeitoper* based on a modern marital misunderstanding (*Intermezzo*, 1924). It was even too ordinary for Hofmannsthal, who thought that it lacked psychological depth and literary quality. Going his own way, Strauss wrote the libretto and composed the music for the opera, garnering even Schoenberg's admiration.[22] Indeed, much of the spirit of *Intermezzo* is to be found in other contemporary operas of the period, such as Schoenberg's *Von heute auf morgen* (1929) and Hindemith's *Neues vom Tage* (1929), both of which deal with the problems of modern marriage. With its lively subject and unique cinematic qualities, *Intermezzo* proved a moderate success, but it was always Strauss's intention to return to Hofmannsthal, which he did with *The Egyptian Helen*.

In their mutual exploration of a subject that seems at first glance so banal, Strauss and Hofmannsthal articulated a theme of everyday marriage with far larger ramifications. Indeed, that theme seems to have connected with other post-World War I German modernist movements, such as die Neue Musik (the New Music) associated with Schoenberg and die Neue Sachlichkeit (the New Objectivity) associated with Weill and Hindemith. The larger question, which gained significant resonance after the war, was the very nature of the modern human being in a postwar age of technology and sociopolitical turbulence, where death, dismemberment, and destruction had to be dealt with on a daily basis. We might even read Strauss and Hofmannsthal's postwar project *The Egyptian Helen* (set just after the Trojan War), with its ironic tonalities driven by jazz or popular music, as another aspect of their third-way modernism. Here the third way was a course charted between Neue Musik (atonality and serialism) and Neue Sachlich-keit (the turn toward the ordinary and everyday).

Although Strauss and Hofmannsthal had both supported their empires and were disappointed in defeat and uneasy about the new republics that followed, their personal reactions to contemporary events differed signifi-cantly. Part of this divergence can be explained by their respective nation-alities and cultures, but more importantly these two artists were entirely dissimilar men. Letters between them show a temperamental, thin-skinned, neurotic librettist. Time and again Hofmannsthal expressed offense at Strauss's abruptness, his lack of intellectual depth, his pettiness, and his ap-parent coolness, even lack of empathy. How much of this is true we shall never know, for the Bavarian Strauss took Socratic delight in appearing un-reflective and pretending that composing was just another job. We do know, however, that Strauss was obsessed with work, composed every day, and found artistic activity as natural as breathing. For the temperamental Viennese Hofmannsthal, by contrast, artistic creation required special cir-cumstances, whether it was perfect weather or an inspired frame of mind.

Hofmannsthal was a true believer in the Austro-Hungarian Empire and as a reserve officer was recalled to the war ministry. For the self-absorbed Strauss, the war was mainly a nuisance, keeping his librettist from working on *Woman without a Shadow*. "Poets ought to be permitted to stay at home," Strauss observed, adding, "There is plenty of cannon fodder available: crit-ics [as well as] stage producers who have their own ideas."[23] The composer could never fully comprehend his poet's bitter disillusionment at the fall of the Austro-Hungarian Empire, especially the loss of the cultures of the East. For Hofmannsthal, the empire was an ideal amalgam of the Occidental and Oriental (das Abendländische and das Morgenländische), and after the war he was fixated on the possibility of its reunification, if only in the imagina-tive realm of literature and opera.

Strauss saw the crisis on a far more personal and practical level. With the collapse of the monarchy and the economic difficulties that ensued, the shift from imperially run to state-run musical institutions had disastrous effects in terms of day-to-day management, with Strauss himself calling the newly ad-ministered Berlin Opera "ein Narrenhaus" (a mad house).[24] The composer's solution to crises, however, was to immerse himself in work, reinventing him-self by composing, which in this case led to the proto-*Zeitoper Intermezzo*, an autobiographical domestic comedy dealing with love and intrigue. Although

both composer and librettist now lived in Vienna, they had never been further apart, and it was not clear that they would ever collaborate again, in
which event their third-way modernism might never have emerged. Surrealism and expressionism were the most popular movements in the early to
mid-1920s, though, at bottom, they were rooted in the Sturm und Drang of
Wagnerian *Liebestod*.[25] *Intermezzo* offered something fresh and new, as
Strauss explained in his preface to the opera: "By turning its back upon the
popular love-and-murder interest of the usual opera libretto, and by taking
its subject matter perhaps too exclusively from real life, this new work
blazes a path for musical and dramatic composition, which others after me
may perhaps negotiate with more talent and better fortune."[26]

On the Way to Reconciliation

It was a seemingly insignificant idea of Strauss (the self-proclaimed modernist, the Griechische-Germane) that rekindled their relationship. In July
1921, he asked Hofmannsthal whether he would be interested in creating a
treatment for a possible ballet to be based on Beethoven's *The Ruins of Athens*
and *The Creatures of Prometheus*.[27] The idea resonated deeply with the poet,
who saw the project as an allegory for postwar cultural revival. The work
would be set in Greece to which—in Hofmannsthal's thinking—one could
trace the Occidental roots of Austro-German culture. In a critical scene invented by Hofmannsthal, a character named the Wanderer, a German artist
"of half-forgotten days," muses on the ruins of the past in a deserted Athe-
nian market at sundown. In the manner of Goethe's "Prometheus," the Wanderer asks Athena, "Let me go up to your citadel, my goddess. Will you receive me with all the light of your evening?"[28]

Strauss treated this text as a melodrama and seemed less possessed by
Goethe than by Beethoven as he underscored the text with excerpts from
the latter's Third and Fifth Symphonies. The piece is, admittedly, a modest
pastiche of Beethoven, but it paved the way for Strauss and Hofmannsthal's
first opera after World War I, *The Egyptian Helen*, where the East, lost with
the fall of the Austro-Hungarian Empire, is reunited with the West. Hofmannsthal's third and final mythological work (after *Elektra* and *Ariadne auf
Naxos*) was rooted in the realities of personal and global trauma. His experience in World War I had exposed him to the horrors of sustained European
conflict and, more broadly, had shattered his faith in the Habsburg Empire.
But, as the essays and speeches of the 1920s demonstrate, he was not a ni-
hilist. He envisioned a unique "Austrian Idea," a "United States of Europe,"

whose center would be Austria—more specifically Vienna—and it was this idea of a renewed, utopian embrace of ancient Greece that he sought to realize in *The Egyptian Helen*.[29]

One important aspect of Strauss and Hofmannsthal's third-way modernism was to embrace classical mythology for the new century and to embrace it in a manner that was neither tragic nor satirical. For this there was no precedent in German opera. Paradoxically, although *Elektra* is usually cited as Strauss's most modern work via the path-to-atonality paradigm, both Hofmannsthal and Strauss viewed it as old-fashioned and overwrought, tied to a darkly Dionysian (read Nietzschean) worldview. Hofmannsthal wanted a mythology without gods and metaphysics (as did Strauss), with modern costumes taken from *Vogue* and events depicted "as if [they] had happened two or three years ago, somewhere between Moscow and New York."[30] *The Egyptian Helen* is a work where myth meets *Zeitoper*, with fashionable costumes and an omniscient seashell as a spoof of the radio, or perhaps even the telephone. Hofmannsthal himself suggests that it might amuse "if the Sea-Shell were to sound distorted like a voice on the telephone when one stands beside the receiver."[31]

The librettist wanted the audience to recognize the post–Trojan War period as an analogy for current European conflict. Indeed, the opera concerns itself with what Hofmannsthal calls the "terrible and redeeming experiences" immediately following war, when Menelas experiences a kind of shell shock familiar to many veterans of the First World War.[32] In a state "close to insanity," Menelas arrives at Poseidon's palace with Helen, whom he would have killed but for Aithra, who pacifies him with a lotus potion. By the end of act 1, she has convinced Menelas that the Helen he thinks he knows is a phantom and that the "real" Helen is now asleep in an adjacent room; thus he retires to her bed as they drift toward the Atlas Mountains.

If it had stopped there, Hofmannsthal explains, it would have ended as an operetta, "a short, frivolous comedy."[33] *Ariadne auf Naxos* demonstrates that the movement from comic to serious was always an integral part of Hofmannsthal's creative process. If act 1 is about the dominance of the past and its ramifications with and without anesthesia, then the second and final act is about the present and those characters who can live on, make the transition from past to present and so survive. Menelas and Ariadne are able to make this change, while Elektra is not. But the artificial, drug-induced tranquility between Helen and Menelas fails to make an honest or authentic connection between yesterday and today.

The lotus potion may protect Helen's life, but, having robbed her of her past with Menelas, it leaves her half dead. Just before Menelas returns from a hunt, Helen orders Aithra to make him a potion of remembrance, which will either result in her death or enable her to live a fuller and more honest life. She has reached the critical hour, the one also reached by Ariadne, where life might turn into death but—more important—death might become life ("Tot-Lebendige! Lebendige-Tote!").[34] In his preface to the libretto, Hofmannsthal maintains that Helen's strength is "that she must possess completely the man to whom she belongs," and a tranquilized Menelas is only half a man (just as Bacchus in *Ariadne* is only half a god).[35] As in *Ariadne*, the goal of transformation or renewal is reached by forgetting while remembering, by finding each other without losing sight of the past:

> Half-forgetting
> makes for sweet remembering
> you will feel a deep assurance
> of your divine lover's return!
>
> (Ein halbes Vergessen
> wird sanftes Erinnern;
> du fühlest im Innern
> dir wiedergegeben
> den göttlichen Mann!)[36]

Helen must bring him back to the deadly point he reached the night before. Returned to lucidity (and anger), Menelas raises his dagger but then lets it drop, falling into her arms. Hofmannsthal observes that a poet "can make his characters grow above and beyond themselves into gigantic proportions, for this is what mortals do in rare moments."[37] In this decisively modern moment, Helen moves far beyond the passivity of the fin-de-siècle femme fatale. She insists on winning Menelas through her strength—not merely her beauty—but the latter and the former are ultimately reconciled in her dynamic nature.

In his preface, Hofmannsthal reminds us that Menelas and Helen represent opposite allegorical-geographical poles, the Occident and the Orient respectively, following the lines of contemporary masculine-feminine (Apollonian-Dionysian) conceptions: object-subject, light-dark, outward-inward, marriage-hetaerism. But there is an asymmetry to these reductive binaries, insofar as marriage itself may be said to symbolize these dualities

in each of us. For both Hofmannsthal and Strauss, marriage represents equilibrium, which they regarded as socially and politically desirable in the wake
of World War I. Philip Graydon sees *The Egyptian Helen* as "a critical document of Hofmannsthal's post-war, cultural-restorative mission: as no mere
l'art pour l'art libretto or opera, no mere re-hash and re-mix of timeless subject matter, it stands instead as Hofmannsthal's modern attempt to encap-
sulate the conflict and contradictions of his era."[38] It is, as Hofmannsthal
asserts, "This influx of Orient and Occident into our self, for the immense
inner breadth, these mad inner tensions, this being here and elsewhere,
which is the mark of our [modern] life. It is impossible to catch all this in
middle-class modern dialogue. Let us write mythological operas. Believe me
it is the truest of all forms"—far truer, he believed, than a bourgeois, marital
comedy such as Strauss's *Intermezzo*.[39]

Romain Rolland observes that Hofmannsthal could never write pure
comedy because he always ended by believing his own irony. In a work such
as *Der Rosenkavalier*, Hofmannsthal delighted in casting out threads of comedy and irony but rightly realized he had a responsibility to tie them up by
midway through act 3. The pace of that third act suffers for that reason.
Rolland may well be right, but it is also true that for Hofmannsthal comedy
always meant the integration of the social, something he found lacking in
his own tragedies, including *Elektra*. The ruins of contemporary Europe
were never far from his mind as he was writing his opera about the fall of
Troy; Menelas and Europe were a fractured whole.[40] To Hofmannsthal's
thinking, the Orient was the foundation of Greek civilization, which in turn
was the bedrock of modern Europe.

With a certain linguistic nostalgia, he called for a new postwar *Ausgleich*,
or "compromise" (as had once been established in 1867), between East and
West to be centered in Austria (on the threshold of the Eastern Realm) and
founded upon a renewed sense of Greek antiquity. The mission was reconciliation and rejuvenation for a united Europe, with Austria at its center,
Hofmannsthal's self-described *Heimat* in which a new Europe would be his
Vaterland.[41] *Helen* sets the stage for Strauss's next and far better-known
opera, *Arabella*, another marriage of West (Arabella) and East (Mandryka).
But despite Hofmannsthal's assertion at the end of the preface to *Helen* that
a modern American playwright could have written the myth with the work
taking the form of "psychological drawing room play," Hofmannsthal did
just that in *Arabella*: "Anything mythical [in the old fashioned way] or hero-
ical makes a modern audience uneasy, anything somber and grand (which,

moreover, tends to conjure up associations with the *Ring*) terrifies them to the marrow of their bones: but give them a hotel, lounge, ballroom, betrothel, officers, cabbies, tradesman, and waiters, and they know where they are."[42]

Hofmannsthal wanted an opera set around the Gründerzeit (roughly 1850-73), a time of growing prosperity (and financial speculation) combined with political instability, which culminated in the Ausgleich of 1867. The interface of East and West, whether in the form of Menelas and Helen or of Mandryka and Arabella, continued to be the central theme of Hofmannsthal's final project with Strauss, *Arabella*. In the wake of its defeat after the Austro-Prussian War in 1866, Hungary had seen the opportunity for secession from a weakened Habsburg Empire, which Franz Joseph II curtailed by compromise in the form of a so-called dual monarchy, recognizing Hungary as a kingdom in a new Austro-Hungarian Empire. Its very name is a hyphenation of East and West (like Mandryka-Arabella). But that hyphen, which meant both union and separation, was not as symmetrical as it appeared to be, for although each kingdom had its king, there was only one emperor. The compromise promised new stability, and there was a new sense of economic optimism. There was also the recognition, however, that this optimism might be false, as evidenced by the overspeculation of the liberal class, which led to the stock market crash of 1873—a year before Hofmannsthal was born—and which set the tone for the decade of his formative boyhood years.

The economic collapse after World War I only brought back Hofmannsthal's childhood memories in the form of *Arabella*. The poet saw an entire continent in not only economic but also cultural turmoil, noting that Europe's "collapse . . . [was] a shattering experience."[43] For Hofmannsthal, as for many Austrians and Germans of his generation, Europe was neither a political nor a geographical entity but a cultural one. To his thinking, the task for the future of Europe (by which he meant only the Continent) was a uniquely Austrian one. Thomas Mann articulates a similar view in his *Reflections of a Non-political Man* (1918), where art, music, and literature exist in a sacred space removed from the everyday, politicized world. The German *nation*, as a cultural phenomenon, could nurture an individual, but the German *state*—the product of consensus and compromise—could only rob artists of their individuality. However, whereas Mann ultimately reversed his opinion in 1922, embracing democracy and the Weimar Republic, Strauss and Hofmannsthal held on to their nostalgic, antirepublican views.

We shall never know how Hofmannsthal's views might have evolved, given his untimely death in 1929. Strauss, of course, decided to participate as president (1934-35) of the Reichsmusikkammer during the National So-cialist regime but soon discovered that it was, for him, even worse than Weimar-era democracy. For Hofmannsthal, the Austrian mission was the only hope for Europe. Republican France was out of the question; Prussia was too homogeneous, too uncompromising and unwilling to assimilate with the East.[44] "This Europe that wants to give itself new form needs an Austria," writes Hofmannsthal. "It needs Austria in order to comprehend the polymorphous East."[45] Austria was the model for Europe's future, and its historic fluidity of borders was integral to this model, as Hofmannsthal explains in his 1917 essay "The Austrian Idea" ("Die österreichische Idee"), which in his mind could just as easily have been called "The New European Idea": "The primary and fateful gift for compromise with the East—let us say it precisely: toward compromise between old European, Latin-German and the new European, Slavic world—this only task and *raison d'être* of Aus-tria, had to experience a kind of eclipse for European consciousness during the decades 1848-1914."[46]

The action of *Arabella* takes place on Shrove Tuesday, when carnival he-donism is about to give way to Lenten sobriety, as the mass consumption of Moët et Chandon ("halb trocken, halb herb") ordered by Arabella's mother in act 2 is replaced by the abstemious glass of water that ends act 3.[47] On a historical level, the hedonism of speculation gives way to the stock market crash of 1873. *Arabella* represents a prophetic warning to post-World War I culture that Austria's shift from liberalism to conservatism might return during the late 1920s. Within this vital political context, the musical quota-tions of Slavic folk songs in the *Arabella* score are far more than superficial local color—at least for Hofmannsthal, who had read thoroughly an anthol-ogy published just a few years earlier of Slavic folk songs gathered by Pavel Eisner.[48]

Compared to the economically corrupt Viennese liberals and their spec-ulative gambling, the Slavs offered the poet a sense of rustic purity. To Hof-mannsthal's thinking, a Slav such as Mandryka needs no money in his world and opens his pocketbook to Arabella's needy gambler father without flinching. Hofmannsthal's essay "Czech and Slovak Folksongs" suggests how such spiritual essence and "authenticity" may be preserved in their lyrical outpourings. Such an authentic outpouring is the tender love duet between Arabella and Mandyka in act 2 that is based on a Slavic-Croatian love song ("Und du wirst mein geliebter sein / Ci ja je ono djevojka").[49] Creating these moments of Eastern lyricism was central to Hofmannsthal's project, and Strauss was surely delighted with their exotic flair, but I doubt he understood their richer cultural meaning as Hofmannsthal did, especially in the sense that they became an essential part of the latter's postwar Austrian ideal.

In summer 1929, significant dramaturgical work remained to be done on acts 2 and 3; Strauss pointed them out, and Hofmannsthal was hardly in disagreement. But their first act with the added monologue of Arabella at the end was perfect, and Strauss sent his poet a telegram to express his pleasure on July 15, 1929. However, Hofmannsthal never opened it. Two days earlier Hofmannsthal's son had shot himself, and while preparing to attend his funeral, Hofmannsthal suffered a fatal stroke, marking the end of this fruitful collaboration of several decades.

The opera that outlived Hofmannsthal—it was performed in 1933— shows that his views on language had significantly evolved from the days of his youthful *Chandos Brief* ([1902] *The Chandos Letter*), which expresses such skepticism about words as the sole bearer of expressive or emotional content. The older he got, the less he saw language and gesture as a zero-sum game. Language, especially Eastern language, had moved far beyond the so-called *Sprachkrise* (language crisis) of 1902.[50] In his postwar nostalgia, in his essays, and in his "Czech and Slovak Folksongs," he envisioned a language that could be purer than German.

Gesture may have trumped language in *Elektra* (1908) and in those marvelous prewar Strauss-Hofmannsthal operas that followed. But after World War I, when German *Kultur* had become exhausted and powerless for Hofmannsthal, the embrace of the East was not necessarily "a weakening" but rather a new synthesis, a new strength for postwar modern Europe. Of course, the ensuing years proved Hofmannsthal to be entirely wrong. Operas such as *The Egyptian Helen* and *Arabella* were hardly reflections of a grand European tradition, mythological or not, in Hofmannsthal's imagination. Indeed, after the premiere of *Arabella* on July 1, 1933, little about Europe seemed great. In the wake of the World War I, the rest of the world got to see the sad underside of that "grand" tradition, whether in the examples of Spanish and Italian Fascism, German Nazism, or Soviet Communism.

In Germany alone many operas failed the Nazi censors. In Strauss's case, *The Silent Woman* (1935) was cancelled after four performances because its librettist, Stefan Zweig, was a Jew. Strauss's *Day of Peace* (1936), conceived by Zweig as a last hope of reconciliation and carried out by the uninspiring

Joseph Gregor, was banned after the invasion of Poland (1939) because it sent the "wrong message." *The Love of Danae* (1939), the most Wagnerian of his operas, with its focus on love versus gold, never made it past a dress rehearsal in Salzburg in 1944.[51] At the same time, Kurt Weill, who was a Jew, faced similar losses after the Reichstag fire in March 1933. His opera *The Pledge* was banned within a year of its premiere in 1932 and his *Silver Lake* premiered in February 1933, a little more than two weeks after Hitler became Reichskanzler of Germany. Schoenberg's stage works of the 1910s and 1920s were banned, and he and Weill ultimately emigrated to the United States. Korngold, another Jew and the interwar celebrity opera composer of Vienna, was promised a Vienna premiere of his fifth opera, *Die Kathrin* (1938), but the date coincided with the Nazi annexation of Austria on March 12, 1938. These are but a few examples of a negation of Hofmannsthal's nostalgic grand plan for a Europe that had passed him by after his death in 1929.

Hofmannsthal was, however, not the only Austrian to have postwar dreams for a United States of Europe, though the center would be not Vienna but Berlin. With Hitler's rise to power, both Neue Musik and Neue Sachlichkeit emigrated to the United States, the United Kingdom, and other countries. The short-lived third way simply collapsed with the death of Hofmannsthal.[52] Curiously, the Salzburg Festival—a by-product of Hofmannsthal's nostalgic grand plan, which many anti-Semites viewed as Jewish inspired—continued after Austria's annexation because of the support of Strauss and others. Flashing forward seventy years from the end of World War II, the 2015 Salzburg season has moved well beyond the so-called ideology of styles, featuring such diverse composers as Schoenberg, Weill, Strauss, and Boulez. If modernism, like opera, "is dying in the hope of being reborn," then we are clearly in a new manifestation of *das Neue* where first-, second-, and third-way modernisms can be equally appreciated at the same venue.[53]

Notes

1. Albright 16.

2. See Kowalke. Bryan Gilliam expanded from Weill to Hindemith, Krenek, and others in *Music and Performance of the Weimar Republic*. These and other books such as Susan Cook's *Opera for a New Republic* firmly established a secondary musical modernism in the study of Austro-German music of the twentieth century.

3. Strauss, *Betrachtungen und Erinnerungen* 182. My translation.

4. Major figures from this school of thought were Cosima and her son Siegfried Wagner, Hans von Wolzogen, and Alexander Ritter, among others.

5. It is as if Kunrad, the hero of *Feuersnot*, were the Walther in an act 3 of *Meistersinger* who ended the work with "Nicht Meister, nein."

6. Strauss once remarked to Otto Klemperer that he was puzzled by Mahler's focus on redemption: "I don't know what I am supposed to redeemed from. When I sit at my desk in the morning and an idea comes into my head, I certainly don't need redemption" (Klemperer 147–48).

7. Adorno, "Richard Strauss at Sixty" 407.

8. For a different account of Schoenberg's view of German idealism, see Richard Begam's "Schoenberg, Modernism, and Degeneracy" in this volume.

9. Adorno, "Richard Strauss at Sixty" 408.

10. Bloch 37.

11. Botstein, "Enigmas," 22.

12. Adorno, "Social Character" 15.

13. Ibid.

14. By this yardstick we recognize a strong anti-Wagnerism in Strauss's first opera, *Guntram*.

15. Strauss to Stefan Zweig, 3 May 1935, in Strauss, *A Confidential Matter* 85–86.

16. The profits from *Salome* paid for his villa in Garmisch.

17. Music historians might ponder how Strauss's reception might have changed if Strauss had first produced his comedy and then composed *Elektra*.

18. Krause. See the chapter "Abysses," 295–311. The translator is not cited.

19. Strauss, of course, had set Hofmannsthal's play, *Elektra*, to music, though Hofmannsthal had little to do with the operatic process, save adding some verses so that Strauss could round out the final scene with his powerful music.

20. Leading Viennese music critic Julius Korngold decries the opera as being devoid of the German idealism that had informed *Meistersinger* in "Strauss and the Music Critics" (350).

21. Richard Strauss, "To Hofmannsthal," 28 July 1916, Hofmannsthal and Strauss 259; Richard Strauss, "To Hofmannsthal," 16 Aug. 1916, Hofmannsthal and Strauss 262.

22. Gilliam, "Richard Strauss's *Intermezzo*" 283.

23. Letter to Gerty von Hofmannsthal, 31 July 1914, quoted in Kennedy, 58.

24. Strauss, *Chronik zu Leben und Werk* 402 (13 Nov. 1918).

25. Arnold Schoenberg's *Erwartung* (1909/24), Alban Berg's *Wozzeck* (1922/25), Hindemith's *Cardillac* (1926), and Weill's *Royal Palace* (1926), among many others exemplify these trends.

26. Gilliam, "Richard Strauss's *Intermezzo*" 263.

27. May, p. 48.

28. Strauss, *Die Ruinen von Athen* 16.

29. See David S. Luft's translated essays in his collection, *Hugo von Hofmannsthal and the Austrian Idea*. The Austrian idea is a call for conservative revolution that is consonant with the *rappel-à-l'ordre* movement in France. I recommend Malachi Haco-

hen's 2009 essay, "The Culture of Viennese Science and the Riddle of Austrian Liberalism," which puts Hofmannsthal's conservative revolution in a darker pre-Nazi context.

30. Hofmannsthal, preface 305.

31. Hofmannsthal and Strauss 371. Hofmannsthal goes as far as to suggest that with the removal of the mythological elements, the magic tricks and the like, an American playwright could have written it as a modern "psychological drawing room play" (preface 311).

32. Hofmannsthal, preface 302. Spellings of Menelas or Menelaus are inconsistent in the correspondence. I have chosen this spelling as it is indicated in the score.

33. Ibid. 309.

34. Hofmannsthal, libretto 86.

35. Hofmannsthal, preface 310.

36. Hofmannsthal, libretto, 37.

37. Hofmannsthal, preface 312-13.

38. Graydon 193.

39. Hofmannsthal, preface 313.

40. Hofmannsthal, "The Idea of Europe," 90.

41. Hofmannsthal, "The Austrian Idea," 101.

42. Hofmannsthal, preface 311; Hofmannsthal to Strauss, 18 Oct. 1928, in Schuh 510.

43. Hofmannsthal, "The Idea of Europe," 90.

44. Hofmannsthal was not a politician, and he could visualize his idea only artistically. The foundation of the Salzburg Festival (along with support from Max Reinhardt and Strauss) had an international intent, though based in the most Austrian of cities. It also served as an alternative Bayreuth, which at that time was a conservative German festival.

45. Hofmannsthal, "The Austrian Idea," 101.

46. Ibid.

47. See Werley 130.

48. Eisner.

49. Kuhač 1:15.

50. For a discussion of Hofmannsthal's *Chandos Letter* and the language crisis of 1902, see Gilliam, *Rounding Wagner's Mountain* 91.

51. With Goebbels's declaration of "total war" (1944), music festivals were closed throughout the Reich. The politics of persuasion allowed for the exception of the dress rehearsal for invited guests only.

52. Much of the spirit of *Die Liebe der Danae* (The love of Danae [1939]), however, is steeped in Hofmannsthal's original scenario (1920); the work made it to a Salzburg Festival dress rehearsal (1944).

53. See Begam and Smith's introduction to this text, 1.

Bibliography

Albright, Daniel. *Modernism in Music, Literature, and Other Forms.* Chicago: University of Chicago Press, 2000.

Adorno, Theodor W. "Richard Strauss at Sixty." *Richard Strauss and His World.* Ed. Bryan Gilliam. Trans. Susan Gillespie. Princeton: Princeton UP, 1992. 406-15.

———. "Social Character." *In Search of Wagner.* Trans. Rodney Livingstone. London: Verso, 1985.

Bloch, Ernst. "Philosophy of Music." *Essays on the Philosophy of Music.* Trans. Peter Palmer. Cambridge: Cambridge University Press, 1986.

Botstein, Leon. "The Enigmas of Strauss: A Revisionist View." *Richard Strauss and His World.* Ed. Bryan Gilliam. Princeton: Princeton UP, 1992. 3-32.

Cook, Susan. *Opera for a New Republic.* Rochester, NY: University of Rochester Press, 1988.

Eisner, Pavel. *Volkslieder der Slawen: Ausgewählt, Übersetz, Eingeleitet und Erläutet.* Leipzig: Bibliographisches Institut, 1926.

Gilliam, Bryan. *Music and Performance of the Weimar Republic.* Cambridge: Cambridge University Press, 1994.

———. "Richard Strauss's *Intermezzo*: Innovation and Tradition." *Richard Strauss: New Perspectives on the Composer and His Work.* Ed. Bryan Gilliam. Durham, NC: Duke University Press, 1992. 259-84.

———, ed. *Richard Strauss and His World.* Princeton: Princeton UP, 1992.

———. *Rounding Wagner's Mountain: Richard Strauss and Modern German Opera.* Cambridge: Cambridge University Press, 2014.

Graydon, Philip Robert. "*Die* Ägyptische *Helena* (1927): Context and Contemporary Response." Diss. Queen's University Belfast, 2005.

Hacohen, Malachi. "The Culture of Viennese Science and the Riddle of Austrian Liberalism." *Modern Intellectual History* 6.2 (2009): 369-96.

Hofmannsthal, Hugo von. "The Austrian Idea." *Hugo von Hofmannsthal and the Austrian Idea.* Ed. David S. Luft. Purdue, IN: Purdue University Press, 2011. 99-102.

———. "The Idea of Europe." *Hugo von Hofmannsthal and the Austrian Idea.* Ed. David S. Luft. Purdue, IN: Purdue University Press, 2011. 89-98.

———. Libretto. *Die ägyptische Helena.* Decca CD 430 381-2.

———. Preface. *Die ägyptische Helena* (1928). *The Essence of Opera.* Ed. Ulrich Weisstein. New York: Norton, 1969.

Hofmannsthal, Hugo von, and Richard Strauss. *The Correspondence between Richard Strauss and Hugo von Hofmannsthal.* Trans. Hanns Hammelmann and Ewald Osers. Cambridge: Cambridge University Press, 1980.

Kennedy, Michael. *Richard Strauss.* New York: Schirmer Books, 1988.

Klemperer, Otto. *From Klemperer on Music.* London: Toccata Press, 1986.

Korngold, Julius. "Strauss and the Music Critics." Trans. Susan Gillespie. *Richard*

Strauss and His World. Ed. Bryan Gilliam. Princeton: Princeton University Press, 1992. 311-71.

Kowalke, Kim. *Essays on a New Orpheus: Kurt Weill*. New Haven: Yale University Press, 1986.

Krause, Ernst. *Richard Strauss: Gestalt und Werk*. Leipzig: Breitkopf und Härtel, 1963. English translation, Boston: Crescendo, 1969.

Kuhač, Franjo K., ed. *Collected South Slovakian Folksongs for Voice and Accompaniment in Four Volumes*. Agram: K. Albraecht, 1878-82.

Luft, David S., ed. and trans. *Hugo von Hofmannsthal and the Austrian Idea*. Purdue, IN: Purdue University Press, 2011.

May, Jürgen. "Hugo von Hofmannsthals und Richard Strauss' Festspiel *Die Ruinen von Athen* nach Ludwig van Beethoven—mehr als ein Kuriosum?" *Richard Strauss und das Musiktheater*. Ed. Julia Liebscher. Berlin: Henschel, 2005. 45-60.

Schuh, Willi, ed. *Richard Strauss-Hugo von Hofmannsthal: Briefwechsel*. Zürich: Atlantis, 1978.

Strauss, Richard. *Betrachtungen und Erinnerungen*. Ed. Willi Schuh. Zurich: Atlantis, 1981.

———. *A Confidential Matter: The Letters of Richard Strauss and Stefan Zweig 1931-1935*. Berkeley: University of California Press, 1977.

———. *Richard Strauss: Chronik zu Leben und Werk*. Ed. Franz Trenner and Florian Trenner. Vienna: Richard Strauss Verlag, 2003.

———. *Die Ruinen von Athen* in *Der Unbekannte Strauss*. Koch CD 3-6536-2.

Werley, Matthew. "Analysing *Arabella*'s Past: The Cultural Politics of the Waltz and Austrian History." "Historicism and Cultural Politics in Three Interwar-Period Operas by Richard Strauss: *Arabella* (1933), *Die schweigsame Frau* (1935) and *Friedenstag* (1938)." Diss. Oxford University, 2010.

Adorno's Shifting *Wozzeck*

Bernadette Meyler

Although Alban Berg's 1924 opera *Wozzeck* furnished the first full-length atonal work of its kind and was publicly received as a radical departure from extant operatic tradition, several features of its composition seem to controvert its claim to an uncompromising modernism. Rather than searching out the newest of dramatic works to set to music, Berg resorted for his source material to Georg Büchner's early nineteenth-century play *Woyzeck*. Rather than emphasizing the fragmentary disposition of the parts of this work—never completed during the playwright's lifetime and reconstructed only posthumously—Berg insisted upon regimenting the disparate components into three acts, each divided into precisely five scenes. Rather than producing new musical structures for the opera, Berg deployed the classical tools of absolute music, such as sonata form, and the resources of popular music, such as conventional dances and folk tunes. Rather than demanding an avant-garde staging, Berg specified a meticulously realist approach to the dramatic action. And, rather than casting aside all residues of Wagner, Berg employed that most characteristic of Wagnerian techniques, the leitmotif.

Given these features, one might anticipate that Theodor Adorno, that most rigorous of dialectical critics, ever insistent upon the necessity for art—including music—to accord with its historical situation, would critique *Wozzeck* as he did even Schoenberg and certainly Stravinsky. And it is true that Berg does not entirely escape Adorno's scathing pen in *The Philosophy of New Music*. Yet almost every time that Adorno treats *Wozzeck*, from his 1925 essay on the opera for its Berlin premiere to his 1929 writing on the work to the 1968 book *Alban Berg: Master of the Smallest Link* to a radio address soon before Adorno's own death the following year entitled "Alban Berg: Oper und Moderne" (Alban Berg: Opera and modernity), he accords the opera the highest praise. What, then, accounts for Adorno's attitude toward *Wozzeck*? Does Adorno simply ignore those aspects of the opera that might seem to conflict with its claims to modernism, his critical vision succumbing to his personal association with Berg, or does *Wozzeck*, despite or perhaps because of its anachronisms, fulfill Adorno's vision of the necessary relation between art and history?

An intense reverence for Berg, whom Adorno first encountered at the 1924 premiere of fragments of *Wozzeck*, certainly emerges from the pages of *Alban Berg: Master of the Smallest Link*.[1] After meeting Berg, Adorno began studying music composition with him, and a friendship developed, although the relationship may have been of more importance to Adorno than to Berg.[2] Despite the somewhat neurotic affection evinced by Adorno's letters to Berg and the suggestion within these epistles that Adorno's writings on *Wozzeck* were designed to promote the merits of the work to the opera-going public and allay criticisms of the composer, these pragmatic and personal considerations remain insufficient to account for the depth and durability of Adorno's engagement with *Wozzeck*.

In fact, the title of Adorno's final treatment of *Wozzeck*—"Alban Berg: Opera and Modernity"—suggests the philosopher's effort to understand the particular form of modernity represented by his friend's works. In this radio address, Adorno acknowledged Berg's adherence to aspects of the past, admitting that "a traditional element exists from the outset in Berg" while also claiming that "the advanced and the past interlock in him as in no other composer of his time at a comparable level."[3] Through his successive explorations of *Wozzeck*, Adorno progressively illuminated the initial and enduring modernity of the opera. Nor did these engagements simply represent further elaborations upon a work fixed in amber. Rather, Adorno considered the persistence of *Wozzeck*'s modernity even decades following its premiere. In accordance with his prescient observation in a letter to Berg from 1925 that "there will certainly be a history of *Wozzeck* interpretation, just as Büchner's drama had its history," Adorno as rigorously interpreted the significance of *Wozzeck*'s posthistory as he did the posthistory of *Woyzeck* that *Wozzeck* realized.[4]

At the same time, *Wozzeck* continued to challenge Adorno himself and provoke developments in the philosopher's thought.[5] When attempting to fulfill Berg's request for a new piece on the opera in 1926, Adorno explained, again in a letter, that he was unable to compose the essay at the time because of the transformations his philosophy was undergoing. As he wrote to Berg, although he would not have abandoned the points made by his already-published writing for the *Wozzeck* premiere, "I am in the process of adding to them: from the metaphysical points of departure via epistemology through a positive philosophy of history and political theory," remarking that "to tell you that politically it has brought me decisively closer to communism perhaps offers a drastic clarification of the development."[6] The shift in Adorno's own philosophy and increasing orientation toward the political-historical import of the aesthetic rendered it impossible for him to write again immediately about *Wozzeck*. At the same time, however, *Wozzeck* itself had, in part, prompted the alteration. As Adorno claimed, "The interpretation of the text [*Wozzeck*] led me to the problem of the recurrence of external reity [*Dinghaftigkeit*]—which dissolved in language—in music (incidentally in *Wozzeck* as in Mahler: the way in which the choice of a drama *that already has its own history* corresponds exactly to the choice of the Wunderhorn poems and to the objective intention, for example, that draws Kraus to Matthew Claudius)."[7] From this problem, and "the connection 'proletarian tragedy-opera,'" Adorno claimed to have "arrived at a new theory of opera *toto genere* based on *Wozzeck*," one that was still, however, not ready for its airing in relation to *Wozzeck* itself.[8] Nor was the dynamic relation Adorno depicts between the opera and his theoretical writings restricted to this particular episode. After each successive attempt to capture *Wozzeck* philosophically, a residue of the work remained to provoke Adorno's further inquiry. What Adorno concluded about the relationship between philosophy and music generally in his essay on the subject—that "critique reveals itself as what it has always secretly been, the law of form of the works themselves"—describes with particular aptness his relation to *Wozzeck*.[9] Despite Adorno's continued efforts to apply his critical approach to the opera, the work persisted in demonstrating the inadequacy of these attempts, constantly prompting further critique while suggesting that such critique should be derived from the opera's own self-deconstruction.

After outlining the aspects of *Wozzeck* that Berg's contemporaries and subsequent scholars have considered less than modern, this chapter turns to Adorno's successive engagements with *Wozzeck* and his account of the paradoxical modernity of the opera. It then examines in more detail two particular aspects of Adorno's account of *Wozzeck*'s modernity—Berg's treatment of the relation between language and music and the connection between the temporality of the opera itself and its temporality within history. The chapter concludes with an account of Adorno's changing conception of the "caesura" within *Wozzeck*; the shift in his analysis of the caesura—a term borrowed from Benjamin's reading of Hölderlin reading *Oedipus*—both indicates the influence of *Wozzeck* itself upon Adorno's aesthetics and demonstrates the affinities between *Wozzeck* and even later avant-garde works, like the plays of Samuel Beckett.

The Anachronism of *Wozzeck*

A number of features of Berg's opera undermine its claims to a thoroughgoing modernity, among them its choice of source text, its rearrangement of the material furnished by that source into a more coherent structure, its deployment of seemingly archaic musical forms, its use of leitmotifs, and Berg's insistence on a realistic presentation of the piece. According to one of Berg's students, the composer conceived the intention to compose an opera based on Georg Büchner's *Woyzeck* upon first seeing the Viennese premiere of the play in 1914.[10] Despite having been written in the early nineteenth century, *Woyzeck* had received its first performance only a year earlier in Munich.[11] The text itself had been left uncollated and unperformed by Büchner's untimely death in 1837 at the age of twenty-four, and it was written in an almost illegible hand.[12] Only the editorial efforts of Karl Emil Franzos succeeded in bringing the work into print, although even his version was plagued with textual errors, including the misreading of Woyzeck as Wozzeck.[13] This mistake accounts for the discrepancy between the title of the play and that of the opera, although Berg's composition followed Paul Landau's 1909 edition of Büchner's works, which retained Franzos's text but rearranged the scenes, the ordering of which continues to be disputed to this day.[14] On first glance, Berg's selection of the source for his initial operatic effort appears somewhat regressive, as he resorts not to emerging avant-garde drama but instead to a relic of the nineteenth century.

Nor did Berg retain what is arguably the most modernist aspect of Büchner's play—its fragmentation. Despite the fact that "Schoenberg had already composed his revolutionary 'expressionist' monodrama *Erwartung* in the 'disconnected, kaleidoscopic technique' of the so-called athemic style," Berg deemed it necessary to organize the material furnished by Büchner's play in tightly regimented form.[15] As the composer explained, "Text and action alone could not guarantee . . . unity; certainly not in a work like Büchner's *Wozzeck* which, as is well known, consists of many (twenty-three) loose, fragmentary scenes."[16] Instead, Berg reduced the disparate components of the play into three acts of five scenes each and insisted upon a symmetry between the first and third acts.[17] Starting out in act 1 with "five character pieces," act 2 features a "symphony in five movements," and act 3 includes "six inventions."[18]

As the subdivisions of the acts demonstrate, Berg employs forms derived from "absolute music," a phrase that, as Roger Scruton has written, "names an ideal of musical purity, an ideal from which music has been held to depart in a variety of ways; for example, by being subordinated to words (as in song), to drama (as in opera), to some representational meaning (as in programme music), or even to the vague requirements of emotional expression."[19] Importing structures like those of the symphony, sonata, or passacaglia into the context of an opera not only situates these seemingly "absolute" forms within a dramatic frame but also hearkens back to classical compositional models. At the very moment when Arnold Schoenberg complained about his disciples' failure to compose larger-scale pieces, Berg resorted to "traditional forms . . . in restoring the possibility of coherent large-scale structure which the dissolution of the classical tonal system had destroyed."[20]

Not simply content with availing himself of these techniques of absolute music, Berg also employed the leitmotif, a device intimately associated with the works of Richard Wagner. As George Perle classifies the leitmotifs in his comprehensive analysis of *Wozzeck*, they include "any characteristic musical idea that occurs in more than one scene and that acquires an explicit referential function in the drama through its consistent association with an extra-musical element."[21] Hence, they correspond not only with particular dramatis personae but also with other recurring topoi of the opera, from the Captain, to a military march, to the cry, "Wir arme leut!" (We poor people!), initially uttered by Wozzeck in the first scene.[22]

In treating Wagner's deployment of the leitmotif, Adorno levied several criticisms against the technique, accusing it of serving a mnemonic "commodity-function, rather like that of an advertisement," and claiming that the recurrence of leitmotifs destroyed temporal extension.[23] Elaborating upon the latter point, Adorno writes that "every repetition of gestures evades the necessity to create musical time; they merely order themselves, as it were, in time and detach themselves from the temporal continuum that they seemingly constituted."[24] Wagner's operas are thereby deprived of a dialectical character; instead, "identical materials put in an appearance as if they were something new and thereby substitute the abstract succession of bars for the dialectical progression of substance, its inner historicity."[25] The leitmotif thus becomes identified both with commodification and disconnection from historical temporality. One might therefore extrapolate that Adorno would view Berg's return to the leitmotif in a less than favorable light.

Finally, despite the ongoing innovations in techniques of staging, like those of German expressionism or Erwin Piscator's epic theater, Berg opted definitively for a realistic production. In his observations in "The Preparation and Staging of *Wozzeck*," Berg insists that it is necessary for "a realistic representation [to] prevail throughout . . . so that an immediate and unambiguous recognition and overall view of the place in which each scene is set is assured."[26]

Adorno Addresses *Wozzeck*

From the beginning of his engagements with *Wozzeck*, Adorno addressed the retrospective character of Berg's music. In his essay on the premiere of *Wozzeck*, written before he had seen the opera, Adorno aimed, as he asserted in a letter to Berg, to stop "this prattling on about the 'Schoenberg pupil'" by demonstrating "the impossibility of forming a 'school' from his own stance" as well as "to account for the choice of text."[27] In doing so, he emphasized the connection between Berg's work and nineteenth-century music, particularly the symphonies of Gustav Mahler. According to Adorno, who here begins a focus on transformation and variation that would characterize many of his writings on *Wozzeck*, "Berg's technique of transformation concurs closely with Mahler's."[28] Furthermore, the tension in his work between decomposition "towards the smallest unit of a motif, to the single note," which is then used "as a means of connection," and "the call for a larger form as a contrast" presents an analogy with Beethoven's contrast "between rhythmic motif and symphonic movement."[29] Nevertheless, through his "free choice" (*im freier Wahl*), Berg submitted himself to Schoenberg.[30] Hence, in the effort to refute the claim that Berg was simply a member of the school of Schoenberg and a minor adjunct of the latter, Adorno elaborates upon Berg's affinity with the tradition of the nineteenth century.

Were Berg entirely beholden to the nineteenth century, however, *Wozzeck* would remain inadequate to its historical moment. Already here Adorno identifies the obsolescence of the aesthetic tradition emanating from the nineteenth century, tying that obsolescence to the increasing disconnection between art and society. Toward the beginning of the essay, he writes that "the radical problem of the relation [*Beziehung*] between art and society [*Gesellschaft*] in the entire breadth of musical life excludes any connection other than that of free choice [*Wahl*], since the preeminent unity of a school erects itself upon an aesthetic tradition, the social ground of which has wasted away [*verfiel*]."[31] Despite the resonance between Berg's works and those of Mahler and Beethoven, Berg can no longer serve as an inheritor of an aesthetic tradition.

Instead, through his "free choice" (*im freier Wahl*), he was led to Schoenberg. This choice Adorno associates with the opposition between "personality" (*Personalität*) and "tradition" (*Tradition*), mutually constitutive concepts that he then maps onto the contrast between "technical self-sufficiency" (*technischer Autarkie*) and "expressive determination" (*expressiver Bestimmtheit*). Becoming a personality itself entails seeking the tradition yet abolishing it at the same time. This process necessitates the exercise of "personal responsibility [*Verantwortung*] in light of the chaotic broken [*zerspellten*] forms."[32] One of the noteworthy aspects of Adorno's discussion here is its hermetic treatment of the aesthetic tradition, despite his reference in passing to society on the first page. Unlike Adorno's later writings, this essay considers the dynamics of aesthetic inheritance and renewal largely on its own, in a manner recalling T. S. Eliot's 1921 essay, "Tradition and the Individual Talent."

As the dichotomy between "technical self-sufficiency" and "expressive determination" might suggest, considerations of psychology also make their appearance in this essay, considerations that would emerge transmogrified in Adorno's 1929 piece on the opera. It was perhaps not incidental in this regard that Adorno was concurrently completing his first, unaccepted, Habilitation, on the topic of the concept of the unconscious in the transcendental theory of the psyche, which he presented and then withdrew in 1927.

In 1929, on the other side of the shift in Adorno's political thought and after he had had the opportunity to see *Wozzeck* performed—in the company of Walter Benjamin—this interest in psychology led to a discussion of the opera as itself a work of psychoanalysis. Other hallmarks of his essay "The Opera *Wozzeck*" include its increased engagement with the work of Richard Wagner and a concomitant effort to differentiate Berg's opera from the Wagnerian "music drama," particularly *Tristan und Isolde*, as well as an increased focus on the relationship between music and language within the operatic medium.[33] Most notable, however, is the piece's rejection of the internal approach to aesthetic tradition that Adorno's initial writings on *Wozzeck* had taken and its embrace, instead, of a socially situated history of the trajectory from *Woyzeck* to *Wozzeck*. Precisely this focus on the historical positions of *Woyzeck* and *Wozzeck* calls forth the necessity of treating the music's relation to its source and to the language of that source.

Evidence of Benjamin's impact on Adorno's understanding of *Wozzeck* marks both this essay and Adorno's remarks on *Wozzeck* in his "Berliner Opernmemorial" of the same year. In particular, these pieces find Adorno grappling with Benjamin's notion of the "caesura," most fully articulated in the latter's interpretation of Hölderlin's views on tragedy, contained in his essay on Goethe's *Elective Affinities*, published in 1924-25. Writing to Adorno retrospectively of their discussion at the performance of *Wozzeck*, Benjamin explained, "You know that whenever we talked about music, a field otherwise fairly removed from my own, it was really only when his work was under discussion that we reached the same level of intensity as we usually do in our discussions on other subjects. You will certainly still remember the conversation we had following a performance of Wozzeck."[34] As Adorno had observed in a letter to Berg exactly ten years earlier, his conversation with Benjamin about the opera had illuminated for him "the great scene in the inn." As he elaborated then, "It is certainly no coincidence that this scene stands precisely where it does: it is a caesura in Hölderlin's senses, and one which thereby allows the 'expressionless' to break into the music itself."[35] Although Adorno would subsequently employ the criterion of the caesura to evaluate a range of other artworks, including Beethoven's compositions, as Michael Spitzer has shown, and Schoenberg's *Moses und Aron*, as Philippe Lacoue-Labarthe has discussed, it was here, in the context of *Wozzeck*, that he first used it as an analytic category.

Whereas none of his earlier accounts delves into great depths in its musical analysis of *Wozzeck*, Adorno expresses some delight at having based his conclusions about the opera in *Alban Berg: Master of the Smallest Link* on detailed engagement with compositional technique. In the intervening years, Adorno had continued to write about Berg and *Wozzeck*, devoting particular attention to both in his contribution to Willi Reich's 1937 biography of Berg that followed the composer's death, material that formed the substrate of his later book on Berg.[36] Nevertheless, most of his treatments of Berg during these intervening years were contained in works focused on other composers—as is the case with *The Philosophy of New Music*—or considering conceptual problems—such as the 1956 essay "Music, Language, and Composition." His late book on Berg both accentuates the historical dimensions of *Wozzeck* that he had earlier outlined in 1929 and insists upon a refinement of his previous take on Berg's approach to transition. As he summarizes this second development:

> The Berg analyses which I wrote some thirty years ago, directly after his death, were traditional analyses of the kind which brings the "whole" down to the small-est possible number of what one calls germinal cells and then shows how the music develops out of them. . . . However, as I came to revise and prepare the book last year, and so to occupy myself with Berg's music with renewed intensity, I saw something that I had, of course, dimly sensed for a long time: namely, that Berg's music is not at all a Something [Etwas] which forms itself, so to speak, out of a Nothingness [ein Nichts] of the smallest possible, undifferentiated component ele-ments. It only seems like this at first glance. In reality it accomplishes within itself a process of permanent dissolution rather than achieving a "synthesis." . . . Its Becoming, if I may term it thus—at all events, where it crystallizes-out its idea in its purest form—is its own negation. This means that such a structuring of the inner fiber of a music also calls for an analytical practice completely different from the long-established motivic-thematic approach.[37]

While Adorno had identified distinctions between Berg's and Schoenberg's modes of transition in his essay on the premiere of *Wozzeck*, only in the later work does he explain that the dissolution of music into its components re-sults not in a reconstruction but in another successive dissolution. It is Adorno's account of this quality in Berg's work on which David Durst fo-cuses in his chapter "The Art of Disappearance: Adorno's Aesthetics of Modernism and Alban Berg's Music." As Durst argues, *Wozzeck* becomes paradigmatic of modernism for Adorno precisely because Berg "reshap[es] music itself into an 'image of vanishing' (*Bild der Verschwindens*)."[38] Through furnishing the image of vanishing, *Wozzeck* exemplifies the "dialectic of non-simultaneity," which for Adorno, Durst contends, names "a dynamic his-torical process by which archaic nature and traditional social relations are violently effaced by capitalism's insatiable will to the identity of exchange."[39] Similarly focusing on the way in which Berg's music encourages a "perma-nent dissolution [*permanente Auflösung*], rather than achieving a synthesis," Max Paddison interprets this emphasis in Adorno's account of Berg as indi-cating that "Berg's great achievement, the *tour de force* of his music, was at one and the same time to have undermined traditional formal norms while apparently reinstating them. Berg's 'smallest transitions' serve to reveal the transience and instability of formal norms, genres and schemata through dissolving them back into their smallest constituent elements."[40]

Adorno's last treatment of *Wozzeck*, in "Alban Berg: Oper und Moderne," both exemplifies the detailed analyses that Adorno prepared for his book on Berg and confronts head-on the question of Berg's continued modernity in the face of what Adorno had already, in the title of a 1955 piece, identified as "the aging of the new music." As Adorno explains in "Oper und Moderne," "Among musicians, especially the advanced ones, it is not infrequently believed that [Berg] has been overtaken: falsely believed, as I hope to show you."[41] To demonstrate his point, Adorno "undertak[es], as a method, to work from a relatively simple, if you will, general analysis, in order that [he] should be able to take out what is buried there, the concretization of music and the form of Berg's advancements and finally to communicate to [the listener] a knowledge of what that—[he] would almost like to say: unsecularized—modernity of Berg's consists."[42] In this account, Adorno furnishes concrete musical examples of the technique Berg employed in *Wozzeck* but emphasizes more than in his book on Berg the especially dramatic nature of Berg's opera.

While considering the dissolution of the motif down to the most minimal component here as well, Adorno further elaborates upon the dramatic significance of the instant for Berg, a significance tied to the continued tension between harmony and melody. Reformulating what he had earlier seen as the distinctions in variation form between Schoenberg and Berg, Adorno here presents the differentiation in terms of their relations to the persistence or lack thereof of harmony:

> [Schoenberg] wanted to say that harmonics was a mere result of melody formation and of this derived counterpoint, no longer a parameter of its own law. The specific difference between Berg and Schoenberg lies precisely in this, that he never really bowed before this dictum. The verticality, thus that which is sounding at the same time in an instant, is to him precisely the carrier of the musical process as horizontality and the nexus of horizontalities. His music knows that the drama has its center in the instant. Single sounds, chords maintain for Berg his whole compositional life through their weight. That is, however, something of expression: in the single sound it implodes with highest intensity, each part is an expressive microcosm that unloads itself dramatically.[43]

Whereas Schoenberg assimilated harmony with melody, Berg insisted upon harmony for temporal and dramatic reasons.

Similarly, Adorno emphasizes the significance of the general pause in *Wozzeck*—a pause that persists at the end of act 2 even after the curtain comes down.[44] For Adorno, Berg "brought to the fore, like hardly any composer before him, the silence of the power of expression."[45] In this regard, it is not incidental that Adorno sees Berg as advanced for his time and more comparable to Samuel Beckett than to Berg's own contemporaries. Not only does Beckett's language decompose itself into ever more minute units, but silence and its duration—particularly after the end—take on extraordinary importance in the performance of his plays.

Woyzeck and Wozzeck

Despite the span of almost a century dividing Büchner's writing of Woyzeck and Berg's composition of Wozzeck, the tightness of the ties between the two works underpins Adorno's admiration for the opera. On the one hand, the opera furnishes the opportunity for "doing justice" to this long-neglected play. As Adorno writes in Alban Berg: Master of the Smallest Link, "Just as Büchner obtained justice for the tortured, confused Wozzeck, who, in his human, dehumanized state, objectively represents all soldiers, so it is the intention of the composition to seek justice for the drama."[46] The reference to justice is not simply fortuitous. Büchner's Woyzeck is not a wholly fictional character but instead based on the case of Johann Christian Woyzeck, executed in 1824 following trial for the murder of his mistress.[47] Despite considerable evidence of the defendant's insanity, the psychiatrist who examined Woyzeck, Hofrat Dr. Clarus, declined to determine that he had acted with diminished responsibility.[48] Although notoriously difficult to interpret, the character of Woyzeck in Büchner's play could be understood as staging the reasons for believing that the historical Woyzeck lacked agency with respect to his fate, making manifest the potential causes of his insanity and the erratic behavior that resulted. On this account, as Adorno suggests, Woyzeck poetically undoes the injustice of the historical verdict against Woyzeck.

The play itself was likewise denied the favorable verdict of history through its relegation to obscurity until its first performance in the early twentieth century. Berg's opera thus aims at finally bringing Büchner's play into harmony with the historical situation and endeavors to do it justice through the transformation of its medium. The music "seek[s] to comfort the drama over its own despair."[49] As Adorno writes, when transmuted into operatic form, "Büchner's tragedy completely absorbs the profound melancholy of the music's south German/Austrian tone, but with such coherence and immanence of form as to give scenic embodiment to expression and pain, serving thereby, purely out of itself, as something like a posthumous court of appeals [*Berufungsinstanz jenseits*]."[50] Although this is the standard English translation of the sentence, the German reveals a fundamental ambiguity as to whether the tragedy or the music takes priority. Since the German reads, "Die abgründige Traurigkeit ihres süddeutsch-österreichischen Tons nimmt das Büchnersche Trauerspiel ganz in sich auf," the subject could as easily be "the profound melancholy of the music's south German/Austrian tone," which absorbs the tragedy, as the reverse. Under this reading, the opera would furnish a posthumous court of appeals for the tragedy rather than the tragedy becoming its own posthumous court of appeals within the context of the opera. The ambiguity of the sentence is, however, revealing, as the relation between opera and tragedy is, for Adorno, insistently reciprocal, one never clearly taking precedence over the other.

Ironically, at the very historical moment when Berg's artwork could do justice to Büchner's earlier masterpiece, the prospects for *Wozzeck* being received justly in the public sphere were, in Adorno's view, low. Following the divergence in the mid-nineteenth century between "great music" and "social functionality," "the composer can no longer count on there being a mediator between himself and the public" (i.e., the critic), and "the avant-garde composer" himself may be the only one capable of looking "the unique questions and antagonisms of the individual work straight in the eye without having any general theory of music or any music history to instruct him."[51] Once "the break between production and consumption [had] become radical," prior to World War I, difficulty of comprehension necessarily ensued, because "art no longer [had] the task of representing a reality that is preexisting for everyone in common, but rather of revealing, in its isolation, the very cracks that reality would like to cover over in order to exist in safety."[52] Hence, only in criticism such as that of Adorno himself—which takes into account the historical situation of the artwork and considers what formal strategies that temporal plight necessitates—can work as difficult as Berg's be properly addressed. For Adorno, "Berg is entitled to the kind of justice dispensed by Karl Kraus. Kraus mercilessly pursued every misplaced comma and yet was prepared to defend the most flagrant infraction of the rules when it resulted from a higher law of creation."[53] His book *Alban Berg: Master of the Smallest Link* is aimed at according Berg that justice.

As already alluded to, far from being one sided, the relation between play and opera runs in the opposite direction as well. If *Wozzeck* does justice to *Woyzeck*, it is the choice of *Woyzeck* and the opera's fidelity to it that

renders Berg's work efficacious. As Adorno claims, "It is the ultimate paradox of the *Wozzeck* score that it achieves musical autonomy not by opposing the word but by obediently following it as its deliverer [salvager] [*als
rettende dieser hörig folgt*]."[54] While sounding in abstractions, this sentence
speaks quite precisely to the technique Berg employed in composing
Wozzeck. Rather than extracting larger themes from *Woyzeck* and interpreting them into an independent libretto, Berg furnished the text for the opera
himself. Aside from omitting some scenes, Berg then almost slavishly followed the language of the play or, at least, the language of the Landau/
Franzos edition.[55] By according itself to the play on precisely the level of
text, the opera achieves aesthetic independence as well as a timeliness that
other approaches might not have permitted. What exactly this means for
Adorno can be demonstrated more clearly through examining first the plot
of *Woyzeck* then Berg's musical treatment of the materials.

On the stratum of plot, *Woyzeck* addresses the predicament of the soldier caught by the snares of financial exigency and subjected to the dehu-
manizing effects of capitalism. The play's material therefore renders tragic a
seemingly base hero and furnishes an implicit critique of bourgeois society
and military life that might be thought to appeal to Adorno's Marxist orientation. Emphasizing the lack of elevation of the characters in Büchner's play,
George Steiner claims that "*Woyzeck* . . . is the first real tragedy of low life.
It repudiates an assumption implicit in Greek, Elizabethan, and neo-classic
drama: the assumption that tragic suffering is the somber privilege of those
who are in high places."[56] Partly for this reason, Arnold Schoenberg initially
objected to Berg's selection of *Woyzeck* as the subject for his opera; as another of Schoenberg's pupils recollected, "Schoenberg disapproved of
Berg's choice . . . and argued that music should deal 'rather with angels than
with batmen.' "[57] To Adorno, however, the formulation of the political concerns within Büchner's play appeared outdated. Whereas Büchner's tragedy
emphasizes the "paralysis of the petit bourgeois individual [i.e., Woyzeck
himself] in the face of his domination by the bourgeoisie," this conflict "has
long since entered into the class struggle," thereby rendering the political
implications of *Woyzeck* somewhat anachronistic at the beginning of the
twentieth century.[58]

What remains salient, however, is the suffering of the individual, the suffering that Büchner extracted from the historical Woyzeck and that Berg
emphasizes in *Wozzeck*. Although prefiguring this emphasis in more general
comments on the relation of Berg's music to suffering in his 1925 essay on

Wozzeck, Adorno alights upon the identification of Woyzeck with suffering in his 1929 foray back to the opera. According to Adorno's account there, "The suffering of the oppressed human being has no more been assuaged by the class struggle, up to now, than art that takes this suffering as its subject is lost."[59] Berg himself, oppressed by his service in World War I, although mostly occupied with a military desk job during that period, identified with the plight of the soldier in the play; as he explained in a letter to his wife, "There is a bit of me in this character.'"[60] Furthermore, despite the precision of the opera's formal construction, Berg expressed his goal as that of conveying the subject of the drama, rather than allowing the audience members to register the virtuosity of the musical composition. This aim he deemed he had accomplished because "no one in the audience . . . pays any attention to the various fugues, inventions, suites, sonata movements, variations, and passacaglias about which so much has been written. No one gives heed to anything but the vast social implications of the work which by far transcend the personal destiny of Wozzeck."[61] Here a potential discrepancy arises between Adorno's interpretation and Berg's understanding of the work; whereas Berg sees the social implications of the opera as paramount, Adorno deems its greatest accomplishment the "adopt[ion of] the stance of a *real humanity*."[62] In *Alban Berg: Master of the Smallest Link*, Adorno would further describe *Wozzeck* as "not the application of the latest achievements to the long since dubious genre of grand opera, but rather the first paradigm [*Modell*] of a music of genuine humanism [*Humanismus*]."[63] As Adorno would indicate in *The Philosophy of New Music*, it is humanism that both renders Berg's works masterpieces and constitutes their ultimate limitation.

Through Berg's techniques of adaptation, the character of Woyzeck speaks to the audience through *Wozzeck*. Two analogies illuminate the composer's method—one proposed by Berg himself and the other by Adorno. For Berg, the role of the operatic composer, particularly in the context of *Wozzeck*, is "to solve the problems of an ideal stage director."[64] This comparison partially explains Berg's insistence on a realistic approach to the actual stage direction of the opera. As Berg writes in his notes on "the preparation and staging of *Wozzeck*," "a realistic representation [must] prevail throughout."[65] Far from disapproving of this choice, Adorno affirms its necessity, contending that "with the surest of instincts Berg the avant-gardist prescribes a 'realistic' staging, no doubt in order not to detract attention from the music as the most essential element."[66] To the extent that the

music furnishes what an ideal stage director would supply, a more innovative production of the opera might conflict with the realization of the play
proposed by the music itself. As Berg explains, the score itself elucidates the
significance of Büchner's stage directions: "The work of the stage-manager
also demands an intimate knowledge of the music. The general meaning of
a stage direction in Büchner is often only made explicit through the music."[67]
Under this account, the music of *Wozzeck* furnishes the kind of interpretation of *Woyzeck* that an ideal production would provide, remaining faithful
to the text but filling in the dimensions that it can never include.

Similarly, the analogy that Adorno proposes, between the operatic composer and the psychoanalyst, entails gathering from the source material
what its own language constitutively cannot state. In his 1925 essay on the
Wozzeck premiere, Adorno goes to great lengths to distinguish Berg's approach
from nineteenth-century psychologism while simultaneously suggesting that
the composer eschewed the opposite pole of complete objectivity. Rather,
he indicates, Berg achieved a psychology beyond psychology. Writing of
Berg's work generally, Adorno proposes:

> The isolation of the individual, his suffering, his desires and his lethargic melan-
> cholia are reflected psychologically. Their very individualism is subject to tradi-
> tion, expressive chromaticism. He regulates the harmonic selection, upon which
> the form is based for the main part. But he also "decomposes" it, since he exposes
> it: because he has used the arbitrariness of the psychological reference as its
> basis. It dissolves into the infinity of psychological moments. A sudden change
> occurs at the moment when the punctual harmony and its constructive form-
> correlate are emancipated from the dictates of psychological expression subject
> to constructive willpower. That which constitutes the form, whose objectivity of
> psychological individualism proves to be distorted, sinks into oblivion. However,
> the individual, who has burst his bonds, is no longer just an individual. He out-
> grows the limits of the sphere of "bad" individualism, because he has broken the
> bonds requiring him to depict them. This is where Berg has historically broken
> with Mahler.[68]

By mediating psychology through construction, Berg avoids both the mere
psychologism of the nineteenth century and the excessive abstractions of
his contemporaries, instead allowing for a new view of the individual. As
Adorno adds, "Wozzeck's line: 'Man is an abyss' is the drama's motto, which
gives rise to the actual story. Berg's music delves into the abyss. To arrive
there, it first has to break through the outer psychological shell."[69] Only in

his 1929 piece on *Wozzeck* does Adorno further elaborate upon the quality of that individual—no longer the "bad" individual—who emerges from Berg's opera.

In this later essay, Adorno argues that, because the stage of history at which Berg's opera was composed has left behind the class concerns of Büchner's play—preoccupied with the relation between the petit bourgeoisie and the bourgeoisie—the work as an entity cannot cohere. Strict fidelity to the text—but not the structure—of the drama permits the music to unveil Woyzeck/Wozzeck's predicament as a human plight: "Music and the word meet in the power of suffering [*Kraft des Leidens*], and the music salvages [*errettet*] a suffering that may have been intended in *Wozzeck*'s words but that the verbal drama no longer supports."[70] The role of the composition here is that of psychoanalysis: "Between *Wozzeck* and psychoanalysis [*Psychoanalyse*] there exists not mere similarity, but a family relationship [*Verwandtschaft*]."[71] The psychoanalytic process involved does not resemble the nineteenth-century version of psychology, focused on private pathology, but instead entails uncovering the "*residues of existence* [Seinsbestände]."[72] Freudian dream work appears, in that, "like analysis, Berg's music begins with sleep and the dream."[73] In keeping with the psychoanalytic approach, the music decomposes the surface of individuality and character to reveal impulses and urges that also pertain to the individual.

Technically, Berg achieves this result through his compositional method and through the "power of transition [Übergang]."[74] As Adorno claims, Berg's "style . . . pulverizes substance into the tiniest particles, in order to create its form from the construction of their transition [Übergang]."[75] Similarly, the Freudian psychoanalytic method focused on the images furnished by the dream material to undermine the explicit narrative of the dream and reconstruct an alternative account of its significance. As Adorno would explain the musical technique in comparing it with the psychoanalytic in a slightly later essay, "On the Social Situation of Music" (1932), "such music . . . decomposes the contours of the surface [of expression] and constructs out of the particles of musical expression a new language by means of musical immanence."[76]

Through the psychoanalytic process of the opera, the subjectivity uncovered is transmuted into an objective form. Hence, "despite all its subjective dynamics, *Wozzeck*, in reality, is an objective act performed in the space of subjectivity."[77] To the extent that Berg captures what is at stake in *Woyzeck*, what emerges as crucial is not simply "the personal destiny of

Wozzeck," as Berg puts it, but instead the objective character of his suffer-ing, a suffering connected with the historical situation: "For this reason, the petit bourgeois individual is needed here once again: his suffering discloses objective characters that are not yet evident today in the action of the col-lective."[78] Adorno's remarks here coalesce with Berg's own account of the opera, emphasizing something beyond Wozzeck's personal characteristics. Furthermore, they connect with Adorno's resistance to certain strains in Marxism, which he believed "over-socializ[ed]" the individual, "whose psy-chological dimension had not been totally obliterated."[79] As Martin Jay writes, "Adorno's philosophical defense of the contingent, suffering, empirical subject, that ethically materialist moment in his thought . . . led him to argue that psychology (although not psychologism in its reductive forms) was a le-gitimate bulwark against that subject's repression in the name of an allegedly higher or more general subject."[80] It may be partly through his engagement with *Wozzeck* that this aspect of Adorno's philosophy developed.

The significance of Berg's treatment of the intersection between words and music in *Wozzeck* is not restricted to its role in ensuring the success of the work. Berg's technique further suggests an alternative to the two poles of modern music, each of which, according to Adorno, ran aground because of their efforts to unmoor music from language. Whereas other attempts to establish the autonomy of music eschewed the resemblance to language, Berg recognized the impossibility of getting beyond language by any means other than through it: "In *Wozzeck*, too, music makes new claims for sover-eignty within opera. But Berg's method is directly contrary to that of the neoclassicists [i.e., Stravinsky]: utter submersion [*rückhaltloser Versenkung*] in the text."[81] As Adorno puts it elsewhere, Berg's "music obeys the text's intentions in every single one of its motions [*jeder Augenblick*] in order to tear the music loose from them once more through the organization of its coherence."[82] The music of *Wozzeck* takes over the text precisely by its ad-herence to it; the text can pose no further resistance to the work once it has been absorbed into the opera as a whole and incorporated into a new form. It is this submersion that enables the second act of *Wozzeck* to be "quite literally a symphony, with all the tension and all the closure of that form, and at the same time at every moment so completely an opera that an un-aware listener would never even think of a symphony."[83]

Following in the wake of his division of twentieth-century compositional approaches into those represented by Stravinsky and Schoenberg in *The Philosophy of New Music*, Adorno's subsequent essay "Music, Language, and

Composition" (1956) explains that both poles endeavor equally to disentangle language and music. In Adorno's words, "The movement that is subsumed under the name of the new music could easily be represented from the perspective of its collective allergy to the primacy of similarity to language."[84] Although selecting different paths, both trajectories fled from the legacy of Richard Wagner, who both "drew vocal music much closer to language than it had ever been before, and did so in a specifically mimetic way, but also assimilated musical construction itself to the gesture of language to the point of exaggerated clarity."[85]

On the one hand, Stravinsky resorted to earlier, seemingly "architectonic" musical models but through this effort to escape language wound up in parody, "something eminently mimetic and thoroughly similar to language," and finally "reverted to sheer historicism."[86] On the other hand, for the more rigorous exponents of new music, like Schoenberg, "the rebellion against musical similarity to language desires nothing less than to catapult itself out of history altogether."[87] Through the effort to terminate "subjectively mediated musical coherence . . . and create tonal relationships dominated by exclusively objective . . . relationships," these composers wound up caught on the opposite horn of the dialectic, thrust back into the realm of "the purely manufactured thing."[88] Even—and perhaps especially—for the most thoroughgoing proponents of this approach, the twelve-tone composers, "with the proscription of everything that is even remotely similar to language, and thus of every musical sense, the absolutely objective product becomes truly senseless."[89] Despite the otherwise radical differences between them, Stravinsky's and Schoenberg's avoidance of language created an impasse in the development of their music.

The only alternative that Adorno proffers in "Music, Language, and Composition" is furnished by Berg's operas. These succeed precisely because of the contradiction that they stage between inheriting Wagner's legacy and insisting upon the musical autonomy that Schoenberg championed. Under this account, Berg's deployment of the leitmotif cannot simply be criticized as in Wagner, but rather furnishes a component of the effort to reconcile language with musical autonomy.[90] Despite the criticisms Adorno levels against the composer in *In Search of Wagner*, the theorist opines that Wagner's approach to the relationship between music and language represented the only way forward "following the irreparable collapse of the traditional formal cosmos" within the nineteenth century.[91] By taking up the Wagnerian tradition in juxtaposition to an insistence on formal structures, Berg thus went furthest toward generating a properly historicized music within the twentieth century. The best new music, for Adorno, "intertwined" the antithetical elements not of language and the extralinguistic but of two disparate linguistic values, that of expression and "the articulation of the whole," or, in another phrasing, expression and construction.[92] *Wozzeck* succeeds in retaining this tension.

Furthermore, the analogies between Berg's activity and those of an ideal stage director or psychoanalyst emphasize what Adorno considers a fundamental aspect of the differential relation between music and language, an aspect that pertains to the respective roles of mediation in the two. Whereas language attains clarity but only through mediation, music addresses immediately but with obscurity: "Music reaches the absolute immediately, but in the same instant it darkens, as when a strong light blinds the eye, which can no longer see things that are quite visible."[93] Through images and dreams, the music of Berg's *Wozzeck* conveys the impact of Woyzeck's suffering to early twentieth-century audiences. Under psychoanalysis, *Woyzeck* does not cash out into a clear narrative but furnishes an existential insight.

Time and History

The temporality of *Wozzeck*, both in its internal structure and in its relation to the trajectory of history, may also partially rescue it from the alienation evident, for Adorno, in the destiny of twelve-tone music. Both Berg himself and Adorno emphasize the "architectural" quality of the composition of *Wozzeck*, yet this architectural disposition, emerging from the deployment of the forms of absolute music to structure the entirety, is far from static or atemporal. Rather, it serves to ensure development within the opera. Here too the text collaborates with the music to bring forth an emphasis on time; even the slight alterations that Berg made to the play for purposes of the libretto accentuate the drama's obsession with a time that seems to be as out of joint as Hamlet's. Berg's selection of source likewise averts the danger posed to new music of exiting the stage of history altogether. Yet because the stage of history in which the work was composed presents irreconcilable contradictions, Berg's "masterpiece's" own perfectly dialectical structure cannot effect a reconciliation and can remain only a brilliant failure, gesturing toward modernity but not fully capable of speaking to it.

Raymond Geuss has criticized Adorno for failing to acknowledge the fundamentally circular temporal implications of the retrograde forms in

Berg's works and has accused the philosopher of attempting to ignore this propensity for philosophical and political reasons.[94] As Geuss explains, "The late nineteenth-century bourgeoisie which (correctly) feels itself threatened by the rising proletariat must give up its ideology of inevitable progress and retreat from history either into the timeless present of 'positivism'— this is, as it were, the 'soft' Western liberal option—or, when the going really gets tough, into cyclical or other mythic forms of historical thought— this is the proto-fascist option."[95] Were Adorno to acknowledge circularity in Berg, he might be allowing his friend to approach too close to the proto-fascist option. In fashioning this argument, however, Geuss neglects the power of the instant—and even silence—in Berg's operas, particularly *Wozzeck*, and the relation between the operatic instant and history.

Adorno elaborates his critique of the temporality of the music of Schoenberg's school in *The Philosophy of New Music* not only on grounds internal to the compositions themselves but also, and relatedly, in their orientation toward history. As Adorno writes, juxtaposing the two, "Late Schoenberg shares with jazz—and, incidentally, also with Stravinsky—the dissociation of musical time. Music drafts the image of a world that—for better or for worse—no longer knows history."[96] The temporal failings of the musical compositions produced by the Schoenberg school are linked with their removal from history through the destruction of the dialectical relation in both contexts. The dialectic to which Adorno subscribes lends itself not to atemporal reconciliations but to a constant movement forward within history. The effect of the most rigorous new music—and, in particular, its realization in the twelve-tone method—is to efface temporal progression and thereby signal its own disconnection from history. Through its efforts to move beyond the late Romantic mechanisms of development and secure new modes of differentiation, twelve-tone music instead devolved into stasis. At the same time, the techniques employed to ensure musical autonomy themselves speak to the technicality of the stage of history and, despite every effort to ignore the historical situation, signal the reality of that situation.[97] Given the social context, however, that signal cannot be heard, and, instead, the new music furnishes "the true message in the bottle."[98]

In the classical form of tonal music, repetition can function properly because it assumes a place within a larger system. By contrast, the twelve-tone "row, valid for one work only, does not possess the comprehensive universality that would, on the basis of the schema, assign a function to the repeated event, which as a reiterated individual phenomenon it does not have."[99] Within the musical composition, the event can emerge only out of a framework in which universality can be unproblematically assumed. Furthermore, the row obscures the differentiation between melody and harmony and, in doing so, destroys the temporal dynamics of the melody itself. As Adorno insists, connecting the melodic function with rendering harmonic space in the form of time, "the true quality of a melody is always to be measured by whether or not it succeeds in transcribing the effectively spatial relations of the intervals into time. Twelve-tone technique fundamentally destroys this relation. Time and interval diverge."[100] Hence, development is frustrated, and it is not incidental that Schoenberg and others show an affinity for earlier forms of variation like the rondo, which are "nondynamic."[101] The same tendency inhibited the production of larger musical structures from within the twelve-tone method: "The construction of truly free forms delineating the uniquely occurring constitution of the work is denied by the unfreedom that is imposed by the serial technique through the ever-recurring appearance of the same."[102]

At the same time, and relatedly, the artwork becomes disconnected from history. Adorno articulates the link between the two levels most thoroughly with respect to a reading of Berg's later twelve-tone opera, *Lulu*, interpreting the work as an allegory of new music's own relation to the historical moment. Referring to "complementary harmony," or the "vertical, block-like dimension of twelve-tone harmony," Adorno writes, "If the twelve-tone chord heard at Lulu's death is taken as the integral of complementary harmony, Berg's allegorical genius stands the test in a historical perspective that is truly vertiginous: Just as Lulu in the world of gapless semblance longs only for the arrival of her murderer and finds him in that chord, so does all harmony of denied happiness . . . long for the fatal chord as a cipher of fulfillment."[103] The chord is fatal to the ambitions of music as well as to the character of Lulu precisely because it deadens the dialectic without reconciling contradictions. In Adorno's words, it is "fatal, because in this chord every dynamic is stilled without being resolved."[104] Just as the twelve-tone treatment of melody is incapable of converting spatial relations into temporal ones, the "complementary harmony" of twelve-tone music likewise renders such compositions inert. By terminating "the musical experience of time," however, complementary harmony simultaneously "enunciates more insistently than the other symptoms a condition of musical ahistoricity, although it remains undecided as to whether this ahistoricity is dictated by the harrowing rigidification of society in the contemporary forms of domination or whether it portends an end to antagonistic society, which has its existence in the mere reproduction of its antagonisms."[105] Three levels here coexist: Lulu's longing for her murderer, represented by the chord, which furnishes only death; the work's harmonic striving for the chord, which brings it stasis, not reconciliation; and the symptomaticity of that chord—a symptomaticity that accords with Adorno's description of the efforts in new music as those of psychoanalytic dream depositions—that signals the rupture between music and history.

Returning to Berg's other opera, *Wozzeck*, its deployment of seemingly outdated musical forms begins to become explicable and even essential to its modernity. The architectural and architectonic impulse manifested in *Wozzeck* aids in temporally organizing what might otherwise remain disconnected fragments. In the absence of a tonal mechanism for ensuring development, a concern with the architecture of composition intervenes to enable the experience of temporal extension. In a 1929 lecture on *Wozzeck*, Berg himself emphasized the necessity of creating formal structures that would unify the opera in the absence of tonality and associated that quest with an architectural drive. And he posed the quandary, "How, without the proven means of tonality and without being able to use the formal structures based on it, could I achieve . . . a sense of self-containedness not only in the small-scale structure of the scenes themselves . . . but also, what was much more difficult, a sense of completeness in the larger structures of the single acts and, indeed, in the *architecture* of the work as a whole?"[106] Throughout the lecture, Berg returned to the term "architecture" and even insisted, "I use the word intentionally."[107] It is this architecture that, in his view, necessitated the resort to earlier forms, especially in order to ensure not simply the global unity of the opera across its three acts but also to guarantee the cohesion of the smaller units. As Berg maintained, "There was not . . . any desire for the 'archaic' in using such forms as variations, or even passacaglia and fugues in this opera"; rather, considerations of unity "led to the use of certain 'old forms.' "[108] There is here in Berg's own words a somewhat Adornian suggestion. As *In Search of Wagner* posits, "Sonata and symphony both make time their subject; through the substance they impart to it, they force it to manifest itself."[109] In accordance with this claim, Berg's employment of such structures might be thought to enhance the capacity of his opera to incorporate development, escaping from the kind of atemporality that Adorno accused Wagner's work of generating.

Even Berg's treatment of Büchner's text demonstrates a concern with temporality. As Douglas Jarman points out in his interpretation of the opera, Berg reshaped the first scene to end with the word *langsam*, or "slowly," which also commences the opera, with the captain's instruction to Wozzeck —in the process of shaving him—"langsam, Wozzeck, langsam!"[110] Berg also added distinct directions pertaining to the time of day to Büchner's scenes and insists in his notes on the preparation and staging of *Wozzeck* that "it is also important to observe the hour represented in the individual scenes. These changing times of the day and night must be clearly recognizable."[111] Jarman's interpretation of the work as a whole builds upon the opera's foregrounding of temporality; for Jarman, the opera stages the problem of "predestination and of man's inability to affect the course of events."[112] The ending of the opera fails to deliver any progress but instead implies the return of the same, the cycle Wozzeck experienced to be repeated in his child.[113] Regardless of the accuracy of this particular interpretation of *Wozzeck*'s relation to temporality, the opera's engagement with its source material demonstrates a pronounced concern with duration that distinguishes it from other endeavors of the Schoenberg school.

Adorno too takes up the architectural image to describe, in part, the composition of *Wozzeck*. Rather than following Berg in emphasizing the effects of older forms in unifying the composition, however, Adorno brings out the extent to which Berg's work builds upon nineteenth-century expressive and thematic traditions—unlike later twelve-tone music—and how its architectural quality contrasts with this feature. Hence, according to Adorno, "Berg's score exists entirely in a state of tension between the surging unconscious and an almost optically architectonic feeling for enclosed surfaces."[114] It was with *Wozzeck* itself, Adorno opines, that these two elements coalesced most successfully, as previously the tendencies had simply stood in contrast to each other: "Much as Berg belonged to the tradition of thematic work and developing variation, that is, to a thoroughly dynamic kind of composition, his musical manner nevertheless had something peculiarly static about it, hesitantly marking time. Not until *Wozzeck* did his composing become more agile. It struck me that such stasis amidst kinetic activity revealed a kinship with [Walter] Benjamin, who was enormously impressed with *Wozzeck*."[115] The combination of a thematic with an architectural sensibility avoids both the extreme of Romantic subjectivity, a subjectivity caught in an abyss of feeling without the possibility of transformation, and the stasis that comes to characterize later twelve-tone music. Instead, the musical style

of *Wozzeck* furnishes a "dialectic," which "everywhere translates the constancy of what has been into the alien perspective of what is becoming."[116]
In explicating the meaning of theme and the "thematic idea" (*Einfall*)
within his work, Adorno elaborates further upon the dialectical structure
internal to the musical composition and the relation between this inner dialectic and history. A crucial footnote to *The Philosophy of New Music* glosses
Einfall—which has been translated by Robert Hullot-Kentor as "thematic
idea" and Rodney Livingstone as "creative idea":

> The "thematic idea" [*Einfall*] is not a psychological category, something of "inspi-
> ration"; rather, it is an element of the dialectical process that occurs in the musi-
> cal form. It marks the irreducibly subjective element in this process and—in such
> indissolubility—the aspect of music as being [*Sein*], while the "thematic elabora-
> tion" represents the becoming and the objectivity that clearly contains this sub-
> jective element in itself as a driving force, just as inversely the subjective element
> has objectivity as being [*Sein*]. Music since romanticism has consisted in the con-
> flict and synthesis of these moments. It appears, however, that they resist this
> unification, just as the bourgeois concept of the individual stands in perennial
> opposition to the totality of the social process. The inconsistency between the
> theme and its modifications is the image of such social irreconcilability. Yet the
> composition must hold firmly to the "thematic idea" if it does not want to annul
> the subjective element and make itself the image of fatal integration.[117]

The frustration of synthesis between "thematic idea" and "thematic elaboration" within music itself is analogous to and furnishes "the image of" the
inevitable inconsistency between bourgeois individual and social process.
Because a synthesis is impossible, the best new music can aspire not to reconciliation but rather to avoiding the false representation of synthesis, a representation that would participate in rather than critiquing ideology. The
function of new music exists not in itself but rather in opposition to the effects of ideology. Hence, as Adorno writes, "So long as an art that is constituted in the categories of mass production contributes to ideology and so
long as its technique is one of repression, that other art, itself functionless, has
its function. It alone, in its most recent, most rigorous products, delineates
the image of total repression rather than its ideology. As the unreconciled
image of reality, that art becomes incommensurable with reality. Thus, it pro-
tests against the injustice of the just verdict."[118]
Here we return full circle to the justice or injustice of a verdict—on the

bourgeois individual, on Büchner's neglected drama, or on new music itself. Just as Adorno's interpretation of *Lulu* operated on three levels, *Wozzeck* addresses three strata. Crucially, the analogy with psychology that Adorno drew in the context of *Wozzeck* depends not on viewing the composer as analyst but instead on seeing as such the musical work itself—which takes its source material as the analysand. This identification becomes more evident in *The Philosophy of New Music*, where Adorno claims:

> The first atonal works are depositions, in the sense of psychoanalytic dream depositions. . . . The scars of this revolution in expression, however, are the disfiguring stains that have become as deeply fixed in the paintings as in the music—in opposition to the compositional will—as emissaries of the id, distressing the surface and as little to be wiped away by subsequent correction as are the traces of blood in a fairy tale. Real suffering has left them behind in the artwork as a sign that it no longer recognizes its autonomy; their heteronomy defies the self-sufficient semblance of the music.[119]

The traces of suffering discoverable here are not simply those of the individual, like Wozzeck, but also those of music itself. The artwork, like "grimaces made by children," presents to its audience both the suffering of its subject and its own suffering, showing that the just verdict can never be just unless and until the historical moment itself enables a just society.[120]

For this reason, despite constituting "masterpieces"—or rather, because they are masterpieces in the sense of being "a work of traditional art"— Berg's operas ultimately cannot, for Adorno, fully succeed.[121] What constitutes their greatest virtue is not their mediation between the temporal and the architectural or their capacity to achieve a "finished structure," but rather the extent to which the traces of suffering evident in them remain unreconciled.[122] After treating *Lulu*, Adorno writes, "The innermost beauty . . . of Berg's late works is due less to the unified surface of their success than to their profound impossibility, to the hopeless self-exertion announced by that surface, the desperately sad sacrifice of the future to the past."[123] Likewise, with respect to *Wozzeck*, he explains, "The impulses of the work, alive in its musical atoms, rebel against the work that they produce. They tolerate no result."[124] The tragedy of *Wozzeck* is not only the tragedy of the condemned soldier or the tragedy of the forgetting of Büchner's work but the tragedy of Berg's opera's own failure.

Paradoxically, that failure is intimately connected with Berg's success, which, as noted earlier, Adorno associates with his humanism. Not only hearkening back to nineteenth-century musical paradigms, Berg remains concerned with characters like Wozzeck, the petit bourgeois individual of the nineteenth century. Even his reworking of Franz Wedekind's play in *Lulu* domesticates the source material through a humanistic interpretation, so that "Berg's humanism, by making the affair of the prostitute his own, at the same time extracts the thorn that makes her so irritating to bourgeois civilization."[125] Nevertheless, Berg does not attempt to resuscitate past bourgeois conceptions, as, "despairingly, his music accepted separation from the bourgeois rather than holding out false hopes of a state beyond the bourgeois, which to this day exists no more than does an alternative society."[126] Instead, *Wozzeck* returns to the suffering of the individual and points to the unresolved persistence of that suffering despite the transformation of the historical situation. By insisting upon the humanity of this figure from the nineteenth century, the opera signals the irreconcilability of the dialectic within Berg's contemporary historical situation and hence the impossibility of closure within the work of art.

The Caesura Revisited

The specificity of Berg's treatment of the relation between language and music and *Wozzeck*'s temporality are both crystallized in Adorno's accounts of *Wozzeck*'s caesura. As noted above, Adorno adopted the language of caesura from Benjamin, with whom he seems to have discussed the caesura of Berg's opera itself when they attended a performance together. In his reading of Hölderlin's reading of *Oedipus* and the role of the caesura in that play, Benjamin identifies the caesura with the "expressionless," or "the critical violence which, while unable to separate semblance from essence in art, prevents them from mingling."[127] This "critical violence," which Benjamin also calls the "sublime violence of the true," resonates with the opposition Benjamin would later draw between mythical and divine violence in "The Critique of Violence," devaluing the former and favoring the latter.[128]

The caesura for Benjamin operates not only as violence but also as harmony; in both the caesura and harmony, "every expression simultaneously comes to a standstill, in order to give free reign to an expressionless power inside all artistic media."[129] The caesura is, furthermore, associated with the "falling silent of the hero" and with the poet's own loss of agency, as "something beyond the poet interrupts the language of the poetry."[130] As Lacoue-Labarthe elaborates in "The Caesura of Religion," "All works are organized as such from the starting point of the caesura inasmuch as the caesura is the hiatus, the suspension or the 'anti-rhythmic' interruption which is not only necessary, as in metrics, to the articulation and the equilibrium of verse . . . but, more essentially, the place whence that which Hölderlin calls 'pure speech' surges forth."[131] Despite its connection with the hero's silence and with a hiatus, Benjamin's caesura, unlike the poetic trope from which it takes its name, does not signal an actual gap in the text. Rather, the two caesurae that Benjamin identifies in *Elective Affinities* are, first, a novella contained within the novel and, second, the brief sentence "Hope passed, like a star falling from heaven, over their heads and away."[132]

Although Benjamin's influence is evident, an examination of the role of the caesura in Adorno's interpretations of *Wozzeck*—and, in particular, his conflicting accounts of where it occurs—demonstrates both Adorno's deviation from Benjamin and how *Wozzeck* itself influenced Adorno's aesthetics. For Adorno, the emphasis of the caesura falls not on the expressionless but on the suffering that this expressionlessness may aid in uncovering. The caesura discloses the persistence of suffering both by interrupting the seemingly ineluctable movement of the dialectic and by invoking a past that is already lost. Most notably, from functioning as an instant within the work, the caesura becomes identified as the silencing of language and music, a silencing that brings together the opera's source and its sound.

A passage on book 22 of the *Odyssey* from Horkheimer and Adorno's *Dialectic of Enlightenment* helps to illuminate the double motion of the caesura in allowing suffering to speak through rendering the narration expressionless. This section deals with the capital punishment of maids who had turned to prostitution. The description of their deaths is short: "For a little while their feet kicked out, but not for long."[133] The caesura follows: "After the 'not for long' the inner flow of the narrative comes to rest. . . . In being brought to a standstill, the report is prevented from forgetting the victims of the execution and lays bare the unspeakably endless torment of the single second in which the maids fought against death. . . . But in the report of the infamous deed, hope lies in the fact that it is long past."[134] Revealing suffering, the caesura simultaneously permits the hearer or reader to hope, on the grounds that history has moved forward. As Horkheimer and Adorno write, "When speech pauses, the caesura allows the events narrated to be transformed into something long past, and causes to flash up a semblance of freedom that humanity has been wholly unable to extinguish ever since."[135]

The hope is vain with respect to Woyzeck, however, as his suffering remains, despite the progress of history. Indeed, in his (accepted) Habilitation on Kierkegaard, Adorno links the caesura itself to the interruption of history, or at least the interruption of its dialectical motion, noting that, at one point in Kierkegaard's work, "sacrifice disappears, and in its place dialectic holds its breath for an instance; a caesura appears in its progress."[136] In *Wozzeck*, the caesura serves both to uncover Woyzeck's long-past suffering and to suggest the unresolved nature of human suffering within the present historical moment.

Adorno's various references to the caesura in *Wozzeck*, however, are caught between the Hölderin/Benjamin understanding of the caesura as the organizing force that renders a work a true tragedy and a potentially more radical account of the rupture of the artwork itself. On the one hand, Adorno sometimes follows his early conversation with Benjamin, where the two apparently concurred that *Wozzeck*'s caesura occurs during the scene at the inn toward the end of act 2. On the other hand, Adorno increasingly—and most prominently in his final radio address on *Wozzeck*—identifies the caesura with the general pause between act 2 and act 3.

Hence, in "Berliner Opernmemorial," he explains, "The scene at the inn is the caesura [*Zäsur*], in a certain sense the masterpiece [*Meisterstück*] of Wozzeck, after the symphonic expansion and, similarly, the human attitude."[137] The same year, however, in "The Opera *Wozzeck*," he insists that "after the second act is the opera's caesura [*Zäsur*], which can be felt in the splendid moments of silence during the curtain's fall, and then at the beginning of the third act during its rise. If music, always and forever, has utilized the pause as an element of its form—Berg was the first to make silence into a musical actor, the empty beating of time. In seconds, the expressionless. . . ."[138] Despite Benjamin's own identification of two caesurae in *Elective Affinities*, the concept of the caesura as the organizing force of the tragedy implies that there is only one. So which is the caesura of *Wozzeck*? The scene at the inn—not even the final moment of act 2—or the space concluding and beginning the penultimate and last acts?

It is possible to glean some of the reasons Benjamin and Adorno might have considered the scene at the inn the opera's caesura both from an analysis of the scene itself and from Adorno's remarks in "Berliner Opernmemorial." During the episode at the inn, Wozzeck witnesses Marie dancing with the Drum Major and finally comprehends her infidelity, a realization that precipitates him into the already looming abyss. Significantly, his words in this scene are spoken, not sung. Wozzeck recites, "Him! Her! The devil! On we go, on we go [*Immer zu*]! Twisting, turning! Why does not God put out the sun now? Everything twists and turns in lechery, Man and Woman, and Beast! Woman! Woman! Woman is fire, is fire, fire! How he mauls her with his hands—touches her body! And she just laughs. . . . On we go [*Immer zu*]! On we go! Damnation!"[139]

The contrast between the crucial phrase "Immer zu" as first sung by Marie and as then echoed by Wozzeck further emphasizes the spoken character of Wozzeck's lines. Here Wozzeck's utterances fulfill the logic of the caesura both by interrupting the musical continuity of the opera and by furnishing the "pure speech" that Hölderlin invoked. Although the hero does not fall silent, he speaks outside of the register of music. It is precisely by the refusal of song that Wozzeck's suffering—and his humanity—manifests itself most perspicuously. Hence, Adorno writes with respect to this scene of the "consummation of subjectivity," which "collapses into the groundless abyss," in which, "after Wozzeck's word, the human being appears."[140]

At the same time, however, the musical form of the scene is not simply incidental. Rather, it is here that Berg's deployment of traditional forms becomes most significant. According to Adorno, in the scene at the inn, "here finally was written the [symphonic] scherzo, which Mahler fought for his whole life long, the scherzo in which the old emaciated and not wholly suppressed a priori of the dance form is apprehended, made wholly fulfilled."[141] Although Adorno does not add any caveats here, one might wonder why this fulfillment does not represent a regressive aspect of the opera. It may be precisely because Wozzeck remains so at odds with the symphonic scherzo in which Marie and the Drum Major dance that the audience can witness the fulfillment of the form of the Romantic symphony but remain simultaneously alienated from it. The pastness of the past form is thereby foregrounded at the same time it is being perfected. This mournful relation to the image of the past is characteristic of the caesura in its interruption of the dialectic of history.[142]

By the time Adorno pens "Alban Berg: Oper und Moderne," however, he no longer refers to the inn scene in relation to the caesura, which has for him, by this point, definitively shifted to the silence. As Adorno explains in that final engagement with *Wozzeck*, "The indescribable effect of the end of [act 2], as of the beginning of the act, is musical, namely bound together through his time-unit-organized silences [*Pausen*]. That is one of the undespicable reasons that speak against the idea of performing Wozzeck unbroken, cinematically, without caesura [*Zäsur*]; only through the intermission between the last two acts will the composed silences be discussed."[143] The caesura, which is composed, may even last longer through a staging that breaks after the penultimate act. This silence of language and music itself produces another kind of language, the discussion of the audience. Having appropriated Benjamin's understanding of the caesura, Adorno reintroduces to the caesura the poetic connotation of an actual pause. Through this modification Adorno does not, however, simply fall back upon a traditional conception of the caesura but instead augurs a postmodern aesthetics of silence.

Indeed, Adorno's account of *Wozzeck's* caesura here to some extent addresses the critique Lacoue-Labarthe levies against Adorno for the latter's analysis of Schoenberg's *Moses und Aron*. In discussing Adorno's critique of Schoenberg for failing to make the caesura music, Lacoue-Labarthe suggests that Adorno neglects the actual rupture in Schoenberg's compositional process, by which he managed to "only write the text of one scene, the scene where Moses, who reaffirms his 'idea,' pardons Aaron or at least orders that he not be executed."[144] As Lacoue-Labarthe insists, "If, dramaturgically, one must take into account this rupture of this hiatus and the passage to simple speech . . . then there is indeed a caesura."[145] Already in his earlier writings, Adorno had identified the inn scene, where Wozzeck speaks rather than sings, with the caesura, but in his later work, Adorno further indicates how an extramusical element can both furnish the caesura and itself be made music. In this respect, it is significant that the silence ending act 2 and beginning act 3 is, in fact, a composed silence, a silence both within and outside of the musical fabric. Furthermore, the silence operates equally on the registers of text and music, the gap that simultaneously renders the melding of the two media possible and frustrates both forms of signification.

It is, however, not only in adjusting the location of *Wozzeck's* caesura that Adorno departs from Benjamin in "Alban Berg: Oper und Moderne." Whereas Benjamin had insisted on the role of the caesura as emanating from the expressionless (*Ausdruckslose*), Adorno insists instead on its expressive content (*Ausdrucksgehalt*), as opposed to some "airless objectivity [*Sachlichkeit*]."[146] It is precisely through such moments of counterintuitive expressivity that Berg's opera both transcends the expressive tradition of the nineteenth century and sets itself in opposition to other modernist movements, such as the Neue Sachlichkeit. Intimately tied to Berg's form of expressivity was his opera's treatment of its source text and the individual at the heart of that text; indeed, as Adorno points out, the caesura occurs in *Wozzeck* only "after [Wozzeck] is brutally mistreated by one of his rivals, the Drum Major." That mistreatment calls forth the broader theme of Wozzeck's suffering, with which almost all of Adorno's considerations of *Wozzeck* were concerned.

Precisely by decomposing the individual into an instant of his suffering, Berg's *Wozzeck* intervenes within modernity, avoiding both a reduction back into the petit bourgeois individual of the nineteenth century and another kind of reduction associated with ignoring the particular entirely in pursuit of the class struggle. *Wozzeck*'s achievement in this regard depends on both the relation between the opera and its source material and the opera's internal and external temporalities. Adorno identified the details of these aspects of *Wozzeck*'s modernity gradually over the course of his engagements with the opera and, in turn, appears to have responded to the force of the music itself by allowing it to operate critically on his own prior conceptions. Far from simply justifying *Wozzeck* for modernism on account of his friendship with Berg, Adorno predicated his understanding of true modernism on *Wozzeck*.

Notes

1. Adorno, *Alban Berg* ix. Hereafter abbreviated *AB*.

2. *AB* ix–xi.

3. Adorno, "Alban Berg: Oper und Moderne" 652. Hereinafter abbreviated "Oper und Moderne." Thanks to Matthew Smith for assistance with the German of Adorno's untranslated essays.

4. Adorno and Berg 27.12.1925, 33–34.

5. Several recent works have addressed some of the themes of this essay, but none considers the full trajectory of the development of Adorno's responses to *Wozzeck*, including the late radio address. Stephen Decatur Smith's brilliant essay "'Even Money Decays': Transience and Hope in Adorno, Benjamin, and *Wozzeck*" analyzes the specific temporality Adorno discerned in *Wozzeck* and furnishes a compelling analysis of how what Walter Benjamin identifies as the "caesura" of a work of art in his essay "Goethe's *Elective Affinities*" features in Adorno's analysis of *Wozzeck*. Likewise, chapter 4 of Marc Simon Brooks's dissertation "Precision and Soul: The Relationship between Science and Religion in the Operas *Wozzeck* and *Arabella*" argues that "the interaction of the new score with the old text goes some way towards re-situating [the] confrontation [with the limits of conscience . . . when faced with the brute reality of time and nature] within the philosophical debate of the 1920s and 1930s" (102). Although both make use of Adorno's 1968 *Alban Berg: Master of the Smallest Link*, the focus remains on the philosophical concerns of the 1920s and 1930s.

6. Adorno and Berg 30.3.1926, 50.

7. Ibid. 50.

8. Ibid. 50-51.

9. Ibid. 158.

10. Jarman 1.

11. Perle 22.

12. Ibid.; Franzos 117.

13. Jarman 8.

14. Perle 25, 27.

15. Ibid. 37.

16. Jarman 154.

17. Ibid. 41-42.

18. Ibid. 42.

19. Scruton.

20. Perle 17.

21. Ibid. 94.

22. Ibid. 96, 101, 97.

23. Adorno, *In Search of Wagner* 21.

24. Ibid. 27.

25. Ibid. 32.

26. Perle 205.

27. Adorno, "Alban Berg: Zur Uraufführung des *Wozzeck*." Hereinafter abbreviated "Uraufführung"; Adorno and Berg 23.11.1925, 27-28.

28. "Uraufführung" 461.

29. Ibid. 458-60.

30. Ibid.

31. Ibid. 456.

32. Ibid. 461-62.

33. Adorno, "The Opera *Wozzeck*." Hereinafter abbreviated "OW."

34. Adorno and Benjamin 27 Dec. 1935, 119.

35. Adorno and Berg 27 Dec. 1925, 120.

36. *AB* xiii.

37. "On the Problem of Musical Analysis" 176-77.

38. Durst 106-07.

39. Ibid. 110.

40. Paddison 171, quoting from "On the Problem of Musical Analysis," and 174.

41. "Oper und Moderne" 650.

42. Ibid.

43. Ibid. 656-57.

44. *Wozzeck* score, act 2, mm. 815-18.

45. "Oper und Moderne" 660.

46. *AB* 84.

47. Segar 15.

48. Ibid.

49. *AB* 85.

50. Ibid.

51. Adorno, *Philosophy of New Music* 11.

52. Adorno, "Why Is the New Art So Hard to Understand?" 131.

53. *AB* 20.

54. *AB* 87. Here, as elsewhere, Adorno invokes salvaging *Rettung* in a Benjaminian sense. In "The Caesura of Religion," Lacoue-Labarthe explains Adorno's indebtedness to Benjamin for both *Rettung* and "caesura" (72).

55. Jarman 11-12.

56. Qtd. in Perle 37.

57. Perle 192n23.

58. "OW" 619.

59. Ibid.

60. Jarman 66.

61. Berg, "A Word about *Wozzeck*" 153.

62. "OW" 620.

63. *AB* 6.

64. Berg, "A Word about *Wozzeck*" 152.

65. Perle appendix 1, 205.

66. *AB* 88.

67. Jarman 206.

68. "Uraufführung" 461-62.

69. Ibid. 463.

70. "OW" 619.

71. Ibid. 621.

72. Ibid., emphasis in original.

73. Ibid.

74. Ibid. 624.

75. Ibid. 621.

76. "On the Social Situation of Music" 401.

77. "OW" 622.

78. Ibid. 622.

79. Jay 87.

80. Ibid. 88.

81. *AB* 87.

82. "Music, Language, and Composition" 124.

83. *AB* 87.

84. "Music, Language, and Composition" 118.

85. Ibid. 122.

86. Ibid. 120.

87. Ibid. 120.

88. Ibid. 121.

89. Ibid. 122.

90. Adorno writes similarly in *The Philosophy of New Music* that "the twelve-tone technique of *Lulu* and the musical means of altogether different provenance—such as the leitmotif and the summoning up of large instrumental forms—help secure the consistency of the composition" (84–85).

91. Adorno, *In Search of Wagner* 123.

92. Ibid. 119.

93. Adorno, "Music, Language, and Composition" 116.

94. Geuss 48–49.

95. Ibid. 49.

96. Adorno, *Philosophy of New Music* 50.

97. By contrast, in Wagner's work, Adorno had identified the simultaneous increase in and concealment of the technical aspects of the artwork. As he writes, "The greater the progress in the technicization of the work of art, the rational planning of its methods and hence of its effects, the more anxiously is Wagner intent upon making his music appear spontaneous, immediate and natural and upon concealing the controlling will" (*In Search of Wagner* 39–40). Despite also entailing ever-greater technicality, Wagner's operas, unlike twelve-tone music, thus dissimulate their relation to the stage of history.

98. Adorno, *Philosophy of New Music* 102.

99. Ibid. 73.

100. Ibid. 59.

101. Ibid. 58. As we saw earlier, this was not, Adorno believed, the case for Berg, who insisted, unlike Schoenberg, on not assimilating melody and harmony, or the horizontal and vertical elements of music.

102. Ibid. 76.

103. Spitzer 65; Adorno, *Philosophy of New Music* 64–65.

104. Ibid. 65.

105. Ibid.

106. Jarman 154; emphasis mine.

107. Ibid. 166.

108. Ibid. 158.

109. Adorno, *In Search of Wagner* 26.

110. Jarman 12.

111. Perle appendix 1, 206.

112. Jarman 65–66.

113. Ibid. 64.

114. John 37.

115. *AB* 14. One of the critiques that Adorno levies against Wagner is that "Wagner knows about motivs [including the leitmotif] and large-scale forms—but not about themes" (*In Search of Wagner* 31).

116. "OW" 624.

117. Adorno, *Philosophy of New Music* 180n46.

118. Ibid. 87-88.

119. Ibid. 35.

120. Ibid. 102.

121. Ibid. 30.

122. Ibid. 31.

123. Ibid. 85.

124. Ibid. 30-31.

125. Ibid. 175n2.

126. *AB* 8.

127. Benjamin 340.

128. Ibid. 340.

129. Ibid. 341.

130. Ibid.

131. Lacoue-Labarthe 72-73.

132. For a detailed discussion of these two caesurae, see N. K. Leacock, "Character, Silence, and the Novel: Walter Benjamin on Goethe's *Elective Affinities*," 295-99.

133. Horkheimer and Adorno 61.

134. Ibid. 62.

135. Ibid. 61.

136. Adorno, *Kierkegaard* 121.

137. Adorno, "Berliner Opernmemorial" 274.

138. "OW" 625. Stephen Decatur Smith notes the alteration from Adorno's 1925 identification of the caesura to his 1929 identification in "The Opera *Wozzeck*," although he does not observe that the "Berliner Opernmemorial," also of 1929, returns to the 1925 account. Decatur Smith associates the change with a falling away from Benjamin's understanding of the caesura (235-36). One might instead, as this essay suggests, see the alteration as representing a development in and deepening of Adorno's own idea of the caesura.

139. Berg, *Wozzeck* 307-14.

140. Adorno, "Berliner Opernmemorial" 274-75.

141. Ibid. 274.

142. Decatur Smith makes a similar point about the importance of the return to Mahler at the point that Benjamin and Adorno identify as the opera's caesura. As he writes, "If what Adorno and Benjamin call the expressionless invades Berg's music at this point, it does so in the decomposition of Mahler's forms. It is in this sense that

Berg 'sounds [the] final lament' of the tradition of nineteenth-century music," a lament that yet allows for a certain hope (238).

143. "Oper und Moderne" 660.
144. Lacoue-Labarthe 73.
145. Ibid. 75.
146. "Oper und Moderne" 660.

Bibliography

Adorno, Theodor. *Alban Berg: Master of the Smallest Link*. Trans. Juliane Brand and
Christopher Hailey. Cambridge: Cambridge University Press, 1991.

———. "Alban Berg: Oper und Moderne" (1969). *Gesammelte Schriften*. 20 vols. Ed.
Rolf Tiedemann with Gretel Adorno, Susan Buck-Morss, and Klaus Schultz.
Frankfurt am Main: Suhrkamp Verlag, 2004. 18:650-72.

———. "Alban Berg: Zur Uraufführung des *Wozzeck*" (1925). *Gesammelte Schriften*. 20
vols. Ed. Rolf Tiedemann with Gretel Adorno, Susan Buck-Morss, and Klaus
Schultz. Frankfurt am Main: Suhrkamp Verlag, 2004. 18:456-64.

———. "Berliner Opernmemorial" (1929). *Gesammelte Schriften*. 20 vols. Ed. Rolf
Tiedemann with Gretel Adorno, Susan Buck-Morss, and Klaus Schultz. Frankfurt
am Main: Suhrkamp Verlag, 2004. 19:267-75.

———. *In Search of Wagner*. Trans. Rodney Livingstone. New York: Verso, 2009.

———. *Kierkegaard: Construction of the Aesthetic*. Trans. Robert Hullot-Kentor. Minneapolis: University of Minnesota Press, 1989.

———. "Music, Language, and Composition" (1956). Trans. Susan H. Gillespie. *Essays on
Music*. Ed. Richard Leppert. Berkeley: University of California Press, 2002. 113-26.

———. "On the Contemporary Relationship of Philosophy and Music" (1953). Trans.
Susan H. Gillespie. *Essays on Music*. Ed. Richard Leppert. Berkeley: University of
California Press, 2002. 135-61.

———. "The Aging of the New Music" (1955). Trans. Robert Hullot-Kentor and Fred-
eric Will. *Essays on Music*. Ed. Richard Leppert. Berkeley: University of California
Press, 2002. 181-202.

———. "The Opera *Wozzeck*" (1929). Trans. Susan H. Gillespie. *Essays on Music*. Ed.
Richard Leppert. Berkeley: University of California Press, 2002. 619-26.

———. "On the Social Situation of Music" (1932). Trans. Wes Blomster. Rev. Richard
Leppert. *Essays on Music*. 391-436.

———. *The Philosophy of New Music*. Trans. and ed. Robert Hullot-Kentor. Minneapolis: University of Minnesota Press, 2006.

———. "Why Is the New Art So Hard to Understand?" *Essays on Music*. Ed. Richard
Leppert. Berkeley: University of California Press, 2002. 127-134.

Adorno, Theodor, and Walter Benjamin. *Theodor Adorno and Walter Benjamin: The
Complete Correspondence: 1928-1940*. Ed. Henri Lonitz. Trans. Nicholas Walker.
Cambridge, MA: Harvard University Press, 1999.

Adorno, Theodor, and Alban Berg. *Theodor Adorno and Alban Berg Correspondence, 1925-1935*. Ed. Henri Lonitz. Trans. Wieland Hoban. Cambridge: Polity Press, 2005.

Benjamin, Walter. "Goethe's *Elective Affinities*" (1924-1925). *Walter Benjamin: Selected Writings*. Ed. Marcus Bullock and Michael W. Jennings. Cambridge, MA: Harvard University Press, 2004. 1:297-360.

Berg, Alban. "A Word about *Wozzeck*," *Modern Music* (Nov.-Dec. 1927). Rpt. in Derek Jarman, *Alban Berg:* Wozzeck. Cambridge Opera Handbooks. Cambridge: Cambridge University Press, 1989. 152-53.

————. "The Preparation and Staging of *Wozzeck*." *The Operas of Alban Berg*. Vol. 1, *Wozzeck*. Ed. George Perle. Los Angeles: University of California Press, 1980. Appendix 1.

————. *Wozzeck*. Universal Edition No. 12100.

Brooks, Marc Simon. "Precision and Soul: The Relationship between Science and Religion in the Operas *Wozzeck* and *Arabella*" Diss. King's College London, 2011.

Durst, David C. "The Art of Disappearance: Adorno's Aesthetics of Modernism and Alban Berg's Music." *Weimar Modernism: Philosophy, Politics, and Culture in Germany 1918-1933*. Lanham: Lexington Books, 2004. 105-34.

Eliot, T. S. "Tradition and the Individual Talent." *Selected Prose of T. S. Eliot*. Ed. Frank Kermode. New York: Harcourt, 1975. 37-44.

Franzos, Karl Emil. "Georg Büchner." *Alban Berg*: Wozzeck. Ed. Douglas Jarman. Cambridge Opera Handbooks. Cambridge: Cambridge University Press, 1989. 111-129.

Geuss, Raymond. "Berg and Adorno." *The Cambridge Companion to Berg*. Ed. Anthony Pople. Cambridge: Cambridge University Press, 1997. 38-50.

Horkheimer, Max and Theodor Adorno. *Dialectic of Enlightenment: Philosophical Fragments*. Ed. Gunzelin Schmid Noerr. Trans. Edmund Jephcott. Stanford: Stanford University Press, 2002.

Jarman, Derek. *Alban Berg:* Wozzeck. Cambridge Opera Handbooks. Cambridge: Cambridge University Press, 1989.

Jay, Martin. *Adorno*. Cambridge, MA: Harvard University Press, 1984.

John, Nicholas. *Wozzeck*. English National Opera Guide 42. London: John Calder, 1990.

Lacoue-Labarthe, Philippe. "The Caesura of Religion." *Opera through Other Eyes*. Ed. David Levin. Stanford: Stanford University Press, 1993. 45-78.

Leacock, N. K. "Character, Silence, and the Novel: Walter Benjamin on Goethe's *Elective Affinities*." *Narrative* 10.3 (2002): 277-306.

Leppert, Richard. "Commentary." *Essays on Music*. Ed. Richard Leppert. Berkeley: University of California Press, 2002. 391-436.

Paddison, Max. *Adorno's Aesthetics of Music*. Cambridge: Cambridge University Press, 1993.

Perle, George. *The Operas of Alban Berg*. Vol. 1, *Wozzeck*. Los Angeles: University of California Press, 1980.

Scruton, Roger. "Absolute Music." *Grove Music Online*. <http://oxfordindex.oup.com/view/10.1093/gmo/9781561592630.article.00069>.

Segar, Kenneth. "Georg Büchner's *Woyzeck*: An Interpretation." *English National Opera Guide 42*. London: John Calder, 1990. 15-22.

Smith, Stephen Decatur. "'Even Money Decays': Transience and Hope in Adorno, Benjamin, and *Wozzeck*." *Opera Quarterly* 29.3-4 (2014): 212-43.

Spitzer, Michael. *Music and Philosophy: Adorno and Beethoven's Late Style*. Bloomington: Indiana University Press, 2006.

6 Many Modernisms, Two Makropulos Cases

Čapek, Janáček, and the Shifting Avant-Gardes of Interwar Prague

Derek Katz

Leoš Janáček's 1926 opera *The Makropulos Case* (*Věc Makropulos*), based on Karel Čapek's 1922 play of the same title, constitutes a de facto collaboration between the most renowned composer and most celebrated playwright of the Czech First Republic. Although the two men did not actually work together—Čapek, in fact, took a rather dim view of the play's prospects as an opera—Janáček's libretto was assembled by extracting sections of Čapek's script, generally preserving Čapek's words verbatim, with almost all changes consisting of eliminating clauses and lines to compress the libretto to a manageable length. The plot is very much the same in both versions. A world-famous soprano, Emilia Marty, arrives in modern-day Prague just as a long-standing legal dispute over an inheritance is about to be resolved. Marty arouses the sexual interest of the protagonists on both sides of the dispute and proves to have suspiciously detailed knowledge of events from centuries past. Eventually, she reveals that she was born in the sixteenth century and she has been kept alive by a potion created by her father, an alchemist at the court of Rudolf II. She has been wandering Europe, singing to ever-greater acclaim, and assuming different identifies and nationalities, while always retaining the initials E.M. Now, in the 1920s, the potion is wearing off, and she has come to Prague to find her father's formula and renew its effects. Although she does finally recapture the ancient document, she renounces it, and both play and opera end with the recipe going up in flames.

The differences between play and opera have been well documented in the Janáček literature. The most frequently discussed alteration to Čapek's drama is the omission of a substantial discussion near the end of the opera of the possible social implications of the Makropulos formula. This is Čapek at his most Shavian. Each character takes a distinct point of view, reflecting his or her social status, and declaims a position paper, much like dutiful pupils in a school debate. In Caryl Emerson's description, "The men who have found out her secret discuss the implications of her 300-plus-years lifespan from the perspective of Romantic utopianism, Malthusian economics, Henri Bergson's élan vital, and Nietzschean elitism."[1] This discussion— in addition to a later passage in which Marty offers the Makropulos formula to each of the other protagonists—is absent from the opera, save for a few lines in which Marty makes a general offer of the formula to her onlookers and unsuccessfully attempts to foist it on a younger singer. In addition to this large-scale excision, Janáček removed a certain amount of other social commentary, much of it dealing with money. Only Čapek's characters say things like "only paupers have enough. The rich never." Or "in our world even a fairy-tale prince expects his share."

Less often noted is that Čapek is funnier than Janáček. A listener familiar with Janáček's opera but not with Čapek's play may well be puzzled by the composer's designation of the opera as being "after the comedy by Karel Čapek." The opera is certainly not without humor, and there are a few lines that reliably elicit laughs in the theater, especially in act 2. The short and awkward dialogue between Emilia Marty and a tongue-tied and love-struck Janek Prus, in which Janek answers all of Marty's questions—including, "Is there anything else you can say but 'yes'?"—with the single word "yes," is one such moment. Another comes after the bizarre interaction between Marty and the feeble-minded Hauk-Šendorf, in which the heretofore near-emotionless Marty all but seduces the old man. Hauk shuffles offstage, and, after a long pause (Janáček did have some sense of comic timing), Marty asks, "Next. Who wants what?" as if Hauk were merely another autograph-seeker. Nonetheless, it is very difficult to regard *Makropulos* as a predominantly comic opera.

One way out of this apparent conundrum is to apply a more nuanced conception of comedy. As Emerson writes, "*Věc Makropulos* is indeed a comedy—in the sense that Shakespeare's comedies, even the terminally stressful ones like *All's Well that Ends Well*, *The Merchant of Venice*, and *Measure for Measure*, are also comedies: the winning values in them are youthfulness, fertility, escape from death, survival in all its aspects."[2] On a more obvious level, though, even allowing for the notorious subjectivity of humor, Čapek's play is much funnier than Janáček's opera. To some extent, this is an inevitable consequence of the generic transposition. Singing jokes is an inherently unnatural act, and all of the qualities of opera that militate

against comprehension of libretto texts in general similarly obscure potentially humorous moments.[3] However, it also the case that Janáček's pruning
of Čapek's text for his libretto eliminated nearly all of the most obviously
humorous moments.

Janáček does not seem to have been greatly interested in either social
commentary or jokes. Instead, he appears to have been almost solely interested in the plight of the play's protagonist, Emilia Marty. Janáček saw
Čapek's play during its first run in Prague's Vinohrady Theater, and his correspondence about the play (and about the gestation of the opera) consistently focuses on its "icy" heroine, whom Janáček planned to "warm" with
music. Critical opinion has tended to concur with this view, finding that
Janáček's lush, lyrical music for Marty, especially in the final scenes, human-
izes her, making her a much more sympathetic character than her counter-
part in Čapek's play.[4]

Rather than going over this ground again, though, this chapter uses the
two Makropulos works as an opportunity to examine the relationships between different Czech modernisms in the 1920s. Čapek is situated in the
context of the Czech literary and theatrical worlds, and Janáček is located
against the background of the musical polemics of the time. A comparison
of the places of Čapek's *The Makropulos Case* and of Janáček's operatic setting within Czech modernism inevitably touches on many issues, some inherent in the works themselves and others related to larger cultural concerns. Among these are shifts in Czech perceptions of Čapek between 1922
and 1926, Czech critical opinions about cosmopolitan modernism in music,
and the reception of Janáček's music, both by Prague critics and by younger
Czech composers. Ultimately, the status of either play or opera as a modernist document may rest more on the mutable aesthetic and political
stances of small, self-consciously avant-garde groups in interwar Prague
than on the works themselves.

Čapek as Literary Modernist

Arguments for Čapek as a modernist tend to take one of two forms. The
first, which primarily comes from a Czech perspective, emphasizes Čapek's
enthusiasm for new cultural trends in France, especially cubism, in the second decade of the twentieth century and on his influence on a younger
generation of more radically experimental writers in the 1920s, chiefly
through his translations of modern French poetry. The other argument,
which is prominent in Anglo-American writings on Čapek, focuses on his

dramas and novels of the early 1920s and privileges the subject matter of those works, stressing their engagement with contemporary social and scientific issues and highlighting Čapek's apparent fascination with science fiction. However, both of these perspectives are easily problematized.

By Čapek's own account, in the years before World War I, he was immersed in a wide range of European literature, philosophy, and art, with little heed for politics. He was, as he put it in a 1932 essay, "a cultural citizen of the world, intoxicated and satiated by the evaporations of that witch's cauldron where all the great and peculiar literatures of the world were bubbling up."[5] The decisive biographical event of this period was a 1911 trip to Paris, where he spent the summer with his brother Josef, returning fired with enthusiasm for Bergson and for recent French literature and art. In particular, the brothers Čapek were enamored of cubism, with Josef beginning to paint in a cubist style and Karel attempting to find an analogue for his writings, going so far as to describe himself as a "literary cubist."[6]

During the war, however, Čapek's "cultural citizenship" became contingent on his political allegiances. His many translations of French poetry were not only an extension of his Paris infatuations but also an expression of his sympathy with the Allied cause. Looking back in another 1932 essay, Čapek writes, "He sought comfort at least in that he tried to organize a collective anthology of modern French poetry, sweating over translations day and night. He had a somewhat mystical feeling that, in doing so, he was somehow helping those out there on the Somme or at Verdun."[7] These translations, especially that of Apollinaire's "Zone," were an enormous influence on the generation of Czech poets born around the turn of the century, in particular those belonging to the avant-garde Devětsil group formed around Karel Teige in 1920. The Devětsil poets made a veritable cult figure of Apollinaire, and the magazine published by the Brno wing of Devětsil (beginning in 1924) was called *Pásmo*, the title of "Zone" in Čapek's translation.

As William Harkins has pointed out, the importance of Čapek's translations is not that he had made modern French poetry available to the younger Czech poets, who, for the most part, were perfectly capable of reading it in the original French, but rather that he created a Czech poetic style that was roughly equivalent in its revolutionary formal qualities to that of the poets that he was translating.[8] In his introduction to the 1936 second edition of Čapek's translations, Vítězslav Nezval, arguably the most significant of the Devětsil poets and a founder of Czech surrealism, wrote, "Never before Čapek's encroachment into poetry was such a tone heard in the Czech language. None of his literary predecessors gave us poetry in which iambs and dactyls would lose their numerical pathos so completely as they do in Čapek's."[9] Peter Steiner also credits Čapek with stimulating Czech structuralist investigations into the semantics of meter (Roman Jakobson was a member of Devětsil during his time in Czechoslovakia).[10]

Despite the consequence of these translations for the Devětsil group, Čapek continued neither to translate poetry nor to compose his own poetry after the war, leaving the further development of his stylistic innovations to younger poets. Čapek's literary output in the early 1920s was centered on prose and drama. If it was Čapek the poet and translator who was a hero of the Czech interwar avant-garde, it was Čapek the playwright who was the darling of audiences and readers outside of Czechoslovakia, especially in the English-speaking world. Čapek's plays were noted not for their formal or stylistic novelty but rather for their use of fantastic and scientific plot elements in the context of current social and political issues. Although Čapek strenuously denied the direct influence of George Bernard Shaw's *Back to Methuselah* on *The Makropulos Case*, it is Shaw, G. K. Chesterton, and H. G. Wells who provide the most apt context for Čapek's plays of this era.

The most famous of Čapek's plays, *R.U.R. (Rossum's Universal Robots)*, premiered in Prague in January 1921 and was quickly translated and performed throughout Europe as well as in the United States and Japan, becoming a staple in anthologies of modern European drama for generations. Best known for its introduction of the word "robot" (originally coined by Josef Čapek) into the international vernacular, the play was hotly debated as a statement about the role of technology in society.[11] *R.U.R.* was hardly the only Čapek work from this period to dabble in science or science fiction, though. Čapek's first novel, *The Absolute at Large* (1922), takes as its premise that the industrial production of atomic energy induces a sort of religious ecstasy, while his next, *Krakatit* (1924), centers on a powerful and destructive explosive created by releasing atomic energy, and, of course, the plot of *The Makropulos Case* is driven by an immortality formula.

Both views of Čapek as a modernist, however, to some extent privilege his utility as a name to conjure with for later constituencies over his own intentions, or over the intrinsic qualities of the works themselves. As already noted, by his own account, his impetus for translating French poetry was political as much as aesthetic, and, while his translation of "Zone" was a treasured touchstone of the Devětsil poets, Čapek did not see fit to include it in the first edition of the collection, published in 1920.[12] Čapek largely lost interest in French poetry after 1920, and his early enthusiasm seems to have had little consequence for his later work. Somewhat similarly, Čapek has long been happily adopted as a founding father of science fiction by devotees eager to extend the lineage of the genre back in time and across to Europe—novelist Cara Hoffman's 2011 tribute to *The Absolute at Large* for NPR is just one, entirely typical, example—but the premises of *R.U.R.*, *The Absolute at Large*, and *Krakatit* are essentially conceits that allow Čapek to explore more mundane social and political issues.[13] Čapek responded in print to a public discussion of *R.U.R.* in London that included Shaw and Chesterton, complaining of the discussants, "It seems to me that, so far as my play was concerned, their chief interest was centered upon Robots. For myself, I confess as the author I was much more interested in men than in Robots."[14]

Later in this same letter, Čapek describes *R.U.R.* as a "comedy of truth," in which the attitudes of different characters toward the robots—seeing them as emancipators of man from physical labor or as demoralizers of human society, welcoming industrialization or fearing machinery—are all in some sense true and valid. In Čapek's words:

> All of them are right in the plain and moral sense of the word. . . . I ask whether it is not possible to see in the present social conflict of the world an analogous struggle between two, three, five equally serious verities and equally generous idealisms? I think it is possible, and this is the most dramatic element in modern civilization, that a human truth is opposed to another truth no less human, ideal against ideal, positive worth against worth no less positive, instead of the struggle being, as we are so often told it is, one between noble truth and vile selfish error.[15]

This impassioned plea for recognition of simultaneous truths was a product of Čapek's firm adherence to the principles of pragmatism. Shortly after completing his doctoral studies in philosophy and aesthetics at Prague's Charles University, Čapek wrote a lengthy essay on pragmatism, publishing it in 1918.[16] Just as his translations of French poetry were at least partially instigated by Čapek's sympathies with the Allied war effort, so too was his study of William James and John Dewey motivated by wartime politics. As Čapek wrote in 1932, "When Wilson was giving an ultimatum to Germany, the young intellectual was sending to the press a book on Anglo-American pragmatism. It wasn't, dear friends, 'the philosophy of a generation.' It was politics; it was an intellectual alliance with Wilson's America; it was, in its

own way, a tiny crumb of what's called the home resistance."[17] Here the
similarity ends, however, for, while Čapek's infatuation with French poetry
quickly waned after the war, he remained a staunch adherent to pragmatism. To use a biblical metaphor favored by Čapek, he saw life as a choice
between the path of Mary, who devoted herself to a single, absolute truth
(the teachings of Jesus), and that of Martha, who actively engaged with
worldly problems. Čapek, despite Jesus' rejection of Martha in the Gospel
of Luke, openly sided with her, both in his 1932 story "Martha and Mary"
from the *Apocryphal Stories* and in his essays.[18]

Čapek and Czech Theater

Čapek's most intense involvement with theater came in the early 1920s.
It was the January 1921 premiere of *R.U.R.* at the National Theater, directed
by Vojta Novák and designed by Bedřich Feuerstein, that brought international acclaim to Čapek and to postwar Czech theater. Both *The Insect Play*
(*Ze života hymzu*), written with his brother Josef, and *The Makropulos Case*
were produced the following year. In addition, Čapek was active as a director
at Prague's Vinohrady Theater (a state-supported theater, second only to the
National Theater in the pecking order of Prague theaters) from 1921 to 1924,
directing a dozen productions of works ranging from Aristophanes to Molière
and Shelley. Among the works directed by Čapek at the Vinohrady was the
premiere of *The Makropulos Case*. The Čapek brothers collaborated again on
Adam the Creator (*Adam stvořitel*), produced at the National Theater in
1927, but this was not as successful as their earlier works, and Čapek
stopped writing plays for a decade, not returning to the theater until his
anti-Nazi dramas of the late 1930s.

The enormous success of *R.U.R.* notwithstanding, Czech theater in the
1920s was dominated not by playwrights but by directors and stage designers. With the exception of Čapek, who was an international celebrity, and
perhaps also of František Langer, whose *A Camel through the Needle's Eye*
(*Velbloud uchem jehly* [1923]) and *Fringe Area* (*Periferie* [1925]) were popular
in Prague and noted abroad, the Prague theater scene was shaped largely by
productions rather than plays. Even Čapek was only briefly primarily a man
of the theater, and he would soon be immersed in novels, journalism, and
politics to the exclusion of drama.

The first major figure of twentieth-century Czech theater was Jaroslav
Kvapil (1868–1950), who was the head of drama from 1911 to 1918 at the

Prague National Theater, where he had been directing since the turn of the century. Kvapil had seen productions directed by Otto Brahm and Max Reinhardt at Prague's Neues Deutsches Theater, as well as the work of Konstantin Stanislavsky and of the Munich Artists' Theater, and had read Edward Gordon Craig. Although not an innovator or a radical by broader European standards, Kvapil transformed the National Theater from an actors' theater into a director's institution, with productions that, while still based in psychological realism, featured atmospheric stagings with impressionist and symbolist elements.

At roughly the same time, the man who would eventually succeed Kvapil at the National Theater, Karel Hugo Hilar (1885-1935), was working at the Vinohrady Theater, where he began directing in 1911 and where he became chief of drama in 1914. To an even greater extent than Kvapil, Hilar (a generation younger) saw the director as the main creative force in theatrical production, in the manner of Craig, Reinhardt, or Meyerhold. As he writes, "In a word, to be a director means to be a poet who, instead of making experiences fictive, materializes the given fictions. A poet is an artist who from the visible world creates symbols. A director is a poet who creates from symbols a visible world."[19] Hilar's Vinohrady productions restricted actors to a limited and stylized repertoire of gestures and, during the war, increasingly tended toward a type of expressionism that emphasized extremes of emotional display, strong contrasts of lighting, and grotesque satire. Hilar became head of drama at the National Theater in 1921, remaining there until his death in 1935. By the early 1920s, Hilar's direction had become even more stylized. As one National Theater actor lamented in an official complaint (one that no doubt would have pleased Craig), "We're the marionettes of every healthy and sick attempt. . . . [W]e're asked to be mere material, clay and color, sound, the final form of which can be anything."[20] Hilar's productions displayed many elements typical of contemporary German expressionism and were often compared to those of Leopold Jessner.

Hilar's most vital period, which coincided with Čapek's most concentrated involvement with the theater, came in his first years at the National Theater, before suffering a stroke in 1924. Hilar directed the 1922 premiere of *The Insect Play*, a production radical and successful enough that he was invited to direct it on Broadway, as well as *Adam the Creator*.[21] To the extent that Čapek's plays of the 1920s form part of the history of European theatrical modernism, it is much more due to Hilar's direction, and to the stage

designs of Feuerstein and Josef Čapek, than to the texts of the plays themselves.[22]

Čapek's *Makropulos*

The Makropulos Case premiered at Prague's Vinohrady Theater in November 1921, under Čapek's own direction. Like *R.U.R.*, *The Makropulos Case*
was swiftly translated into English and successfully performed on Broadway
(1926) and in London (1930). Also like *R.U.R.*, *Makropulos* has a premise
rooted in the fantastic. From the first, discussions of the play have centered
on the provenance of the central conceit, the longevity formula created
by Marty's father, to the exclusion of other elements. The appearance of
The Makropulos Case in the same year as the publication of Shaw's *Back to
Methuselah* caused enough of a furor to raise talk of a plagiarism lawsuit,
and Čapek felt obliged to include a preface in the published edition, dis-
avowing any connection to Shaw's pentateuch, which he had not read, and
claiming instead to have been inspired by the work of Ilya Ilyitch Mechnikov, a Nobel Prize-winning biologist who had theorized that aging was
caused by toxic bacteria in the digestive system.[23] A 1923 *Times Literary
Supplement* review of the English translation noted the coincidence with
Shaw, while also suggesting connections to František Langer's story "Eternal
Youth" and mentioning Frankenstein and the Wandering Jew.[24] Frank Chandler's 1931 monograph on modern European drama adds Swift and Tennyson to the mix, and, more recently, Harkins argues for the play as a response
to H. G. Wells's *The Food of the Gods*.[25]

Despite all of this attention to the immortality theme, the document that
contains the magic formula is a MacGuffin, existing to motivate characters
and incite them into conflict with each other, and even the idea of radically
extended life is little more than a debating point, allowing Čapek's characters to argue about its moral, economic, and emotional consequences. The
crux of the play comes near its end, when the drama's action comes to a
grinding halt, allowing each character on stage to deliver a position paper
about the implications of such longevity. Here, as in *R.U.R.*, Čapek is much
more interested in pragmatism than in science fiction, presenting multiple
truths in the hope that they can productively coexist, rather than encouraging us to choose among them.

For all of the similarities to *R.U.R.*, *The Makropulos Case* never quite attained the earlier play's critical or popular success. As noted above, *Makropulos* did make its way into print in English and was produced in British and

American theaters, but critical responses were not uniformly positive. The *New York Times* review of the 1926 Broadway production, for instance, was lukewarm, complaining that the play (at least in this performance) "rarely stirs the audience to laughter" and that withholding of the protagonist's secret until the end could "result in tedium."[26] Czech reception of *Makropulos* was noticeably cooler than that of the Anglophone press, with comparisons to Shaw drawn to Čapek's disadvantage.[27] Although *Makropulos* followed not even two years after the triumph of *R.U.R.*, Čapek's involvement in drama had peaked. He would direct for two more years at the Vinohrady, but his only other play of the decade would be the unsuccessful *Adam the Creator*.

By the second half of the 1920s, Čapek had almost entirely lost his relevance to modernist efforts in Czech drama and literature. As detailed above, his plays of the 1920s, while generally popular, were, if perceived as progressive at all, seen as such mostly on account of the directorial and scenic properties of their Prague productions. Even more importantly, though, Čapek had become politically unacceptable to the self-appointed leaders of the Prague avant-garde, most of whom were about a decade younger than he was. In particular, the Devětsil group, formed in 1920, was dominated by artists born around the turn of the century, notably Karel Teige (1900-51), Vítězslav Nezval (1900-58), and Jaroslav Seifert (1901-86). As discussed above, Čapek's translations of French poetry were central to the Devětsil group, which had strong Francophile leanings. Teige traveled to Paris in 1922, where he met Le Corbusier, and returned in 1924 with Seifert in tow. Seifert wrote that the entire Teige generation was following in the footsteps of Apollinaire, and Nezval's preface to the 1936 second edition of Čapek's collection demonstrated its gratitude for Čapek's pioneering translations.[28]

The Devětsil group, however, also had a Marxist orientation. Neither its initial commitment to proletarian literature nor its later adherence to Teige's doctrine of poetism (which advocated a joyful liquidation of existing artistic categories and institutions under the influence of modern technology, popular culture, and sports), had any place for Čapek, who was disqualified both by his politics and by his entrenched positions in the Czech literary and dramatic establishments. Čapek was closely associated with T. G. Masaryk, whose government had been explicitly rejected by the Devětsil Marxists. Čapek published an essay entitled "Why Am I Not a Communist?" in 1924, while Seifert had joined the new Communist Party of Czechoslovakia in 1921.[29] By the time that Janáček's opera premiered in 1926, Čapek was a

household name, a leading figure in Prague's cultural, journalistic, and political circles, but largely irrelevant to the avant-garde.

Janáček and Czech Musical Modernism

The relations between music and modernism in interwar Prague were
extremely complex and resist easy summary. The vigorous ideological debates of this time have been thoroughly and heroically chronicled by Brian
Locke, and the following discussion will highlight some of the more prominent issues and controversies.[30] The most immediate consequence of
Czechoslovak independence for Prague musical life was its separation into
distinct Czech-speaking and German-speaking institutions. Already in the
fall of 1918, the Czech faculty of the Prague Conservatory had pushed for
both expulsion of their German colleagues and also the resignation of the
(Czech) aristocrats who administered the institution. In early December,
the Deutsche Akademie für Musik und darstellende Kunst in Prag opened,
leaving the Prague Conservatory a Czech-speaking institution, serving the
Czech musical community.[31] Barely two years later, in November of 1920,
the Deutsches Landestheater was forcibly entered by a Czech-speaking
mob, claimed as Czech territory with a performance of Smetana's *The Bartered Bride*, and annexed to the National Theater, leaving the Neues
Deutsches Theater (under the direction of Alexander Zemlinsky) as the
main outlet for German opera in Prague.[32] Similarly, German Bohemians
were expelled from the Czech Philharmonic. Within this newly constructed
and purified realm of Czech musical life in postwar Prague, the crux of discussions of musical modernism was the most appropriate way for composers to be both modern and national. Unlike the literary world—where the
use of the Czech language itself could link a work to national culture—art
music, especially instrumental music, needed to link itself to Czech culture
through stylistic traits.

   This perceived need for Czech music to be simultaneously modern and
national was inextricably linked to the forbidding model of Bedřich Smetana.
Already by the time of his death in 1884, Smetana was largely accepted as
the single composer whose works embodied both a fulfillment of the cultural aims of the National Revival and also the stylistic traits of European
musical progressivism. Smetana's stature only grew in the following decades, with this unique position amongst Czech composers accepted across
most of the political spectrum. In the early decades of the twentieth century, Smetana's legacy continued to be the standard to which living compos-

ers were held—and, generally, found wanting. The main figure in promoting Smetana as an exemplar of Czech musical modernism was Zdeněk Nejedlý, a critic and musicologist who lectured at Charles University (and eventually became the first minister for culture and education of the Czechoslovak Socialist Republic in 1948). Nejedlý's deployment of Smetana as an ideological instrument peaked in 1917, when a *Smetana Exhibition* curated by Nejedlý opened at the Prague Ethnographic Museum. This exhibition was very popular with the wartime Czech public and solidified the perception of Smetana as a uniquely national composer just as the Czech lands were on the cusp of independence. This led to the paradoxical situation of a composer dead for more than three decades being accepted as a stylistic model for Czech composers after the war.[33] As Erwin Schulhoff wrote in 1925, what distinguished the Czech Republic from the rest of Europe was that Wagner's model had elsewhere been almost completely repudiated, while in the Czech lands reverence for Smetana caused Wagnerian principles to extend into the new century.[34]

Astonishingly, when the International Society for Contemporary Music granted Prague the orchestral portion of its 1924 festival, the Czechoslovak section's contribution included a cycle of new productions of Smetana's operas. This was an obvious gesture of celebrating Smetana's centennial but a puzzling answer to the premiere of Schoenberg's *Erwartung*, conducted by Alexander Zemlinsky at the same festival. Nejedlý, in particular, argued that modern trends in European composition were incompatible with the Smetanian ideal, and he was openly hostile to the Spolek pro moderní hudbu (Society for Modern Music), founded in 1921 at the urging of Vítězslav Novák to explore and promote exactly those trends.[35] Beyond Nejedlý, however, the 1924 Prague ISCM festival occasioned debate across the ideological spectrum about the extent to which cosmopolitan musical modernism was compatible with Czechness.[36]

Another legacy of the musical polemics of the National Revival years was a reflexive mapping of musical politics onto social politics. In the last quarter of the nineteenth century, Smetana, a putative Wagnerian and therefore a progressive in terms of Austro-German musical ideology, was associated with the Young Czech Party. Conversely, Antonín Dvořák, a nominal Brahmsian, was regarded as a musical conservative and as an avatar of the principles of the Old Czech Party. Similarly, it was taken for granted in the 1920s that the political Left would be sympathetic to more radical compositional styles and production choices. The 1924 Smetana cycle, for instance, was controversial on account of the modernist stagings of Ferdinand Pujman. Criticism of Pujman and of Otakar Ostrčil (the opera director at the National Theater and a protégé of Nejedlý) was a sufficiently public issue to be debated in Parliament, with detractors and defenders breaking down along politically partisan lines, as members of the Agrarian Party attacked the productions and liberals supported them.[37]

These various ideological forces converged most dramatically in November 1926, when Alban Berg's *Wozzeck* was produced at Prague's National Theater (the first staging of *Wozzeck*, after its Berlin premiere). The third Prague performance, on Tuesday, November 16, was the occasion of a *Rite of Spring*-quality demonstration (including police involvement) during the second act that forced the clearing of the theater and the cancellation of the rest of the opera.[38] Opposition to the production stemmed from a variety of sources, including the garden-variety displeasure of a conservative, middle-class opera audience (Tuesday night audiences were dominated by subscribers, most of whom were wealthy businesspeople) when confronted with a new and difficult work and the presence of a large contingent of fascist students and workers hired to whistle at a prearranged moment.[39] The production, staged by Pujman, offended many of the same critics already displeased by his Smetana cycle.

In broader ideological terms, responses to the opera broke down along political and generational lines. Conservative papers and critics attacked *Wozzeck* for being musically, politically, nationally, and even racially unacceptable. Predictably, Berg's music was subjected to stock antimodernist critiques, with, for instance, Antonín Šilhan of the National Democratic *Národní Listy* (the very paper that Čapek had left in 1921 when the National Democrats refused to support Masaryk) comparing Berg's singers to "alcoholics erupting into desperate, delirious shrieks."[40] Šilhan also accused the National Theater of musical bolshevism, on the grounds that avant-garde music was inherently Leftist, that Ostrčil was politically suspect by virtue of his close association with the Marxist Nejedlý, and that the next production of *Wozzeck* was to be in Leningrad.[41] Furthermore, Šilhan suggested that the apparent success of the first Prague performance was attributable to the presence of a disproportionate number of German speakers in the audience (his review was entitled "In Foreign Service").[42] Berg was even described as a "Berlin Jew" by a right-wing critic (in Berlin, Berg had been rumored to be a "Czech Jew").[43]

Strong support for Berg came, however, from the younger generation of composers at the Prague Conservatory. Although the composers born in the first decade of the twentieth century, like Iša Krejčí (1904-68), Jaroslav Ježek (1906-42), and Emil František Burian (1904-59), were oriented toward the neoclassicism of Stravinsky and Les Six rather than toward Viennese expressionism, they still saw attacks on Berg as opposition to cosmopolitan musical modernism in general and rallied in support of *Wozzeck*. Krejčí, Ježek, and Burian, along with a number of young musicians and prominent members of the Prague avant-garde (including Devětsil members like Nezval, Seifert, and Teige) signed a public letter in support of Ostrčil.[44]

Janáček's relationship to these various polemics was oddly tangential. In purely geographical terms, as a Brno resident whose connections with Prague musical life were minimal (Janáček did give master classes for the Prague Conservatory from 1920 to 1925, but all of his operas after 1920 were premiered in Brno), he was generally not implicated in the ideological debates surrounding the National Theater and other Prague institutions. He did run afoul of Nejedlý when *Jenůfa* was produced in Prague in 1916. Nejedlý's animus toward Janáček was probably motivated by resentment of Janáček's alleged support of Smetana opponents in the 1880s but manifested itself in criticism of Janáček's "speech-melodies" and of his links to verismo and naturalism, and regionalism.[45] These attacks, though, did little to hamper the success of *Jenůfa* or to deter further productions of Janáček's operas in Prague (including a production of *Kát'a Kabanová* as part of the Czechoslovak contribution to the 1924 ISCM festival).

Janáček (born in 1854) was not only almost two generations older than Krejčí, Ježek, and Burian but also significantly older than the composers who made up the old guard in postwar Prague, like Josef Suk (1874-1935), Novák (1870-1949), and Ostrčil (1879-1935). Despite this, he was accepted as a fellow traveler by the younger composers. Schulhoff described him as "belonging to the latest generation of composers, whose struggle he has also fought," and credited him with breaking the Smetana-Wagner stranglehold on Czech music.[46] Janáček also seems to have been accepted as a generationally displaced musical modernist by exactly those Devětsil members who considered Čapek old-fashioned.

In principle, the Devětsil members held that the arts had evolved beyond the institutions that had traditionally supported them, with the visual arts, for instance, ending with the *Black Square* of Kazimir Malevich. According to Seifert's memoirs, when he and Teige were in Paris together, Teige forbade him to visit the Louvre, and, while they did visit some galleries of modern art, their cultural activities were largely focused on sitting at side-walk cafés and attending circuses and wax museums.[47] In the realm of music, jazz was the touchstone of the Devětsil poets, and classical music in general was viewed as a commodity obsolete in the modern world. Seifert, for instance, in his "All the Beauties of the World" (from *Sheer Love*, 1923), requests, "Be silent violins and ring you horns of automobiles/aeroplanes, sing the song of evening like a nightingale."[48]

Nonetheless, just as galleries showing cubist or futurist works were more palatable than the Louvre to Teige in Paris, so too were some modern composers of art music more acceptable than others. Just as Teige had declared the Louvre off limits to Seifert, so too did Teige discourage him from seeing Smetana's *The Bartered Bride* at the Prague National Theater.[49] Teige, however, approved of Stravinsky, Milhaud, Satie, and, in general, of Les Six.[50] Nezval was a proficient pianist who frequently played at Devětsil gatherings, and Seifert describes "stormy" renditions of works by Janáček and Bohuslav Martinů, including a salon at Teige's apartment when Nezval played and sang *Jenůfa*.[51]

Despite these seals of approval from Devětsil members, Janáček's credentials as a musical modernist are suspect. Janáček did sympathize with the plight of Berg during the Prague "*Wozzeck* Affair," exclaiming in a 1928 interview, "Wronged—wronged! They wrong *Wozzeck*, Berg has been deeply wronged!"[52] He was also flattered by suggestions that he belonged in the company of the leading modern composers of the day, like Arnold Schoenberg and Franz Schreker.[53] There is, however, no evidence that he had any interest in any of the stylistic experiments of the 1920s, be it Schoenberg's method of composition with twelve tones, Stravinskian neo-classicism, or, closer to home, Schulhoff's dalliances with jazz and American dance music and the experiments with quarter tones of Alois Hába and his students in the department of microtonal music that Hába established at the Prague Conservatory in 1924. If his reputation as a modernist was much more firmly established than that of Čapek, it rested almost entirely on his departures from older styles, rather than his proximity to newer ones.

Nor does Janáček seem to have been interested in the modernist possibilities of the theater. His one experience with a leading modernist producer was foisted on him against his will. Ostrčil chose Pujman for the 1925 Prague production of *The Cunning Little Vixen* over the objections of Janáček. Janáček had seen—and hated—Pujman's 1921 production of Debussy's *Pelléas et Mélisande* at the Prague National Theater, writing that the staging made him leave the theater "in disgust." Predictably, Janáček was displeased by Pujman's work on *Vixen* (although he was happily taken with Josef Čapek's sets and costumes). When offered a choice of producers for the Prague staging of *The Makropulos Case*, Janáček explicitly rejected Pujman.[54]

Ultimately, though, the fact that the Janáček-Čapek *Makropulos Case* turned out to be something of a nonevent in the history of Czech modernism is no surprise. Trivially, the ages and modest modernist credentials of the playwright and the composer would be enough to all but eliminate the prospect of a truly radical work. However, perhaps more meaningfully, the cultural moment during which Czech modernism seemed to be a viable and identifiable concept was brief and rested upon fragile personal relationships among a very small group of people. By the time of the—highly successful —1928 Prague production of *The Makropulos Case*, alliances between the members of Prague's literary and musical avant-gardes were slipping and shifting.

Seifert was expelled from both the Communist Party and Devětsil in 1929 for criticizing the Czech Communist Party, and Devětsil, which had already ceased operating in Brno, would grind to a halt altogether by 1931. Some of the Devětsil members, led by Nezval, reorganized under the banner of surrealism, forming the Czech Surrealist Group in 1934 (Teige would join them later). Nor would the group of young composers at the Prague Conservatory who had so vigorously defended Berg's *Wozzeck* continue to form a cohesive group. Burian, although he continued to compose, would become much more closely associated with the theater than with the concert hall. He appeared as an actor in the Prague Dada Theater, where he also unveiled his "Voiceband," which performed a sort of syncopated choral recitation of poetry in 1927. In the early 1930s, he worked in cabaret and founded his own experimental theater, D 34, in 1934, becoming one of the most important Czech avant-garde directors of the decade. Similarly, Ježek, without forsaking composition, would become famous for something other than concert works, becoming the composer and pianist-bandleader for the antifascist Liberated Theater of Jiří Voskovec and Jan Werich in 1928, and achieving a Gershwin-like status in the Czech Republic for his satirical cabaret songs. Like the Devětsil members, the musicians would continue to shift alliances and form groups. Shortly before Nezval founded the Czech Surrealist Group, a circle of musicians, including Ježek, Krejčí, and Martinů, inaugurated the Mánes Music Group with a December 1933 concert of settings of Nezval's poetry. The Mánes Group, modeled loosely on Les Six, was oriented toward French music and neoclassicism, reflecting the inclinations of these composers in their student days.

This brief sketch of the protean relationships among the cultural figures who came of age in interwar Prague hints at how elusive a coherent sense of the modern or of avant-garde would be during this period. A few months after the December 1926 Brno premiere of *The Makropulos Case*, the *New York Times* published a report on the production from Rosa Newmarch. Newmarch, a great advocate of Janáček's music who had brought him to London earlier in 1926, was unsurprisingly enthusiastic about his most re- cent opera. However, while she was willing to assure American readers that the opera was a spellbinding drama that would become a repertoire staple in Europe, even Newmarch made no claims for theatrical or musical innova- tion, instead writing that, "musically, the opera does not reveal any fresh technical departure" and that Janáček had "relieved the play of much of its grotesque and weird element" in the service of creating a "'conversational' opera." Newmarch's only assertion of novelty is the suggestion that this might be the first appearance of a telephone on the operatic stage.[55] Newmarch was prescient in predicting a place for the opera in the international repertoire— even if the wait for its success was longer than she had anticipated—and perceptive in finding it a work more closely allied with Janáček's previous operas than with Čapek's drama. Janáček's *Makropulos Case* is modern in the very loose sense that its musical textures demonstrate some distance from nineteenth-century precedents and that it is set in 1920s Prague, but it is difficult to find meaningful points of contact between the opera and any of the contemporary efforts to establish distinct and progressive movements in Czech theater, poetry, and music.

Notes

1. Emerson 190.
2. Ibid. 191.
3. Robinson 330-38.
4. For references to further literature and an expanded discussion of this reading, see Katz 121-36.
5. Čapek, "About the Čapek Generation" 31.
6. Harkins 27. The earliest example of Čapek's "literary cubism" would be his story "The Luminous Depths," written with Josef in 1911 or 1912 and published in 1916. See Harkins 49.
7. Čapek, "About the Čapek Generation" 37.
8. Harkins 30.

9. Klíma 35-36.

10. Steiner 71. For more on Čapek's translations of French poetry, see Rubeš.

11. The subtitle is in English in Čapek's original. See Harkins 90-91, for instance, for an account of a 1923 public discussion in London with Shaw and Chesterton.

12. It appeared for the first time in the 1936 edition. See Rubeš 62-63.

13. Hoffman.

14. Harkins 90.

15. Ibid. 90-92.

16. Čapek, "Pragmatismus Čili filozofie praktického života."

17. Čapek, "About the Čapek Generation" 37.

18. Steiner, 86-89. See also Čapek, "About Relativism" 290.

19. Translation from Burian, "K. H. Hilar" 68.

20. Ibid. 70; Burian, *Creators* 15.

21. Hilar's *Regiebuch* was used as the basis of the October 1922 Broadway production, although he did not come to America to direct it (Burian, "K. H. Hilar" 64; Burian, *Creators* 8).

22. Material about Kvapil and Hilar from Burian, *Modern Czech Theatre* 20-40; and Burian, "K. H. Hilar." The latter is largely reprinted in Burian, *Creators* 1-19.

23. Mechnikov won the Nobel Prize in Medicine 1908 for his work in immunology. Most of the Čapek preface is translated into English in Harkins 111-12.

24. "A Czech Dramatist" 74.

25. Chandler 458; Harkins 111.

26. Atkinson 12.

27. Bradbrook 61. Even Ivan Klíma's 2001 biography of Čapek is noticeably less kind to *Makropulos* than is recent American and British criticism (103-07, esp. 106).

28. For more on the importance of Paris to the Prague avant-garde in the 1920s, see Kuhlman.

29. Čapek, "Why Am I Not a Communist?"

30. Locke, *Opera and Ideology in Prague.*

31. Ibid. 140.

32. Ibid. 140-42. See also Demetz 340.

33. Locke, *Opera and Ideology in Prague* 63.

34. Schulhoff 52.

35. Locke, *Opera and Ideology in Prague* 119.

36. Ibid. 152. Also Beckerman.

37. Locke, *Opera and Ideology in Prague* 151.

38. For a detailed account of this incident, see Locke, "The '*Wozzeck* Affair.'"

39. Ibid. 81.

40. Ibid. 72.

41. Ibid. 71.

42. Ibid. 71, 73.

43. Ibid. 74.

44. Ibid. 86.

45. Locke, *Opera and Ideology in Prague* 62-63. For more on "speech-melodies," see Katz 13-29. For more on Janáček, verismo and naturalism, see Katz 8-10.

46. Schulhoff 51-52. For Janáček and generational displacement, see Katz 4-5.

47. Seifert, *Poetry* 243.

48. Seifert, *Early Poetry* 91.

49. Seifert, *Všecky Krásy Světa* 119.

50. Ibid. 119.

51. Ibid. 119, 246.

52. Tyrrell 773.

53. Katz 6-7.

54. Tyrrell 390, 532-33, 544, 741.

55. Newmarch X7.

Bibliography

Atkinson, J. Brooks. "The Play: Longevity Drawn Out." *New York Times* 22 Jan. 1926: 12.

Beckerman, Michael. "In Search of Czechness in Music." *19th-Century Music* 10 (Summer 1986): 61-73.

Bradbrook, Bohuslava R. *Karel Čapek: In Pursuit of Truth, Tolerance and Trust.* Brighton: Sussex Academic Press, 1998.

Burian, Jarka M. "K. H. Hilar and the Early Twentieth-Century Czech Theatre." *Theatre Journal* 34.1 (Mar. 1982): 55-76.

———. *Leading Creators of Twentieth-Century Czech Theatre.* London: Routledge, 2000.

———. *Modern Czech Theatre.* Iowa City: University of Iowa Press, 2000.

Čapek, Karel. "About Relativism." *Believe in People: The Essential Karel Čapek; Previously Untranslated Journalism and Letters.* Ed. Šárka Tobrmanová-Kühnová. London: Faber and Faber, 2010. 287-90.

———. "About the Čapek Generation." *Believe in People: The Essential Karel Čapek; Previously Untranslated Journalism and Letters.* Ed. Šárka Tobrmanová-Kühnová. London: Faber and Faber, 2010. 30-36.

———. "Pragmatismus Čili filozofie praktického života." *Karel Čapek: Univerzitní studie.* Prague: Československý spisovatel, 1987. 263-315.

———. "Why Am I Not a Communist?" *Believe in People: The Essential Karel Čapek; Previously Untranslated Journalism and Letters.* Ed. Šárka Tobrmanová-Kühnová. London: Faber and Faber, 2010. 269-79.

Chandler, Frank W. *Modern Continental Playwrights.* New York: Harper & Brothers, 1931.

"A Czech Dramatist," *Times Literary Supplement* 1 Feb. 1923: 74.

Demetz, Peter. *Prague in Black and Gold: Scenes from the Life of a European City.* New York: Hill and Wang, 1997.

Emerson, Caryl. "*Čapek*, Janáček, That Makropulos Thing, and a Word about Sacrificed Women in 20th-Century Slavic Opera." *Festschrift for Michael Henry Heim.* Ed. Craig Cravens, Susan Kresin, and Masako Fidler. Ann Arbor, MI: Slavica, 2008. 189-98.

Harkins, William E. *Karel Čapek.* New York: Columbia University Press, 1962.

Hoffman, Cara. "Lit Novelist Confesses Nerd Love for Sci Fi Classic." NPR July 14, 2011. Accessed 9 Sept. 2011. <http://www.npr.org/2011/04/21/135241076/a-rollicking-critique-of-absolute-religious-fervor>.

Katz, Derek. *Janáček beyond the Borders.* Rochester, NY: University of Rochester Press, 2009.

Klíma, Ivan. *Karel Čapek: Life and Work.* Trans. Norma Comrada. North Haven, CT: Catbird Press, 2002.

Kuhlman, Martha. "Prague Meets Paris: The Reception and the Representation of the 'Eiffelka.'" *Modernism/modernity* 14.2 (2007): 291-308.

Locke, Brian S. *Opera and Ideology in Prague: Polemics and Practice at the National Theater, 1900-1938.* Rochester, NY: University of Rochester Press, 2006.

———. "The '*Wozzeck* Affair': Modernism and the Crisis of Audience in Prague." *Journal of Musicological Research* 27.1 (2008): 63-93.

Newmarch, Rosa. "Janacek's *Makropulos*: Opera by Czech Composer, Using Capek's Play as Text, a Success." *New York Times* 8 May 1927: X7.

Robinson, Paul. "Reading Libretti and Misreading Opera." *Reading Opera.* Ed. Arthur Groos and Roger Parker. Princeton: Princeton University Press, 1988. 328-46.

Rubeš, Jan. "Constructing Modernity—Čapek's Translations of French Poetry." *On Karel Čapek: A Michigan Slavic Colloquium.* Ed. Michael Makin and Jindřich Toman. Michigan Slavic Materials 34. Ann Arbor: Michigan Slavic, 1992.

Schulhoff, Erwin. *Erwin Schulhoff: Schriften.* Ed. Tobias Widmaier. Vol. 7 of *Verdrängte Musik.* Hamburg: von Bockel, 1995.

Seifert, Jaroslav. *The Early Poetry of Jaroslav Seifert.* Trans. Dana Loewy. Evanston, IL: Northwestern University Press, 1999.

———. *The Poetry of Jaroslav Seifert.* Trans. Ewald Osers and George Gibian. North Haven, CT: Catbird Press, 1998.

———. *Všecky Krásy Světa.* Prague: Československý spisovatel, 1982.

Steiner, Peter. "Radical Liberalism: *Apocryphal Stories* by Karel Čapek." *The Deserts of Bohemia.* Ithaca, NY: Cornell University Press, 2000. 69-93.

Tyrrell, John. *Janáček: Years of a Life.* Vol. 2, *(1914-1928): Tsar of the Forests.* London: Faber & Faber, 2007.

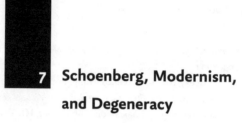

7 Schoenberg, Modernism, and Degeneracy

Richard Begam

Between 1927 and 1932, Arnold Schoenberg composed what is arguably modernism's most revolutionary opera, *Moses und Aron*. The music—Schoenberg's longest twelve-tone composition—is startlingly original, filled with auditory effects that have no precedent and little afterlife. The voice of God, as ventriloquized through the Burning Bush, floats and flutters, a kind of acoustic impalpability, the wind of the Sinai refined into metaphysical abstraction. The scene with the golden calf is a savage rewriting of Stravinsky, *Le sacre du printemps* purged of its primitivist stylizations and restored to the dark and bloody breast of Dionysus. Finally, there are those passages of minimalist serialism—discrete plops, plinks, and plunks that sound arbitrary and aleatory but have all the inexorable logic of a Beethoven symphony or a Jackson Pollock painting. And yet, if the opera's music astonishes in its radicalism, its text astonishes in its conservatism, focusing as it does on the central events of Exodus: God's summons to Moses, Moses and Aaron leading the Jewish people out of Egypt, the travail in the wilderness, the worship of the golden calf and its destruction. Of course, it is not unusual for a modernist work to draw its narrative from the literature and myth of antiquity, but *Ulysses*, *The Waste Land*, and *The Cantos* speak in a multiplicity of voices, voices whose heterogeneity serves to challenge Europe's Judeo-Christian heritage. Schoenberg's opera, on the contrary, draws not on a variety of texts but on a single book, one that purports to be The Book; and it relates not just any story but the founding story of the Jewish people. How does Schoenberg reconcile his radical music with his conservative text? How, in other words, does he reconcile his modernism with his Judaism?

The short answer to this question—one that I will spend much of this chapter elaborating—is to be found in the second commandment, with its famous prohibition against the making of images. Now, in the Middle East of 1500 BCE, the Jewish God is unique among the reigning deities: an iconoclast with a hammer, he is committed to shattering all divine likenesses, especially his own.[1] Modernism, as we know, is also celebrated for its iconoclastic fervor, its hostility to representation. In the German-speaking world of Schoenberg's youth, the avant-garde dedicated itself with almost obsessive singularity to assaulting traditional mimesis, most notably through its experiments in expressionist and abstract art. Schoenberg himself composed two expressionist operas, exhibited his oil paintings in *Der Blaue Reiter* exhibition of 1911, and contributed an article and a musical composition to their 1912 almanac.[2] He also knew and admired such antirealist painters as Oskar Kokoschka, Egon Schiele, Franz Marc, and Wassily Kandinsky.[3] It was precisely the kind of art produced by these men, art that distorted or eliminated "natural" forms, that would later be condemned by National Socialism.

Nazi hostility to modernism was a matter of public knowledge as early as the mid-1920s, but it was most fully and emphatically exemplified in the *Entartete Kunst* (Degenerate art) and *Entartete Musik* (Degenerate music) exhibitions in Munich in 1937 and Düsseldorf in 1938.[4] For the Nazis, "degenerate" referred to art that was not simply morally suspect but mimetically deficient, indeed to any representation that "degenerated" or—to use a more contemporary term—deconstructed the "natural" and "objective" forms of reality. The degeneration of these forms was, according to Nazi ideology, a quintessentially Jewish phenomenon.[5] Hitler himself is quoted to this effect in the *Entartete Kunst* catalogue, where he describes modern art as a collection of "misformed cripples and cretins, women who can inspire only aversion, men who are more like beasts than men, children, who, if such were to live, must instantly be considered the accursed of God! And this these completely inhuman dilettantes dare to present to our present world as the art of our time, that is to say, as an expression of that which the contemporary epoch forms and upon which [it] impresses the seal."[6] The phrase "cripples and cretins" is modified in the original German by *missgestaltete*, a word that derives from *Gestalt* (shape, form, figure) and carries obvious aesthetic connotations.[7] At the same time, by calling such "misformed" creatures "the accursed of God!" Hitler reverses the notion that the Jews are the "chosen people," even as his characterization of modern art as an "expression" of the "contemporary epoch" connects them with expressionism. Elsewhere in the catalogue, Hitler makes even more explicit the affiliation between the Jews and modernism: "The Jews understood, especially through exploitation of their place in the press, with help from the so-called critics, not only how to confuse step by step the natural conceptions [*natürlichen Auffassungen*] about the essence and the lessons of art as well as the purpose, but moreover to destroy the common healthy perceptions in these matters."[8] In what was to become a familiar formulation, the Jew is presented as the enemy of the normative and the organic, a shifty rhetorician who bends and shades the truth, thereby undermining "natural conceptions" about the "essence" of art.

Needless to say, the connection between Judaism and modernism that the Nazis drew was entirely factitious. Jews were arguably more interested in the arts than some groups, but the notion that they constituted an aesthetic fifth column that used modernism to undermine the *völkish* values of Germany was a pure fabrication. In point of fact, out of the 112 artists shown in the *Entartete Kunst* exhibition, only 6, or approximately 5 percent, were Jews.[9] The story was much the same in music. According to the 1933 census, of the 93,857 Germans who listed themselves as career musicians, only 1,915, or about 2 percent, were Jews.[10] Despite these small numbers, after Hitler came to power in 1933, there was a wholesale purging of Jews from musical positions in Germany. Eminent conductors such as Otto Klemperer and Bruno Walter were chased from the podium by Alfred Rosenberg's Combat League for German Culture.[11] Schoenberg, who held an appointment at the prestigious Prussian Academy of the Arts in Berlin, resigned his post in March 1933 after the academy's president, Max von Schillings, publicly deplored the "Jewish influence" at the institution.[12] In April of that year, the passage of the Civil Service Restoration Act, which officially denied jobs to "non-Aryans," led to the dismissal of even more Jews.[13] By May 1933, Schoenberg had fled Germany, traveling first to France and then to the United States, where he would spend the remainder of his life. But if Schoenberg was finished with Germany, Germany was not finished with him. He was later prominently featured in the *Entartete Musik* exhibition in a display disparagingly entitled "The Jew, Arnold Schoenberg."[14]

Given the fact that *Moses und Aron* was the last major work Schoenberg composed before emigrating from Europe, it may be worthwhile to consider the opera in light of the National Socialist discourse on *entartete Musik*.[15] I will argue that, as a matter of polemical provocation, Schoenberg not only accepts the equation of modernism with Judaism but goes on to do what the Nazis have not: he advances a substantive argument for this claim.

Hence, modernism begins not with the narrative experiments of Joyce and Woolf, the painterly innovations of Picasso and Braque, or the revolutionary philosophizing of Nietzsche and Bergson but some 3,400 years earlier with the patriarch Moses and the second commandment's prohibition against representation. But Schoenberg does not stop here. In a brilliant dialectical reversal, he develops two further lines of argumentation that would have outraged the Nazis even more. First, the critique of representation develops not simply from outside German culture, through the "alien influence" of the Jew, but from within that culture, indeed in its very heart and soul: its great philosophical tradition. Second, degeneracy in art—especially insofar as it promotes the "primitivism" and "atavism" that the Nazis deplored— results not from the rejection of mimesis but from its idolatrous and fetish- istic worship, as the episode of the golden calf so vividly demonstrates. In other words, Schoenberg takes over the Nazi rhetoric on aesthetics and moral degeneracy, but he turns it on its head. Degeneracy is the product of the cult of the image, particularly the image conceived of in ritualistic terms, the image as the incarnation of a higher or deeper reality. It is perhaps also worth mentioning that the early 1930s was a time when a number of artists and thinkers in the German-speaking world became deeply suspicious of the power of representation and spectacle, especially as it was invested in the image, from Walter Benjamin's demystification of the "auratic" to Bertolt Brecht's development of the *Verfremdungseffekt* to Ludwig Wittgenstein's rejection of the "picture theory."[16] *Moses und Aron* participates, then, in the broader critique modernism mounted against a mimesis that, in the German-speaking world, had begun to assume negative, even nightmarish, political implications. Following World War II, Theodor W. Adorno further elabo- rated on that critique in his discussion of "metaphysics after Auschwitz," explicitly connecting it to the *Bilderverbot*, or "prohibition against images."[17]

Toward a Critique of Representation

Virtually all commentators agree that *Moses und Aron* is preoccupied with the issue of representation.[18] The opera begins with Moses' invocation of God as "singular, eternal, omnipresent, imperceptible and unimaginable" (einziger, ewiger, allgegenwärtiger,/unsichtbarer und unvorstellbarer) (112).[19] But the answer Moses receives dramatically illustrates just how problematic representation is. For, despite the fact that God is *einziger*—singular, uni- tary, one—he responds in *six* different voices, three sung and three spoken, thereby immediately calling into question his true nature and man's ability to represent him. Indeed, the opera's central conflict—between Moses and Aaron—develops into a philosophical dialogue on the relation of the noumenal to the phenomenal, of abstraction to representation. Moses the idealist is, on the one hand, dedicated to a truth that is metaphysical and absolute, a truth that will remain doctrinally pure only as long as it remains rigorously abstract. It is therefore appropriate that his role is performed in *Sprechstimme*, a stylized form of speech that eschews the intensity and lyricality of song.[20] Aaron the pragmatist is, on the other hand, committed to God's mandate to liberate the Jewish people, a task that requires the ability to communicate in vivid language, in words that function as pictures. It is therefore equally appropriate that his role is performed as a bel canto tenor whose singing is dramatic and highly colored.

Schoenberg was deeply interested in philosophy, particularly the writings of Kant, Schopenhauer, and Nietzsche, which were crucial in shaping his thinking, and a few words here about how these philosophers criticized traditional notions of reality will be useful.[21] For Kant it is impossible to know the underlying nature of reality, what he calls the *Ding an sich*, or "thing-in-itself," and all knowledge is necessarily limited to the *representations* humans make of reality: "Although I have no notion of such a connection of things in themselves [*Dinge an sich selbst*], how they can either exist as substances, or act as causes, or stand in community with others . . . we have yet a concept of such a connection of representations [*Vorstellungen*] in our understanding and in judgments generally."[22] It is important to understand that what Kant calls a *Vorstellung*—a representation in the philosophical sense—is nothing more than a mental construct of reality, a sensory datum that is defined by the categories of mind available to the perceiving subject. As Kant observes in *Critique of Pure Reason* (1787), "We have within us presentations [*Vorstellungen*] of which we can also become conscious. But no matter how far this consciousness may extend and how accurate and punctilious it may be, they still remain forever only presentations [*Vorstellungen*], i.e. inner determinations of our mind in this or that time relation."[23]

Schopenhauer, who owed a great debt to Kant, renders the Kantian notion of *Vorstellung* even more tenuous and uncertain in his magnum opus, *The World as Will and Representation* (*Die Welt als Wille und Vorstellung* [1818/1844]). Kant distinguishes between *phenomenal* reality—those sensory representations that are accessible to humans—and *noumenal* reality or the thing-in-itself.[24] For Schopenhauer, the ultimate reality, the Kantian *noumenon*, is Will, the unbounded and unformed energy that courses through the universe: "Eternal becoming, endless flux, belong to the revelation of the essential nature of the will."[25] Humans give shape and substance to reality by arresting the "endless flux," by transforming the "eternal becoming" into a stable and predictable world of Representation. But the categories of mind that we apply to reality, the representations that lend our experiences their solidity and objectivity, are illusory: "In truth everything objective is already conditioned as such in manifold ways by the knowing subject with the forms of its knowing, and presupposes these forms; consequently it wholly disappears when the subject is thought away."[26] No doubt Schoenberg was also greatly interested in Schopenhauer's view that music comes closer than any of the other arts to expressing the "endless flux" and "eternal becoming" precisely because it is less invested in representation than is painting or literature.[27]

In *The Birth of Tragedy* (1872), Nietzsche pushes Schopenhauer's argument further by associating Will with Dionysus and Representation with Apollo. Citing a passage from Schopenhauer that compares the Will to "a stormy sea" that is "unbounded in all directions" and Representation to the "*principium individuationis*," Nietzsche identifies Apollo as the "divine image" of this principle and Dionysus with its "collapse."[28] Later, in characterizing the tragic stage, Nietzsche speaks in terms that are unmistakably Kantian and Schopenhauerian in describing the relation between perception and reality: "We must understand Greek tragedy as the Dionysian chorus which ever anew discharges itself in an Apollinian world of images [*Bilderwelt*] . . . the scene [on stage], complete with the action, was basically and originally thought of merely as a *vision*; the chorus is the only 'reality' [*Realität*] and generates the vision."[29] Again, the dynamic and amorphous energy of nature is identified with a Dionysian "reality," the *Bilderwelt* of bounded and individuated images with the Apollinian realm of *Vorstellung*.[30] It also would not have escaped Schoenberg's attention that the original edition of *The Birth of Tragedy* bore the subtitle *Out of the Spirit of Music*, that the volume was dedicated to Richard Wagner, and that it implicitly compared Greek tragedy—which integrated the visual, musical, and verbal arts—with Wagner's *Gesamtkunstwerk*. Since Schoenberg's library included Nietzsche's *The Case of Wagner* and *Nietzsche contra Wagner*, he also knew that, four years after the publication of *The Birth of Tragedy*, Nietzsche radically revised his conception of Wagner, coming to see the composer not as the savior of modern music but as one of its most destructive influences.[31]

While Nietzsche's evaluation of Wagner and the influence it exercised

over Schoenberg are interesting in themselves, what needs to be emphasized here is that Schoenberg was intimately acquainted with a German
philosophical tradition that rejected representationalism, a tradition that regarded reality as unknowable in itself and that treated *Vorstellungen* as con-
structions that enable humans to constitute the world. Modernism's antirepresentationalism was, then, not an alien phenomenon imported by Jews
but a highly developed critique that emerged from within the very citadel
of German culture—the philosophy of Kant, Schopenhauer, and Nietzsche.
It is also worth remarking that not only was Nietzsche—whom National
Socialism distorted to the point of parody—one of the favorite philosophers
of the Third Reich but so too was Schopenhauer.[32]

The philosophical category of *Vorstellung*, most often presented in its
adjectival form (*vorstellbar* and *unvorstellbar*), as well as related metaphors
of seeing, picturing, and making visible, dominates *Moses und Aron*.[33] Act 1
of the opera begins with Moses invoking an "unsichtbarer und unvorstellbarer Gott" (imperceptible and unimaginable God; 112), and act 2 ends with
the same invocation: "Unvorstellbarer Gott" (194). Throughout the libretto
we encounter words like *Bild* and *bilden* (picture, to picture; 118, 166, 168,
182, 184, 186, 190, 194, 196, 198, 202), *Gebild* (vision; 118), *Abbild* (copy;
174), *Vorbild* (model; 174, 178), and *Form* (form; 158), along with variations
on *Vorstellung* and *vorstellbar* (112, 118, 120, 134, 146, 148, 156, 160, 194),
indicating how crucial the problem of philosophical representation is, especially *Vorstellung* conceived on the analogy of picture making. Indeed, these
words occur with such frequency that they begin to constitute something
like the equivalent of a verbal tone row, which Schoenberg permutes and
transmutes throughout the opera.

The fullest exposition of the Kantian and Schopenhauerian background
to *Moses und Aron* is to be found in Pamela White's *Schoenberg and the God-
Idea*, which focuses on such key words as Idea (*Gedanke*), Representation
(*Vorstellung*), and Language or Word (*Wort*).[34] In her view, the opera is Platonic in its philosophy, dividing the world between a transcendent reality
epitomized by *eidoi*, or Forms, and the phenomenal realm of everyday life
where we encounter the shadows of these Forms: "The concept of Idea is
used in this context as similar to the Platonic archetype—the artist draws
from another 'plane' where archetypal images are eternally pre-existent."[35] On
this reading, the God whom Moses attempts to know is equivalent to the
Truth that Plato seeks to discover. White's commentary is valuable for docu-

menting Schoenberg's philosophical borrowings from Kant and Schopenhauer, but I do not share her Platonic interpretation and argue—to the
contrary—that Schoenberg advances the critique of representationalism I
have traced in Kant, Schopenhauer, and Nietzsche.

As we have observed, the opera opens with Moses addressing God as
single and unitary—qualities attributed not only to the Hebrew deity but
also to Plato's World Creator in the *Timaeus*.[36] Hence, God's polyvocality
undermines both the Mosaic and Platonic understanding of the divine. Plato
regards the eidetic as accessible through reason, and while this realm can be
communicated only by analogy, it nevertheless is knowable.[37] By calling
into question Moses' account of a single and unitary God, indeed by directly
contradicting Moses (and at the all-important level of music), Schoenberg
aligns himself with Kant rather than Plato. For the former, the thing-in-itself
cannot be known, and therefore all sensory constructs or projections are
just that, the *Vor-stellung* or "placing-before" the subject of a constructed
world. In other words, implicit in Kant, developed in Schopenhauer, and
fully articulated in Nietzsche is a conception of reality that is not idealist but
constructionist.[38] As Nietzsche writes in "Truth and Lies in the Nonmoral
Sense," "The various languages placed side by side show that with words it
is never a question of truth, never a question of adequate expression; otherwise, there would not be so many languages. The 'thing in itself' (which is
precisely what the pure truth, apart from any of its consequences, would
be) is likewise something quite incomprehensible to the creator of language
and something not in the least worth striving for."[39] This constructionism is
also implicit in *The Birth of Tragedy* and explicit in other works by Nietzsche,
some of which Schoenberg owned.[40] Speaking more generally, we may say
that Schoenberg's opera takes up the post-Kantian critique of representationalism and examines it in depth. While both Moses and Aaron reject a
realist or objectivist conception of truth—the view that our sensory perceptions directly correspond to reality—each emphatically differs from the
other in the approach he takes to the problem of *Vorstellung*. It is to these
differences, and the debates that follow from them, that I now turn.

Noumenon versus Phenomenon

As we have observed, the central conflict in the opera turns on Moses'
commitment to the noumenal and Aaron's commitment to the phenomenal. Schoenberg takes a decidedly Kantian perspective in the first scene

between the brothers, a scene that dramatically illustrates the incommuni-
cability of these two realms as Moses and Aaron deliberately speak past one
another:

> MOSES: Other [gods] are to be found only in men, only in their representation
> [*Vorstellung*]. But it [the imagination] is not spacious enough to contain the
> Almighty.
>
> AARON: Form [*Gebilde*] of the loftiest imagining [*Phantasie*], how grateful it
> should be that you entice it to take shape [*zu bilden*].
>
> MOSES: No picture [*Bild*] can give you a picture [*Bild*] of the unrepresentable
> [*Unvorstellbaren*].
>
> AARON: Love will never weary of making a model of itself [*sich's vorzubilden*].
> Happy is the people that thus loves its God.
>
> MOSES: A people chosen to know the Unseen [*Unsichtbaren*], to think the Un-
> imaginable/Unrepresentable [*Unvorstellbaren*]. (118)

Here Schoenberg applies techniques of serialism to his text, focusing on
two words (*Vorstellung* and *Bild*) that he then permutes and transmutes (*Unvorstellbaren, Gebilde, bilden, vorbilden*) in ways that shift and alter their se-
mantic values—just as each iteration of a tone row plays variations on its
prime form.[41] Hence, Moses begins by observing that pagan deities can be
reduced to *Vorstellung* (in the sense of representation) but that for this reason they have existence only in *Vorstellung* (in the sense of imagination).
Aaron, seeming not to have heard his brother, commends the latter's desire
to give material shape (*bilden*) to a Form (*Gebilde*) of such lofty immateriality,
while Moses replies by reducing his language to its simplest terms, emphasizing the contradiction involved in attempting to make a picture (*Bild*) of
what cannot be pictured (*Unvorstellbaren*). Once more Aaron ignores Moses,
celebrating the power of love to produce a model (*vorbilden*) of itself, as
Moses celebrates the charge of the Jews to know what is Unseen (*Unsicht-
baren*) and think what is Unimaginable (*Unvorstellbaren*).

The following scene (act 1, scene 3) also foregrounds the problem of
Vorstellung as the Chorus describes the approach of Moses and Aaron:

> CHORUS: Does Aaron now stand by Moses?
> No, he hurries before him!
> Does Aaron walk by Moses' side?
> In front of him or behind him?
> They do not move in space.

Are closer,
Are further,
Are deeper,
Are higher,
Have completely vanished!
See Moses! See Aaron!
They are now here! (132, 134)

In this passage, the brothers function not as divine messengers so much as vaudeville philosophers, whose metaphysical pratfalls take apart those categories of time and space that Kant constructs at the beginning of *Critique of Pure Reason* and that he explicitly identifies with *Vorstellung*.[42] The larger effect of the scene—which plays a *fort-da* game with the a priori conditions of reality—is to show how fully the Jewish God is equated with, indeed seems to be the product of, Moses and Aaron. Hence, the two brothers enact not only the categories that make perception possible—stasis and kinesis, time and space, presence and absence—but also the limits of those categories, which they transcend by simultaneously standing and moving, being close and far, high and low—in short, all-in-all. But if this scene suggests that God—or the nature of reality—is constituted by the human mind (i.e., that it is nothing more than the construct of these brothers), then clearly Moses was wrong when he earlier asserted that the Jewish deity cannot be contained by the imagination (*Vorstellung*; 118). To the contrary, the Divine or Transcendent is a projection of consciousness, the placing-before or *Vorstellung* of Moses and Aaron. It is therefore appropriate that God is presented as the operatic analogue of the two brothers: just as he combines *Sprechstimme* and *Singstimme* in communicating with Moses, Moses and Aaron combine these two forms in communicating with each other.

Yet no matter how the Chorus views Moses and Aaron, the brothers themselves continue their debate on *Vorstellung* in the next scene (act 1, scene 4). Moses insists on the impersonality and abstractness of God ("Der . . . Unsichtbare, Unvorstellbare" [The invisible, unimaginable; 134]), while the people reject a deity they can neither see nor hear, and Moses complains that his "thought [*Gedanke*]" has become "powerless in Aaron's word" (140). Aaron responds by asserting the equivalence of saying and doing ("I am the word and the deed"; 140), an assertion he proves by using words to perform the deeds attributed to Moses in Exodus—in this case the transformation of the rod into the serpent, the healthy hand into the leprous hand,

and the water into the blood.[43] The performative notion that language can compel reality, that Aaron can translate *das Wort* into *die Tat*, is crucial to this scene, with the result that a transcendental abstraction becomes a concrete representation. As the chorus of men proclaims:

> So this God becomes imaginable [*vorstellbar*] to us,
> The symbol [*Sinnbild*] grows into the copy [*Abbild*] . . .
> Through Aaron Moses lets us see
> How he himself beholds God,
> So this God becomes imaginable [*vorstellbar*] to us,
> Attested by visible [*sichtbare*] wonders. (148)

But there is a problem. Although Aaron may understand his conjuring in purely allegorical terms, the people believe his miracles are real; for them the "symbol" (*Sinnbild*) becomes the literal representation or copy (*Abbild*) of the thing-itself.[44] As we shall see, Schoenberg regards such representational literalism as dangerous, since it enables a political leader to deceive the people through the manipulation of powerful or sensational images.

As act 2 opens in the wilderness, the Jewish people have grown restive waiting for Moses to return from the Mountain of Revelation. Again, the complaint turns to the problem of *Vorstellung*:

> Forty days we have now waited for Moses,
> And still no one knows justice or law!
> The unimaginable [*Unvorstellbares*] law of an unimaginable [*unvorstellbaren*]
> God! (156).

To placate the people, Aaron constructs the golden calf, but significantly, he does not treat it as the representation of a transcendent reality:

> This image [*Bild*] testifies
> That in everything that is a God lives . . .
> It little matters what shape [*Gestalt*] I have given it.
> Worship yourselves in this symbol [*Sinnbild*]. (166)

Any shape would have sufficed not because transcendent reality can be comprehended by an image but precisely because it cannot. Indeed, the notion that any number of images could have been substituted for the golden calf suggests the logic of the tone row—where no one note has priority over any other—and this in turn suggests the larger antimimetic logic of serialism, which by undermining traditional diatonic and chromatic composition undermines musical pictorialism of the kind one encounters in the Wagnerian leitmotif and the Straussian tone poem. But, again, it is important that the people neither regard the form of the calf as extrinsic to its meaning nor treat it as merely one in a series of interchangeable instantiations. Representational literalists, they view the calf as the material manifestation of the god, an *Abbild* rather than a *Sinnbild*, and they worship it with the expectation that it will perform miracles and demand sacrifices.

The return of Moses and the destruction of the golden calf set in motion the climactic confrontation between the brothers. Moses triumphantly proclaims, "Your image faded before my word" (184), to which Aaron responds:

> Your word [*Wort*] was formerly [*sonst*] denied images [*Bilder*]
> And miracle [*Wunder*], which you disdain.
> And yet the miracle [*Wunder*] was nothing more
> Than image [*Bild*]
> When your word [*Wort*] destroyed my image [*Bild*]. (186)

The passage owes its complexity to its simplicity: the fact that key words are repeated—much as the prime row is repeated in diverse forms—but in such a way that their meanings are permuted and varied. Hence, while Aaron observes that Moses has finally experienced the illocutionary power of language—the ability of words (his utterance that the golden calf "begone") to compel things—it is worth noticing that *Wunder* itself undergoes a subtle transmutation. In the first sentence, the word refers to the "miracle" of language's transformative power, its ability to effect change in the world, whereas in the second sentence it is the equivalent of Aaron's *Bild*, the golden calf that its worshipers regard as a "wonder" or "miracle." Indeed, by the conclusion of the speech, *Wunder*, *Bild*, and *Wort* have become interchangeable, the performative consequences of manipulating tools within a language game.

As the debate continues, it becomes evident that Moses, the philosophical idealist, is dedicated exclusively to his abstract God, while Aaron, the philosophical pragmatist, feels a genuine commitment to the Jewish people:

> MOSES: Do you begin to grasp the omnipotence of
>   Thought over words and images?
> AARON: Here is what I understand:
>   This people shall survive.
>   But a people can only know through their senses.[45]

I love this people,

I live for them,

And will save them. (186)

Moses counters that he "loves" and "lives for" his "idea" (*Gedanken*; 186), which he identifies with the tablets of the Decalogue. But Aaron points out that the tablets undermine the transcendental nature of the idea, since as material and verbal entities they are "also an image" and therefore a metonym for God—a mere "part of the idea." While Moses responds by destroying the Decalogue, his brother observes that the tablets are the "images of your thought," indeed that they *are* the thought ("they are it"; 190). Once more, Aaron has demonstrated that there is no outside to the language game—that even ideas depend on words and images.

With the appearance of the pillars of fire and cloud that will guide the Jewish people out of the Wilderness, Moses' idealism is finally undone. For him these manifestations are "Götzenbilder" (194), not images of God but the idols of pagan worship. Of course, the audience knows that the pillars of fire and cloud are not false appearances but true signs sent to lead the Jewish people to the promised land—which means that Moses is himself refuted by the text of Exodus. As the people abandon Moses, he turns to God and utters the concluding words of act 2:

Unimaginable [*Unvorstellbarer*] God!

Inexpressible and ambiguous thought!

Do you permit this interpretation [*Auslegung*]?

May Aaron, my mouth, fashion this image [*Bild*]?

I too have made an image [*Bild*],

False,

As an image [*Bild*] can only be!

Thus am I defeated!

Thus, everything that I thought

Was madness

And cannot and must not be spoken!

O word, thou word, that I lack!

(*He sinks despairing to ground.*) (194)

Moses' usual address to God consists of the formula, "Singular, eternal, omnipresent, imperceptible and unimaginable" (112). But here the stately

procession of adjectives is reduced to a single, overdetermined word—
Unvorstellbarer—as Moses internalizes this "omnipresent" being, treating
him as a thought so vague ("Inexpressible and ambiguous") as to resist ver-
balization and therefore conceptualization. In effect, Moses half admits
what Aaron has long asserted: that pure intellection does not exist; that *any*
effort to conceive or describe God relies on sensory categories, which is to
say on the contingency of representation. Unable to reconcile his idealism
with Aaron's nominalism, Moses cries out for what he lacks—revealingly
not a thought but a word. In acknowledging his defeat, he acknowledges
that language is the prior category.

How to approach act 3 of the opera poses serious problems in terms of
both interpretation and staging. Schoenberg never scored the act, but
shortly before his death indicated his willingness to have it "performed
without music, simply spoken."[46] The scene is set in the wilderness, before
the Jews have entered the Promised Land, and Aaron, a prisoner in chains,
has been accused of corrupting the youth of Zion. We hear nothing of the
serious debate that the brothers carried on earlier. Aaron utters a few words
in his defense, but Moses peremptorily cuts him off, using his power to silence dissent. Still, it appears that Moses has modified his earlier position,
since the charge against Aaron is not that he uses word and image but that
he uses them inappropriately; that in his case "images . . . govern / The idea
instead of *expressing* it," suggesting that the latter is permissible (202; emphasis mine). As Moses elaborates:

> Images lead [*führen*] and rule
> This people, whom you have freed,
> And foreign [*führen*] wishes are their gods,
> And lead [*führen*] them back to the slavery
> Of godlessness and pleasure. (202)

Again, the objection that Moses raises is not against images per se but
against those that lead astray, especially alien or foreign images that have a
corrupting influence. Such language obviously invokes the discourse against
degenerate art, suggesting uncomfortable analogies between Moses' doctrinal and aesthetic purity and that of the Nazis. It should also be pointed out
that Moses is no longer the abstracted idealist but a leader who understands
the efficacy of political rhetoric, even of judicial clemency. Thus, when the
soldiers ask whether they should execute Aaron, Moses replies, "Set him

free, and if he is able, he will live" (204). For no apparent reason, Aaron is
unable to live and collapses at his brother's feet. Moses concludes by com-
mending his people:

> But in the wilderness you are invincible
> And will reach your goal: atonement with God. (204)

The last act appears to represent the triumph of Moses' idealism over
Aaron's pragmatism, but this triumph is heavily qualified, if not decisively
undercut. First, there is the lack of music. It is difficult to believe that at
some level this was not intentional on Schoenberg's part. From 1932 when
he "interrupted" his work on the opera until his death, Schoenberg had
nineteen years in which to score approximately four and half pages of text.
Nor were these years of diminished productivity, including as they did the
Violin Concerto (1934-36), String Quartet no. 4 (1936), Kol Nidre (1938), the
Chamber Symphony (1939), Ode to Napoleon (1942), the Piano Concerto
(1942), the Prelude for Orchestra (1945), A Survivor from Warsaw (1947),
Driemal Tausend Jahre (1949), and De profundis (1950). Surely, if he had
wanted to score the brief coda that is act 3, he could have managed this
task. Obviously, we can only speculate on why Schoenberg did not "finish"
his greatest masterpiece, but one explanation is that it was already finished
—that the musical silence of this final scene is both deliberate and eloquent.[47] For in leaving act 3 unscored, Schoenberg reveals that Moses' triumph means the suppression of the sensuous and therefore the suppression
of music itself. As long as Moses' asceticism was counterbalanced by Aaron's
aestheticism—as long as Sprechstimme was answered by Singstimme—the
music continues. But, once song is vanquished, we are left with only text,
an outcome that suggests Schoenberg was not of Moses' party.

Another feature of act 3 that appears to undercut Moses' triumph is its
bizarre conclusion. In an opera that has not participated in the conventions
of melodrama, indeed that has resolutely resisted baroque or flamboyant
plot elements, Aaron's abrupt and unmotivated death strikes a decidedly
false note. One way to make sense of this otherwise puzzling ending is to
read it as an ironic rewriting of the final scene of Parsifal, an opera that
Schoenberg himself links with Moses und Aron.[48] It will be remembered that
Parsifal concludes as the title hero heals Amfortas and restores to him his
lance, whereupon Kundry collapses and dies. In Wagner's most Christian
opera, spiritualism represented by Parsifal triumphs over sensuality represented by Kundry. Indeed, Kundry's sudden death makes dramatic sense

only if we assume that she has in some sense chosen it, that in being converted to Parsifal's spiritualism she has abandoned her bodily existence. A
similar kind of logic seems to be at work in the case of Aaron, who appears
to die on cue when Moses "magnanimously" grants him his freedom, while
ominously warning that he will live only "if he is able" (204). In other words,
Schoenberg appears to reproduce the *staginess* of Kundry's death, but
where Wagner strives to incorporate this death into the dramatic texture of
his story, Schoenberg underscores its forced, even ludicrous, theatricality.
The result is ironically to distance the audience from Schoenberg's own
conclusion, thereby further undercutting Moses' victory.[49]

Finally, act 3 ends with this proclamation, addressed by Moses to the
Jewish people:

> But in the wasteland [*Wüste*] you are invincible
> And will reach your goal:
> Atonement with God. (204)

Confronted with these words, the audience cannot fail to realize how thoroughly Moses has misunderstood the historical destiny of the Jewish people, which is to become a nation by establishing a homeland. Since the end
of act 1, Moses has preferred the wasteland to the homeland ("In the wasteland purity/Of thought will nourish, sustain and advance you"; 150), and
the fate he now conceives for his people ("Atonement with God") is exclusively spiritual. Yet the audience knows both from Exodus and from the
beginning of the opera that Moses has misinterpreted his divine mandate
(*Auftrag*; 114), which is presented in practical and political terms: "You must
free your people from [their enslavement]" (112). In other words, Moses'
insistence on ideological purity above all else constitutes a betrayal not only
of the Jewish people but also of God himself.

The reading I have developed in this section is more critical of Moses and
more sympathetic toward Aaron than many commentaries on the opera.[50]
Here I would like to emphasize two points, one historical and one philosophical. In Schoenberg's drama, *Der biblische Weg* (*The Biblical Way* [1926]),
written the year before he started work on *Moses und Aron*, he makes clear
how fully committed he was to the establishment of a Jewish homeland.
The hero of the play is Max Aruns, a name that serves as a composite of
Moses and Aaron. While Schoenberg's play acknowledges the difficulty of
reconciling the beliefs of these two strikingly different characters, it also
recognizes that some combination of idealism and pragmatism is necessary

if the Jews of Europe are to deliver themselves from an impending catastro-phe.[51] For Schoenberg, Moses' allegiance to Jewish law and thought is ad-mirable, but his obsession with doctrinal purity is ultimately destructive, a point Schoenberg emphasizes not only in his drama but also in his political writings.[52]

From a philosophical perspective, the debate between Moses and Aaron turns on the problem of *Vorstellung*, in which Moses plays the Platonic ideal-ist and Aaron the Nietzschean pragmatist.[53] But Moses' position, even from a Platonic perspective, is extreme. He believes, at least through the first two acts, that any representation of a transcendent reality is a misrepresen-tation and therefore to be condemned, a position far more absolutist than Plato's.[54] As we have seen, Aaron favors a contingent system of representa-tion, images (*Bilder*) that function not as literal copies (*Abbilder*) but as con-structed symbols (*Sinnbilder*), a view consistent with the philosophical cri-tique initiated by Kant and carried forward by Schopenhauer and Nietzsche.

The aesthetic consequences of the critique of representation are compli-cated. Both brothers reject a simple mimesis, the idea that there is a direct correspondence between *Vorstellung* and the *Ding an sich*. Schoenberg does not, however, align himself with either of his title characters. Moses' com-mitment to abstraction is so uncompromising that it ultimately leads to the end of music, exemplified both by Moses' use of *Sprechstimme* and an un-scored third act. By way of contrast, Aaron understands better than his brother the contingency of representation, but Schoenberg is equally criti-cal of his penchant for conjuring up striking images, for pursuing a mimesis that is dangerously incarnational. What Schoenberg seeks and his opera delivers is a compromise between Moses' rigorous abstractionism and Aar-on's seductive pictorialism. Twelve-tone composition made available pre-cisely that compromise. On the one hand, such composition decisively un-dermines the tonality that enabled late nineteenth-century and early twentieth-century composers to paint sound pictures. On the other hand, Schoenberg's music retains enough expressive force that it can register emotions, even suggest objects and events, without falling into the vulgar mimesis of musical realism or naturalism. In other words, Schoenberg's mu-sical evocations stand, as it were, in quotation marks, carrying within them-selves their own *Verfremdungseffekt*. Precisely how Schoenberg achieves the delicate balance between abstraction and expression, between Moses and Aaron, is deeply implicated in his opera's engagement with a composer much admired by both Schoenberg and the Nazis—Richard Wagner. And this engagement with Wagner returns us to the question with which we began: How is Schoenberg's modernism related to his Judaism?

Modernism and Judaism

Schoenberg's interest in Judaism has been extensively documented, and while the story is familiar it will be useful to touch upon some of the high points here.[55] Although Schoenberg was born to Jewish parents and his birth was recorded in the register of the Viennese Jewish community, he converted to Protestantism in 1898, probably under the influence of his friend Walter Pieau, who acted as his godfather at the baptism ceremony. Schoenberg's relation with the Lutheran Dorotheerkirche lasted approximately three and a half years, until he moved to Berlin in 1902. As White notes, "Schoenberg's Christianity appears to have been more formal than deeply convicted: his involvement with Dehmel and the expressionistic group shortly after this time and through the 1920s led him easily through various stages of existentialism, German rational philosophy, theosophy, mysticism, and other diverse modes of religious and philosophical thought."[56] A decisive shift in Schoenberg's sense of his religious and ethnic identity occurred, however, in 1921 in Mattsee, Austria, when he was denied a room at a resort hotel because of his Jewish background. Goldstein observes, "That experience proved so traumatic that two years later he turned down a very desirable invitation from his friend Wassily Kandinsky to join the Bauhaus cultural center in Weimar because of reports of antisemitism."[57] In a letter to Kandinsky, he wrote, "For I have at last learnt the lesson that has been forced upon me during this year, and I shall not ever forget it. It is that I am not a German, not a European, indeed perhaps scarcely even a human being (at least, the Europeans prefer the worst of their race to me), but I am a Jew. I am content that it should be so!"[58] So consequential did the issue of European Jewry become for Schoenberg that around this time he began to conceive *The Biblical Way*, which explicitly deals with the founding of a new Jewish homeland. The hero of the work is modeled after Theodor Herzl, and the play dramatizes Schoenberg's view that assimilation was a failed strategy for European Jews and that their only hope for salvation lay in the establishment of a Jewish state.

After fleeing to Paris in 1933, Schoenberg reconverted to Judaism in a well-publicized act, but, as he wrote in a letter to Alban Berg the conversion had effectively taken place years earlier, "As you have doubtless realised, my return to the Jewish religion took place long ago and is indeed demonstrated by my published work ('Thou shalt not . . . Thou shalt') and in 'Moses and Aaron,' of which you have known since 1928, but which dates from at least five years earlier; but especially in my drama 'Der biblische Weg' [*The Biblical Way*] which was conceived in 1922 or '23 at the latest, though finished only in '26-'27."⁵⁹ "Thou shalt not, thou must" is the second of "Four Pieces for Mixed Chorus," composed in 1925, and its reference to the second commandment's prohibition against making images reveals how fully he identified Judaism with antirepresentationalism. Indeed, the text of the song, written by Schoenberg himself, sounds like a preview to *Moses und Aron*:

> Thou shalt make no image!
> For an image confines
> limits, grasps
> what should remain unlimited and unrepresentable [*unvorstellbar*].⁶⁰

In other words, by the time Schoenberg began to write *Moses und Aron*, he was committed not only to Judaism but also to the cause of Jewish liberation, which is of course the central theme of Exodus.

In *Reinscribing Moses*, Goldstein speculates that Schoenberg composed *Moses und Aron* in response to "experiences of growing antisemitism and the rise of National Socialism."⁶¹ She goes on to observe that the "prohibition against making images is especially important not merely for a person returning to Judaism . . . but for those who had everything to fear from the Nazis and their preoccupation with symbols, ritual, and worship of heroes and idols" (165). I have argued that of central importance to Schoenberg's experiences of this time was the Nazi assault on antirepresentationalism in modernism, an assault that was already under way well before the *Entartete Kunst* and *Entartete Musik* exhibitions of 1937-38. In the area of musicology, two works were of crucial importance in defining what the Nazis regarded as the Jewish influence on music. In 1926, Hans Pfitzner published *Die neue Aesthetik der musikalischen Impotenz* (The new aesthetic of musical impotence), a work that, according to Michael Meyer, took "an alarmist reaction in the 1920s to the disintegration of tonality—dissonance, twelve-tone theory, and alien jazz."⁶² Meyer continues, "Pfitzner spoke for many, and anticipated an important argument of the National Socialists, when he attributed this 'musical chaos,' a symbol of threats to civilization itself, to an active anti-German international conspiracy. His radical conservative defense of traditional harmony, melody, and inspiration (all claimed as characteristically German) and his attack on subversive atonality and jazz (identified with Bolsheviks, Americanism, and Jews) were reformulated in racialist terms by the Nazis with little violence to the original."[63] The other work that helped provide a background for the exhibitions of 1937–38 was Richard Eichenauer's *Musik und Rasse* (Music and race), published in 1932. As Meyer observes, Eichenauer "associated 'degenerate' modern music with the Jews, who were 'following a law of their race.' Music was assumed to reveal fixed, racially defined German characteristics and their Jewish opposites."[64]

Of course, standing behind Pfitzner and Eichenauer was the paterfamilias of musical anti-Semitism, Richard Wagner, who in 1850 published "Judaism in Music," which he revised and reissued in 1869. So vicious and vituperative is Wagner's essay that it is easy to dismiss it as nothing more than a toxic piece of anti-Semitism, yet the essay repays analysis since it brings together all the elements of the National Socialist polemic against Jews and music. Wagner begins with the question, "Why does the European feel '*involuntary repellence*' toward and 'instinctive repugnance' against 'the Jew's prime essence'?"[65] The answer, he suggests, is to be found in the unnaturalness of the Jew, an "unpleasant freak of Nature" (83) who is incapable either of "purely human expression" or "mutual interchange of feelings" (85). Wagner develops this claim within a musical context, observing that while "Song is just Talk aroused to the highest passion" and "Music is the speech of Passion," the "Jew is almost [altogether] incapable of giving artistic enunciation to his feelings" (86).[66] Yet, despite an incapacity for artistic expression, the Jew has been able "to reach the rulership of public taste," even to extend his influence to performance and composition through a talent for imitation (87). Hence, he mimes musical forms and intonations, "as parrots reel off human words and phrases" but with as little "feeling and expression as those foolish birds" (89), listening to "the barest surface of our art, but not to its life-bestowing inner organism" (92). What ultimately emerges from Wagner's essay is a familiar portrait of the Jew as cosmopolitan. A wanderer on the earth, cut off from the rhythms of the land and isolated from the restorative life of the "people," he creates an etiolated kind of art, an artificial, hothouse growth that is kept alive by a coterie of connoisseurs, who prefer abstraction to emotion, form to substance. What Wagner describes as the degenerate art of the Jew—all effect and no affect—the Nazis gave another name. They called it modernism.[67]

Deconstructing Wagner

In 1935 Schoenberg opened a lecture on the "Jewish situation" with these remarks:

> When we young Austrian-Jewish artists grew up, our self-esteem suffered very much from the pressure of certain circumstances. It was the time when Richard Wagner's work started its victorious career, and the success of his music and poems was followed by an infiltration of his *Weltanschauung*, of his philosophy. You were no true Wagnerian if you did not believe in his philosophy, in the ideas of *Erlösung durch Liebe*, salvation by love; you were not a true Wagnerian if you did not believe in *Deutschtum*, in Teutonism; and you could not be a true Wagnerian without being a follower of his anti-Semitic essay, *Das Judentum in der Musik*, "Judaism in Music."[68]

Schoenberg greatly admired the musical genius of Wagner, whom he counted among his chief influences, but his relation to the composer was complicated. Certainly Wagner's chromaticism did more than any other development in the nineteenth century to break the back of musical tonality, thereby opening the way for the New Music of Bruckner, Mahler, Debussy, Strauss, and Schoenberg.[69] Yet Wagner's operas, with their nationalist emphasis on Teutonic mythology and their celebration of epic heroism and, later, Christian virtue, stand at a great distance from Schoenberg's own sensibility. A particular source of ambivalence is the leitmotif. For Schoenberg this repeating element—which he compares to the tone row—was a brilliant formal innovation, which enabled Wagner to write longer operas that nevertheless retain their musical coherence.[70] But Schoenberg believed that the leitmotif is musically regressive insofar as it functions as an aural signature, music at its most reductively descriptive and mimetic. The galumphing march of the giants, the flowing strains of the Rheinmaidens, the fiery and mercurial dance of Loge all seem to mime reality, particularly the primal forces of nature. With the leitmotif, especially as it is used in *Der Ring des Nibelungen*, representation and reality appear to coalesce, as though music is finally performing the task Schopenhauer assigned it: rendering transparent the inner structure of the universe, the Will that underlies and animates all things.

Of course, Schoenberg's own music, even those compositions written in the dodecaphonic style, possesses descriptive and emotive force.[71] The problem with Wagnerian pictorialism is not its expressive or mimetic character but its claim to representational transcendence, as though it has ascended, Erda-like, from the chthonian depths and is singing the music of nature itself. With the leitmotif, representation, so far from acknowledging its own contingency, treats itself as a substitute for, indeed as a manifestation of, the thing-itself. Such representational literalism is from Schoenberg's perspective philosophically naïve, musically vulgar, and politically dangerous.[72] Needless to say, National Socialism offers no methodical account of the epistemology of representation, but the Nazis' *Blut und Boden* ideology assumes that art can directly connect the viewer or auditor with the deep structure of reality, whether this consists of the primal patterns of Nature or the enduring wisdom of *das Volk*. It is also worth remembering that Wagner's music played a central role in the Nazi propaganda effort to fuse ritual and myth with politics. In this regard, the leitmotif is a remarkably effective tool. The ease with which it is recognized makes it well suited for a mass audience, and its musical literalism ("heavy" music for the giants, "light" music for Loge) gives the impression that Wagner has, in a few deft phrases, disclosed the types and symbols of eternity.

It will be remembered that in responding to the Nazis' polemic on *entartete Kunst*, Schoenberg argues that it is not modernism's rejection of the image that leads to moral degeneracy but precisely the opposite: the summoning up of images that are treated as revelations of the thing-itself. In *Moses und Aron*, the two most obvious examples of this kind of representational literalism are the conjuring that Aaron performs in the first act and the construction of the golden calf in the second act. It is no accident that these scenes, which equate degeneracy with image making, both involve allusions to the man who invented the leitmotif—that ultimate act of musical conjuring. Of course, Schoenberg had a long history of drawing upon Wagner's music, and such early compositions as *Verklärte Nacht* (1899), *Gurre Lieder* (1901), and *Pelleas und Melisande* (1903) are unmistakably Wagnerian in their inspiration and construction.[73] But by the time Schoenberg composed *Von heute auf morgen* (1929), the twelve-tone opera that immediately precedes *Moses und Aron*, he was no longer imitating Wagner but quoting him directly and to devastatingly ironic effect.[74] Schoenberg adopts a similar approach in *Moses und Aron*, but here the allusions are not identified in the text, and they involve travesties of Wagner's music rather than direct citations. It is also significant that the allusions focus on passages drawn from *Der Ring des Nibelungen*, Wagner's most nationalist and anti-Semitic opera.

Figure 7.1. Dragon motif, *Siegfried*

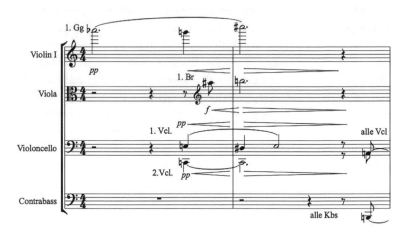

Figure 7.2. Rod and snake motif, *Moses und Aron*

The first of these allusions occurs in act 1, scene 4, where Schoenberg employs (mm. 706–07) a parodied version of the Dragon motif from *Siegfried*, as Aaron transforms Moses' rod into a snake (figs. 7.1 and 7.2).[75] In Wagner the semitone movement in the first half of the phrase, combined with the slow tempo (dotted half notes), gives the impression of something gradually unfolding, while the resolution of the phrase in a minor third emphasizes the dragon's menacing and demonic quality. Schoenberg briefly quotes this passage in truncated form in the violins, preserving the dotted half note, only in his version (he has shifted registers) he begins on the second note of the Dragon motif. To preserve the Wagnerian progression, the phrase should be G-Ab-G-Bb, but Schoenberg displaces the final note to a C#, producing a diminished fifth rather than a minor third. He then gives us the full Wagnerian phrase in inverted form in the cellos (E-D#-E-A), again displacing the minor third with a fifth.

Underlying Schoenberg's musical allusion to Wagner is a textual analogy. Just as Fafner has transformed himself into a dragon (or *Wurm* in German), Aaron has transformed the rod into a snake. When we forget the metaphoric status of words, when we insist on turning an abstraction (the power of Moses' rod) into a concrete object (a snake), we begin to act as mere conjurers. Eduard Hanslick, the music critic, whose writings Schoenberg knew and admired, had condemned Wagner for being more magician than musician—for employing cheap stage tricks to achieve theatrical effects— and here the leitmotif functions as a wonderful device for bodying forth the ominously uncoiling dragon.[76] In other words, Wagner's use of the leitmotif is the equivalent of Aaron's conjuring, which means that the devotees of Bayreuth are no less credulous than are the Jews of the Sinai. Especially noteworthy are the reactions of three characters to Aaron's sorcery. The Girl rapturously affirms that "[Moses] will free us" (144), while the Young Man swears fealty to his "Führer" (142) with the words "we want to serve him" (144), as the Man promises to "make a sacrifice to him" (144). Schoenberg's point is especially revealing in the context of 1930s Germany: a naive mimeticism that collapses the distinction between the figurative and the literal exposes a people to political manipulation that is dangerous and potentially despotic.

The second allusion I want to discuss centers on the scene with the golden calf, when a character called the Naked Youth carries off a woman whom he is about to rape, as he proclaims:

In your image, gods,
We live up to love! (178)

There follows in measure 918 in the woodwinds and strings, and in measure 921 in the woodwinds and brass, a figure that parodies the Siegfried leitmotif from the opera of that title. Figures 7.3 and 7.4 show the passages from Wagner and Schoenberg.[77] The Siegfried motif is built around a G-major triad, beginning with an arpeggiated chord in which the notes are played in the 1-5-3 positions, followed by a series of triplets that ascend the scale, ultimately returning to the tonic G. Schoenberg begins with Wagner's 1-5-3 triad but contracts the fifth by a whole step and the third by a half step, producing a distorted and diminished version of Siegfried's rousing motif. He then parodies Wagner's climbing triplets, substituting a series of rising notes that alternately point toward and displace harmonic resolution. Schoenberg begins his ascent on a B♭, establishing—however fleetingly—a tonal center around the E♭ triad. He then undermines that tonal center with a minor second (B♭ to B), seems to reclaim it with a major second that repeats itself (B to D♭, D♭), and then instead of converging on the tonic an

Figure 7.3. Siegfried motif, *Siegfried*

Figure 7.4. Naked Youth motif, *Moses und Aron*

octave up (as Wagner does) plunges his motif into the crashing dissonance of a seventh (D♭ to E). Musically speaking, the effect of Schoenberg's rewriting of Wagner is to take a noble and gracefully articulated hunting call and reconfigure it as a hectic and lecherous hoot. At the level of text, Schoenberg has worked a similar transformation. By equating Siegfried with the Naked Youth, Schoenberg reimagines Wagner's ideal warrior hero—and by extension the Nazi ideal of German manhood—as a brutal gang rapist. Again, it is significant that the Naked Youth's degenerate behavior results from his exposure not to the intellectual bohemianism of abstract art but to its opposite—a vulgar and kitschy representationalism, embodied by the golden calf.

The last musical travesty of Wagner also occurs in the golden calf scene and involves another one of the Nazis' most cherished symbols. If Siegfried represents an ideal of German masculinity, the Rheinmaidens represent an ideal of German femininity, identified through their flowing music with nature and the Life Force. Wagner uses two related motifs to describe his water nymphs—the Rheinmaidens motif and the "Rheinmaidens' Song"— but it is the latter, sung at the end of *Rheingold* (see fig. 7.5), that becomes the focus of Schoenberg's parody.[78]

The "Rheinmaidens' Song" is constructed around an A-♭ triad, beginning with a stately and declamatory rhythm (dotted half and quarter notes give emphatic shape to the refrain "Rhein -gold!"), as the melody coyly hovers above the triad moving between the sixth and the fifth, before relaxing into quarter and eventually eighth notes that flow into the tonal center of the motif (in the third and fourth measures shown in fig. 7.5, we move from A♭

Figure 7.5. "Rheinmaidens' Song," *Das Rheingold*

through G and F to E♭ and then down to C). Schoenberg parodies the "Rheinmaidens' Song" in his own "Song of the Four Naked Virgins" (fig. 7.6). Textually, the passages are closely related. The Rheinmaidens open with "Rhein-gold! Rhein-gold!" (250), while the Four Naked Virgins open (at mm. 780–85) with "Oh gol-den-er Gott, oh Prie-ster gol-de-ner Göt-ter" (176), and both proceed to sing the praises of the gold they worship. Because Schoenberg coordinates four singers rather than three and gives each a separate melodic line, it is difficult to hear the quotation of Wagner, but even the casual listener is struck not only by the similarity in text but also by the choral effect of multiple female voices. The more attentive listener will also detect in Schoenberg's Virgins a recurrent use of precisely the same A♭ triad that dominates the "Rheinmaidens' Song." Schoenberg has, however, introduced a crucial modification. By expanding the three voices to four, he is able to bend and distort Wagner's triadic structure. Hence in measure 780, which opens the scene with the Naked Virgins, three of the voices sing a chordal version of the A♭ triad, which is then knocked off tonal center as the second alto adds a dissonant D. In measure 785, Schoenberg produces almost the same chordal progression, only he displaces it further from the A♭ triad, converting the C♭ to a C# and the D to an F. In measure 786, he works another variation on measure 780, but here he combines the decentering D with an A as opposed to an A♭ chord. He further elaborates the A♭ triad—now in arpeggiated form at measures 787 and 788—where the second soprano sings A♭–D–E♭ (taking the third of the triad up a whole), and then E♭ and an emphatically repeated A♮, producing a slightly displaced version of the triad's dominant and tonic. Finally, measure 796 offers a chordal version of the A♮ triad with an A♭ sounded by the second soprano.

    Equating the Rheinmaidens and the Four Virgins has much the same effect as equating Siegfried and the Naked Youth. Schoenberg plays the Rhein-

Figure 7.6. "Song of the Four Naked Virgins," *Moses und Aron* (a) m. 780,
(b) m. 785–88, and (c) m. 796

maidens but off key, treating them not as emanations of nature or acolytes
of solar joyfulness but as fetishists for whom the gold has become a form of
idolatrous celebration. And again, the degeneration into mass hysteria and
ritualistic bloodletting that follow are inspired not by the destruction of the
image but by its cultic worship, especially the worship of an image that
represents the primal forces of nature.

The three moments of travesty I've examined are revealing because they
illustrate Schoenberg's critique not only of Wagner but also of the emerging
aesthetic of National Socialism. This aesthetic invested tremendous importance in a vulgar pictorialism, which for a critic like Hanslick was exemplified by the leitmotif. Again, while Schoenberg recognizes the musical genius
of Wagner, he was uneasy with the latter's representational literalism, which
too often presented itself as naturalism. That naturalism took on special
meaning, given Wagner's pronouncements on the denatured and deracinated
Jew, whose cosmopolitanism, Wagner believed, would have made it impossible for a composer like Schoenberg to create significant or original music.

Representing the Unrepresentable

In the foregoing pages, I have argued that *Moses und Aron* mounts an
extended critique of the Nazi polemic on *entartete Kunst*, a polemic that
identified modernism with antirepresentationalism and antirepresentationalism with the Jew. By deliberately embracing these facile and false equa-
tions, Schoenberg connects the second commandment's prohibition against
image making with one of the most influential traditions in German phi-

losophy, the post-Kantian critique of *Vorstellung* that would eventually open the way to Wittgenstein's language game. Schoenberg's opera aligns itself neither entirely with Moses' perspective nor with Aaron's. Moses' abstractionism leads to the end of sensuous art, a third act in which the music has fallen silent; while Aaron's pictorialism leads to the end of serious art, a debased and vulgar mimeticism, the kind of sensationalism that took its inspiration from Wagner's *Gesamtkunstwerk* and found its ultimate expression in Leni Riefenstahl's mythological cinema and Albert Speer's monumental architecture.

In *Language and Silence*, George Steiner suggests that Moses' concluding utterance in act 2—"O word, word that I lack!"—acknowledges the inability of language to articulate the historical horror looming on the European horizon.[79] What I have attempted to show, contra Steiner, is how amply and eloquently Schoenberg resists a discourse that sought to destroy not only modernism but also European Jewry. Confronted with crises that were political, cultural, and philosophical, Schoenberg nevertheless found the words and the music to image forth an experience that would soon become, in the fullest sense, *unvorstellbar*—inconceivable, unimaginable, unrepresentable.

Notes

I would like to thank Michael Bane for his valuable comments and criticisms on this essay.

1. 1500 BCE is a rough approximation of the Mosaic era.

2. Reich 42. Schoenberg's expressionist operas are *Erwartung* (1909) and *Die glückliche Hand* (1913). Schoenberg's contributions to the almanac were his composition *Herzgewächse* (op. 20) and the essay "Das Verhältnis zum Text," later published as "The Relationship to the Text" in Schoenberg, *Style and Idea* (141-45).

3. Reich 40-42, 84, 105, 124-25. When Schoenberg contemplated turning his opera *Die glückliche Hand* into a film, he considered both Kokoschka and Kandinsky as possible set designers (Reich 84). For Schiele's wonderfully evocative portrait of Schoenberg, see Reich 53.

4. See especially Hans Pfitzner's *Die neue Aesthetik der musikalishen Impotenz* [The new aesthetic of musical impotence], published in 1926, which equated atonality with Jewishness and "musical impotence" (*Gesammelte Schriften* 101-281). Also important, although it did not appear until 1932, was Richard Eichenauer's *Musik und Rasse* [Music and race], which specifically mentions Schoenberg as an example of the "Jewish" trend in music (273). Of course, the discourse on *Entartung* may be traced back to Max Nordau's book of that title (published 1892). There is a certain irony in

the fact that Nordau, who was Jewish and regarded both Nietzsche and Wagner as instances of "degeneration," is largely responsible for inaugurating the discourse of *Entartung* in the German-speaking world. See Nordau. For an excellent account of *Entartete Kunst* and *Entartete Musik* exhibitions, see Barron, *"Degenerate Art."*

5. The *Entartete Kunst* catalogue connected modernism not only with Jewish influences but also with Africanism and Bolshevism; see *Entartete Kunst*.

6. Ibid. 16.

7. In German, to be *gestalterisch* is to be "creative" or "artistic."

8. *Entartete Kunst* 20.

9. In Barron, "Modern Art and Politics in Prewar Germany" 9.

10. The census figures are quoted in Meyer, "A Musical Facade for the Third Reich" 172.

11. Ibid.

12. Schoenberg's letter of resignation was dated 20 Mar. 1933 (Reich 187).

13. Meyer 172-73.

14. Ibid. 173.

15. Schoenberg completed the second act of *Moses und Aron* in 1932. His only other musical compositions before leaving Germany were an arrangement of a concerto by Georg Matthias Monn and three songs (op. 48); see Reich 184-85. Although his focus is not specifically on "degenerate art," Herbert Lindenberger's *"Moses und Aron, Mahagonny*, and Germany in the 1930s: Seventeen Entries" demonstrates with great specificity how fully Schoenberg's opera responded to the history and culture of the period (*Opera in History* 191-239).

16. See Benjamin; Brecht; Glock; Wittgenstein.

17. Adorno discusses the *Bilderverbot* in various works, including *Negative Dialectics* and *The Dialectic of the Enlightenment*, as well as examining this theme in Schoenberg in his essay "Sacred Fragment: Schoenberg's *Moses und Aron*" in *Quasi una Fantasia: Essays on Modern Music*. As Elizabeth Pritchard writes, "Adorno's endorsement of the *Bilderverbot* is a qualified one. Adorno points out—long before his critical successors—the political liabilities of the image ban. Adorno observes that the *Bilderverbot*, which was to serve the ends of demythologization, had itself recoiled into myth" (297).

18. While commentators agree that the opera deals with the crisis of representation, their emphases are different: Adorno focuses on the inability to achieve a totalizing representation or image in a secularized and fragmented world (*Quasi una Fantasia* 225-58); Albright views the opera as a self-reflective examination of the tension between representation and imagination; Janik and Toulmin (102-12), along with Botstein, stress the importance of language to epistemology in relation to Viennese language-critique; Goldstein is principally concerned with "communicating the idea of an ineffable deity through language" ("Word, Image, Idea" 152; "Schoenberg's *Moses und Aron*"); HaCohen links the opera's "phenomenological and semiotic con-

siderations" to its aesthetic of "irresolution" (112); Lacoue-Labarthe connects the crisis of representation to the Kantian category of the sublime (129-33); Steiner identifies the silence of the opera's third act as the only legitimate response to the experience of the "unspeakable" (163); and White explores a number of these themes in their historical and biographical contexts. For other articles of interest, see Cherlin; and Latham. Wörner's study provides valuable historical, formal, and thematic analysis and includes the opera's libretto.

19. All references are to the libretto included in Wörner. The English translations are my own.

20. *The Harvard Concise Dictionary of Music and Musicians* gives the following definition of *Sprechstimme*: "A use of voice midway between speech and song. In general, it calls for only the approximate reproduction of pitches and in any case avoids the sustaining of any pitch" (Randel 629).

21. White has documented the contents of Schoenberg's private library, which included Kant's first and third critiques and his *Prologomena to Any Future Metaphysic*, Schopenhauer's *Sämtliche Werke* (Reclam edition of 1891), as well as an extensive collection of Nietzsche (68-69). White writes, "It may be seen from these data that Schoenberg's interest in Schopenhauer, Kant, and Nietzsche was well developed by 1913" (69). Reich and Stuckenschmidt also discuss the influence of Kant, Schopenhauer, and Nietzsche on Schoenberg.

22. Kant, *Prolegomena for Any Future Metaphysics* 58; *Prolegomena zu einer jeden künftigen Metaphysik* 81.

23. Kant, *Critique of Pure Reason* 266; *Kritik der reinen Vernunft* 218.

24. See sections 32 and 33 of *Prolegomena*.

25. Schopenhauer 164. Will expresses itself in inorganic matter as gravity, electromagnetic energy, rigidity, impenetrability, fluidity (130); in animals it expresses itself principally through hunger and sex (108).

26. Ibid. 28.

27. Ibid. section 52, 255-67. One suspects Schopenhauer's crude mimeticism would not have appealed to Schoenberg, as when the philosopher identifies the "ground-bass" with "inorganic matter" (258) or equates the departure from the tonic in music to "desire" and the return to it as "satisfaction" (260).

28. Nietzsche, *The Birth of Tragedy* 36.

29. Ibid. 64-65; *Geburt der Tragödie* 44-45.

30. That Nietzsche was himself thinking in the phenomenological terms proposed by Kant and Schopenhauer is evident from his unpublished essay "Truth and Lies in the Nonmoral Sense" (1873), which he wrote the year after he published *The Birth of Tragedy*. In that essay, Nietzsche argues that, in returning to the primitive Dionysian world of our linguistic origins, we discover that the categories or metaphors that enable us to define and shape reality are merely human inventions. See Nietzsche, *Philosophy and Truth* 86.

31. As Nietzsche wrote in *Nietzsche contra Wagner*, "By the summer of 1876, during the time of the first *Festspiele*, I said farewell to Wagner in my heart" (*The Portable Nietzsche* 675).

32. For a discussion of the Nazi misappropriation of Nietzsche, see Kaufmann 285-306. Of course, one need only read Nietzsche himself to realize how preposterous was the Nazi distortion of his thought, something Schoenberg himself would have understood from Nietzsche's writings on Wagner; see, for example, the numerous anti-German remarks in *The Case of Wagner* ("Wagner's stage requires one thing only—*Teutons!*—Definition of the Teuton: obedience and long legs"; 180) or Nietzsche's revulsion with anti-Semitism as expressed in *Nietzsche contra Wagner* ("since Wagner had moved to Germany, he had condescended step by step to everything I despise—even to anti-Semitism"; 676). Nietzsche's hatred of both German nationalism and anti-Semitism has been amply documented in numerous studies and biographies; in addition to Kaufmann, see Cate and Safranski. Schopenhauer, on the contrary, had more typically German views of his time on the subject of the Jews, and he is approvingly cited in Hans Pfitzner's polemical *Die Neue Aesthetik der musikalischen Impotenz*.

33. Pamela White translates *Vorstellung* as Idea and *Darstellung* as Representation. In common German usage *Vorstellung* can refer to the presentation one makes in a courtroom, a performance one gives on stage, as well as the imagination, an idea, conception, or mental image. The notion of the mental image comes closest to the philosophical application of the term, which carries with it the implication of an object-category (i.e., the epistemic category of a table, a chair, a leaf, etc.). In philosophical writing, one of the standard translations of *Vorstellung* is "representation" (as in E. F. J. Payne's translation of Schopenhauer's *Vorstellung* as Representation), and obviously the notion of *Vorstellung* as a mental image of the world is deeply implicated in the whole problem of mimesis or representationalism.

34. White, see especially 67-76.

35. Ibid. 75.

36. Plato, *Timaeus* 20-21 (sections 31a and b).

37. "Of that region beyond no one of our earthly poets has ever sung, nor will any ever sing worthily. Its description follows, for I must dare to speak the truth, especially since the nature of the truth is my theme. It is there that Reality lives, without shape or color, intangible, visible only to reason, the soul's pilot; and all true knowledge is knowledge of her" (Plato, *Phaedrus* 30, section 247).

38. Nietzsche makes his explicitly anti-Platonic position clear in "Truth and Lies in the Nonmoral Sense":

Every concept [*Begriff*] arises from the equation of unequal things. Just as it is certain that one leaf is never totally the same as another, so it is certain that the concept [*Begriff*] "leaf" is formed by arbitrarily discarding these individual differences and by forgetting the distinguishing aspects. This awakens the idea [*Vorstel-*

lung] that in addition to the leaves, there exists in nature the "leaf": the original model [*Urform*] according to which all the leaves were perhaps woven, sketched, measured, colored, curled and painted—but by incompetent hands, so that no specimen has turned out to be a correct, trustworthy, and faithful likeness [*Abbild*] of the original model [*Urform*].

Nietzsche, *Philosophy and Truth* 83; "Über Wahrheit und Lüge im aussermoralischen Sinne" 492.

39. Nietzsche, *Philosophy and Truth* 82.

40. For examples of such constructionism, see Nietzsche, "How the 'True World' Finally Became a Fable"; and Nietzsche, "Four Great Errors" in *Twilight of the Idols* in *The Portable Nietzsche* 463-563.

41. Obviously, the analogy I am drawing here is approximate, but reversing (R), inverting (I), and reversing and inverting (RI) the prime row are forms of permutation that Schoenberg also applies to individual words in his text. Since these four versions of the row are susceptible to further transposition by beginning on a different pitch in the row, the variations become almost infinite. Clearly, there are more tonal permutations than verbal permutations, but it is striking how consistently certain words are repeated in the libretto (constituting a kind of verbal row) and then submitted to variation and elaboration.

42. "Space is a necessary a priori presentation [*Vorstellung*] that underlies all outer intuitions" (Kant, *Critique* 78; *Kritik* 73), and "time is a necessary presentation [*Vorstellung*] that underlies all intuitions" (Kant, *Critique* 86; *Kritik* 80).

43. In Exodus, Aaron acts as Moses' assistant and the miracles are performed before Pharaoh, while in Schoenberg's opera, Aaron initiates the miracles, which are performed before the Jewish people. See Exodus 7.

44. Although Moses' rod is nothing more than the "symbol" of his authority, insofar as it inspires his followers, its power is "real." But obviously this is not the same as saying the rod possesses supernatural properties that literally enable one to perform miracles.

45. In the original German, the line reads: "Aber ein Volk kann nur fühlen." *Fühlen* combines the ideas both of having "feelings" and "perceiving" through the senses.

46. Noted in the libretto of the enclosed booklet in Schoenberg, *Moses und Aron & Chamber Symphony* 122.

47. Albright notes that the "mechanism of the drama can be compared to a wind-up toy, a black box out of which, when one turns a switch on, a small hand reaches to turn the switch off; Schoenberg has made a gesture that is accomplished only for the sake of its own termination, has designed a song that intensifies silence" (44).

48. See Schoenberg, "Art and the Moving Pictures" in *Style and Idea* 154. Although I know of no commentary that has drawn a parallel between the deaths of Kundry and Aaron, a number of critics have noted significant connections between *Moses*

und Aron and *Parsifal*; see Adorno, "Sacred Fragment" 239; Botstein 176-79; Lacoue-Labarthe, *Musica ficta* 121-22; and Steiner 153. Lacoue-Labarthe treats *Moses und Aron* as the "negative (in the photographic sense) of *Parsifal*" (121), a description that aptly describes the relation between Wagner's and Schoenberg's respective endings. Also of interest is Steiner's discussion of the Golden Calf scene: "Thus the Golden Calf is both the logical culmination of, and a covert satire on, that catalogue of orgiastic ballets and ritual dances which is one of the distinctive traits of grand opera from Massenet's *Hérodiade* to *Tannhäuser*, from *Aida* and *Samson et Dalila* to *Parsifal* and *Salome*" (160).

49. The "ludicrous" has often been viewed as a sign of the kind of theatricality that is associated not only with Wagner in particular (see Matthew Smith's chapter in this volume) but also with opera in general. In this sense, Schoenberg's ironic ending is deeply antitheatrical.

50. Most critics believe that Schoenberg himself identifies with Moses (Adorno, "Sacred Fragment" 226, Botstein 169, Lindenberger 221), but Goldstein ("Schoenberg's *Moses und Aron* 176-78) and HaCohen (131) view Schoenberg's sympathies as more divided between the two brothers, and Albright observes, "I do not think Schoenberg intends all virtue to be on Moses' side" (39).

51. A dying Aruns believes that God has "smitten" him for presumptuously attempting to be "both Moses and Aron in one person" (Schoenberg, *Der biblische Weg/The Biblical Way* 319). The play was published as a bilingual text.

52. In a "A Four-Point Program for Jewry," which dates from 1938, Schoenberg insists on the need for "practical politics" (55), and while he acknowledges that Mandate Palestine is the historic homeland of the Jews (56), he nevertheless believes that the Uganda Project offered a practical solution for European Jewry at a time of political crisis (56).

53. Here I have in mind the account of Nietzsche that emerges in "Contingency of Language," in Rorty; see also Vattimo and Nehamas.

54. See, for example, Plato's qualified defense of a representational system such as writing in *Phaedrus* 73-74 (sections 276-78).

55. For accounts of Schoenberg's relation to Judaism, see Goldstein, "Word, Image, Idea" 137-49; Botstein 162-67; White 51-55.

56. White 54.

57. Goldstein, "Word, Image, Idea" 138.

58. Schoenberg, *Letters* 88.

59. Ibid. 184.

60. Text quoted from liner notes for Schoenberg, *Das Chorwerk* 66.

61. Goldstein, "Word, Image, Idea" 165.

62. Meyer 171.

63. Ibid.

64. Ibid.

65. Wagner, *Judaism in Music* 80, emphasis in the original, 82. Subsequent citations appear in the text.

66. In the original 1850 version of the essay, Wagner writes that the "Jew is altogether incapable [*durchaus*] of giving artistic enunciation to his feelings," which he softens in the 1869 version to "almost."

67. For an excellent discussion of the relation of cosmopolitanism to modernism, see Walkowitz.

68. Schoenberg, *Style and Idea* 502–03.

69. In "New Music: My Music," Schoenberg writes, "Not a single note written by any of the 'new classicists,' 'folklorists,' 'new objectivists,' and 'community-art' musicians would be possible without Wagner the musician" (*Style and Idea* 105); and in "Criteria for the Evaluation of Music," he writes, "Wagner's entirely new way of building, expressing, harmonizing and orchestrating" has the effect of "revolutionizing music in all its aspects" (*Style and Idea* 133).

70. As Schoenberg remarks in "Twelve-Tone Composition" (1923), "I believe that when Richard Wagner introduced his leitmotif—for the same purpose as that for which I introduced my Basic Set—he may have said: 'Let there be unity'" (*Style and Idea* 244).

71. Helen White demonstrates not only that Schoenberg employs expressive and affective devices in his music but also that he makes use of a fairly elaborate structure of leitmotifs (see chapter 5 and appendices 2 and 3). Schoenberg's leitmotifs are, however, sufficiently stylized that no one would imagine that they are direct musical manifestations of the person, thing, or event with which they are associated.

72. In writing against music designed to produce specific subjective impressions or "psychological" effects, Schoenberg observes that "certain dance music goes where it belongs—to the feet." He continues, "Certainly *Forest Murmurs* and the *Moonlight Sonata* do not go to the feet—not, at least, as their principal target. It is less hard to imagine someone on whom the waltzes from *Die Meistersinger* . . . have such a narrowly 'psychological' effect—but one may not feel obliged to view it as a virtue worth mentioning" (Schoenberg, "New Music" in *Style and Idea* 139).

73. In "My Evolution," Schoenberg writes, "In my *Verklärte Nacht* the thematic construction is based on a Wagnerian 'model of sequence' above a roving harmony. . . . [T]he treatment of instruments, the manner of composition, and much of the sonority were strictly Wagnerian" (*Style and Idea* 80).

74. In mm. 693–94 of *Von heute auf morgen*, the Singer praises the Wife's "radiant eyes" ("der Schein von . . . Ihren strahlenden Augen") in a lyrical run up the scale, which inspires the Husband's harshly ironic dissonance (dropping from B♭ to A to C♭) when he points out that the Singer is merely quoting *Rheingold* ("Siehe *Rheingold*!"). The humor is even richer if we realize that the text being quoted (the music is not) comes from Fasolt's love-sick mooning over Freia toward the end of the opera ("Weh! Noch blitzt ihr Blick zu mir her; des Auges Stern strahlt mich noch an"). The

other Wagner allusion in *Von heute auf morgen* occurs at m. 997 ("Schmecktest du mir ihn zu!") and involves a direct quotation of both music and text from act 1, scene 1 of *Walküre*. Here the irony is, if anything, greater than in the earlier allusion. Instead of a heroic and wounded Siegmund who accepts a restorative drink from Sieglinde, we are confronted with a vain and puffed-up tenor who tells the Wife that a cup of coffee poured by her hand would taste as good as gin ("schmeckt ein Milchkaffee sicher wie Gin!"). See Schoenberg, *Von heute auf morgen*.

75. Schoenberg, *Moses und Aron: Oper in drei Akten*. The Dragon motif is quoted in Newman 545.

76. For a discussion of Hanslick, see Janik and Toulmin 103-07. Janik and Toulmin write, "Wagner was offensive to Hanslick because, in personal as well as musical matters, he was always the conjurer, always the entertainer"; they go on to cite the leitmotif as an example of this "conjuring" (104).

77. The Siegfried motif is quoted in Newman (546).

78. For the "Rheinmaidens' Song," see Richard Wagner, *Das Rheingold* 250.

79. Steiner, 162-63.

Bibliography

Adorno, Theodor W. *Negative Dialectics*. Trans. E. B. Ashton. New York: Continuum, 1973.

———. "Sacred Fragment: Schoenberg's *Moses und Aron*." *Quasi una Fantasia: Essays on Modern Music*. Trans. Rodney Livingstone. London: Verso, 1992. 225-48.

Adorno, Theodor W., and Max Horkheimer. *Dialectic of Enlightenment*. Trans. John Cummings. London: Verso, 1997.

Albright, Daniel. *Representation and the Imagination: Beckett, Kafka, Nabokov, and Schoenberg*. Chicago: University of Chicago Press, 1981.

Barron, Stephanie, ed. *"Degenerate Art": The Fate of the Avant-Garde in Nazi Germany*. New York: Harry N. Abrams, 1991.

———. "Modern Art and Politics in Prewar Germany." *"Degenerate Art": The Fate of the Avant-Garde in Nazi Germany*. Ed. Stephanie Barron. New York: Harry N. Abrams, 1991. 9-24.

Benjamin, Walter. "The Work of Art in the Age of Mechanical Reproduction." *Illuminations*. Ed. Hannah Arendt. Trans. Harry Zohn. New York: Schocken Books, 1968.

Botstein, Leon. "Arnold Schoenberg: Language, Modernism and Jewish Identity." *Austrians and Jews in the Twentieth Century*. Ed. Robert S. Wistrich. New York: St. Martin's Press, 1992.

Brecht, Bertolt. "Alienation Effects in Chinese Acting." *Brecht on Theatre: The Development of an Aesthetic*. Ed. and Trans. John Willett. New York: Hill and Wang, 1957.

Cate, Curtis. *Friedrich Nietzsche*. Woodstock, NY: Overlook Press, 2002.

Cherlin, Michael. "Schoenberg's Representation of the Divine in *Moses und Aron*." *Journal of the Arnold Schoenberg Institute* 9.2 (1986): 210-16.

Eichenauer, Richard. *Musik und Rasse*. Munich: J. S. Lehmanns Verlag, 1932.

Entartete Kunst: Führer durch die Ausstellung. Original German with accompanying English translation. Trans. William C. Bunce. Redding, CN: Silver Fox Press, 1972.

Glock, Hans-Johann. *A Wittgenstein Dictionary*. Oxford: Blackwell, 1996.

Goldstein, Bluma. "Schoenberg's *Moses und Aron*: A Vanishing Biblical Nation." *Political and Religious Ideas in the Works of Arnold Schoenberg*. Ed. Charlotte M. Cross and Russell A. Berman. New York: Garland, 2000. 159-92.

———. "Word, Image, Idea: Schoenberg and Moses—a Tragic Coexistence." *Reinscribing Moses: Heine, Kafka, Freud, and Schoenberg in a European Wilderness*. Cambridge, MA: Harvard University Press, 1992. 137-67.

HaCohen, Ruth. "Sounds of Revelation: Aesthetic-Political Theology in Schoenberg's *Moses und Aron*." *Modernist Cultures* 1.2 (2005): 110-40. <http://www.js-modcult .bham.ac.uk>.

Janik, Allan, and Stephen Toulmin. *Wittgenstein's Vienna*. Chicago: Elephant Paperbacks, 1996.

Kant, Immanuel. *Critique of Pure Reason*. Unified ed. (1781/1787). Trans. Werner S. Pluhar. Indianapolis: Hackett, 1996.

———. *Kritik der reinen Vernunft*. Berlin: Mayer & Müller, 1889.

———. *Prolegomena for Any Future Metaphysics*. Rev. of the Carus trans. by Lewis White Beck. Indianapolis: Bobbs-Merrill, 1950.

———. *Prolegomena zu einer jeden künftigen Metaphysik*. Hamburg: Felix Meiner Verlag, 2001.

Kaufmann, Walter. *Nietzsche: Philosopher, Psychologist, Antichrist*. Princeton: Princeton University Press, 1974.

Lacoue-Labarthe, Phillipe. *Musica ficta (Figures of Wagner)*. Trans. Felicia McCarren. Stanford: Stanford University Press, 1994.

Latham, Edward D. "The Prophet and the Pitchman: Dramatic Structure and Its Elucidation in *Moses und Aron*, Act 1, Scene 2." *Political and Religious Ideas in the Works of Arnold Schoenberg*. Ed. Charlotte M. Cross and Russell A. Berman. New York: Garland, 2000. 131-58.

Lindenberger, Herbert. *Opera in History: From Monteverdi to Cage*. Stanford: Stanford University Press, 1998.

Meyer, Michael. "A Musical Facade for the Third Reich." *"Degenerate Art": The Fate of the Avant-Garde in Nazi Germany*. Ed. Stephanie Barron. New York: Harry N. Abrams, 1991. 171-83.

Nehamas, Alexander. *Nietzsche: Life as Literature*. Cambridge, MA: Harvard University Press, 1985.

Newman, Ernest. *The Wagner Operas*. Princeton: Princeton University, 1991.

Nietzsche, Friedrich. *The Birth of Tragedy* and *The Case of Wagner*. Trans. Walter Kaufmann. New York: Vintage, 1967.

――. *Geburt der Tragödie*. Vol. 1 of *Werke in Zwei Bände*. Munich: Carl Hanser Verlag, 1973.

――. *Philosophy and Truth: Selections from Nietzsche's Notebooks of the Early 1870's.* Ed. and Trans. Daniel Breazeale. Atlantic Highlands, NJ: Humanities Press International, 1979. 79-97.

――. *The Portable Nietzsche*. Ed. and Trans. Walter Kaufmann. New York: Penguin, 1983.

――. "Über Wahrheit und Lüge im aussermoralischen Sinne." *Die Geburt der Tragödie und Schriften der Frühzeit*. Leipzig: Alfred Kröner Verlag, 1924. 487-504.

Nordau, Max. *Degeneration*. Trans. unknown. Lincoln: University of Nebraska Press, 1993.

Pfitzner, Hans. *Gesammelte Schriften*. Vol. 1. Augburg: Filser Verlag, 1926.

――. *Die Neue Aesthetik der musikalischen Impotenz*. Munich: Verlag der Süddeutschen Monatshefte, 1920.

Plato. *Phaedrus*. Trans. W. C. Helmhold and W. G. Rabinowitz. New York: Macmillan, 1956.

――. *Plato's Timaeus*. Trans. Francis M. Cornford. Indianapolis: Bobbs-Merrill, 1959.

Pritchard, Elizabeth A. "*Bilderverbot* Meets Body in Theodor W. Adorno's Inverse Theology." *Harvard Theological Review* 95.3 (2002): 291-315.

Randel, Don Michael, ed. *The Harvard Concise Dictionary of Music and Musicians*. Cambridge, MA: Belknap Press of Harvard University Press, 1999.

Reich, Willi. *Schoenberg: A Critical Biography*. Trans. Leo Black. London: Longman, 1971.

Rorty, Richard. *Contingency, Irony, and Solidarity*. Cambridge: Cambridge University Press, 1989.

Safranski, Rüdiger. *Nietzsche: A Philosophical Biography*. Trans. Shelley Frisch. New York: Norton, 2002.

Schoenberg, Arnold. *Der biblische Weg/The Biblical Way*. Trans. Moshe Lazar. *Journal of the Arnold Schoenberg Institute* 17.1-2 (1994): 162-329.

――. *Das Chorwerk*. Conducted by Pierre Boulez. CD. New York: Sony Classical, 1990.

――. "A Four-Point Program for Jewry." *Journal of the Arnold Schoenberg Institute* 7.1 (1979): 49-67.

――. *Letters*. Ed. Erwin Stein. Trans. Eithne Wilkins and Ernst Kaiser. Berkeley: University of California Press, 1987.

――. *Moses und Aron: Oper in drei Akten*. Score and text. Mainz: B. Schott's Söhne, 1958.

――. *Moses und Aron & Chamber Symphony no. 2, op. 38*. Cond. Pierre Boulez. CD. New York: Sony Classical, 1993.

———. *Style and Idea.* Ed. Leonard Stein, Trans. Leo Black. Berkeley: University of California Press, 1984.

———. *Von heute auf morgen.* Score and text. Mainz: B. Schott's Söhne, 1961.

Schopenhauer, Arthur. *The World as Will and Representation.* Vol. 1. Trans. E. F. J. Payne. New York: Dover, 1969.

Steiner, George. "Schoenberg's *Moses und Aron.*" *Language and Silence.* London: Faber and Faber, 1958. 150-63.

Stuckenschmidt, H. H. *Schoenberg: His Life and Work.* Trans. Humphrey Searle. London: John Calder, 1977.

Vattimo, Gianni. *The End of Modernity: Nihilism and Hermeneutics in Postmodern Culture.* Trans. Jon R. Snyder. Baltimore: Johns Hopkins University Press, 1988.

Wagner, Richard. *Judaism in Music and Other Essays.* Trans. William Ashton Ellis Lincoln and London: University of Nebraska Press, 1995.

———. *Das Rheingold.* Score and text. Frankfurt: C. F. Peters, 1942.

Walkowitz, Rebecca L. *Cosmopolitan Style: Modernism beyond the Nation.* New York: Columbia University Press, 2006.

White, Pamela C. *Schoenberg and the God-Idea: The Opera "Moses und Aron."* Ann Arbor: UMI Research Press, 1985.

Wittgenstein, Ludwig. *Philosophical Investigations.* 3rd ed. Trans. G. E. M. Anscombe. New York: Macmillan, 1968.

Wörner, Karl H. *Schoenberg's "Moses and Aaron."* Trans. Paul Hamburger. London: Faber and Faber, 1963.

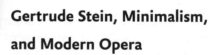

8 Gertrude Stein, Minimalism, and Modern Opera

Cyrena N. Pondrom

Unlike her avant-garde literary colleague Ezra Pound, who tried his hand at opera, Gertrude Stein wasn't particularly musical and (again unlike Pound) she made no pronouncements on music theory. Yet she undoubtedly has made the far larger impact on modern opera. It is well known that she profoundly influenced Virgil Thomson and that their collaboration on *Four Saints in Three Acts* produced one of the most popular American operas of the 1930s (not to speak of their further collaboration on *The Mother of Us All* in the 1940s). Mabel Dodge Luhan enthusiastically prophesized it would "finish modern opera just as Picasso had finished old painting," and though it did not do that, it did offer during the period of high modernism a compellingly intermedial example that would help to prompt essential parallels in the opera of late contemporary modernism.[1] Much has been reported about *Four Saints*, but the story that generally is not told is this later one, when the practices of systematic repetition, use of the vernacular, hammering rhythm, stern reductionism, absence of narrative, and sometimes aleatory composition that Stein instantiates in literary form reappear in American minimalism, where they may be found today in some of the most significant and best known contemporary operas, like Philip Glass and Robert Wilson's *Einstein on the Beach* (1976) or John Adams's *Nixon in China* (1987).

The connection between Stein and contemporary opera is complex and may usefully be mediated through the work of John Cage and Steve Reich. But it is equally interesting to work backward and consider how some ideas in musical set theory and other ways of talking about contemporary minimalist music can also illuminate the practices of Stein. In this chapter I briefly consider Thomson's debt to Stein and the way some practices of her text and his music may be seen as antecedent to minimalism, and note the evidence for the transmission of her influence through Cage and Reich.

Then I explicate the ways in which "phase-shifting" pieces in the work of Reich, which have been seen to combine "a repeated pattern with a delayed statement of the same pattern in another voice" and to vary "the temporal interval of imitation between original and imitated voices . . . systematically," are in many ways analogous to the repetition with variation that one finds in Stein's libretto to *Four Saints in Three Acts*.[2] The chapter concludes with much briefer looks at other analogies between Stein's work and prominent characteristics in modern music, particularly with reference to recent opera.

Thomson recalled that he had been "addicted from Harvard days to *Tender Buttons* and to *Geography and Plays* (almost no other of her books was yet in print)" and had begun to try to set some of the poems of *Tender Buttons* to music before he sailed for France the second time in September 1925.[3] As yet musically unknown, he did not seek Stein out. The opportunity to meet her arose in January 1926, when George Antheil—then exciting comment with his experimental music—insisted that Thomson accompany him to one of Stein's frequent peremptory invitations to newly rising stars to join her for the evening. Stein responded to Thomson favorably, but Toklas remained cool. Afterward Thomson did not approach the pair until the summer of 1926, when they exchanged notes, and he was not to meet Stein again until December, when he attended a Christmas Eve party thrown for Sherwood Anderson and others at her residence.[4] Thus emboldened, on New Year's Day he delivered to the door of the Stein atelier his composition of music for piano and voice for the poem "Susie Asado," the opening piece of Stein's *Geography and Plays*.[5] The response was prompt and enthusiastic: "Thanks so much I am delighted, I like its looks immensely. . . and when can I know a little other than its looks. . . you and the Susie. . . do come in soon we will certainly be in Thursday afternoon. . . ."[6]

Although her response suggests that Stein may not have been able to read music—she confessed, "Miss Toklas who knows more than looks says the things in it please her a lot"—it was the rhythm of her language that had attracted Thomson to the task of setting her words to music.[7] He explained:

My hope in putting Gertrude Stein to music had been to break, crack open, and solve for all time anything still waiting to be solved, which was almost everything, about English musical declamation. My theory was that if a text is set correctly for the sound of it, the meaning will take care of itself. And the Stein texts, for prosodizing in this way, were manna. With meanings already abstracted, or absent, or so multiplied that choice among them was hopeless, there was no temptation toward tonal illustration, say of birdie babbling by brook. . . . You could make a setting for sound and syntax only, then add, if needed, an accompaniment equally functional. I had no sooner put to music after this recipe one short Stein text than I knew I had opened a door. I never had any doubts about Stein's poetry; from then on I had none about my ability to handle it in music.[8]

He became a frequent visitor to 27 rue de Fleures and by February had proposed to Stein that they collaborate on an opera (and in the next several months he composed settings for Stein's brief "Preciosilla" and lengthier "Capital Capitals").[9] Stein found the beginning difficult—she wrote Thomson on March 30, 1927, "I think I have got St. Therese onto the stage, it has been an awful struggle . . . ," but by mid-June Stein was able to send Thomson the virtually completed manuscript.[10] Because of some preplanned excursions, Thomson was unable to start on the music until November.[11] He finished composing the score in June 1928; his partner, Maurice Grosser, finished the scenario in 1929, and the opera was finally first produced in Hartford, Connecticut, on February 8, 1934.[12] The text was quite unlike the libretto of any extant opera and startled Thomson by lacking both assignment of parts and stage directions.

True to Thomson's hope that the scenario would present "the working artist's working life, which is to say, the life we both were living," the entire first section is "a narrative of prepare for saints in narrative prepare for saints," which is to say, a metacritical performance of the process of bringing a creative text into being.[13] Stein understood the act of creation to take place in a period of intense awareness of the present moment. "The business of Art," she writes in "Plays," "is to live in the actual present . . . and to completely express that complete actual present."[14] It was a high calling to which she clearly presumed her friend Virgil Thomson also aspired. Stein thought ordinary drama normally made such a state of mind impossible for the audience to share. "The . . . scene as depicted on stage . . . is almost always in syncopated time in relation to the emotion of anybody in the audience," she explains, and she sought to create drama in which this syncopation did not exist.[15] She began partially to apprehend a solution to the dilemma while watching Strauss's opera *Elektra* and after a period of incubation sought to put her ideas into practice in her first play, *What Happened: A Five Act Play* (1913). There and in other early plays she sought "to tell what could be told if one did not tell anything . . . to make a play the essence of what happened."[16] She calls such plays "landscapes." They avoid narration and seek a completely synchronic relationship between the audience and the textual performances of the play or libretto. Both the act of creation and the relation of the audience to her landscapes invokes oblivion to ordinary diachronic time, a state of "timelessness" we might call synchronic. Carried to its symbolic conclusion, such a state presumably mimes the synchronicity of all time caught up as one—the state of the saints. Or as Stein herself says:

> In Four Saints I made the Saints the landscape. All the saints that I made and I made a number of them because after all a great many pieces of things are in a landscape all these saints together made my landscape . . . the play really is a landscape.
>
> A landscape does not move nothing really moves in a landscape but things are there, and I put into the play the things that were there.[17]

Stein was hardly unaware of the symbolic overtones of the language she chose to use; she elaborates, "Magpies are in the landscape. . . . [T]hey hold themselves up and down and look flat against the sky. . . . They look exactly like the birds in the annunciation pictures the bird which is the Holy Ghost and rests flat against the sky very high."[18]

Thus, when Stein launches *Four Saints in Three Acts* as "a narrative of prepare for saints in narrative prepare for saints," she captures the tremendous struggle of the working artist to achieve that state of acute awareness only of the present moment, which is the precondition of genuine creation. The process is intense. Unable initially to reach that state of mental synchronicity—to realize Saint Therese—she begins again and again, struggling against the diachrony of narrative. The section is a kind of prologue occupying some five pages before act 1 is announced. In it many—maybe even most—of the characteristics that would come to define minimalism in American music are enacted.

Insistent, almost hypnotic, repetition; use of a small number of simple phrases within brief passages of contiguous lines; creation of "development" through minor changes in repeated phrases; an emphasis on ordinal numbers, visible in the text both literally and in the number of repeated words and phrases; use of a hammering simple rhythm implicit in both the sound and the syntax of words and lines; interruption of the rhythm by a succession of unstopped words that creates the sense of a single held or continuously repeated note; frequent rhyming and punning, which have the effect of repetition; emphasis on process in the text rather than its destination or climax (the final two lines of the libretto are "Last Act. / Which is a fact"); self-reflexive performance of the act of performing or writing—all these characteristics of minimalism are visible and audible within Stein's first two pages.

The first nineteen line phrases in this prologue constitute a unit. For the purposes of analysis I am defining as a "line phrase" all those words that begin a line indented at the left of the page, following a period ending the previous line phrase, and continuing until another period is followed by a line break and indention. (These units are maintained from printing to printing. The literal number of lines varies from printing to printing depending on page size and type face.) The opera begins:

> To know to know to love her so.
> Four saints prepare for saints.
> It makes it well fish.
> Four saints it makes it well fish
> Four saints prepare for saints it makes it well well fish it makes it well fish
> prepare for saints.[19]

The opening lines are in iambic tetrameter, one of the most hypnotic rhythms in English-language poetry. Iambic metrical units are only two beats (or syllables), the first unaccented and the second accented: "To knów / to knów // to lóve / her só." The second line shifts to trimeter and substitutes for the first two feet an even simpler unit: a spondee, or two stressed syllables (here monosyllables), before the caesura: "Fóur sáints // pre páre / for sáints." (Note that the line finishes with two iambs). Using this form of scansion, the next line is again trimeter, with a catalectic foot (that is with the final syllable truncated), reversing the rhythm of the previous line by using the sequence iamb, iamb, spondee: "To máke / it wéll / físh [-´]." Musically, this is a retrograde. The last of these four lines bookends the group by returning to the tetrameter of the first line, but it incorporates the substituted spondee from line 2 and the cataleptic spondee from line 3 for the beginning and ending feet: "Fóur sáints / it mákes / it wéll / físh [-´]."[20] The rhythmic repetition of the first two lines is increased by the homology (or near homology) of "four" and "for," and one sees an example of repetition with minimal change not unlike that in beat set theory in the reversal of the rhythm of the second and third lines. One also sees an example of repetition that seems very similar to phase shifting, with a second voice repeating a first but displaced by one or more measures, as in a canon. That is, the fourth line starts a repetition of "four saints" but is interrupted in the second measure by an exact repetition of the third line, "it makes it well fish." And just as with a canon, the counterpointed voice "finishes" a measure later, even though this lengthens the line. These practices are staples of early minimalist music and suggestive of the work of Steve Reich in pieces like "Music for Two or More Pianos" (February 1964). Of this piece Keith Potter explains:

> The score consists simply of a sequence of nine five-, six-, and seven-note chords. . . .[T]hese chords are, as the score says, to "be repeated as many times as performers feel appropriate." . . . While "[c]hords may be arpeggiated or broken in any way," . . . Reich requires his players to "remain with any chord for as long as desired, but as soon as any performer moves from one chord to the next, all performers should move on similarly, as soon as possible." The result is a kind of close canonic playing of the chord sequence.[21]

In setting the libretto to music, Thomson had some of the same freedom as would the performers of the Reich piece; he could divide the texts among multiple voices, and he could decide which words to stress, though he scored all the words as they stood. In the second and third lines, he chose to treat "it makes it well fish" as a syntactic unit that has a contrapuntal relationship to the metric scansion of the line ("it mákes it well / físh). He also scored this nineteen-line unit for chorus and both male and female voices, beginning with a choral opening and shifting to solo voices at the seventh line, although Stein gives no indication of speakers in the text.

The opening line, "To know to know to love her so," is usually read as simultaneously an invocation both to the opera's Saint Therese and to Stein's lifelong partner, Alice B. Toklas, whose faithful encouragement, praise, and practical support contributed inestimably to Stein's literary experiments.[22] The next lines shift to a description of the task at hand: to *prepare* the opera, to *make it well*, to *fish* for her subject. After the first four lines in this opening nineteen-line unit of text, Stein abandons the gesture toward metrical form of the first four lines (which are actually inset as a unit in some printings of the text). The fifth line unit has twenty-one syllables and nineteen words, which are verbally broken into six syntactical units in the opera. It ruptures any pretense of metrical regularity, while it maintains its emphasis on the lexically and rhythmically minimal. *Nineteen* words with only *twenty-one* syllables! Only the crucial word "prepare" has more than one syllable; every other word is a monosyllable, and the same has been true of the previous four lines.

In the six lines that follow, one more crucial word is permitted to be multisyllabic, the word "narrative."

In narrative prepare for saints.
Prepare for saints.
Two saints.
Four saints.
Two saints prepare for saints it two saints prepare for saints in prepare for saints.
A narrative of prepare for saints in narrative prepare for saints.[23]

Just before undertaking *Four Saints*, Stein had been writing narrative and exploring its meaning. When she turned to a play (or libretto), she sought to generate a "landscape," which she believed should simply be "there," a performance without chronological progression, having existence in the present moment. But she found she could not easily achieve this state in her libretto, and her efforts to achieve it keep turning into a narrative: "in narrative prepare for saints." She continues, however, in a fashion that presages the operatic minimalists, to keep her insistence on simple ordinal numbers and a similar number of syllables: "Two saints. // Four saints." The text continues in this way through the first nineteen lines of the prologue, when Stein seems to interrupt herself and give in completely to the attractiveness of narrative:

What happened today, a narrative.
    We had intended if it were a pleasant day to go to the country it was a very beautiful day and we carried out our intention. We went to places that we had been when we were equally pleased and we found very nearly what we could find and returning saw and heard that after all they were rewarded and likewise. This makes it necessary to go again.[24]

Scored to be sung in a monotone until three bars before the end of the unit, these words have much of the character identified in the very earliest minimalist texts of La Monte Young, whose "Trio for Strings" in 1958 relied on long sustained notes, or a tonal drone.[25]

    The relapse into narrating "what happened today" does not relieve her block on bringing the saints to the stage, and Stein finds "this makes it necessary to go again." The tonal drone that follows is even more extreme: two word sequences, the first a "sentence" of 162 words in which all but 23 are monosyllabic, followed by the abrupt conclusion: "This is how they do not like it."[26] For seven lines of the printed text, Thomson's setting reflects this maintenance of a single sound or rapid vocal drone. After the expression of dislike of this narrative, Stein returns to her efforts to conjure the saints in simple rhythms, successive repetitions with minimal change, retrograde repetitions, and an emphasis on ordinal numbers. We may note also what seems like phase-shifted voices, with lines 2, 3, and 4 in the following quotation having four syllables, ending with "in the sun," and lines 5 and 6 having the same ending but respectively with five and six syllables:

> Imagine four benches separately.
>
> One in the sun.
>
> Two in the sun.
>
> Three in the sun.
>
> One not in the sun.
>
> Not one not in the sun.
>
> Not one.[27]

Stein and Thomson accomplish here by the manipulation of voices what Reich declares he "discovered . . . by accident" in "It's Gonna Rain" (January 1965) and "Come Out" (1966) by the use of taped voices played in unison and then permitted to go slightly out of phase.[28]

La Monte Young, along with Terry Riley, was one of the figures who provided some of the creative inspiration for Steve Reich, and both were members of the avant-garde group of young musicians clustered around the New School in New York, where between 1956 and 1958 Cage's classes in music composition fueled the beginnings of "the happenings theater."[29] Cage had been launched into radical composition in part by an exposure to the work of Gertrude Stein similar to Thomson's. In his second year at Pomona College, in 1929, he started reading Stein, abandoning his initial interest in the ministry.[30] By the spring of 1930 he had begun to write his examinations in an imitation of Stein's style, and at the end of the semester, he set out for Paris.[31] The experience of the new arts in Paris freed him from any commitment to practicing or honing a traditional compositional style. He now believed, his biographer says, "that he could not only write, but also paint, compose, even dance, without any technical training."[32] He returned to his parents' home in California in fall of 1931 and began to develop a new improvisational method of composition, using Stein's writings as one element of his inspiration: "He set to music experimental writing from *transition* magazine, texts by Gertrude Stein, and choruses from the *Persians* by Aeschylus. He also wrote . . . songs from Ecclesiastes. . . . 'These compositions were improvised at the piano,' Cage explains, and quickly notated before they were forgotten. 'The style of the songs are [sic], so to speak, transcriptions in repetitive language put to repetitive music.'"[33] According to his biographer, Cage was also drawn initially to a kind of mathematical composition, a practice extended in a somewhat different way when he began exploring in *Sonata for Two Voices* (1933) "two ranges of two chromatic octaves" in which the upper octave of one and the lower octave of the other were the same, no pitch of the shared octave to be repeated until "eleven other pitches had intervened" and "no pitch in either of the unique octaves could be played until all twenty-five notes of its two-octave chromatic range had appeared."[34] This practice, David Revill argues, is more like Cage's own earlier mathematical experiments in composition than Schoenberg's serialism.[35] Cage was still carefully keeping up with Stein in 1940, when the second movement of his composition *Living Room Music*, "Story," uses the opening lines of Stein's August 1939 children's tale "The World Is Round."

Simpler than serial compositional techniques, Stein's own fascination with numbers and the abstraction they introduce into the composition is extremely prominent in *Four Saints in Three Acts*. "How many . . . are there in it?" is the repeated question of the libretto. "How many saints are there in it?" is asked twice on page 597, again on 604 and 610, and five times on 611, the penultimate page. This is paired with fifteen occasions in which the text asks how many nails, windows, doors, or floors are in it (594, 602) and eight times "how many acts are there in it" (610–11). This latter occasion offers another of the numerous examples of repetition that suggests phasing:

> How many acts are there in it. Acts are there in it.
> Supposing a wheel had been added to three wheels how many acts how many how many acts are there in it.[36]

This almost obsessive insistence on counting is buttressed by literary and sometimes both literary and musical allusion to nursery counting rhymes. One encounters just before act 2 (592) the verbal rhythms of "Partridge in a Pear Tree" and shortly thereafter both the verbal and musical allusion "One two three four five six seven all good children go to heaven some are good and some are bad one two three four five six seven" (594), an allusion repeated in truncated form three further times (596, 610, 611).[37] In considering recognizable parallels in later operatic minimalism, listeners familiar with Glass and Wilson's *Einstein on the Beach* will doubtless remember its beginning, in which the section "Knee Play 1" is dominated for all 3′52″ by the repeated chanting of the ordinal numbers "one two three four five six seven eight" over a three-note range (slowly drowned out by a hymn-like chorus and the crackling static of background voices).[38] Indeed, many of the subsequent sections of this opera use these ordinal numbers (or in "Knee 4," do re mi fa so) as a substantial part of the spoken or sung text.

The parallels with later minimalism extend well beyond repetition, phased language, vernacular allusion, and fascination with ordinal numbers, however. The structures of both Stein's libretto and the scenario by Maurice Grosser also are suggestive of some structural practices of the minimalist opera of the 1970s and later, which revolve around a series of set scenes or storyboards. Grosser's scenario stages act 1 of *Four Saints* at Avila as a "pageant on the steps of the cathedral" structured by an opening scene and seven tableaux:[39] Therese seated in the gardens painting large eggs (23); Therese with dove, being photographed by St. Settlement (35); Therese seated and Ignatius kneeling, playing the guitar (38); Ignatius presenting flowers to Therese (42); Ignatius showing Therese "the model of a Heavenly Mansion" (47); Therese "in ecstasy, seated, with angel hovering" (53); and Therese "with halo, pretending to hold a baby in her arms" (57). Acts 2 and 3 also have something of the quality of tableaux, though they are not explicitly performed as they are in act 1 by the presentation of each successive pose in a "portal, . . . the small curtain being pulled aside for each presentation."[40] The second act is staged as a garden party and ends after the appearance in the sky of a "Vision of a Heavenly Mansion" (93) like that presented as a model in tableau 6 of the first act. Act 3, set in the garden of a monastery, centers on Ignatius's description of the Heavenly Mansion and his prediction of a Last Judgment. The final, very brief, act 4 offers a full-stage tableaux of all the saints assembled, presumably in heaven, singing. Each of these scenes or tableaux can be seen as a timeless present moment, something that just "is there," which Stein calls a landscape, a present that "was in the beginning, is now and ever shall be." Although few can do it some of the time and no one all of the time, Stein seemed to believe that if we could but be fully present to the present moment, we would all live like the saints, as if in the absolute time of a kind of Heavenly Mansion.[41] Certainly, Stein associates such moments of intense consciousness of the present with the life of the working artist, or at least those few who could "make it as it is made," or successfully present their own time.[42]

The significance of replacing narrative chronology with a series of tableaux of inexplicit relationship is emphasized by Stein's flagrant violation of the normal progression of acts and scenes. The performance of the writer's struggle to present Saint Therese is presented in five full (prologue-like) pages of text labeled neither prologue nor act 1. When act 1 does appear, it is immediately followed by brief passages labeled "Repeat First Act" and "Enact End of An Act." Only then does a brief parody of "progression" appear: we leap directly to "Scene Two" and "Scene III" [sic].[43] This apparent advance is followed immediately by a second "Scene III" and "Scene IV," followed in turn by *another* "Scene III" and "IV" before "Act Two" is enumerated. But this act 2 is illusory; it consists of a mere three syllables and a scene 1 consisting of three brief verbal units, concluding with an allusion to the artist's central struggle to prepare the main character: "Saint Therese preparing in as you might say" (593). So we return to "Act One." Finally, the writer's efforts realize a kind of fruition, and the appearance of Saint Therese is celebrated: "Saint Therese has begun to be in act one" (593). This permits a shift to a second act 2, which will be shared with Saint Ignatius, announced with the opening line, "Saint Ignatius was very well known" (594). Although he had been "meant and met" in the prologue, where another nineteen saints are listed (585–86), now in the second act 2 we have "Saint Ignatius finally" (594). The frontal attack on dramatic progression continues throughout the remainder of the opera. This second act 2 has a scene 2, a "Scene III and IV," "Scene IV" twice, and "Scene V" eight times before briefly lapsing into a more normal sequence. All of these "stage directions" for acts and scenes are clearly sung in the opera, so that the audience is unable to ignore this illogical assembly of progression, regression, and stasis. When *Four Saints in Three Acts* discovers a final fourth act, the audience may be partially prepared for the setting to portray the synchronic time of the Heavenly Mansion, with all the saints assembled and singing, with fanfare, "when this you see remember me," and to meditate on the meaning of the lines, sung in a melody not unlike that with which the opera begins:

> They have to be.
> They have to be to see.
> To see to say.
> Laterally they may. (612)

The staging of this opera, ironizing narrative progression, is in some respects mirrored by the staging of Glass and Wilson's *Einstein on the Beach*. Anna Fishaut explains, "The two chose their subject jointly—Albert Einstein becoming the mythic focus around which images of motion, space travel, and justice in the twentieth century circled—and then Wilson led the discussion regarding the visual structure. It was not until that dialogue had been mostly completed that Glass began to compose his minimalist, mathematically measured score."[44] Glass describes the collaboration this way: "I put [Wilson's notebook of sketches] on the piano and composed each section like a portrait of the drawing before me. The score was begun in the spring of 1975 and completed by the following November, and those drawings were before me all the time."[45] The result of this process is an operatic structure as fully lacking in narrative, history, characterization, logic, or causality as is the first opera by Stein and Thomson. Musicologist Robert Palmer explains:

> *Einstein on the Beach* . . . revolves around three recurring visual images, each of which has its corresponding music. There are trains . . . a trial scene . . . a spaceship . . . and Einstein himself . . . fiddling. . . .
>
> The organization, the patterning, the décor, along with the images themselves, make up the content of Wilson's work, serving the functions that plot, characterization, and narrative exposition serve in more conventional operas.[46]

Similarly, *Four Saint in Three Acts* fuses the words, the music, and Florine Stettheimer's lavish and fantastic stage sets into a single transportive experience, in which the presentation of the libretto as surtitles would have been interruptive to the reception of the event. After an "invited dress rehearsal," Carl Van Vechten wrote to Stein on February 8, 1924, "Four Saints, in our vivid theatrical parlance is a knockout and a wow. . . . I haven't seen a crowd more excited since *Sacre du Printemps*. The difference is they were pleasurably excited."[47] New York art critic Henry McBride chimed in with similar emphasis in a letter to Stein March 20, 1934:

> When we went up to Hartford for the premier we were expecting some kind of a good time, naturally, but we were totally unprepared for the unearthly beauty that the first curtain disclosed and which mounted and mounted as the thing went on and finally left all the hard-boiled and worldly connoisseurs in tears at the end. . . . It is indeed indescribable. With all this, the regular music critics (who knew nothing of painting) did not "get" it. . . . Even so, the event has upset New York as nothing else has this winter.[48]

After performances in Hartford and New York City had closed, Thomson's own reflections on the opera's reception were more measured but equally insistent on its intermediality and the impact it had on the audience. He wrote Stein April 21, 1934, "Of course there were some who didnt [sic] like the music and some who didnt like the words and even some who didnt like the décors [sic] or the choreography but there wasnt anybody who didnt see that the ensemble was a new kind of collaboration and that it was unique and powerful and I wish you could have seen the faces of people as they watched and listened."[49] The "unique and powerful" collaboration in-cluded Stettheimer's stage images, which were glittering, fantastic, and some would later argue, surreal. Thomson described the set to Stein on December 6, 1933:

> Miss Stettheimer's sets are of a beauty incredible, with trees made out of feathers and a sea-wall at Barcelona made out of shells and for the procession a baldachins of black chiffon & bunches of black ostrich plumes just like a Spanish funeral. St. Teresa comes to the picnic in the 2nd Act in a cart drawn by a real white don-key & brings her tent with her and sets it up & sits in the door-way of it. It is made of white gauze with gold fringe and has a most elegant shape. My singers, as I have wanted, are negroes, & you cant imagine how beautifully they sing.[50]

Of necessity Thomson had a relatively free hand in the selection of the stage setting, for most of the decisions about those designs were made during the one period (January 21, 1931–May 30, 1933) during which Thomson had been cut off from interaction—a quarrel resulting from his role as an inter-mediary in Stein's dispute with Georges Hugnet over publication of a book of his poems with English paraphrases in her distinctive style. Stein did, however, participate in the discussions of what would be sought toward the end of the arrangements with Stettheimer, responding on June 6, 1933, "I am entirely agreed that the stage setting of out of doors scenery would be the best, and I hope there will be the [o]xcarts, (with the [nuns?]), and the river and the landscape."[51]

Thomson's music, too, avoids melodramatic narrative, focusing instead on the smaller vocal units of the libretto itself. Somewhat nonplussed by the reaction of some of those experimenting with serial music and extreme atonality, Thomson mused that they failed to see the deliberate, nearly pa-rodic excess of his "willful harmonic simplicities" as a revolution against a prescription in modern music for atonality.[52] In its own way, in the context of the time his music was nearly as extreme as Stein's text. He uses "an elaborately-fitted-to-the-text vocal line" and "the plainest musical language"

and maintains those textual structures throughout. Thomson saw that setting "a text of great obscurity . . . had forced me to hear the sounds that the
American language really makes when sung, and to eliminate all those re-
courses to European emotions that are automatically brought forth when
European musicians get involved with dramatic poetry, with the stage."[53]
Alternating among recitative lines that intoned the text exactly or sang it to
the simplest of repetitive melody, and brief flashes of lyric arias or choral
passages, Thomson's music parallels the struggle between the diachronic of
narrative and the synchronic of "landscape" that Stein's text presents.[54]

Interestingly, given Thomson's insistence that the performers in *Four
Saints* be African American (at a time when only "black" parts were ordinarily made available to them), one of his first experiences in such acute "hearing" of English came in what he described as the "esthetic experience"
of a "Negro tent meeting." In summer 1925 he had written close friend
Briggs Buchanan, "I learned more about the rhythm of the English language
in a half-hour than I had ever known before. Also African scales. You see,
the sermon was intoned. And fitted into a regular rhythmic scheme. Basic
rhythms (clapping, swatting Bible, jumping) very simple. Complex and
syncopated rhythms to fill in the spaces. These determined by language,
but sufficiently exaggerated that they are recognizable apart from the language. The extraordinary thing to me, however, was their aptness to the
language."[55] This experience came at the same moment in his Harvard
years that he was beginning to experiment with setting some Stein pieces
to music.[56]

The trajectory of Thomson's development here is paralleled in some respects by that of Steve Reich. Beginning in his earliest years with looped
tapes of African American voices—street preacher Brother Walter in "It's
Gonna Rain" and an imprisoned black teenager in "Come Out"—by 1981
Steve Reich was seeking in *Tehillim* to match his music perfectly to the
human voice, invoking many of the same considerations that influenced
Thomson in setting Stein's text.[57]

Seeking a "universal text" to set that would represent his own tradition,
Reich selected verses from Psalms 19, 34, 18, and 150 for the vocal texts,
both because it seemed natural to him and because, he told an interviewer,
"as opposed to the Torah and the book of Prophets, which have traditional
melodies, the traditional melodies for singing the Psalms have been lost in
all the Ashkenazic . . . traditions. . . . Therefore it was a kind of green light

for me to compose . . . without having to ignore or incorporate some pre-existing melody."[58] This freed him to compose directly to the sound of the words:

> While the four-part canons in the first and last movements may well remind some listeners of my early tape pieces "It's Gonna Rain" and "Come Out," which are composed of short spoken phrases repeated over and over again in close canon, *Tehillim* will probably strike most listeners as quite different from my earlier works. There is no fixed meter or metric pattern in *Tehillim* as there is in my earlier music. The rhythm of the music here comes directly from the rhythm of the Hebrew text and is consequently in flexible changing meters.[59]

This method also resulted in withholding a grand dramatic structure, just as Thomson and Stein do in *Four Saints*. Asked, "Is there an underlying structure to the whole work?" Reich responded, "Not really. What is underlying the whole piece and what really makes it work is basically the use of groups of twos and threes in a totally free arrangement. This was done entirely by ear, depending on how my ear heard the syllables of the Hebrew."[60] The ending, however, offers a resolution to the canonic structure. Reich notes, "When the canonic process returns to unison . . . it's a perfect way to end. *Tehillim* is very traditional Western music, key-wise. . . . Hallelujah in D major certainly seems like a good place to end."[61]

Similarly, Thomson uses 3/4, 4/4, 3/2, 4/4, and 5/4 time in the first ten bars of the score alone. In the brief act 4 of *Four Saints*, all the singers are summoned on stage to sing in a celebratory chorus what Thomson calls "the saints' hymn"—"when this you see remember me," roughly an equivalent of "Hallelujah in D major." Nonetheless, this gesture toward traditional closure is not left as the final emotion, as Stein, the rigorous observer of the present moment, requires the flat final statement "Last Act./Which is a fact."

We have seen thus that as a prototype of later minimalism *Four Saints in Three Acts* offers important parallels at both a micro and a macro level. To repetition, phased language, tone drone, vernacular allusion, and fascination with ordinal numbers is added an associative structure which abandons plot, narrative, and logical coherence. Moreover, it shares with later minimalists an alteration in the method of making meaning. Rather than being *referential*, Stein's opera is *performative*—not in the obvious sense of being presented by singers and dancers in the theater but in the sense given the word by J. L. Austin in *How to Do Things with Words*, that the utterance *is* the action, and in the related sense given in *Gender Trouble* by Judith Butler, that a series of repeated actions actually construct, actually bring into being, the quality or state referred to.

The experience of hearing and seeing the opera and reflecting as one does so—however one does reflect—constructs an experience of intense consciousness in the present moment. For Stein, this experience of genuinely living in the present constitutes something much like what some would call an experience of the divine—an experience of sharing ever so slightly in the life of the saints in the Heavenly Mansion. Necessarily, such a text means multiple things and will be received differently by different members of the audience. It has to be what Robert Wilson calls "open . . . a dialogue with the public."[62] Wilson also says the theater is "a forum . . . a way of hearing, a way of seeing—a mental landscape for thinking."[63] (Or as Robert Palmer argues, *Einstein on the Beach* and other Wilson operas are "meditations, with their central figures serving as mantras."[64]) Whether it is *Four Saints in Three Acts* or *Einstein on the Beach*, the apprehension of the words and the music and the scenery on stage are all quintessentially a part of the experience—or, put another way, of the "meaning" or purpose of the opera. The intermediality and performativity of high modernism can be seen again in late contemporary modernism. It should surprise no one that when Robert Wilson was asked by the Houston Grand Opera to direct a revival of *Four Saints in Three Acts* in January 1996, followed by performances in New York and Edinburgh, the opera was again the talk of the town.[65]

Keith Potter places Steve Reich at the foundation of the development of contemporary minimalist music and its progeny. "While the tape recorders via which Reich discovered the technique of phasing may have soon been set aside by him in the pursuit of instrumental music," he writes,

> the transferral of phasing from tape to live performance must count among the major influences which electronic music has had on the development of music for players of conventional Western instruments. The composer's use of the sounds of American vernacular speech as a basis for composition has inspired a host of others, whether they wished to explore this territory in similarly experimental ways . . . or in the more conventional Western contexts of opera and song (for instance, John Adams). The advent of what we now call "sampling" in the mid-1980s not only gave a new lease of life to the use of tape . . . in the composer's own more recent output . . . but has also led to the re-evaluation of *It's Gonna Rain* and *Come Out* as pioneering examples of a technique central to late twentieth-century composition.[66]

Philip Glass, however, rejects the idea that he is indebted to Reich in this way, asserting that the two "had been developing our own music in our own distinctive ways."[67] Potter interprets "this remark [as] presumably intended to assert an already existing interest in reductive repetition developed before 1967, entirely independent of Reich."[68] Potter concludes that "such disputes concerning intellectual property can never be fully resolved; it is easier to conclude . . . [with] Robert T. Jones . . . that . . . 'It was an eruption of the times.'"[69] It is certainly true that the development of recording tape succeeded the first presentation of *Four Saints in Three Acts* in 1934, but what is missing from these assessments is a common denominator shared by John Cage, Steve Reich, Philip Glass, and Robert Wilson—an early fascination with the writings of Gertrude Stein, familiarity with the work of Virgil Thomson, and an acquaintance with the radically experimental opera they produced in 1934. And *this* is a heritage that both Philip Glass and Robert Wilson freely acknowledge. In a panel discussion with Virgil Thomson in 1987, Glass said, "The kind of operas that are now becoming part of this new generation of music theater really do begin with the Gertrude Stein-Virgil Thomson operas, which were theatrical without being bound to exactly telling a story in a usual way. They were also very visual . . . very much about movement . . . about color."[70] And in the playbill for his revival of *Four Saints in Three Acts* for the Houston Grand Opera in 1996, Wilson explains, "In the early sixties I began to read Gertrude Stein's work and I . . . heard the recordings of her speaking. That was . . . before I began to work in the theater and it changed my way of thinking forever. . . . I felt a creative dialogue with her, especially her notion of seeing a play as a landscape. The architecture, the structure, the rhythms, the humor—they invited mental pictures."[71]

These mental pictures—this state of mind, whether imaginative, Zen-like, or ecstatic—when successfully elicited, transport the participant into a state of being temporarily separated from the diachronic world and the means-end teleology of everyday existence. In pointing the direction toward the practices by which later minimalist writers and composers could enable audiences to enter similar states, the importance of this powerful opera of 1934, *Four Saints in Three Acts*, has become anything but "minimal."

Establishing the connection between Gertrude Stein and minimalism substantially broadens our understanding of Stein's impact on twentieth-century culture. Most literary scholars should be aware of Stein's importance in two periods. The first, 1909-14 and the years immediately following, were the years in which Stein published the story "Melanctha" in *Three Lives* (1909), the early "difficult" works "Matisse" and "Picasso" in Alfred Stieglitz's *Camera Work* in 1912, and *Tender Buttons* in 1914. As a consequence of these publications, the distribution by Mable Dodge of her *Portrait of Mabel Dodge at the Villa Coronia* at the New York Armory Show in February 1913, and the popularity of her weekly "at home's" in her rue de Fleures atelier hung floor to ceiling with Picasso, Matisse, and other modern artists, Stein at that time was seen as the literary parallel to the move to abstraction in art and atonality in music.[72] Although they professed to ridicule the "American lady" whose manuscript of *Tender Buttons* they seem to have seen in 1913, the circle of Cocteau and Apollinaire was soon to follow her with newly radical abstraction in French; e. e. cummings made her work central to his lecture "The New Art" at his graduation from Harvard in 1915, Edith Sitwell brought her to give the influential lecture "Composition as Explanation" at Oxford and Cambridge in 1926, and writers as varied as Ernest Hemingway and Sherwood Anderson took her narrative style as a model for their far less experimental writings.

In the second period, that of the mid-1930s, Stein had become influential in quite a different way. Instead of being ridiculed for her abstraction, Stein in 1934-35 was barnstorming the United States, speaking at colleges and arts organizations in the East, Midwest, South, and West following the widespread acclaim for *The Autobiography of Alice B. Toklas* (published 1933, excerpted and serialized in the *Atlantic Monthly*) and the smashing success of *Four Saints in Three Acts*.[73] The reputation she generated teaching a seminar at Chicago and speaking at institutions as varied as the Museum of Modern Art, Harvard, Amherst, Bryn Mawr, Princeton, the Universities of Virginia, North Carolina, Minnesota, Wisconsin, Michigan, and Indiana, Tulane, and a variety of public and private settings in Dallas, Austin, Los Angeles, and San Francisco made her a newsworthy figure for many years to come.[74]

Setting the record straight on the sources of operatic minimalism in Stein and Thomson's *Four Saints in Three Acts* confers a similar breadth of influence by Stein in the last decades of the twentieth century. Literary figures from John Cage to the L=A=N=G=U=A=G=E school to OuLiPo have found inspiration in Gertrude Stein. To recognize but one example among many possible, one can turn to Joan Retallack's experiment in "writing through" Gertrude Stein in her "Steinzas in Mediation" in *How to Do Things with Words* (1998) or her prolonged reflection on Stein's poetics in "The Difficulties of Gertrude Stein I & II" in *The Poethical Wager* (2003). Now it is clear that Stein's inspiration extends to minimalist music and stage performance as well.

Notes

I want to express my great thanks to research assistant Lauren Hawley, whose bibliographical work on this topic proved invaluable and contributed directly to its final form.

1. Gallup, 228.

2. Roeder 275.

3. Thomson, *Reader* 54; Watson 29.

4. Thomson, *Reader* 54.

5. Watson 38.

6. 3 Jan. 1927, Holbrook and Dilworth, *Letters* 23.

7. Ibid. 23.

8. Thomson, *Reader* 55.

9. In addition, Thomson set to music Stein's "Portrait of F.B.," the film scenario "Deux soeurs qui ne sont pas soeurs," and of course the later, less abstract opera, *The Mother of Us All* (Thomson, *Reader* 61).

10. Holbrook and Dillworth, *Letters* 27, 36.

11. Thomson, *Reader* 61-62.

12. Gallup 225; Dydo 173, 175.

13. Thomson, *Reader* 55; Stein, *Four Saints* 581. The play has been reprinted in several collections, including *Operas and Plays* (Paris: Plain Edition, 1932); *Last Opera and Plays*, ed. Carl Van Vechten, introd. Bonnie Marranca (New York: Rinehart, 1949; Baltimore: Johns Hopkins University Press, 1995); and *Selected Operas and Plays of Gertrude Stein*, ed. John Malcolm Brinnin (Pittsburgh: University of Pittsburgh Press, 1970), but it has never received scholarly publication after comparison with extant manuscripts. I am citing the version in *Selected Writings* because, of the readily available literary editions, it is the closest to the libretto used in the complete recording and very slightly shorter than the texts in either *Last Opera and Plays* or *Selected Operas and Plays*.

14. Stein, "Plays" 104-05.

15. Ibid. 93.

16. Ibid. 117, 118-19.

17. Ibid. 128-29.

18. Ibid. 129.

19. Stein, *Four Saints* 581.

20. One could also argue that the second line and fourth line remain iambic tetrameter, with stressed monosyllables substituting for the first two iambs in both lines and the fourth line augmented by a monosyllabic foot. (That argument leaves

the third line unaccounted for.) This potential ambiguity accords with Reich's own lack of concern to establish a preselected structure. See Kim 349.

21. Potter 162.

22. Bridgman 177; Dydo 186; Watson 44.

23. Stein, *Four Saints* 581.

24. Ibid. 581-82.

25. Stein and Thomson, *Four Saints*, complete vocal score 3.

26. Stein, *Four Saints* 582.

27. Ibid.

28. Reich 20-22.

29. Ibid. 20; Kostelanetz, *Cage* 19.

30. Revill 33.

31. Ibid. 34.

32. Ibid. 37.

33. Ibid.

34. Ibid. 37, 42.

35. Ibid. 42.

36. Stein, *Four Saints* 610.

37. Moreover, Bonnie Marranca claims that "John Cage counted at least thirty-eight allusions to nursery rhymes in the score" (54).

38. The Reisman "recording. . . contains all the music, lyrics and speeches from the original production as performed in Europe in the summer and autumn of 1976 and at the Metropolitan Opera House, New York, in November, 1976." Glass, CD notes 4.

39. Stein and Thomson, *Four Saints*, complete vocal score. Page numbers that follow come from the same score.

40. Maurice Grosser, untitled preface to Stein and Thomson, *Four Saints*, complete vocal score, n.p.

41. One should be aware, however, that Stein's insistence on the absolute present possesses none of the vision of a literal Heavenly Mansion of fundamentalist religion—a difference Thomson explicitly notes in his "Portrait of Gertrude Stein" for the *New York Review of Books*. He attributes to Toklas the statement "Gertrude was right, of course, to believe that 'when a Jew dies, he's dead'" (*Reader* 78).

42. Stein, "Composition as Explanation" 514.

43. Stein deliberately emphasizes inconsistency by shifting from words to roman numerals to number the acts and scenes.

44. Fishaut.

45. Shyer 220.

46. Palmer 5-6.

47. Gallup 275.

48. Ibid. 278-79.

49. Holbrook and Dilworth 233.

50. Ibid. 221.

51. Ibid. 211.

52. Kostelanetz, *Reader* 177.

53. Ibid. 177, 277, 212.

54. Here I must disagree with the emphasis on conflict between Thomson's music and Stein's text in Brad Bucknell's thoughtful discussion of the opera in *Literary Modernism and Musical Aesthetics*. He argues, "Thomson's very structured tonality and rhythms *suggest* the image of a syntactical and ordered progression and acceptable *social* structure. The *language* on the other hand . . . keeps drawing up possible images and scenes, and then dissolving them" (202). He offers important insight, however, when he identifies beginning again and again as "the primary musical technique of the opera" and argues that "in doing so [Thomson] really adopts for tonal music a Steinian technique" (196).

55. Page 62.

56. Ibid. 63.

57. "Black Pentecostal preaching hovers between speaking and singing. The phasing process intensifies this—taking one little phrase, the vowel pitches, and the consonantal noises that go with them. As I recorded Brother Walter, a pigeon took off near the microphone, and it sounds like a beating drum. So you've got a kind of drum beat, a low rumble of traffic going in Union Square, and then Brother Walter's words—all of this going against itself at a constantly varying time rate" (Reich 21).

58. Kim 349.

59. Reich 101.

60. Kim 349.

61. Ibid. 353.

62. Wilson 121.

63. Ibid. 115.

64. Palmer 5.

65. With Robert Wilson as director, the opera was performed in Houston January 26–February 7, at New York's Lincoln Center August 1–3, and at the Edinburgh Festival August 29–31, 1996. The influence of *Four Saints in Three Acts* continues today, for it was revived under the direction of Mark Morris as recently as March 1–3, 2012, in New York City. It had also received abbreviated performance in 2011 in both New York and San Francisco in connection with the exhibition *The Steins Collect: Matisse, Picasso, and the Parisian Avant-Garde*.

66. Potter 247.

67. Page 67, cited by Potter 262, 356.

68. Potter 262–63.

69. Ibid. 263.

70. Clark 185–86.

71. Wilson, "Director's Notes." Cited by Bay-Cheng 135, 199.

72. Rudnick 67.

73. "Interest in Stein's memoir was so great that when *The Autobiography of Alice B. Toklas* was released on September 1, the entire first printing of 5400 copies had already been sold. The *Autobiography* was the September selection of the Literary Guild, the Book of the Month Club's largest competitor, and thus a second printing was automatically distributed to homes throughout the United States. The book ran to four printings by 1935, and a French translation by Bernard Faÿ was published in 1934. The publication of the *Autobiography* was considered such news that Stein appeared on the cover of *Time* magazine on September 11" (Leick 147).

74. Mellow 496. See entire chapter, 454-97.

Bibliography

Adams, John. *Nixon in China*. Libretto by Alice Goodman. Orchestra of St. Luke's. Cond. Edo de Waart. CD#791772. New York: RCA/Nonesuch, 1987.

Albright, Daniel. "An Opera with No Acts: *Four Saints in Three Acts*." *Southern Review* 33.3 (1997): 574-604.

Bay-Cheng, Sarah. *Mama Dada: Gertrude Stein's Avant-Garde Theater*. New York: Routledge, 2004.

Bridgman, Richard. *Gertrude Stein in Pieces*. New York: Oxford University Press, 1970.

Bucknell, Brad. *Literary Modernism and Musical Aesthetics: Pater, Pound, Joyce and Stein*. Cambridge: Cambridge University Press, 2001.

Clark, J. Bunker, ed. and transcriber. "The Composer and Performer and Other Matters: A Panel Discussion with Virgil Thomson and Philip Glass, Moderated by Gregory Sandow." *American Music* 7.2 (Summer 1989): 181-204.

Dydo, Ulla, with William Rice. *Gertrude Stein: The Language That Rises 1923-1934*. Evanston, IL: Northwestern University Press, 2003.

Fishaut, Anna. "Robert Wilson." Stanford Presidential Lectures in Arts and Humanities. Accessed 18 Oct. 2012. <http://prelectur.stanford.edu/lecturers/wilson/>.

Gallup, Donald, Ed. *The Flowers of Friendship: Letters Written to Gertrude Stein*. New York: Knopf, 1953.

Glass, Philip. *Einstein on the Beach*. Scenario by Robert Wilson. Philip Glass Ensemble. Cond. Michael Reisman. CD #88697985152. New York: Sony, 1978.

Holbrook, Susan, and Thomas Dilworth, eds. *The Letters of Gertrude Stein and Virgil Thomson: Composition as Conversation*. New York: Oxford University Press, 2010.

Kim, Rebecca Y. "From New York to Vermont: Conversation with Steve Reich." *Current Musicology* 67-68 (Fall 1999): 345-66.

Kostelanetz, Richard. *John Cage (ex)plain(ed)*. New York: Simon & Schuster / Schirmer, 1996.

———. *Virgil Thomson: A Reader—Selected Writings 1924-1984*. New York: Routledge, 2002.

Leick, Karen. *Gertrude Stein and the Making of an American Celebrity*. New York: Routledge, 2009.

Marranca, Bonnie. "Hymns of Repetition." *Performing Arts Journal* 18.3 (Sept. 1996): 42–47.

Mellow, James R. *Charmed Circle: Gertrude Stein & Company*. New York: Avon, 1974.

Page, Tim. "A Conversation with Philip Glass and Steve Reich." *Music from the Road: Views and Reviews 1978–1992*. New York: Oxford University Press, 1992. 66–67.

Page, Tim, and Vanessa Weeks Page, eds. *Selected Letters of Virgil Thomson*. New York: Summit, 1988.

Palmer, Robert. "*Einstein on the Beach* on Stage." Liner notes for Philip Glass, *Einstein on the Beach*. Scenario by Robert Wilson. Philip Glass Ensemble. Cond. Michael Reisman. CD #88697985152. New York: Sony, 1978. 5–6.

Potter, Keith. *Four Musical Minimalists: La Monte Young, Terry Riley, Steve Reich, Philip Glass*. Cambridge: Cambridge University Press, 2000.

Reich, Steve. *Writings on Music 1965–2000*. Ed. Paul Hillier. New York: Oxford University Press, 2002.

Revill, David. *The Roaring Silence: John Cage; A Life*. New York: Arcade, 1992.

Roeder, John. "Beat Class Modulation in Steve Reich's Music." *Music Theory Spectrum* 25.2 (Autumn 2003): 275–304.

Rudnick, Lois Palken. *Mabel Dodge Luhan: New Woman, New Worlds*. Albuquerque: University of New Mexico Press, 1984.

Ryan, Betsy Alayne. *Gertrude Stein's Theatre of the Absolute*. Ann Arbor: UMI Research Press, 1984.

Shyer, Laurence. *Robert Wilson and His Collaborators*. New York: Theatre Communications Group, 1989.

Stein, Gertrude. "Composition as Explanation." In *Selected Writings of Gertrude Stein*. Ed. Carl Van Vechten. New York: Random-Vintage, 1990. 513–23.

———. *Four Saints in Three Acts*. transition (June 1929). Rpt. in *Selected Writings of Gertrude Stein*. Ed. Carl Van Vechten. New York: Random-Vintage, 1990. 581–612.

———. "Plays." *Lectures in America*. 1935. Boston, Beacon Press, 1985. 93–131.

Stein, Gertrude, and Virgil Thomson. *Four Saints in Three Acts*. Orchestra of Our Time. Cond. Joel Thome. Complete recording 79035-2. New York: Elektra-Nonesuch Records, 1982.

———. *Four Saints in Three Acts: An Opera by Gertrude Stein and Virgil Thomson*. Scenario by Maurice Grosser. Complete vocal score. New York: Music Press and Arrow Music Press, 1948.

Strickland, Edward. *Minimalism: Origins*. Bloomington: Indiana University Press, 1993.

Thomson, Virgil. "Langlois, Butts, and Stein." *Virgil Thomson* (1966) by Virgil Thomson. Rpt. in *A Virgil Thomson Reader*. New York: Dutton, 1984. 50–62.

———. "A Portrait of Gertrude Stein." *New York Review of Books* 7 July 1966. Rpt. in *A Virgil Thomson Reader*. New York: Dutton, 1984. 69–78.

———. *A Virgil Thomson Reader*. Introduction by John Rockwell. New York: Dutton, 1984.

———. *Virgil Thomson*. 1966. New York: Plenum/Da Capo, 1977.

Watson, Steven. *Prepare for Saints: Gertrude Stein, Virgil Thomson, and the Mainstreaming of American Modernism*. New York: Random House, 1998.

Wilson, Robert. "Director's Notes." Houston Grand Opera Stagebill (Winter 1996). Byrd Hoffman Foundation Collection.

Wilson, Robert, and Fred Newman. "A Dialogue on Politics and Therapy, Stillness and Vaudeville. Moderated by Richard Schechner." *Drama Review* 47.3 (Fall 2003): 113-28.

Zamsky, Robert. "'A Narrative of Prepare for Saints': Lyric, Narrative, and the Problem of Nationalism in *Four Saints in Three Acts*." *Modernism/modernity* 11.4 (Nov. 2004): 723-44.

III Opera after World War II
Tensions of Institutional Modernism

9 Stravinsky, Auden, and the Midcentury Modernism of *The Rake's Progress*

Herbert Lindenberger

The "Beautiful"

Interviewed on a BBC television documentary about his librettist W. H. Auden fourteen years after *The Rake's Progress* was first performed (1951), Igor Stravinsky looked back at their joint project with the following words: "As soon as we began to work together I discovered that we shared the same views not only about opera, but also on the nature of the Beautiful and the Good. Thus, our opera is indeed, and in the highest sense, a collaboration."[1] Those who have studied the Strauss-Hofmannsthal collaborations or the collaborations of Verdi with his various librettists are more aware of tensions and differences than they are of the solid harmony that marked Stravinsky's work with Auden—or, more precisely, his work with Auden and his partner Chester Kallman, who drafted roughly half of the libretto.[2]

If this harmony between Stravinsky and Auden was made possible by their agreement "on the nature of the Beautiful and the Good," as well as about the genre within which they were working, it is clear that they shared both an aesthetic and an ethical framework that might shed some light on what has now, after more than sixty years, emerged as one of the great classic operas. I start with the aesthetic framework guiding *The Rake's Progress*. Both Stravinsky and Auden at the time of composition could be called neoclassicists. Although this designation had long been used to characterize the composer during the more than thirty-year period preceding the opera, there is no generally recognized classification of the poet, for British and American critics have traditionally been resistant to period terms, such as baroque and neoclassicism, that are drawn from other art forms. Stravinsky is often described as the founder of musical neoclassicism, although the aesthetic's defining characteristics were anticipated by others, most notably by Ferruccio Busoni, whose "Sketch of a New Aesthetic of Music" (first published in 1907) laid the ground for what Busoni would later call his New Classicality (Neue Klassizität).[3] Flanked by his so-called "Russian" and serial periods, neoclassicism marked the longest and most productive of the three phases of Stravinsky's career. And *The Rake's Progress* is the most large-scale and complex and also the final work of this composer's neoclassical period. Perhaps the most conspicuous mark of his neoclassical phase is its self-consciousness about the musical past, which manifests itself in imitations of earlier musical forms—for example, Bach inventions, sonata-type movements—forms that he had obviously eschewed in the works that established his fame during his "Russian" period. Some of Stravinsky's neoclassical works are essentially remakings of compositions by a specific composer, as *Pulcinella* (1920), which rewrote a number of pieces that Stravinsky took to be by Pergolesi, and *Le baiser de la fée* (1928), a loving homage to Tchaikovsky. Yet the listener is always reminded, by means of the dissonances and rhythmic irregularities of a neoclassical piece, that the composer is not simply reproducing the past but rather interpreting it in a characteristically contemporary way.

Auden's neoclassicism manifests itself most obviously in the dazzling array of English and classical poetic forms that he borrowed and rethought. For example, two of his finest poems from widely separated parts of his career use Greco-Roman ode stanzas: "In Memory of Sigmund Freud" (1939) is written in alcaics, "River Profile" (1966) in sapphics. Note the following stanza from the latter poem:

> Disemboguing from foothills, now in hushed meanders,
> now in riffling braids, it vaunts across a senile
> plain, well-entered, chateau-and-cider-press country,
> its regal progress . . .[4]

Just as Stravinsky distorts earlier musical idioms through unexpected dissonances and rhythmic changes, so Auden here strains the English language in his attempt to approximate the long and short syllables of Greek and Latin verse. The unexpected locutions ("disemboguing," "senile plain"), together with the distorted syntax, challenge readers of poetry in ways similar to those that listeners to Stravinsky's neoclassical works experienced. Indeed, one might describe neoclassicism in both poetry and music as the employment of traditional forms—often going back to the earliest traditions within each medium—to work as familiar containers within which the poet or composer can then complicate and distort the language and the music in totally unfamiliar ways. For example, Joseph N. Straus, in studying Stravinsky's sketches for *The Rake's Progress*, has found that the composer started with "rhythmically square and harmonically rudimentary" ideas that "have the appearance of a simple, classical prototype," with "the 'classical' com[ing] first chronologically and the 'neo' emerg[ing] as the compositional process unfolds."[5] But Stravinsky's "neo" games extend as well to undoing the natural accent in his librettist's text: as Richard Taruskin has pointed out after examining the composer's sketches, Stravinsky first set Anne's line "Although I weep, it knows no loneliness" to scan regularly, but he then crossed out his initial version and decided to stress such syllables as the "al" in "although" and the pronoun "it."[6] And in the second stanza of Anne's aria, he even chose to mangle Auden's syntax.

The forms appropriated by Auden in the course of his career encompass the whole history of English poetry. His early poem "The Wanderer" (1930), from its opening line, "Doom is dark and deeper than any sea-dingle" (62), invokes Anglo-Saxon alliterative verse. "Letter to Lord Byron" (1936) borrows the tone of the addressee's *Don Juan*, though it shifts from the latter's ottava rima to rhyme royal because, as the poet jokes, the former proved too difficult for him (85). "New Year Letter" (1940) renews the convention of the verse epistle in rhymed octosyllabics. *The Sea and the Mirror* (1944), which Auden calls a "commentary" on Shakespeare's *The Tempest*, contains a whole plethora of earlier poetic forms, for example, Petrarchan sonnet (Ferdinand's speech, 412); terza rima (Antonio's speech, 410-12); sestina (Sebastian's speech, 419-20); villanelle (Miranda's speech, 421-22), Shakespearean-style songs (406-22), not to speak of the late Henry Jamesian prose of "Caliban to the Audience" (422-44), the work's longest section.

It is little wonder that Aldous Huxley, Stravinsky's friend and neighbor, suggested Auden as librettist when the composer sought his advice after determining to create an opera out of William Hogarth's eight-painting narrative entitled *A Rake's Progress* (1734). "The making of poetry he seemed to regard as a game," Stravinsky later remarked of Auden. "All his conversation about Art was, so speak, *sub specie ludi*."[7] Much the same could be said of the composer's attitude toward his own work, at least during his neoclassical phase. Indeed, many readers, listeners, and critics during this time complained that, instead of making major pronouncements or stirring up big emotions, neoclassical composers and poets teased their consumers by

doing little more than playing games. Although most of the significant composers and poets during this period played the neoclassicist game, their
consumers, however attentive to their work, often felt a bit let down. I can
speak for this myself, having become quite familiar with both Stravinsky's
and Auden's work during the 1940s—before the creation of *The Rake's Progress*. For example, "interesting" as a work such as Stravinsky's *Symphony in
Three Movements* seemed when I first heard it about 1946, I could not feel
the same excitement that the great works of his "Russian" period—above
all, *The Rite of Spring*—generated. Similarly, although I could "appreciate"
the verbal ingenuity of, say, "Mundus et infans" (324-25), it could not "do"
the things for me that I had come to expect from such "exciting" high modernist poets as Yeats, Eliot, and Pound.

I did not, to be sure, assent to the outright rejection of the neoclassical
Stravinsky common among many music critics at the time. For example, the
veteran *New York Times* reviewer Olin Downes characteristically decried
each new Stravinsky piece of the period with terms such as "dry" and "un-
inspired"—while reminding his readers that this was the composer who had
once thrilled his listeners with works such as *The Firebird* and *Petrushka*. It
had clearly become difficult to experience works in the neoclassical mold,
whether musical or literary, within the same frame of mind that one assumed for high modernist ones. And, as a study of the reviews following
the opera's Venice premiere demonstrates, its early critics made much the
same complaint, while the serialist establishment, typified by the young
Pierre Boulez's remark, "what ugliness," found its own, predictable mode of
rejecting the new opera.[8]

The irony in all this is that, whatever the differences in frame of mind
demanded from the listener, the composer's "Russian" and seemingly antithetical neoclassical works issued from the same sensibility, whose differences in style during these two periods today seem less radical than they did
half a century ago.[9] Auden, in contrast, was born too late to participate in the
high modernist revolution. A full generation younger than the composer, his
poetry, despite some workmanlike early imitations of Eliot, remained neoclassical throughout his career. And it is no accident that, well before the opera
project with Stravinsky had entered his life, he had expressed his preference
for the composer's neoclassical over his "Russian" works.[10]

Even if listeners and readers did not yet possess the necessary frame of
mind, we can now look back to neoclassicism as the dominant among several competing trends in all the arts between 1920 and 1950. Even Picasso

had a brief neoclassical fling during the 1920s (he had, as well, collaborated with Stravinsky in the *Pulcinella* production), and viewers of his neoclassical nudes needed a different frame of mind from that demanded by *Les demoiselles d'Avignon* or the cubist paintings of the first decade of the century. In music neoclassicism encompassed a wide variety of composers in all Western countries—Poulenc, Milhaud, Hindemith, Weill, Martinů, Copland, to name only a few—and was propagated widely through the teachings of Nadia Boulanger. Even Schoenberg, whom Stravinsky for strategic reasons chose to ignore for most of his life, had his neoclassical period during the 1920s in works that, within his new twelve-tone style, imitated the likes of Bach-style suites and sonata-type compositions. At one point Stravinsky described the music that Schoenberg, Berg, and Webern composed during the 1920s as neoclassic but added that, in contrast with his own practice, in which historical references were "overt," theirs were "elaborately disguised."[11] Indeed, Robert Craft reports a brief crisis in confidence on the part of Stravinsky: remembering a recent performance by Craft of Schoenberg's *Septet* (op. 29 [1927]; a suite of baroque-like dance movements in twelve-tone form), on a car trip to the Mojave desert, the Russian composer came close to weeping—less, apparently, from the effect of the music than from the fact that the Austrian had beat him at his own game.[12] (Stravinsky resolved the crisis by himself picking up the twelve-tone method from its now safely dead creator—though his compositions in this mode sound far less like those of the second Viennese school than they do like the earlier Stravinsky pieces we have long known.)

And, within Anglophone poetry at midcentury, neoclassicism (even though nobody used this or any common name) was pretty much the only game in town. A restrained tone, traditional syntax, clever rhyming—all this in contrast with the free and obscure verse of the preceding generation— characterized an array of otherwise diverse poets: Robert Lowell (at least up to his confessional period), Marianne Moore, John Crowe Ransom, Stanley Kunitz, Louise Bogan, Yvor Winters, and such British Movement poets as Donald Davie and Philip Larkin. Many, like Auden, revived elaborate verse forms. And even so oracular, otherwise un-Audenesque a poet such as Dylan Thomas forced his obscure syntax into elaborate stanzaic patterns.

The apparent "coolness" characterizing midcentury modernism can be applied to art in other media, for instance, to the cinematic work of Ingmar Bergman, whose 1961 stage production of *The Rake's Progress* in Stockholm Stravinsky called "the most original and beautiful realization of any of my theater pieces that I have ever seen on any stage."[13] What drew the composer to Bergman is evident in his statement that "[Bergman's] way of thinking is close to mine. His very severe, very hot-cold way of expressing himself fascinates me."[14] Indeed, Stravinsky's own neoclassicism, as he suggested in this remark, helps make sense of the "severe" and "hot-cold" aesthetic behind such great Bergman films as *The Seventh Seal* and *Persona*. And this same "hot-cold" mode of expression is equally applicable to the severely controlled passion emanating from Auden's poetry.

It thus seems natural that Auden and Stravinsky proved so successful a match aesthetically—and that both the libretto and music of *The Rake's Progress* should take neoclassical practices to an extreme. The libretto alone, as Willard Spiegelman has shown, is encyclopedic in the references to earlier literature that it brings together.[15] Not that the listener is necessarily aware of these references. To be sure, the various myths that Auden invokes—the Faust story by means of Nick Shadow's Mephistophelian relationship to Tom Rockwell, Mother Goose in the brothel scene, Venus and Adonis in the final scene—are pretty obvious on the surface. Yet he also includes a plethora of literary allusions—to Milton, the eighteenth-century satirists, Wordsworth, Keats, among many more—that, even though they might not be discernible in the opera house, would look familiar in a reading of the libretto.

Similarly with the music. Stravinsky has ransacked the history of opera—at least the history of "number" opera—without demanding that his listeners recognize his allusions. Some, like the myths cited above, are obvious. Every serious opera-goer thinks of the *Don Giovanni* epilogue while hearing *The Rake*'s epilogue, and the latter opera's cemetery scene, if only by virtue of its setting, recalls the scene in which Don Giovanni first confronts the Commendatore's statue. But who would necessarily hear the opening of Monteverdi's *Orfeo* in Stravinsky's opening bars? This early opera, indeed, was known largely to musicologists at the time Stravinsky composed *The Rake's Progress*. During the brief period in late 1947 that Auden spent in the Stravinsky household planning the opera, the two collaborators attended a two-piano performance of *Così fan tutte* that later elicited the composer's remark, "An omen, perhaps, for *The Rake* is deeply involved in *Così*."[16] And, to be sure, *Così*, not to speak of *Don Giovanni*, is mentioned frequently in musicological commentaries on Stravinsky's operas.[17] Opera-goers attending *The Rake* will doubtless feel at various points that they have heard this *kind* of music before—Mozart? Monteverdi? Donizetti? Verdi?—but without the dissonances that this "neo-minded" composer has injected.

Imitation of earlier operatic forms came easily to *The Rake*'s creators, for both Stravinsky and Auden were steeped in the operatic repertory. As a child, the composer had sat through innumerable performances at the Marinsky, where his father was a principal bass. Auden began attending opera regularly in New York after his relationship with Kallman, already an opera buff, started in 1939. Echoing the operatic past for *The Rake's Progress* must have been a pleasure for both the composer and the librettists. Indeed, the one time I met Auden, at a faculty reception following a reading he gave during the mid-1950s, he wanted to talk about nothing but opera once he discovered that I knew a thing or two about this topic; attempts by my colleagues to introduce other topics of conversation were stifled by our distinguished guest.

To illustrate some of the ways that a listener can react to one of the long-antiquated forms employed in *The Rake*, consider the cabaletta to Anne Trulove's aria at the end of act 1:

I go, I go to him.
Love cannot falter,
cannot desert;
Though it be shunned
or be forgotten,
though it be hurt,
if love be love
it will not alter.
O should I see
My love in need,
It shall not matter,
What he may be.
Time cannot alter
A loving heart,
an ever loving heart.[18]

As one reads these words without the music, it is instantly clear that Auden, recognizing the difference between libretto style and poetry as such, would never have written this passage as an independent poem. Everything is exaggerated—much as it was in the Italian libretti that Auden knew so well. Anne expresses the constancy of her love in the traditional discourse of the many constancy arias that span the history of opera. Who would expect anything except the most outrageous clichés ("If love be love, / It will not alter") from a soprano voicing the steadfastness of her love?

Moreover, the section is carefully marked "cabaletta" in the score (120)—
just as the other set pieces—duettino, trio, aria, recitative, and the like—are
explicitly marked. Although the score contains a number of arias, each in an
individual style, only Anne's aria contains a cabaletta. It is as though the librettist and composer are telling us that we are experiencing a cabaletta in
its most essential, most archetypal form. The monosyllabic opening, with
its almost banal vocal line (G-E-C, F-D-B) outlining two obvious chords
(121), reflects at once the simplicity of the heroine and the simplicity at the
heart of any cabaletta (one remembers how the aging Verdi often expressed
his embarrassment about having to compose cabalettas for his singers). And
look at the line "It will not alter," which Stravinsky repeats four times with
different ornamentations (122-25). (Had the opera been composed two decades later—after the bel canto revival had begun—one suspects that the ornamentations would have been even more extravagant.) And although the cabaletta had originally ended with a lower note, Auden, quite conscious of the
need for a cabaletta to show off a singer's higher range, talked the composer
into a high C (129). Indeed, the whole idea behind a high C had a special meaning for Auden, who once wrote, "Every high C accurately struck utterly demol-
ishes the theory that we are the irresponsible puppets of fate or chance."[19]
    When I first attended *The Rake's Progress* about a year after its premiere
I took Anne's cabaletta to be simply a parody of its form. But I later came to
realize that it was far more than that, for Auden and Stravinsky are telling us
many things: that the cabaletta form and its exaggerations are central to the
nature of opera; that we are to see Anne both as silly and, through the ear-
nestness of her vocalizing, as utterly serious; that in the extravagance of
both text and music—here and in a multitude of other passages, for example, Baba's farewell aria—opera reveals itself as at once noble and foolish.
Anne's cabaletta, one suspects, also makes a statement about the many real-
life people who choose to lead their lives in an overtly operatic way. As I
listen to it now after attending many diverse productions, I hear it as the
cabaletta to end all cabalettas. (I can think of no cabalettas in subsequent
operas, but then the convention had been dead for well over half a century
before *The Rake's Progress*.)
    Among the productions I have attended, none seems as appropriate to
the Auden-Stravinsky aesthetic as the one designed by David Hockney for
the Glyndebourne Festival in 1975 and subsequently seen in several opera
houses. Hockney's sets pretend to be engravings in the style of those that
Hogarth authorized to reproduce his paintings for *A Rake's Progress*. The

exaggerated cross-hatchings that Hockney devised within each scene revisit, with an appropriate ironic distance, the world of eighteenth-century
engraving.[20] Moreover, the cross-hatching affects not only the walls and windows, but also the curtains and many of the costumes. Together with the
words and the music performed within these settings, the audience here experiences a neoclassical, thoroughly un-Wagnerian *Gesamtkunstwerk*.

The "Good"

If the completed opera embodies its creators' conception of "the Beautiful," how does it give voice to that other term, "the Good," that Stravinsky
used to indicate their intellectual compatibility? Although it is easy enough
to analyze literary works for their ethical content, finding this content in
music is a tricky endeavor. After all, musical discourse does not make statements that can easily be translated into verbal terms. One could, of course,
cite certain works, for example, Beethoven's *Fidelio* and Ninth Symphony,
whose humanitarian messages are clear to any listener—yet we also possess
the words to which these works are set, words that help clarify the musical
messages that hit audiences in so powerful a way.

Poetry, by contrast, readily reveals its ethical content. And within twentieth-century poetry in English, no body of verse is more ethically laden
than Auden's. One of his most-quoted lines, "We must love one another or
die," is so overtly didactic that the poet's ethical conscience ultimately
found it "inauthentic"—with the result that Auden, after rereading "September 1, 1939," in which the line occurred, decided that the whole poem "was
infected with an incurable dishonesty" and thenceforth banished it from his
collected works.[21]

But making moral statements, even if not so overt as the line "We must
love one another or die," was central to Auden's writing, whether in verse
or prose. The epilogue to *The Rake's Progress* is a brief collection of moral
apothegms, for example, in Tom's lines:

Beware, young men who fancy
You are Virgil or Julius Caesar,
Lest when you wake
You be only a rake. (404–05)

Yet the epilogue, both its words and its music, is, like the opera as a whole,
thoroughly ironic, and determining what real ethical messages come
through this opera would be difficult at best.

To get a more precise hold on this topic, I limit my discussion to the ways that works of art stimulate distinct ethical responses in their audiences. However one might evaluate "September 1, 1939," nobody would question Auden's ability throughout his career—whether during his leftist or his Christian periods—to elicit such responses. For example, his elegy to Yeats, "In Memory of W. B. Yeats" (1939), forces the reader to think about the gap between a poet's morality and the quality of his writing. "The Shield of Achilles" (1952), by juxtaposing Homer's seemingly beautiful shield to descriptions of modern war, reduces the ancient scene to the horrors that Hephaestos's art had sought to disguise.

Literature, whether poetry or fiction, performs its ethical work far more readily—or at least more discernibly—than do the visual arts or music. To be sure, certain visual artists are conspicuous for their ability to elicit ethical responses. Many Rembrandt portraits are notable for the power with which they awaken compassion in their viewers, and Edvard Munch's *The Scream* (1893-1910), with its literal cry for help on the part of the woman at the center—not to speak of the figures contemplating suicide on the bridge behind her—puts to the test the viewer's ability to respond to the plight of others.

Yet there is one form of painting, the narrative cycle, that rivals literary narrative in its ability to draw ethical responses from its viewers. In the innumerable stories of the Passion told in multiple panels in medieval and Renaissance churches, it is clear that the Catholic Church knew that it could communicate its doctrines in visual terms with a special effectiveness to its often illiterate viewers. I bring up the narrative cycle since Stravinsky's opera derives not from an earlier written text but from one of the major narrative cycles in the history of art.

Stravinsky remembered seeing William Hogarth's *A Rake's Progress* at the Chicago Art Institute in 1947.[22] I also saw the Hogarth cycle while it was on loan there; indeed, over the years I have fantasized how wonderful it might have been to follow the composer through the show and observe him looking at each of the eight panels to assess its operatic possibilities.[23]

A Rake's Progress, together with Hogarth's other cycles, *The Harlot's Progress* (known today only through its engravings since the paintings were destroyed in a fire) and *Marriage A-la-Mode*, rivals the work of the painter's literary colleagues Swift, Pope, and Gay in the satirical power with which it uncovers the vices and the hypocrisy of the society around him. And like its literary contemporaries, *A Rake* seeks to awaken its consumers' moral sensibilities. Hogarth's Tom Rakewell, like his operatic descendant, is pictured "progressing" through a series of bad choices—squandering his money, dissipating, marrying foolishly—that culminate in his relegation to Bedlam.

Just as *The Rake* is suffused with allusions to the musical past, so *A Rake* depicts many earlier paintings on the walls as a means of casting an ironic light on its various dramatic situations. For example, painting 2 has a large *Judgment of Paris* that implicitly contrasts Paris's choice of Helen with Tom's choice (in painting 5) of an aging, ugly rich woman whom he marries for financial reasons alone. And the Bedlam scene in the final painting shows Tom in the unmistakable pose of Christ in a pietà. Hogarth alludes not only to painting but to music: painting 2 shows a composer, thought to be Handel or Porpora, playing an operatic score entitled *The Rape of the Sabines*—still another allusion to Tom's dissolute life; the later, engraved version of this painting contains the names of specific singers such as Senesino and Cuzzoni.[24] *A Rake*, moreover, already contains the traces of an opera (or an opera of sorts) in its allusion to *The Beggar's Opera*, from which Hogarth had already painted a scene—Polly Peachum's plea to her father—on at least two occasions.[25] It is no wonder that Stravinsky saw operatic possibilities in the narrative cycle he viewed in Chicago.

Yet the viewer's experience in reading Hogarth's paintings against the earlier paintings depicted in them is considerably different from that of the audience of Stravinsky's opera. Seeing Tom Rakewell juxtaposed to the mythical Paris or posing in a pietà immediately tells us how mediocre this hero is compared to these other figures. By contrast, even if we recognize the opening sinfonia of *Orfeo* in the introduction to *The Rake*, the allusion in itself does not make a moral point; rather, it seeks to establish the latter work as a worthy member of that great tradition originating with Monteverdi's opera. The most explicit references to *Don Giovanni*—the cemetery scene and the epilogue—not only serve, like the *Orfeo* allusion, to tie Stravinsky's work to this tradition, but they also influence our experience of the earlier work: the card game in *The Rake*'s cemetery scene helps us to see the game-like quality of Giovanni's interchange with the Commendatore, while Mozart's epilogue comes to seem even more ironic than we usually take it to be when we place it next to the more blatant ironies with which the characters of the later work bring it to its conclusion. Similarly, Auden's great poem "Musée des Beaux Arts," with its unforgettable opening— "About suffering they were never wrong, / The Old Masters"[26]—has encouraged me, each time I have visited the Brussels museum, to read Auden back into Brueghel's *Fall of Icarus*. And whenever I have visited the Hogarth paintings at Sir John Soane's Museum since first hearing the opera, Stravinsky's catchy short tunes take hold of me. Such reading back and forth in time is endemic to the experience of mid-twentieth-century neoclassicism.

The Hogarth paintings that played most directly into the opera are the tavern scene (painting 3) and the final scene in Bedlam. Both would likely have struck the composer as operatic in character when he first saw them. Many of the changes, including the additions, that he and Auden made were designed to heighten the operatic nature of the work. Most notably, Hogarth made no use of the Faust story, which, after Marlowe's work, did not reenter literature until the late eighteenth century. But the addition of Nick Shadow and his Faustian pact with Tom Rakewell put *The Rake's Progress* squarely within an operatic tradition that, besides those works—by Berlioz, Gounod, Boito, and Busoni—in which Faust is specifically named, includes such Faust-infused tales as Meyerbeer's *Robert le Diable*, Offenbach's *Les contes d'Hoffmann*, and Stravinsky's own, generically unclassifiable *L'histoire du soldat* (1918). It is as though the process of selling one's soul to the devil keeps demanding operatic treatment. Still, whatever ethical problems emerge from Marlowe's and Goethe's literary versions of the story are pretty much lost in their musical embodiments, in which the relation between devil and victim largely assumes the characteristics of a game—and a literal card game, at that, in the cemetery scene of Stravinsky's opera.

Moreover, the two leading female characters in *A Rake* needed operatic uplifting to make them more theatrically viable than they appeared in the paintings. Thus, the lowly Sarah Young, whom Tom has impregnated in *A Rake*, becomes the far classier and chaste Anne Trulove: by raising her class status, Auden and Stravinsky are able to portray a figure of more will than Hogarth's pathetic figure. Yet in both the paintings and the opera this figure is notable for the loyalty she maintains toward her thoroughly unreliable lover. In painting 4, for example, Sarah appears to help Tom escape debtor's punishment by means of the small sum she has earned as a seamstress, and in the Bedlam scene she weeps at his side without Tom's showing any awareness of her presence. And in both the paintings and the opera the loyal woman appears as the only positive figure within an otherwise corrupt world.

The dumpy, middle-aged woman whom Tom takes as his wife in *A Rake* is thoroughly transformed in the opera. Now she becomes the grotesque bearded lady Baba the Turk, the thought of whom supposedly caused

Auden and Kallman to burst into uproarious laughter together. "The quality common to all great operatic roles," Auden wrote soon after *The Rake*, "is that each of them is a passionate and wilful state of being."[27] Although the hero and heroine of *The Rake* scarcely qualify as willful beings (except for the cabaletta that briefly endows Anne with willfulness), Baba surely does. Her fits of temper and her constant posturing represent an unbearable assertion of will, and, like a number of Verdi mezzo figures, Baba ordinarily steals the show.

In the outrageousness of her theatricality, Baba points to an aspect of the opera relevant to this discussion of the work's ethical implications. In an earlier paper, "Anti-theatricality in Twentieth-Century Opera," I discuss four operas—*Pelléas et Mélisande, Moses und Aron, Saint François d'Assise*, and *The Rake's Progress*—to argue that these major works all question the nature of theatricality.[28] The first three of these operas, moreover, display an overt, virtually puritanical disdain for theatricality, which their composers associate with a certain inauthenticity. One may wonder why I included *The Rake's Progress* in this group, for it is as overtly theatrical as any opera in the classic repertory. Its theatrical extravagance is evident especially in scenes such as the visit to Mother Goose's brothel, the cemetery scene, and the attempted sale of Baba the Turk as Tom auctions off his possessions; yet this extravagance also marks such other moments as Anne's cabaletta and the scene with the bogus bread-making machine. At the same time that *The Rake's Progress* demonstrates how wildly operatic it can be, it also asks its listeners to note the extreme artifice at the heart of the form, indeed, to maintain a skeptical stance toward the emotions it purports to convey to its audiences. Although Auden, Kallman, and Stravinsky all dearly loved opera, their very love also enabled them to expose its inauthentic underside. Indeed, the ludicrous element introduced by Kundry's laughter to challenge of sublimity in which *Parsifal* culminates, as Matthew Wilson Smith demonstrates in his chapter in this volume, becomes the dominant tone of Stravinsky's intransigently anti-Wagnerian opera; and the hysteria that Smith pinpoints in Kundry is taken to its most ludicrous extreme—as the librettists' laughter shows—in that most absurdly theatrical of operatic characters, Baba the Turk.

To keep their audience at a distance sufficient to evaluate what is going on, the creators of *The Rake's Progress* maintain their ironic masks throughout the opera. To be sure, this distancing is a hallmark of neoclassical style in both poetry and music, and anybody comfortable with this style would approach the opera without demanding that it speak out to us in a directly emotional way. Yet there is one conspicuous spot in the final scene in which Stravinsky briefly removes his mask: the great lullaby that the ever-faithful Anne sings to her mad Tom in Bedlam (383-85). The voice is marked *dolce*, and the flute accompaniment *dolce e cantabile*. From the opening lines, we recognize that this lullaby is as straightforward as, say, Marie's lullaby to her child in *Wozzeck*:

> Gently, little boat,
> Across the ocean float,
> The crystal waves dividing:
> The sun in the west
> Is going to rest;
> Glide, glide, glide
> Toward the Islands of the Blest. (383)

With its haunting obbligato for two flutes, this lullaby displays a direct lyric expressiveness rare within the otherwise ironic style dominating the opera. Yet in its context it seems entirely appropriate and in no way sentimental— and after all, this great passage is followed directly by the epilogue, which restores the opera's dominant irony. A film version of the opera insists on dropping the epilogue entirely and instead ends with a flashback of Anne repeating her lullaby while hugging Tom in a pastoral landscape[29]—a revision so unconscionable that, as I watched the film, I was sure I could hear the composer turning in his watery Venetian grave.

What we recognize in the lullaby in its proper context is that, amid the theatrical antics that dominate *The Rake's Progress*, a strong emotion such as compassion can still manifest itself and work infectiously on its audience. The forgiveness that the much-wronged heroine grants Tom—as weak and foolish a tenor hero as one can find within the history of opera—provides an ethical lesson that listeners can absorb directly without having to reflect on the action as they do throughout the rest of the work. After attending many productions since 1952, I still leave the opera house not only hearing Anne's melody in my head but also feeling thoroughly moved by the compassion emanating from the music. Indeed, just as I was revising this chapter, I heard a radio interview of the two singers playing Anne and Tom in the Metropolitan Opera revival of spring 2015: both singers, Layla Claire and Paul Appleby, admitted that during rehearsals they could scarcely hold back their tears during the Bedlam scene—in fact, that they needed to exert severe discipline on themselves simply in order to sing the music.[30] And as we look back at the opera from this scene, we come to recognize a certain pathos gradually emerging beneath the irony that has suffused the opera up to this point.

Beyond the opera itself, one can speak of a particular attitude that both Auden and Stravinsky took to their vocation as artists, an attitude, moreover, whose ethical implications are relevant to our understanding of their work. I refer to the fact that both practiced the game of High Art in a self-consciously responsible way. For Auden every word and for Stravinsky every note and chord had to count. Both could be immensely tough on other practitioners who they believed did not meet the standards they set for themselves. "That now so ascendant *Ariadne auf Naxos*?" Stravinsky remarked during the 1950s. "I cannot bear Strauss's six-four chords. *Ariadne* makes me want to scream."[31] Or Auden in his introduction to an edition of selected Tennyson poems: "He [Tennyson] had the finest ear, perhaps, of any English poet; he was also undoubtedly the stupidest."[32] Statements such as these, flippant though they may sound, also indicate the high standards that they characteristically set for their respective art forms. Auden's continuing revising of earlier poems, together with his refusal to allow several of his most famous pieces to appear in his collected editions, testifies to the extraordinary demands that he made on himself. Both Stravinsky and Auden, unlike many of their contemporaries, scrupulously put into practice the famous advice that the perfectionist John Keats gave to his sometimes sloppy fellow poet Percy Shelley to "'load every rift' of your subject with ore."[33]

Neither Stravinsky nor Auden had any patience with the notion that art should be a means of self-expression. The neoclassical aesthetic that they practiced was itself an attempt to expunge whatever Romantic elements they might be tempted to allow into their work; and in his earlier high modernist period Stravinsky had already, unlike his rival Schoenberg, distanced himself from self-expressive indulgences. The notion of poetry or music as a game provided both poet and composer with a metaphor to avoid the leftovers of Romanticism that can be found in many otherwise modernist artists. To the extent that they pursued the game with authority and without compromise, they demonstrated that the Good is by no means incompatible with the games of art.

Notes

1. Griffiths 4.

2. For convenience's sake, I shall refer to Auden alone as the librettist throughout this essay. Despite Kallman's major role in the project, it was Auden who initially worked out the plan for *The Rake's Progress*, which he presented to the composer without mentioning his partner's proposed role. When Stravinsky, already in the midst of composition, learned that Auden was not the sole librettist, he was at first miffed but soon after accepted the arrangement. Kallman adapted himself so comfortably to Auden's style that readers have found it hard to distinguish who drafted which parts. For a list of which partner was responsible for particular passages, see Griffiths 14.

3. See Levitz 69-78.

4. Auden, *Collected Poems* 806. Subsequent references to this edition will be noted in the text.

5. Straus 165, 166.

6. Taruskin 194-96.

7. Stravinsky and Craft, *Memories and Commentaries* 157.

8. See Giaquinta. Boulez's remark appears in a letter from Boulez to John Cage reporting on recent musical developments in Europe (Boulez and Cage 118).

9. Rudolf Stephan has identified a common impulse behind Stravinsky's approach to his compositional models, whether Russian folksong or the music of J. S. Bach, in the concept of defamiliarization developed by Viktor Shklovsky and his fellow Russian formalists early in the century (244-46).

10. Carpenter 350. This statement, made in conversation with the composer Nicolas Nabokov, dates from 1945, two years before he met Stravinsky for the preparation of *The Rake's Progress* libretto.

11. Stravinsky and Craft, *Conversations with Igor Stravinsky* 126.

12. Craft, *Stravinsky* 72-73. Another version that Craft wrote of this incident shows Stravinsky actually breaking into tears. See Craft, "Assisting Stravinsky."

13. Qtd. in Carter 292.

14. Ibid.

15. Spiegelman 101-10.

16. Stravinsky and Craft, *Memories and Commentaries* 158.

17. See, for instance, Hyde 135; and Cross 137.

18. Stravinsky 121-30. Subsequent references to the score will be noted in the text.

19. Auden, "Some Reflections on Music and Opera" 302.

20. For reproductions of Hockney's set designs, together with earlier engravings that inspired them, see Vaccaro 141-56. For an analysis of this production, see Chimènes 157-76.

21. Callan 170-71. To read "September 1, 1939" today, one needs to look in the various anthologies that, despite the poet's rejection, have continued to reprint it.

The poem is available, for example, in *The Norton Anthology of Poetry*, edited by Margaret Ferguson, Mary Jo Salter, and Jon Stallworthy (1474-76). This anthology also contains "Spain 1937" (1466-68), a once-popular poem that Auden removed from his collected works as well.

22. Stravinsky and Craft, *Memories and Commentaries* 154.

23. Although Stravinsky claimed that he had seen the paintings in 1947, my own memory is that I saw the paintings at the Art Institute in late 1946 while they were part of a selection of major paintings by Hogarth, Constable, and Turner sent by Great Britain to the United States. Before I left the exhibition, I bought the catalogue, which lists the exhibition dates as October 15-December 15, 1946. See *Masterpieces of English Painting*.

24. For details on the allusions, see Paulson 20-35. See also Hallett and Riding 86-93.

25. Reproduced in Hallett and Riding 70-71; see Paulson 24-25.

26. Auden, *Collected Poems* 179.

27. Auden, *Prose* 3:299.

28. Lindenberger 196-218.

29. *The Rake's Progress*, dir. Inger Åby.

30. Interview on Sirius XM radio, 29 Apr. 2015.

31. Stravinsky and Craft, *Conversations with Igor Stravinsky* 75.

32. Auden, *Prose* 2:204.

33. Letter of 16 Aug. 1820, Abrams and Greenblatt 1,857.

Bibliography

Abrams, M. H., and Stephen Greenblatt, eds. *The Norton Anthology of English Literature: The Major Authors*. 7th ed. Volume B. New York: Norton, 2001.

Auden, W. H. *Collected Poems*. Ed. Edward Mendelson. Rev. ed. London: Faber and Faber, 1991.

———. "Introduction to *A Selection from the Poems of Alfred, Lord Tennyson*." *W. H. Auden: Prose*. Ed. Edward Mendelson. Princeton: Princeton University Press, 2008. 2:203-11.

———. "Some Reflections on Music and Opera." *W. H. Auden: Prose*. Ed. Edward Mendelson. Princeton: Princeton University Press, 2008. 3:296-301.

———. *W. H. Auden: Prose*. Ed. Edward Mendelson. Princeton: Princeton University Press, 2008.

Boulez, Pierre, and John Cage. *The Boulez-Cage Correspondence*. Ed. Jean-Jacques Nattiez. Trans. Robert Samuels. Cambridge: Cambridge University Press, 1990.

Callan, Edward. "*Disenchantment with Yeats*: From Singing-Master to Ogre." *W. H. Auden*. Ed. Harold Bloom. New York: Chelsea House, 1986. 161-76.

Carpenter, Humphrey. *W. H. Auden: A Biography*. Boston: Houghton Mifflin, 1981.

Carter, Chandler. "Bergman's *Rake's Progress*: How a Director Helped Create an Operatic Masterpiece." *Igor Stravinsky: Sounds and Gestures of Modernism*. Ed. Massimiliano Locanto. Turnhout: Brepols, 2014. 291-99.

Chimènes, Myriam. "Une production de l'Opéra Glyndebourne: Les décors et costumes de David Hockney, la mise en scène de John Cox." *The Rake's Progress*. Ed. J.-M. Vaccaro. Paris: Editions du Centre National de la Recherche Scientifique, 1990. 157-76.

Craft, Robert. "Assisting Stravinsky: On a Misunderstood Collaboration." *Atlantic Monthly* 250.6 (Dec. 1982): 64-74. Accessed 19 Mar. 2013. <http://www.theatlan tic.com/past/docs/issues/82dec/craft82.htm>.

———. *Stravinsky: Chronicle of a Friendship*. Rev. and exp. ed. Nashville, TN: Vanderbilt University Press, 1994.

Cross, Jonathan. "Stravinsky's Theatres." *The Cambridge Companion to Stravinsky*. Ed. Jonathan Cross. Cambridge: Cambridge University Press, 2003. 137-48.

Ferguson, Margaret, Mary Jo Salter, and Jon Stallworthy, eds. *The Norton Anthology of Poetry*. 5th ed. New York: Norton, 2005.

Giaquinta, Rosanna. "*The Rake's Progress*: The Critics' Perception of the World Premiére (Venice 1951)." *Igor Stravinsky: Sounds and Gestures of Modernism*. Ed. Massimiliano Locanto. Turnhout: Brepols, 2014. 441-51.

Griffiths, Paul. *Igor Stravinsky: The Rake's Progress*. Cambridge: Cambridge University Press, 1982.

Hallett, Mark, and Christine Riding, eds. *Hogarth*. London: Tate, 2006.

Hyde, Martha M. "Stravinsky's Neoclassicism." *The Cambridge Companion to Stravinsky*. Ed. Jonathan Cross. Cambridge: Cambridge Univ. Press, 2003. 98-136.

Levitz, Tamara. "Teaching New Classicality: Ferruccio Busoni's Master Class in Composition 1921-1924." Diss. University of Rochester, 1993.

Lindenberger, Herbert. *Situating Opera: Period, Genre, Reception*. Cambridge: Cambridge University Press, 2010.

Masterpieces of English Painting: William Hogarth, John Constable, J. M. W. Turner. Chicago: Art Institute of Chicago, 1946.

Paulson, Ronald. *Hogarth: High Art and Low, 1732-1750*. New Brunswick: Rutgers University Press, 1992.

The Rake's Progress. Dir. Inger Åby. Sveriges Television (later issued by NVC Arts), 1995.

Spiegelman, Willard. "*The Rake's Progress*: Operatic Pastoral." *W. H. Auden*. Ed. Harold Bloom. New York: Chelsea House, 1986. 101-10.

Stephan, Rudolf. "Zur Deutung von Strawinskys Neoklassizismus." *Vom musikalischen Denken: Gesammelte Vorträge*. Ed. Rainer Damm and Andreas Traub. Mainz: Schott, 1985. 243-48.

Straus, Joseph N. "The Progress of a Motive in Stravinsky's *The Rake's Progress*." *Journal of Musicology* 9.2 (Spring 1991): 165-85.

Stravinsky, Igor. *The Rake's Progress: An Opera in 3 Acts*. London: Boosey & Hawkes, 1951.

Stravinsky, Igor, and Robert Craft. *Conversations with Igor Stravinsky*. Berkeley: University of California Press, 1958.

——. *Memories and Commentaries*. Berkeley: University of California Press, 1959.

Taruskin, Richard. "Stravinsky's 'Rejoicing Discovery' and What It Meant: In Defense of His Notorious Text Setting." *Stravinsky Retrospectives*. Ed. Ethan Haimo and Paul Johnson. Lincoln: University of Nebraska Press, 1987. 162-99.

Vaccaro, J.-M., ed. *The Rake's Progress*. Paris: Editions du Centre National de la Recherche Scientifique, 1990.

10 *Gloriana* and the New Elizabethan Age

Irene Morra

This Age hath genius too of high report,
And now, conjoined with some artistic Earls,
    Arts Council gallants
Doe cheer them on to bow before the Court,
As Shakespeare once, and Spenser, Tudor churls,
    Displayed their talents.

It may well be that judges yet unborn,
Will finde these words and musick are as fine
    As any written,
And say of oure Elizabethan morne,
"O dulcet ayres! O, Plomer's mighty line!
    O, rare Ben Britten!"

Sagittarius

In 1952, the satirist Sagittarius (Olga Katzin) drew attention to the dominant (and much-publicized) expectations around Benjamin Britten's forthcoming coronation opera. Not only would *Gloriana* celebrate the new queen, but it would offer a cultural manifestation of a new Elizabethan age. This moment, supported by a glittering court, was to be characterized by individual genius and the proud patronage of a state-funded Arts Council.[1] It would articulate the cultural strength of a modern, emergent Britain, in so doing evoking the achievements of the earlier Elizabethan era.

This rhetoric of a new Elizabethan era dominated the coronation year: promoted in the mainstream press and popular works such as *The New Eliz-abethans* (Philip Gibbs, 1953) and numerous Elizabethan studies by popular historian A. L. Rowse, it emphasized both cultural continuity and national renewal. Just as Elizabethan England had emerged from the shadow of Spain to initiate an era of adventure and artistic might, so too could the new Elizabethans shake off a postwar gloom, embrace modern discovery and adventure, and reflect upon that accomplishment in a new flourishing of the arts. While modern artists were hardly expected to write in the same style and idiom as their Elizabethan predecessors, their work would recapture and replicate the national experience of the genius and energy of that earlier era. In so doing, they would be offering a performative manifestation of a great and modern Britain that had as yet to fully appear: "We are now Elizabethans again. Could we hope for a new Elizabethan era with its flowering of genius, its high spirit of adventure, its golden share in the renaissance of learning and the arts? . . . Well, why not?"[2]

The origins of this rhetoric arguably lie in the 1940s, with the founding of the Arts Council. The self-conscious promotion and encouragement of national art had been a defining motive of the council, and when Covent Garden reopened in 1946, it overtly promoted an ideal of national opera based on vernacular expression and national heritage.[3] By 1953, however, the Arts Council had run afoul of more traditional voices. For Conservatives, the egalitarian approach to society and culture apparently encouraged by the Arts Council and a recently dismissed Labour government repressed the very individual talent and genius that had defined the strength of the nation: "Are we losing our old individualism and independence of character, asking to be pap-fed by a benevolent State? . . . Can we save our souls, our songs, our humour, our laughter, even if we lose our Empire and our former wealth?"[4] Bemoaning the influence of the welfare state as "the bureaucratic and industrial enemy of the sweet pastoral of Deep England," Gibbs hailed the return of Winston Churchill and delighted in the possibilities represented by the new young queen.[5] As Heather Wiebe argues, the coronation celebrations can in many ways be seen as a "Tory response" to Labour's 1951 Festival of Britain, articulating "an optimistic British modernity in self-consciously different terms, emphasising social hierarchy and individual achievement rather than egalitarianism."[6] Melman identifies a similar distinction: the Festival of Britain, supported by the Arts Council, had "evolved around a mundane and everyday people's history," while the coronation "occasioned another revival of a heroic past of monarchs as the focus of people's collective emotions, and as the engine of change."[7] *Gloriana* was written for the coronation year and (like Britten's Festival of Britain opera, *Billy Budd*) supported by the Arts Council.[8] To some extent, therefore, it

could be expected to manifest this apparent conflict between the egalitarian "modernity" of the council and the imperialist nostalgia (and ambitions)
of its conservative, aristocratic audience.[9]

This expectation, however, would overlook the overt—and often exclusive
—nationalism of many of the projects of the Arts Council itself. As Melman
has noted, when the Arts Council panel sponsored an opera competition for
the Festival of Britain, it awarded four works that "punctured definitions of
a homogenous national history."[10] These works were not easily "accommo-
dated within the guiding plan and vision of the Festival," however, and were
not staged until decades later.[11] In the coronation year, the council commissioned *A Garland for the Queen*, a collection of madrigals modeled on the
Elizabethan collection *The Triumphs of Oriana*. Leading poets and composers were invited to treat "contemporary Britain" in its "widest sense."[12]
Nonetheless, the invitation was qualified both by the use of the madrigal
form and by the accompanying prescriptive advice: "A search for modern
parallels with the age of the first 'Oriana' may prove fruitful: the continuing
spirit of discovery; the renascence of music or of the arts as a whole, loyalty
to the monarchy, and compliment to the first lady of the land."[13] Projects
such as *A Garland for the Queen* enforce an unambiguous relationship among
modern artists, the monarchy, and a received ideal of cultural tradition.
They also align those artists with a historical moment whose apparent association with perseverance, discovery, pastoral wistfulness, and cultural
achievement implicitly enshrines their own national and contemporary significance. As Wiebe in particular has indicated, such nationalist practices
are not dissimilar from those promoted by the organizers of the coronation
festivities. Indeed, the madrigals were performed at the coronation concert,
which also included original madrigals, Purcell's *King Arthur*, and Vaughan
Williams's *Tallis Fantasia*. The coronation service similarly "put the English
musical tradition itself on display, surveying music from the sixteenth century to the present."[14] Britten's subsequent involvement in the coronation
opera—not to mention his fortuitous choice of Elizabethan subject—would
implicitly underline similar ideals.

By 1953, the national position of Britten had been firmly established.
Thanks to the immediate success of his 1945 opera, *Peter Grimes*, Britten
had superseded many of his peers to become the next apparent hope for
British musical endeavor. Unlike other European powers, England had never
truly developed and established its own operatic tradition. The success of
Peter Grimes was seen to redress this phenomenon, and its international

reception was received as a recognition both of a reemergent Britain and of its immediate cultural strength. Indeed, not only had the work gone "far to break down the inferiority complex under which English opera had laboured for so many years," but, as Arthur Oldham noted in 1951, "it seemed too good to be true that, after more than two hundred years of disillusionment, England was again to lead the world in this most complicated sphere of musical achievement."[15] This rhetoric of a simultaneous cultural rebirth and dominance echoes much of the language around the new Elizabethan era, positioning Britten simultaneously at the forefront of modern culture and as an ideal composer for a proud nation.

Nonetheless, Britten himself tended to resist the nationalist implications of his recognition, distancing himself from the political and cultural ambitions of the institutions that acclaimed his success. To some extent, this distance was motivated by aesthetic instinct. At the time of both *Peter Grimes* and *Gloriana* (and arguably still today), the idea of national opera tended to be most consistently associated with nineteenth-century grand opera: large scale, melodic, characterized by rousing choruses and the spectacular staging of an informing historical past. Indeed, when Britten and Lord Harewood discussed the national operas of different countries, their list comprised nineteenth-century operas exclusively: "What was 'national' expression in opera, we asked ourselves; what were the 'national' operas of different countries? *The Bartered Bride* obviously for the Czechs, said Ben, *Manon* for the French, *Boris* and all that for the Russians. . . . For the Italians undoubtedly *Aida*, said Ben."[16] Apparently perceiving in the scale and success of *Peter Grimes* a certain recognition of this tradition, Covent Garden and the Arts Council continued to embrace and encourage more large-scale projects, both from Britten himself and from other composers.[17] Britten, however, moved swiftly into smaller works for the English Opera Group, seeing in chamber opera a more progressive future for his own modern aesthetic. Not only did Britten remove himself from the cultural center of London to Aldeburgh, but his English Opera Group became associated with an "opera fringe" that countered "the opera establishment" of Covent Garden and the Arts Council.[18]

This "fringe" identity was further bolstered by Britten's well-known political leanings. An established pacifist known for his work with such left-leaning, "clever" writers as W. H. Auden and Ronald Duncan, Britten may well have been the most famous composer of the day, but he was also associated with suspect values that were as much social (and sexual) as they

were aesthetic.[19] Indeed, as early as 1941, Britten had decried any attempt
to create a national music as "only one symptom of a serious and universal
malaise of our time."[20] The best way to avoid such malaise was to avoid any
adherence to an artificial, constructed ideal of continuous cultural expression: "The English composers of today . . . are avoiding the pitfalls that some
of their musical fathers and uncles have dug for them. It is only those who
accept their loneliness and refuse all the refuges, whether of tribal nationalism or airtight intellectual systems, who will carry on the human heritage."[21]
A year before the premiere of *Gloriana*, Donald Mitchell and Hans Keller had
produced a collection of essays, *Benjamin Britten: A Commentary on his
Works from a Group of Specialists*. A defensive piece on "Britten's Englishry"
highlighted continuing concerns about Britten's musical and social Englishness: "How closely related is Benjamin Britten to the English tradition? Many
will argue that he isn't; that lying outside nationalist musical considerations
he . . . is too clever, too sophisticated, too eclectic, too polished, too heart-
less even—a list of adjectives the opposites of which might add up to the
average Englishman's conception of the national character."[22] While the
book attempted to enshrine Britten as a leading national composer, it also
suggested—like Britten—that vital modern art demands a redefinition of
national culture and identity from those outside of conventional national
institutions.[23]

Such assumptions would have been very much at odds with the dominant rhetoric in the coronation year. Unsurprisingly, perhaps, neither Britten's critics nor his advocates tend to regard *Gloriana* as a complete fulfil-
ment of a single vision: the general (and negative) consensus seems to be
that the opera vacillates between Britten's characteristic instincts and his
half-hearted concessions to the national event. For some, the opera's apparently petulant unwillingness to offer a traditional, nationalist pageant with
hummable tunes rendered it thoroughly unsuitable for the occasion. The
occasion offered "a perfect setting for an all-star production of [Edward
German's 1902 operetta] *Merrie England*. . . . Instead, we had Mr Britten,
which was tough all round."[24] This "once great" queen and "swashbuckling
courtier" are "dwindled, in spite of fine clothes, by such uneasily nervous,
ungenerous music."[25] Many of these complaints centered on the work's simultaneous invocation of a suitable subject and its deliberate subversion of
its Elizabethan mythology: "It was an inept choice for the occasion because
it presented to the young Queen Elizabeth II a portrait of Queen Elizabeth
I, old and raddled, removing her wig to display an almost bald head and

every other sign of decay."[26] This apparent lack of respect for the glorious legacy of Elizabeth I, for the new young queen, and for musical "beauty" confirmed many suspicions about self-consciously clever and modern art and its emphatically negative, willed removal from any positive national zeitgeist. Tory MP Beverly Baxter noted the "apprehensive" demeanor of the Speaker of the House of Commons at the premiere: "How would he respond to this new cacophonous music of the ultramoderns?"[27] Ultimately, his fears were realized: "No melody emerged, no tune, no beauty in the sustained passages"; Britten "[seemed] to be shouting, 'Ugliness is truth, and truth is ugliness!' "[28]

Despite this perception of a hostile and deliberately subversive "ultra-modernism," Britten defenders similarly tend to qualify their praise. In these assessments, Britten's natural, modernist aesthetic was necessarily limited by the national context for which he was writing. *Gloriana* offers Britten's "most conventional operatic structure," revealing an unnatural attempt to be more conservative, to "tap into the national consciousness—to produce a truly 'national' stage work."[29] In a letter to David Webster, Peter Pears asserted that *Gloriana* was a "so-called 'flop'" precisely because "it is not a Covent Garden opera. Ben is incapable of writing 'grandiose,' both sound-wise and stage-wise, and *Gloriana* is in fact much more likely to come off in a smaller theatre than Covent Garden."[30] According to Mitchell, despite such limitations, *Gloriana* remains "obstinately true to [Britten's] genius."[31] Nonetheless, he valuates the work not according to its own singular merits but for its ability to be reassimilated within an implicit Britten canon: "The opera, with its spectacular and festal dimension, was certainly faithful to the occasion. . . . But more interestingly, at the heart of it, the composer remains stubbornly faithful to ideas that were central to his creative life."[32] While the opera's first audiences may have "felt cheated of another *Merrie England*," therefore, those "who knew their Britten better may have been disappointed that he had relaxed so far the musical tension that distinguished [his preceding opera, *Billy Budd*]."[33]

Such responses underline the extent to which "serious" opera was assumed (or expected) to remain on the fringes of the national(ist) stage. In apparent recognition of this incompatibility between his modern art and national institutions, Britten returned to composing smaller chamber operas, away from Covent Garden. According to Harewood, Britten and Peter Pears concluded that they should "in future stick to the public that wanted them, the loyal Aldeburgh friends, and not get mixed up with something

that was none of their concern": "He had made a great public gesture and
the public had, so to speak, rejected him. He had risked writing for other
than 'his' audience."[34]

Gloriana is almost always read as a misguided concession to a nationalist
occasion, an attempt to adhere to social and aesthetic values foreign to Britten's own modernist sensibilities. Nonetheless, the mere fact that *Gloriana*
was an *opera* ensured an immediate break from the ideal of cultural continuity promoted in works such as *A Garland for the Queen*. To some extent, the
very form of the work ensured its vexed national reception. While modern
composers could align themselves with an English madrigal tradition, they
could not position themselves in relation to a national operatic heritage.
Indeed, the idea of national opera as grand opera did not just invoke
nineteenth-century conventions; it suggested an inherently "foreign" tradition. Verdi could create a "national opera" about tragic love in Egypt precisely because the form in which he was writing had become so strongly
associated with Italian cultural expression. Britten had no such indigenous
operatic tradition with which to align his work.

Furthermore, some of the most popular grand operas—particularly Italian opera—had adopted English literary sources or historical material, mythologizing and rewriting Walter Scott and Shakespeare plots within their
distinctly grandiose presentations. As Oldham notes, before *Peter Grimes*,
"we had suffered the discomfort of seeing our literary classics become operatic masterpieces in the hands of an Italian genius and been powerless to
compete."[35] Ironically, the operatic idiom celebrated in works such as
Verdi's *Macbeth*, Donizetti's *Roberto Devereaux*, or Rossini's *Elisabetta, regina
d'Inghilterra* (which aired three times on BBC Radio's Third Programme in
the coronation year) meant that subsequent English treatments of similar
sources or historical moments had to distinguish themselves somehow
from the language of these appropriations.[36] Although the subject of *Gloriana* seemed to advertise the Englishness of the project, it also inevitably
invoked comparison with nineteenth-century Italian and French opera. As
Andrew Porter's appreciative review of *Elisabetta* made clear, the broad narrative of Rossini's opera bears some similarity to that of *Gloriana* and invites
an evaluative comparison: "The tenor is not Essex, but Leicester—also en-
cumbered with a wife, also imprisoned for treachery. But in the end Elizabeth forgives all, turns her back on love and decides to devote herself to
duty."[37]

To some extent, an indigenous English response to the grand opera tradition had already been established by the Savoy operas. Works such as *Merrie England* continued this tradition, simultaneously invoking and parodying the conventional musical language and plot contrivances of the more melodramatic Italian operas. They did so within an emphatically English context, placing considerable emphasis on witty wordplay and downplaying the significance of musical ingenuity, passion, or drama. When archconservatives such as Baxter advocated for *Merrie England* over *Gloriana*, they were implicitly recognizing a more established, populist, and familiar template for national expression in musical theater. In its lighthearted and satirical parochialism, however, operetta is not opera—nor is it national pageant or drama. Furthermore, *Merrie England* may have enjoyed countless amateur revivals in the early 1950s, but by 1953 the Englishness of operetta had been perceptibly transformed by its assimilation within the form of the twentieth-century musical and by a potentially suspect alliance with American popular culture.

With relatively little interest in a new operetta and even less in a new definition of national opera, the many detractors of *Gloriana* seemed to demand an impossible creation. The work's reception suggests a desire for a uniquely English national pageant and drama that would aggrandize both the monarch and a (re)emergent England. Most of these criticisms, however, also seemed to anticipate a familiar form. As Richard Capell argued, "Whether any mortal men could have succeeded in such an enterprise may be doubted. Plomer and Britten have failed."[38] Despite the popularity and familiarity of *Merrie England* at the time, most reviews of *Gloriana* seemed to expect grand opera. Eric Blom commended the work's success in this regard: *Aida* "would in fact have been the last of the kind in operatic history but for the reappearance of 'Gloriana,' the first two acts of which are a kind of *festa teatrale*."[39] Porter similarly recognized "an historical opera (the only one of our time which comes to mind)"; like *Boris Godunov* "it is surely a national work which must win international acclaim."[40] Others were less convinced. Not only did the opera's music make Stanley Bayliss "want to cry out for an enormous orchestral noise," but its excessive reliance on pageantry seemed to prevent conventional moments of traditional, passionate drama.[41] Capell complained simultaneously of "ungenerous music," a surfeit of "galliards and lavoltas, jolly though these are in their way"—and an inability to recognize that "in all the great lyric dramas of the past the characters have been simple, their motives plain to every man."[42] Stephen Williams noted music "that even deviates into melody here and there," but both he and Shawe-Taylor bemoaned an excess of pageantry rather than drama: "Bold manipulation . . . might have produced a taut drama of amorous and political intrigue; but this was not the aim of author and composer."[43]

These reviews reveal not a desire for more pageant or *Merrie England* but an expectation of a traditional, nineteenth-century grand opera transformed into a proudly nationalist English idiom. Ironically, they failed to recognize that it is in these moments of pageantry that Britten seems to be most self-consciously attempting to perform such a transformation. The subject and scale of *Gloriana* invite parallels with *Aida* or *Boris Godunov*. This association is also suggested in the work's large choral set pieces, in its representation of passion amid political intrigue, and in its emphasis on historical spectacle and display. In a letter to Plomer, Britten declared his hope that the opera be "crystal-clear, with lovely pageantry . . . but linked by a strong story about the Queen & Essex—strong and simple. A tall order, but I think we can do it!"[44] At the same time that the opera invokes these conventions, however, it also attempts to assert an Englishness *within* this essentially foreign tradition. In both the extended masque scene and the court dances, Britten engages with Elizabethan musical traditions, all the while attempting to avoid any simplistic "hotch-potch."[45] As Evans argues, in Essex's lute songs, the masque and court dances, and the Ballad Singer's verses, Britten creates "a sound-picture" that "in some way" suggests "the Elizabethan period."[46] Rather than reinventing grand opera within a modern English idiom, Britten inserts signifiers of English musical (but not operatic) identity within this traditional, recognized form.

This musical project, however, conflicts with and disrupts the conventional expectations otherwise invoked by the opera itself. These "English" scenes and musical interludes seem to point up a disjunction between the work's signaled, overt Elizabethanism (both old and new) and its expected nationalist function *as grand opera*.[47] A similar disjunction is signaled in William Plomer's libretto. Unlike Britten's previous, more "difficult" literary collaborators,[48] Plomer adopted a more conventional role: "The music is the thing, and if the composer finds obstacles in the libretto, it is for the librettist to remove them or find a way round them."[49] Nonetheless, Plomer also recognized a need to signal the project's Englishness in his language: he identified in his libretto deliberate "plays on words (an Elizabethan habit), echoes of the Elizabethan love of antithesis, or quotations of Elizabethan plain speaking."[50] Such literary moments are difficult to discern within the context of sung drama, however, and more than one critic lamented Plomer's "stilted lines," which (like Britten's dances and masque) apparently hindered the music from achieving the full expression invited by the form.[51]

Furthermore, when these stylistic "Elizabethanisms" *do* integrate within the operatic form, they seem to lose the very authenticity to which Britten and Plomer were aspiring. Ernest Newman, for example, complained that in its operatic context, the music came across as "hardly more than pastiche, sometimes very clever pastiche, sometimes not so clever."[52] One of the libretto's most prominent, recurrent verses is the choral

> Green leaves are we
> red rose our golden Queen,
> O crownèd rose among the leaves so green.

These lines may have been inspired by notes in an Elizabethan boy's schoolbook, but they become extremely conventional when presented within a choral operatic setting.[53] Plomer attempted to "shun everything that might smack of Wardour Street, Merrie England, good Queen Bess, or the halfbaked, half-timbering of debased twentieth-century 'tudor' styling."[54] Similarly, Britten tried to avoid "hotch-potch." Ultimately, however, by containing moments of Elizabethan "authenticity" within a larger project whose subject and spectacle seemed to promise high romance and drama within the "foreign" idiom of grand opera, both Plomer and Britten rendered themselves susceptible to these very accusations.

According to Capell, *Gloriana* only exposed "the limitations of [Britten's] art": all the "breadth of style, the heartiness, the passionate flow, wanted to represent a sanguine age, are lacking."[55] These ideals of breadth, rhythm, passion, spectacle, and song dominated the rhetoric around a new Elizabethan culture. They also, however, characterized traditional expectations of national grand opera. Britten and Plomer attempted to avoid a simplistic (and "foreign") adherence to the conventions of nineteenth-century grand opera. Instead, they offered what they saw as a celebration of authentic, Elizabethan Englishness within that traditional form. In so doing, however, they moved *Gloriana* further from the anticipated idiom and values of new Elizabethan expression.

For many, the Elizabethan age itself was not history but a performed, expressive, and to some extent operatic art: "England was a nest of singing birds. Poets flashed out like stars above the darkness of men's minds. They were great lovers, though some of them laughed at love because of human frailty. Some of them, like Shakespeare himself, seemed to bleed at the heart with love, and cried out in a kind of mad anguish at love denied."[56] This era was best read both *as* theater and *through* its own theatrical traditions: "The explanation of the miracle that is Shakespeare . . . is that in his work there is more than the man: there is the age."[57] This theater, however, is defined exclusively by its manifestation in the written word. Gibbs, for example, notes that the "poetic spirit" has "seldom been missing for any length of time from our heritage and richness of the written word."[58] Advocating a modern flowering of the arts, he asks, "Shall we have our Shakespeares and Marlowes, our Bacons and Spensers in the literary world? There are lands yet to explore and develop."[59] In such rhetoric, the greatest manifestation of the living spirit and culture of both the old and the new Elizabethan era is to be found in the poetry, song, and theater of the "written word" as manifest on the Shakespearean stage. Unlike madrigals, unlike sonnets, and unlike the masque, this form of Renaissance and Elizabethan pageantry had withstood the vagaries of time, the dissolution of empire, and two world wars. Furthermore, it had spoken directly to and for the people and the nation.[60] This stage embraced spectacle, ambition, individual genius, and energy. It insisted upon a selfless and direct articulation to a large, national audience. In so doing, it apparently manifested all of the ideals of an English grand opera, independently both of music and of any foreign influence.

To some extent, therefore, this rhetoric around the Elizabethan stage rendered the very form of opera redundant; the ideal of an expressive, lyrical, and direct performance of "the age" *already existed* on the Elizabethan stage and as a continuing, living heritage in contemporary culture. Such assertions did not just qualify the national significance of musical expression; they prescribed an ideal for literary and theatrical expression that countered some of the most prominent trends in self-consciously modern literature. Puchner, for example, has identified in modernist theater a resistance to the value of theatricality itself.[61] According to Rowse, this new Elizabethanism also offered a healthy foil to the "mere cerebration" of modernist poets.[62] Gibbs argues that these poets suffer from a tendency not to "write to be understood easily and instantly," contrasting the apparent simplicity of Donne's "Death Be Not Proud" against Dylan Thomas's "Deaths and Entrances."[63] Rowse condemns T. S. Eliot as sadly "symptomatic of our time," a "poet of defeat, of suffering and neurosis" incapable of recognizing the necessary vitality of a new Elizabethan era.[64] These assessments mirror criticisms of *Gloriana*, which was also perceived as defining its "ultramodernism" by avoiding overt theatrical statements of emotion or optimism. Indeed, Rowse's condemnation of Eliot is not dissimilar to Plomer's praise of Britten as "a man of his tragic time" for whom it was consistent "to make use of a tragic story."[65]

Many of *Gloriana*'s critics have attempted to isolate a continuity between that work and the rest of Britten's operatic oeuvre. They tend to do so, however, by focusing almost exclusively on the opera's musical language or on its isolated protagonist. Such valuations risk overlooking the extent to which Britten's opera remains faithful to his *literary* sensibilities—in this case, to the implications presented by the source text of the opera itself.[66] Harewood recounts that he suggested Strachey's *Elizabeth and Essex: A Tragic History* (1928) to Britten, who allowed himself to be guided by the suggestion.[67] Correspondence reveals that Plomer sent the historian J. E. Neale's text to Britten as an apparent corrective to Strachey.[68] Perhaps as a result, some have argued that there is little influence of the Strachey text on *Gloriana*—and most receptions treat the opera as a loose representation of history rather than source.[69] Nonetheless, Michael Holroyd reveals that Plomer told him that Britten "had for some time seen the story as a possible theme for an opera"; Plomer professed that "like Britten, [he had been] impressed on re-reading the book, by its dramatic qualities, its vividness, and Strachey's sense of character and situation."[70] In a separate article, Plomer similarly declared that Britten had "at once" seen the dramatic possibilities of Lytton Strachey's text and that he had done so "long before there had been any thought of the occasion which was to bring 'Gloriana' into being."[71] According to Plomer, they both recognized in that text not just a subject of national interest but that "*Elizabeth and Essex* is almost a sketch for a play and that Strachey's treatment of the story was inspired by and borrowed from the Elizabethan stage": "Whatever its merits or faults, Strachey's book is a work of literature."[72]

It is also possible that Britten saw in *Elizabeth and Essex* a clear mediation between the rhetoric of the (future) new Elizabethans and the more self-conscious, experimental focus of the modern writers with whom he often collaborated. In its celebration of theater as history and history as theater, in its enthusiastic recognition of a simultaneous vitality and variety to the Elizabethan era, Strachey's text to some extent prefigures some of the rhetoric behind the new Elizabethanism that dominated the coronation year. At the same time, however, it is an exercise in the very literary experimentation to which Gibbs and Rowse objected. Variously described as a history, a novel, and a play, the work deliberately disrupts conventional expectations of biography. Using the relationship between Elizabeth and Essex as an overriding framework, it offers a presentation of the age in a tone that is subjective and "historical," familiar and scholarly. Strachey's text seems to encourage an elision of history, Elizabethan literature, and the contemporary language in which that moment is being evoked. This elision is the result of a necessary uncertainty about the past—and a self-conscious awareness of the subjectivity both of the contemporary writer and of his society. The text is self-conscious about this process: it structures statements of speculation against declarations of certainty, descriptive flights against literal facts. It also offers subjective interpolations and moments of psychological analysis, calling attention to the fact that it is both presenting and creating a history that is simultaneously distant and familiar.

To some extent, that very evocation of distance and familiarity mirrors the language of the new Elizabethans, who aspired both to renew the lost spirit of a former age and to assert its continuing presence. According to Strachey, the age "needs no description: everybody knows its outward appearances and the literary expressions of its heart."[73] By "what art," however, "are we to worm our way into those strange spirits . . . ? The more clearly we perceive it, the more remote that singular universe becomes."[74] This simultaneous familiarity and nebulousness is the result both of time and of "the inconsistency of the Elizabethans," which "exceeds the limits permitted to man."[75] Such perceptions are similarly suggested in the new Elizabethan celebration of the contradictions and variety within the "pageant" of the Elizabethan age: "They were mostly a rough lot, coarse, earthy, humorous, violent, passionate, and cruel, apart from saints among them, and martyrs, and 'parfit gentil knyghtes' here and there, like Spenser and Sir Philip Sidney."[76] Strachey chooses to embrace these contradictions within the very style, tone, and changing perspectives of his text: in *Elizabeth and Essex*, he seems deliberately to mirror the complexities that he identifies in the Elizabethans themselves.

Like the new Elizabethans, who admired an age that placed its accent "on creation, not criticism," Strachey celebrates the independent, creative art of the writer.[77] He does so, however, by signaling a literary indebtedness to the complex age he depicts and admires. This indebtedness is signaled most clearly in the text's allusions to theater. Indeed, Holroyd argues that the "structure of this tragic history is nearer to that of a five-act play than a novel."[78] At the end of chapter 2, for example, Strachey uses rhythm and visual description to suggest an appropriate climax for a closing scene: "Looking round, she saw that Essex had come in. He went swiftly towards her; and the Queen had forgotten everything, as he knelt at her feet."[79] Toward the end of the text, Essex is interrupted by Nottingham, "who pressed him backwards. Elizabeth did not stir. There was an appalling silence; and he rushed from the room."[80] In other passages, Strachey includes dialogue, all the while suggesting how these lines could be delivered: "Then he paused, and added gloomily. . . . De Maisse, inwardly noting the curious combination of depression, anger, and ambition, respectfully withdrew."[81] He also alludes to fatalistic omens, which Holroyd likens to Seneca: "Though the cloud had vanished, the sky was subtly changed. A first cloud is always an ominous thing."[82]

Holroyd is particularly assertive of parallels between Strachey's text and Shakespeare's plays, suggesting that Strachey simultaneously pays homage to a Shakespearean era and replicates that moment in his own literary theater.[83] The work "is Lytton's *Antony and Cleopatra*."[84] Another even more prominent presence within the text is that of *Henry IV*. Like Hotspur, Essex is proud and noble, defined by outdated chivalric ideals, "incapable of dissembling."[85] Furthermore, he is unable to recognize a modern age in which nobility is defined by different means: "Why should the heir of the ancient aristocracy of England bow down before the descendant of some Bishop's butler in Wales?" His feelings constitute "the last extravagance of the Middle Ages flickering through the high Renaissance nobleman."[86] This parallel between Essex and Shakespeare's tragically outdated chivalric hero is enforced later in the text, when Elizabeth discovers a *History of Henry the IV* dedicated to Essex—and suspects treason.[87] With this use of theatrical devices and allusions, Strachey can be seen as both invoking and rewriting Shakespeare in order to offer a "new" Elizabethan representation of historical subjects.

In its overt celebration of a complex but vital Elizabethan age, in its clear indebtedness to a "living" Shakespearean theater, Strachey's *Elizabeth and Essex* suggests that not all self-consciously "modern" literary creativity conflicted with the dominant cultural enthusiasms of the new Elizabethan era. At the same time, of course, Strachey contextualizes those enthusiasms within a self-consciously contemporary voice characterized by a fundamental insecurity. It is possible that Britten perceived in the text, therefore, a useful mediation between this essentially modernist sensibility and the traditionalist values of the coronation moment. Where Strachey resists the confines of conventional biography, for example, Britten invokes and subverts the tradition of grand opera. Even a brief comparison of *Elizabeth and Essex* to *Gloriana* reveals a considerable indebtedness to that text. Indeed, the opera's most famous set pieces (Essex's lute song and Elizabeth alone and dewigged) derive from their extended theatrical depictions in Strachey's source.

Most significantly, however, the opera offers a similarly fractured presentation of history and theatrical display, artifact, and art. Both *Elizabeth and Essex* and *Gloriana* signal an appreciation of the historical moment they dramatize, but they do so by representing the impossibility of its full representation. Where Strachey contrasts historical documents with subjective speculation or description, *Gloriana* contrasts the historical words of Elizabeth and Essex with rhyming verse, the tradition of grand opera with galliards and lute songs. Like Strachey's text, the opera also dramatizes its own inability to fully capture and understand the past: its tone and focus vacillate between the inconsistencies of its variously tragic, petulant, and heroic protagonists and the larger inconsistencies of its scheming knights, sulking courtiers, and changeable citizens. Strachey suggests a breadth and a pageantry of characters but constantly dramatizes his inability to render them with full historical or artistic justice. *Gloriana* achieves a similar effect: scenes with a vaguely defined hero, an inconsistent heroine, a "historical" court, and an impoverished ballad singer seem deliberately to compete for attention and fuller representation. Ultimately, both texts signal an ambition to represent both an era and a tragic romance, invoking a variety of established artistic traditions to underline that ambition. At the same time, however, they are equally committed to dramatizing the impossibility of such a project. Both *Elizabeth and Essex* and *Gloriana* seem to suggest that it is just such fragmentary, incomplete representations that offer the most authentic *and* modern artistic manifestations of the Elizabethan age.

Ultimately, many of the complaints leveled against the opera are reminiscent of those directed against Strachey. Holroyd notes that for all its "skilful and entertaining literary devices, the impact of the writing is frequently pale and thin. It is all speed and ease and slotted-in arrangement; the texture is too shiny."[88] He also laments Strachey's overuse of "picturesque adjective and adverbs" as "an apparent attempt to avoid the banal" and to compensate for his inability to write of passion: "Lytton insists upon the importance of passion with all the urgency of a man who has never experienced it full-bloodedly in life."[89] As Antonia Malloy points out, a similar and frequent complaint against the opera was its lack of passion and "restraint of texture."[90] Evans notes a "banal" love melody for Mountjoy to Penelope that is only "surrounded by bewitching orchestral details of colour and figuration," and Malloy contends that Britten "is more at home" when using the orchestra "to portray the picturesque."[91]

Despite these similar perceptions, *Elizabeth and Essex* was extremely popular in its own time, and its criticisms were considerably less damning than the infamously negative reception with which *Gloriana* has been so long associated. This difference is in part the result of context: *Gloriana* was produced for a national occasion. More significantly, however, it is the result of one fundamental difference between the two works. The primary difficulty with *Gloriana* is that it necessarily *translates* a dialogue about the Elizabethan age and its contemporary manifestation into a musico-dramatic form. In *Elizabeth and Essex*, Strachey—like Gibbs and Rowse—recognizes the defining "characteristic" of both the old and the new as resident in a literary theater. As a drama, *Gloriana* is ostensibly in a strong position from which to represent a similar awareness. As a piece of *musical* theater, however, it is emphatically distanced from the traditions and language that so consistently characterize recognitions of national cultural expression. Where Strachey contextualizes his own vacillations and theatricality within an implicitly Shakespearean template, *Gloriana* can only do so by invoking the Italian operatic tradition associated with the inauthentic appropriation of that culture.

To some extent, *Gloriana* signals an awareness of this tension in its epilogue, which prioritizes the spoken words of the historical Elizabeth over musical setting. This moment is arguably inspired by Strachey's insistence that Elizabeth I's "crowning virtuosity was her command over the resources of words."[92] Plomer himself claimed that "Elizabeth I herself was an utterer of phrases superbly memorable for their emotive plainness."[93] He hoped that this "denouement . . . can be seen as a compliment to a young, constitutional monarch on her accession."[94] How words invoking death and an ambivalent attitude toward duty and life could be seen as a compliment to the queen seems ambiguous only outside the context of opera. In these statements, Plomer suggested his awareness that it is words and language that act as the ultimate tribute to the representative of the new Elizabethan era. By foregrounding the historical words of Elizabeth I, the opera arguably celebrates language over any musical "trappings." In so doing, it conforms to the enthusiasms of those new Elizabethans who insist upon literary expression as the primary manifestation of English cultural strength.

What Plomer and Britten failed to recognize, however, is the importance of presenting the significance of words not as history made bare but as *art*, as national poetry and theater. An anonymous review in the *Times* argued that the opera's final "excursion into melodrama with speech intruding upon what operatic convention demands should be sung is always extremely questionable on the fundamental grounds of the aesthetics of opera."[95] In *Elizabeth and Essex*, Strachey does not merely declare the virtuosity of Elizabeth I; he represents it within his own aestheticized language: "Then the splendid sentences, following one another in a steady volubility, proclaimed the curious workings of her intellect with enthralling force; while the woman's inward passion vibrated magically through the loud high uncompromising utterance and the perfect rhythms of her speech."[96] The rhetoric around the new Elizabethan era rendered the translation of this aesthetic into opera virtually impossible. The new Elizabethans celebrated the old Elizabethan era—and particularly Elizabeth I—not as history but as a history disseminated, performed, and consistently manifest in the works and cultural mythology of the Elizabethan poets. To a considerable extent, therefore, the failure of *Gloriana* can be attributed to the fact that the only possible theatrical form in which this subject matter could be received as simultaneously modern, national, and "grand" would be one that similarly foregrounded the poetic majesty and musicality of the spoken word.

In a letter to the *Times*, Vaughan Williams (no great admirer of Britten) hailed the representative function of *Gloriana*: this was "the first time in history the Sovereign has commanded an opera by a composer from these islands for a great occasion."[97] As the vexed reception of the opera suggests, however, *Gloriana* was not able to fulfill this apparent promise. To some extent, this failure can be attributed to a conflict between a nebulous ideal of national opera and the distinct aesthetic sensibilities of one of Britain's most acclaimed modern composers. To an even greater extent, however, it can be attributed to a culture that insisted—and to some extent continues to insist—on identifying an ideal of national art and theater within the confines of an established literary tradition.

In his relative fealty to *Elizabeth and Essex*, Britten signals an awareness of this implicit literary national aesthetic. Indeed, this awareness also characterizes Britten's other works, suggesting a willing recognition of the importance of literary values and a desire to align himself with self-consciously modern, if not modernist, tendencies. Nonetheless, by translating this

awareness into an operatic form, Britten inevitably "traduces" a new Elizabethan era in thrall to an idea of art, music, and society constructed around
a nationalist literary ideal. It is perhaps fitting, therefore, that Britten should
have articulated his subsequent retreat from that national stage by suggesting a redefinition of Shakespeare himself. In 1961, Britten noted that Shakespeare in fact wrote for a "specific public, for a specific purpose." Having
created a "small opera house, in the part of the world where [he] lives,"
Britten now has come to align himself with a similar, implicitly more authentic project: "In my own small experience I have learned that if one concen-
trates on the local, the particular . . . the works can have an actuality, a
realistic quality, which may make the result useful to the outside world."[98]

Notes

1. The project had been enabled by Lord Harewood, the queen's cousin, a friend
of Britten, and the director of the Royal Opera House. As William Walton (at work
on his own opera, *Troilus and Cressida*) complained to Christopher Hassall, "Owing to
Harewood's royal connections he has wangled that the Queen has commanded an
opera for the Coronation season. It is, I need hardly say, not [*Troilus and Cressida*], but
a new one 'Elizabeth & Essex' by Billy Britten. . . . [T]here it is, we've no friends at
Court so we must put on a smiling face and pretend we like it" (219, 222). Billie Melman notes that the opera was at the time "probably the single most expensive state-
sponsored historical spectacle ever staged in the UK" (286).

2. Gibbs 22.

3. As Melman notes, "The definition of national historical opera and the national
institutions supporting it was intertwined with the policy of reviving a past deemed
national" (289).

4. Gibbs 19.

5. Hewison 10.

6. Wiebe, "Now and England" 147.

7. Melman 294.

8. Paul Kildea argues that, when he accepted the commission, Britten seemed
tacitly to accept that "the British public's view of opera was closer to the Arts Council's than to his own" (129).

9. In the Elizabethan era, according to Gibbs, "discoveries, and the dreams of
Empire beyond them, touched the imagination of the English people and especially
of its poets and scholars" (14). As Melman notes, the Coronation's invocation of the
"Elizabethan past called for the inclusion of the Empire and colonies, old and new,
within the collective biography of people and monarch, thus 'modernizing' the notion of the Empire and substituting it with one of the young Commonwealth" (294-
95). Wiebe provides a strong overview of this moment in her book-length study, with

a particular emphasis on state negotiations with the formulation and prescription of an ideal of musical "modernity" (*Britten's Unquiet Pasts*).

10. Melman 289–90. Furthermore, "of the four winners three were immigrant Jews. . . . The one truly 'English' winner transpired to be a Communist: Alan Bush" (290).

11. "The fate of the winning operas discloses a narrow definition of Englishness on the part of the music establishment" (Melman 291).

12. Such self-consciously modern poets and composers as Michael Tippett, Christopher Fry, Clifford Bax, and Louis MacNeice accepted the commission. Both Benjamin Britten and William Walton declined; Britten pleaded a full work schedule, and Walton objected to the request that any humor not be "brittle, sardonic or satirical" (qtd. in Kildea 132).

13. Qtd. in Kildea 132.

14. Wiebe, *Britten's Unquiet Pasts* 125.

15. White 168; Oldham 101.

16. Harewood, *The Tongs and the Bones* 134.

17. Britten produced only two large-scale operas after *Peter Grimes*, and both (*Billy Budd* and *Gloriana*) were composed for national occasions. As Kildea notes, however, "at a time when the economic reasons for mounting chamber operas are absolute, it is Britten's big operas . . . that opera companies, with their existing *and* surviving infrastructure, continue to promote" (147).

18. Ibid. 125.

19. Britten had recently provided a recent reminder of this pacifism in a joint letter to the *Times* that urged less martial display in national celebrations (letter to the editor: "Civilians and Pageantry," *Times* 16 Apr. 1952).

20. Britten, "England and the Folk-Art Problem" 34.

21. Ibid. 35.

22. Mitchell, "The Musical Atmosphere" 9. Britten was deemed particularly suspect for having moved away from the folk idiom so actively promoted by Vaughan Williams and for having embraced the influence of such Continental composers as Mahler and Berg. These suspicions were inevitably further encouraged by Britten's well-known pacifism and his only slightly less well-known homosexuality.

23. Britten possesses "an intensely local, but hardly uncritical patriotism": that he "is very seriously and sincerely concerned with his communal function is not to be doubted, nor should his love for his home ground be underrated" (Mitchell, "The Musical Atmosphere" 52–53).

24. Baxter, rev. of *Gloriana*. *Merrie England*, an oft-revived standard favorite, was broadcast on the BBC Light Programme on coronation day.

25. Capell.

26. Colville 129. Kildea speculates that, "like the Arts Council, audiences would have preferred babbling brooks, sleeping swans, and bold sunrises to a portrait of a bald and dying queen at the end of her reign" (139).

27. Baxter 54.

28. *Evening Standard* 9 June 1953.

29. Kildea 134.

30. 22 April 1966, qtd. in Kildea 139.

31. Mitchell, "Fit for a Queen?" 18. Mitchell speaks of "the real excitement" of a "postponed discovery" of *Gloriana*. Nonetheless, that excitement demands a process of recuperation unlike that required by any of Britten's other operas.

32. Ibid.

33. Evans, *The Music of Benjamin Britten* 188.

34. Harewood, *The Tongs and the Bones* 138, 148.

35. Oldham 101.

36. In this context, Evans's claim that *Gloriana*'s "dependence on some knowledge of the historical background will probably continue to keep it off foreign stages" seems somewhat disingenuous (*The Music of Benjamin Britten* 188).

37. Porter, rev. of *Elisabetta, regina d'Inghilterra* 443.

38. Capell.

39. Blom.

40. Porter, "Opera Diary" 566.

41. Stanley Bayliss, "Not a Great Britten," *Daily Mail* 10 June 1953.

42. Capell.

43. Williams; Shawe-Taylor.

44. Britten, *Letters from a Life* 63.

45. In a letter to David Evans, Britten asserted, "The work is a serious one and has never been planned as a hotch-potch" (*Letters from a Life* 122).

46. Evans, "Britten's Celebration of Musical Englishness" 20-21.

47. Britten himself seems to have recognized this conflict when he later set these pieces for independent performance.

48. Many self-consciously modernist British composers asserted the modernity of their work as much in relation to modernist literary sensibilities as to any exclusively musical aesthetic. This instinct was often reflected in the choice of a literary librettist. As Harewood notes of Britten's decision not to approach Ronald Duncan for *Gloriana*: "Ben felt he had had too many tussles with Ronnie over the shaping of an opera in the past to trust him on his own" (*The Tongs and Bones* 135).

49. Plomer, "The *Gloriana* Libretto" 9. Salfen offers an intriguing qualification to this statement, arguing for an essential tension between the focus of the libretto and its setting by Britten.

50. Ibid.

51. See, for example, Evans, *Music of Benjamin Britten* 199.

52. Newman.

53. See Plomer, "The *Gloriana* Libretto" 9.

54. Plomer, "Notes on the Libretto of *Gloriana*."

55. Capell.

56. Gibbs 17.

57. Rowse 6. Similarly, "to know what the first Elizabethan girls were like one must go again to the works of Shakespeare . . . For the women of the markets, and fairs . . . one may go to Ben Jonson who knew them all" (Gibbs 19).

58. Gibbs 149.

59. Ibid. 11.

60. This simultaneous celebration of Shakespeare, the Elizabethan moment, and the modern nation had been promoted prominently in Laurence Olivier's highly suc-cessful wartime film of *Henry V* (1944) and was continued (in more subtle terms) in his *Hamlet* (1948) and *Richard III* (1955). Even the Hollywood film *The Private Lives of Elizabeth and Essex* (1939) underlines the significance of this tradition to contempo-rary definitions of the era. The end of Maxwell Anderson's original play *Elizabeth the Queen* (itself based on the same source as *Gloriana*), involves an extended perfor-mance of a scene from *Henry IV, Part I*. The Queen interrupts this performance in a pastiche of Shakespearean reference:

My God, my God . . . can one not forget for a moment?
Who are these strangers? What is this interlude?
Go! Go! It's a vile play and you play it vilely!
Go! By my God, will no-one deliver me from this torment? (155)

The film adaptation is less engaged but nonetheless contains a prominent moment in which Elizabeth I confronts her agedness while listening to one of her attendants sing Raleigh's reply to Marlowe's "Passionate Shepherd to His Love."

61. "Modernist drama and theater might be considered to be just that, a theater at odds with the value of theatricality" (Puchner 7).

62. Rowse 9.

63. "It has the true ring of poetry but who can interpret it? Who honestly can say that he understands every line of it?" (Gibbs 137–38).

64. Rowse 10.

65. Plomer, "The *Gloriana* Libretto" 8.

66. Aside from collaborating with many well-known modernist writers, Britten often articulated his own aesthetic in literary terms. In his 1941 condemnation of nationalism and music, for example, he quoted Auden's "A Letter to Elizabeth Mayer" ("England the Folk-Art Problem" 34). In 1961, when asked about his compositional process, he cited Eliot and Forster ("Britten and Pears in Canada" 213). It was a well-known fact by 1951 that "the final impetus to Britten's decision to come back" to England had been "a reading in *The Listener* of an article by E. M. Forster on George Crabbe." Britten's subsequent rewriting of that poem, implicitly informed as much by Forster's assessment as by Montagu Slater's libretto, was translated into *Peter Grimes*, which "marked in many people's opinion the turning of the tide for British

music" (Harewood, "The Man" 4, 5). This awareness of Britten's literary sensitivity has informed many assessments of his work. Mitchell, for example, aligns the "satirical mood" of Britten's *Frank Bridge Variations* with the "joint dramatic productions of Auden and Isherwood"—and traces Britten's subsequent musical development in terms of his change of taste in poetry ("The Musical Atmosphere" 12, 31). By the time of *Gloriana*, Britten was arguably associated as much with contemporary literary sensibilities as he was with music alone. For further discussion, see Morra.

67. "We talked into the night, agreed that Lytton Strachey's Elizabeth and Essex, which I had recently read, would make a good starting point, and then started to face the difficulties" (Harewood, *The Tongs and Bones* 135).

68. In a letter to Plomer, Britten noted, "I haven't got on to the later bits, so I haven't yet felt the 'corrective' to Strachey; but I am learning a lot about the extraordinary woman & times" (*Letters from a Life* 63). It is probable that the "corrective" to which Plomer referred lay in Strachey's much-discussed Freudian treatment of Elizabeth's psychosexual development.

69. Evans, for example, argues that "it remains debatable how much Plomer and Britten drew upon Lytton Strachey's *Elizabeth and Essex* in designing a plot for their opera, though the particular cross-section they chose to treat . . . was obviously comparable to that which Strachey had made his central theme" ("The Number Principle and Dramatic Momentum in *Gloriana*" 77–78). This reception is to some extent encouraged by Plomer's libretto, which tends either toward simplistic or evocative verse or faithful transcription of historical text. Furthermore, Plomer's literary reputation would have been considerably less established in England at the time than that of Britten's previous collaborators—again encouraging critics to consider the work more as a treatment of subject than literary text.

70. Holroyd 613.

71. Plomer, "The *Gloriana* Libretto" 8.

72. Ibid., 8, 9.

73. Strachey 8.

74. Ibid.

75. Ibid. 9.

76. Gibbs 15.

77. Rowse, 8.

78. Holroyd 578. While the action may move generally toward a five-act structure, however, it hardly maintains a consistent tone or focus to imply a unified dramatic tragedy in the sense that Holroyd suggests.

79. Strachey 29.

80. Ibid. 172.

81. Ibid. 162.

82. Holroyd 578; Strachey 33.

83. Thus, the "long meditations attributed to the main characters have their ori-

gin in the monologues of Elizabethan drama"; the use of "omens to Essex's final di-
saster" are devices "of the sort to which Shakespeare was particularly addicted" (Holroyd 578).

    84. Ibid. 579.
    85. Strachey 123.
    86. Ibid. 181.
    87. Ibid. 195-96.
    88. Holroyd 581.
    89. Ibid. 582, 581.
    90. Malloy 61.
    91. Evans, *The Music of Benjamin Britten* 179; Malloy 62.
    92. Strachey 18.
    93. Plomer, "The *Gloriana* Libretto" 9.
    94. Ibid.
    95. *Times Weekly Review* 11 June 1953.
    96. Strachey 18-19.
    97. Vaughan Williams, letter, *Times* 18 June 1953. In fact, Vaughan Williams was
mistaken; the opera had not been commissioned by the queen.
    98. Britten, "On Writing English Opera" 8.

Bibliography

Anderson, Maxwell. *Elizabeth the Queen*. New York: Longmans, Green, 1930.

Baxter, Beverly. "The One Sour Note of the Coronation," *Maclean's Magazine* 1 Sept.
    1953.

———. Rev. of *Gloriana*. *Evening Standard* 9 June 1953.

Blom, Eric. Rev. of *Gloriana*. *Observer* 14 June 1953.

Britten, Benjamin. "Britten and Pears in Canada." *Britten on Music*. Ed. Paul Kildea.
    Oxford: Oxford University Press, 2003. 210-13.

———. "England and the Folk-Art Problem." *Britten on Music*. Ed. Paul Kildea. Oxford:
    Oxford University Press, 2003. 31-35.

———. *Letters from a Life: The Selected Letters of Benjamin Britten 1913-1976*. Ed.
    Philip Reed, Mervyn Cooke, and Donald Mitchell. Vol. 4. Woodbridge, UK: Boy-
    dell Press, 2008.

———. "On Writing English Opera." *Opera* January 1961: 7-8.

Capell, Richard. Rev. of *Gloriana*. *Daily Telegraph* 13 June 1953.

Colville, John. *The New Elizabethans, 1952-1977*. London: Collins, 1977.

Evans, Peter. "Britten's Celebration of Musical Englishness." Liner notes. *Gloriana*.
    Decca, 1993.

———. *The Music of Benjamin Britten*. London: J. M. Dent, 1979.

———. "The Number Principle and Dramatic Momentum in *Gloriana*." *Britten's Glori-
    ana: Essays and Sources*. Ed. Paul Banks. Woodbridge: Boydell Press, 1993. 77-94.

Gibbs, Philip. *The New Elizabethans.* London: Hutchinson, 1953.

Harewood, George Lascelles. "The Man." In *Benjamin Britten: A Commentary on His Works from a Group of Specialists.* Ed. Donald Mitchell and Hans Keller. London: Rockliff, 1952. 4-5.

———. *The Tongs and the Bones: The Memoirs of Lord Harewood.* London: Weidenfeld and Nicolson, 1981.

Hewison, Robert. "'Happy Were He': Benjamin Britten and the *Gloriana* Story." *Britten's Gloriana: Essays and Sources.* Ed. Paul Banks. Woodbridge, UK: Boydell Press, 1993. 1-16.

Holroyd, Michael. *Lytton Strachey: A Critical Biography.* Vol. 2, *The Years of Achievement* London: Heinemann, 1968.

Kildea, Paul. *Selling Britten: Music and the Market Place.* Oxford: Oxford University Press, 2002.

Malloy, Antonia. "Britten's Major Set-Back? Aspects of the First Critical Response to *Gloriana.*" *Britten's Gloriana: Essays and Sources.* Ed. Paul Banks. Woodbridge, UK: Boydell Press, 1993. 49-76.

Melman, Billie. *The Culture of History: English Uses of the Past, 1800-1953.* Oxford: Oxford University Press, 2006.

Mitchell, Donald. "Fit for a Queen? The Reception of *Gloriana.*" Liner notes. *Gloriana.* Decca, 1993.

———. "The Musical Atmosphere." *Benjamin Britten: A Commentary on His Works from a Group of Specialists.* Ed. Donald Mitchell and Hans Keller. London: Rockliff, 1952. 9-58.

Morra, Irene. *Twentieth-Century British Authors and the Rise of Opera in Britain.* Aldershot, UK: Ashgate, 2007.

Newman, Ernest [E.N.]. Rev. of *Gloriana.* Sunday Times 14 June 1953.

Oldham, Arthur. "*Peter Grimes*: The Music; The Story Not Excluded." *Benjamin Britten: A Commentary on his Works from a Group of Specialists.* Ed. Donald Mitchell and Hans Keller. London: Rockliff, 1952. 101-10.

Plomer, William. "The *Gloriana* Libretto." *Sadler's Wells Magazine* Autumn 1966: 8-9.

———. "Notes on the Libretto of *Gloriana.*" *Tempo* 28 (Summer 1953): 5-7.

Porter, Andrew. "Opera Diary: Covent Garden *Gloriana* July 2." *Opera* September 1953: 566.

———. Rev. of *Elisabetta, regina d'Inghilterra. Opera* July 1953: 5.

Puchner, Martin. *Stage Fright: Modernism, Anti-Theatricality, and Drama.* Baltimore: Johns Hopkins University Press, 2002.

Rowse, A. L. *A New Elizabethan Age?* Oxford: Oxford University Press, 1952.

Sagittarius. "The Elizabethans." *New Statesman and Nation* 7 June 1952.

Salfen, Kevin. "Towards a Mechanics of Voice for Plomer and Britten's *Gloriana.*" *Music and Letters* 92.1 (Feb. 2011): 84-113.

Shawe-Taylor, Desmond. Rev. of *Gloriana. New Statesman and Nation* 13 June 1953.

Strachey, Lytton. *Elizabeth and Essex: A Tragic History*. San Diego: Harvest, 1969.

Walton, William. *The Selected Letters of William Walton*. Ed. Malcolm Hayes. London: Faber, 2002.

White, Eric Walter. *The Rise of English Opera*. London: Lehman, 1951.

Wiebe, Heather. *Britten's Unquiet Pasts: Sound and Memory in Postwar Reconstruction*. Cambridge: Cambridge University Press, 2012.

———. "'Now and England': Britten's *Gloriana* and the 'New Elizabethans.'" *Cambridge Opera Journal* 17.2 (July 2005): 141–72.

Williams, Stephen. Rev. of *Gloriana*. *New York Times* 9 June 1953.

One Saint in Eight Tableaux
The Untimely Modernism
of Olivier Messiaen's
Saint François d'Assise

Linda Hutcheon and Michael Hutcheon

On November 28, 1983, the Palais Garnier in Paris was the site of the
world premiere of *Saint François d'Assise*, the first (and only) opera by the
seventy-five-year-old French composer, Olivier Messiaen (1908-92). To
the consternation of many in the audience, perhaps unaccustomed to more
than four hours of idiosyncratic contemporary music, much less more than
four hours of musical theater that staged "the progress of grace in the soul
of a saint," this may not have felt like an opera at all.[1] From the first scene,
in which Francis explains to a fellow Franciscan the meaning of "perfect
joy"—achieved only by taking up the cross of Christ—and well into the
second, which stages a ritual of praise (*Laudes*) of God and his creation,
there is almost no dramatic action the audience would have recognized as
conventionally operatic. The end of the second tableau, though, where
Francis asks God to make him capable of loving that which he loathes and
fears, sets up the psychological and spiritual inner tensions of the next
scene: Francis confronts a suffering leper and is granted the courage to
embrace him—and thus cure him. The second act introduces the Angel, the
only female voice in the work, who appears to the friars as a traveler to
question them about predestination—again, not quite the usual operatic
fare. The Angel then appears to Francis to play for him the "musique de
l'invisible"—making him swoon, "terrassé, anéanti" by the celestial sounds
the audience too has just heard. Scene 6 stages the saint's famous sermon
to the birds, and Messiaen provides more than forty different transcribed
and orchestrated birdsongs as their response. The contrasting next tableau
is one of great physical pain and equally great spiritual ecstasy, as Francis
receives the stigmata, the wounds of Christ. The final scene presents the
saint's farewell to his brethren and the natural world, his welcoming of "Sis-

ter Death" and the invitation by the Angel to enter heaven, where he will hear that "music of the invisible" forever.

At this point, if not earlier, many in the audience no doubt wondered what it was they were experiencing in the theater that night. It seemed more religious ritual than opera. Its composer would later call it a musical spectacle but denied it was an oratorio, despite those eight static tableaux.[2] Later scholars might be forgiven for thinking of it as a prime instance of modernist antitheatricality, as the introduction to this volume explores. We, however, want to call it a symbolist-inspired modernist opera—despite the late date of its premiere. Messiaen, we will argue, used his unique form of musical modernism to symbolist ends: that is, to have his audience experience the "beyond"—the *au-delà*—though a very particular version of it. To demonstrate this, however, we must first back up in time to explore at some length Messiaen's long, complicated, and fraught relationship to musical modernism before the writing of his only opera.

From his earliest days, Messiaen had been considered a modernist composer in the French tradition and had once even been dubbed a "superserialist." He had also been the teacher at the Paris Conservatoire of an entire generation of postwar radical modernists, including Pierre Boulez, Karl-heinz Stockhausen, and Iannis Xenakis. He shared their modernist drive to experiment, their thirst for innovation, but he had always followed his own, distinct pathway through musical modernity, in large part because of his strong Catholic faith. But he had also been both musically and operatically formed by his love for Claude Debussy's symbolist opera, *Pelléas et Mélisande*. He was given the vocal score of the work at age ten in 1919, and a new world opened up for him.[3] Like the earlier generation of symbolists, Messiaen came to believe that the senses offered the way to the spiritual, and the aesthetic the way beyond the phenomenal world, that is, to that *au-delà*. To adapt Northrop Frye's definition of symbol, Messiaen, like his predecessors, sought to represent through material means (musical, verbal, visual) the immaterial—"something *more* or something *else*"—by virtue of association.[4] But unlike the more secular symbolist poets, artists, and musicians before him, the immaterial and the spiritual meant, in his case, something very specific: the mysteries of the Catholic Church. Yet he too offered, in his one opera, a symbolist theater of interiority, of suggestion and evocation, a theater not primarily driven by plot action. His audience, like the symbolists', was to be allowed to move inward, to feel new emotions and sensations, undistracted by any realist representation of contemporary reality.[5] But the move inward here was ideally one into a timeless world of *merveilles* that his faith offered him. And from Baudelaire to Mallarmé to Messiaen, it was a Wagnerian bringing together of all the arts in a *Gesamtkunstwerk* that was seen as the way to achieve such transcendence: "Musique et Poésie m'ont conduit vers Toi" (Music and Poetry lead me toward You) are among Saint Francis's final words addressed to God in the opera. Clearly, Messiaen was not going to be a conventionally antitheatrical modernist.

French symbolism was historically an outgrowth of late Romanticism. Messiaen himself was once called "un adepte militant du romanticisme" (a militant partisan of Romanticism), and there is little doubt that his values would certainly fit into Richard Taruskin's list of those of the Romantic period: "spirituality, sincerity, naturalness, spontaneity, naïveté, pastoralism, and transcendence of the worldly."[6] In fact, Messiaen consciously and deliberately sought to create a musical form that would induce in its listeners a symbolist version of the Romantic sense of awe in the presence of the sublime and the divine. Unlike many of his modernist contemporaries, he would not eschew the emotional for the intellectual but strive to retain both—and put them equally at the service of his faith.

Musical Modernism, French-Style

Of the two centers of early musical modernism in Europe, Messiaen was a product not of Vienna but of Paris. Paris, of course, was the much-vaunted birthplace of the symbolist avant-garde who saw in Wagner's "music of the future" the astonishing modernity, as well as the passion and suggestiveness, to which they aspired in their own work, as Daniel Albright explores in this volume. In documents ranging from Charles Baudelaire's 1861 essay "Richard Wagner et Tannhauser à Paris" in *La revue européenne* to Stéphane Mallarmé's 1885 "Richard Wagner—rêverie d'un poète français" in the *Revue wagnérienne*, it is clear that Wagner's music was central to the symbolist aesthetic. After the French humiliation in the Franco-Prussian War in 1871, however, there was in France a conscious and nationalist shift away from things Germanic.[7] For example, in the music of Erik Satie or even that of Debussy, although deeply influenced by Wagner, this translates into a resistance to Wagnerian thematic development and forward drive; instead of the urge to resolve, there is a static quality to their harmony; traditional tonality itself comes under pressure.[8] Both, like many other composers later, were also attracted to Javanese gamelan music and to the non-Western alternative and novel sophistication it offered.[9] Out of all of this—but filtered through his Catholic faith—came the modernism of Olivier Messiaen.

Messiaen entered the Paris Conservatoire at the age of eleven in 1919, the year after Jean Cocteau had published his French modernist manifesto, *Le coq et l'harlequin*, warning composers to be wary of the "insidious charms" of Debussy, Igor Stravinsky, and Richard Wagner: As one commentator summarized, "What Cocteau wanted was for French music to be true to itself. It must strip off the incrustations of foreign influence."[10] The problem was that in Messiaen's early years—and later—the work of Debussy was clearly important for the young composer; he had also studied Wagner's *Siegfried* and *Die Walküre* from childhood on, and the Stravinsky of *Le sacre du printemps* had suggested important new rhythmic possibilities to him. Even without this core disagreement, Messiaen's fundamental sincerity and seriousness about his religion and his musical vocation would have prevented him from being at all in sympathy with the willed irony, emotional restraint, and urbanity of the Cocteau-influenced musicians of the time— including Satie and Les Six. In fact, he and three colleagues formed a group they nostalgically called, after Berlioz, La Jeune France in the mid-1930s to counter Cocteau's call for an updated music of the day; in contrast, combating what they saw as willed frivolity, they advocated "sincerity, generosity and artistic good faith," as their manifesto, in turn, put it.[11] In his journalism of these years, Messiaen routinely attacked the fashionable, ironic, restrained neoclassicism of Stravinsky and Les Six that had been spawned by Cocteau's manifesto. He protested, among other things, its rhythmic and metrical predictability: "the lamentable bars of three and four that are the habitual sickness of our Parisian concerts."[12] Rhythm and meter, as we shall see, were things the composer felt very strongly about.[13] His own compositions at this time were consciously experimental in both rhythm and harmony, but their intention, in his own words, was always a specifically religious as well as technical one: "Emotional sincerity, put at the service of the dogmas of the Catholic faith expressed through a new musical language."[14]

This "new musical language" was decidedly French and had little to do with what had been developing in that other center of modernist music, Vienna, where Arnold Schoenberg had, in a move that came to be called atonality, gone Debussy one further, abandoning Western tonality completely in the early years of the century. Feeling the need for a compensating structuring principle, he later developed what he dubbed a "method of composing with twelve tones which are related only with one another."[15] Clearly feeding into that broader modernist belief in aesthetic autonomy (and perhaps even its frequent corollaries—hermeticism and esotericism), music composed in this manner risked, as did many other modernist arts, losing its comprehending public. Not that such modernist composers cared. As Hans Werner Henze later explained the modernist dogma he was to reject: "The existing audience of music-lovers, music-consumers, was to be ignored. . . . And any encounter with the listeners that was not catastrophic and scandalous would defile the artist."[16] Or as Schoenberg would put it, "If it is art, it is not for all, and if it is for all, it is not art."[17]

This particular kind of modernist music did not initially have much impact in Paris, where the French tradition had a strong hold on musical training and where resistance to things Teutonic persisted until after the Second World War, when René Leibowitz began teaching the music of the Second Viennese School at the Paris Conservatoire.[18] It was after the war, of course, that the modernist music of Schoenberg and others, which had been banned as *entartet* (degenerate) by the Nazis, took on a politically positive resonance, forcibly dissociated from that compromised past.[19] This ideological acceptance came in part because of (and not despite) its audience-alienating, antipopulist aesthetic of "dissonance, density, difficulty, complexity."[20]

Messiaen the Musical Modernist

Provoked, perhaps, by his radical students, though always open to experimentation and to learning about new musical schools, Messiaen too tried his hand at serial composition.[21] He had come to believe that in Western music it was rhythm that was undertheorized (compared to harmony and melody).[22] Therefore, where other twelve-tone composers used only pitch or tone rows, Messiaen decided to "serialize" everything—duration, dynamics, and attack—in his *Mode de valeurs et d'intensités* (1949).[23] When this premiered at the famous modernist Ferienkurse at Darmstadt, it was greeted as "superserial," and for a brief moment, Messiaen became the darling of the avant-garde, on the cutting edge of this particular kind of musical modernism—a position he would soon readily and quickly relinquish.[24]

The reasons for his turning away from this serial experiment were multiple. While he responded positively to the mathematical systematizing (something he had always enjoyed and, in his own way, indulged in), he also firmly believed not only that music should actually address an audience but that it should also have a real impact on it—indeed, it should bring its listen-

ers into contact with the divine *au-delà*.[25] Therefore, he found that what he
called this "aggressive, intellectual, interesting, gripping" music was nonetheless not sufficiently "moving" (émouvant).[26] Unlike many of his deeply
intellectualist Darmstadt contemporaries, Messiaen saw emotion as well as
reason as being central to music's impact. This kind of modernist music, he
also believed, was not sufficiently "colored." By this he did not mean what
is conventionally associated with musical color, that is, variations in timber
or tone. Not a true synesthetic like Scriabin, Messiaen nevertheless "intel-
lectually" experienced music (whether read in a score or heard) as a series
of colors and, in fact, called himself a "musician of sound-color": "When I
think of chords and sound-complexes, they carry with them combinations
of color. . . . [A] sound-complex has one color—a complicated color or simple color, but it has one. If you transpose it a semitone, it's another color
again."[27] Inspired by Baudelaire's famous poem, "Correspondances," the
symbolist aesthetic too had prized synesthesia's mysterious "confusion ex-
quise" of the senses linked to the spiritual.[28] So too, for Messiaen, would his
music's colors lead his audience to experience spiritual transcendence. But
this was the trouble with most modernist music, according to Messiaen:
"Dodecophony, serial music, atonal music, the result is the same: music
without color, grey and black."[29]

But there was yet another reason Darmstadt modernism was abandoned
by Messiaen. In his resolute openness to new ideas, he came to distrust the
rigidity of what one composer vividly named the "dodecaphonic police."[30]
Witness, for example, the strong position of one of the Darmstadt leaders,
Messiaen's former student Pierre Boulez: "Every musician who has not
felt—we do not say understood, but indeed felt—the necessity of the serial
language is USELESS."[31] One specific form of serialism became dogma at
Darmstadt in these years of the midcentury: that of Schoenberg's student,
Anton Webern. In one critic's succinct assessment of why this happened,
"Webern's few notes, written in a style utilizing pre-classical contrapuntal
devices, seemed a world small, perfect and totally controlled."[32] Webern's
appeal came from his limited emotive field, his deliberately limited technical means and length chosen, and his particular use of interrelated "pre-
formed elements."[33] For example, Boulez, in his version of this practice,
used as preformed elements the pitch order of Messiaen's own *Mode de
valeurs* to compose his 1951 piece, *Structures I*.[34] Messiaen, who would later
praise Webern as "le 'vrai' musicien sériel" (the "true" serialist composer),
was also not uninfluenced by this practice, but we want to argue that he

would find his own idiosyncratic way to work with radically different pre-formed elements.[35]

That he had to find some alternative is suggested by the fact that he appeared to be undergoing a kind of aesthetic crisis or at least facing an impasse in his own composing at this time.[36] Later, he would articulate his feelings in these terms: "In melancholy moments, when my uselessness is brutally revealed to me, when every musical language, whether classical, exotic, ancient, modern or ultra-modern, seems to me reduced to being merely the praiseworthy result of patient research, without anything behind the notes to justify so much labour, what else is there to do except search for the true face of Nature, forgotten somewhere in the forest, in the fields, in the mountains, on the seashore, among the birds?"[37] Given this religious musician's need to feel something "behind the notes to justify so much labour," what this translated into was a new source of "preformed elements"—derived this time not from the human imagination but instead from God's creation, from nature, and specifically birdsong.

Always an amateur birder, he had occasionally used mimetic birdsong in his earlier works. In the 1950s, however, he began to study birdsong seriously enough to consider himself an ornithologist. His fellow operatic modernist, Leoš Janáček, had sat in Czech cafes listening to the rhythm and harmony of the spoken language, transcribing into music the conversations around him; Messiaen went out into the fields and forests and transcribed (and then imaginatively reconstructed) the rhythms, melodies, and timbres of birdsongs, finding in them not only new inspiration and new sonic material but also confirmation of his own theories, both musical and theological.[38] In his own words later in life, "I owe my rhythmic techniques and my refound inspiration to the songs of the birds; this is the story of my life."[39] Birds, the traditional images of sacred messengers, mediating between the human and the divine, now took on both theological and technical importance for the composer.

As may be clear by this point, strange as it may seem, Messiaen's religious beliefs inform and filter all his engagement with musical modernism. In this, he lived out yet another version, an admittedly idiosyncratic one, of the modernist paradox of revolutionary aesthetics married to more conservative ideology.[40] His Catholicism inspired not only his choice of subject matter but his musical techniques as well. It also determined that he, unlike the antipopulist modernists, definitely wanted his music to have an audience.[41] Indeed, he firmly believed that religious experience could be evoked by musical-technical means.[42] He also thought that it could be experienced sensorily by the listener. And the sensual, rich musical textures of *Saint François d'Assise* were the summation of all his attempts to achieve this.[43] Like the symbolist opera composers (and one of their inspirations and sources, Maurice Maeterlinck) before him, Messiaen sought to bring the "beyond" onto the stage.

Modernism, Symbolism, and Opera

That particular kind of technical-theological life summation (and musical trajectory?) may not sound as if it had the makings of a symbolist opera, but it did. Messiaen had the deepest admiration for Debussy's *Pelléas et Mélisande* (1902) and for *Ariane et Barbe-bleue* (1907), the symbolist opera composed by his teacher Paul Dukas. Nevertheless, he had come to be deeply skeptical not of the past but of the future of opera as an art form. Though he had loved opera since he was a child (even asking for scores as Christmas presents) and though he had taught it to several generations of students at the Conservatoire, he believed there were only a handful of operatic masterpieces—and all those from the past.[44] After Berg's *Wozzeck* (1925), he said, he could see no "way forward" for the genre of opera; it had to be reinvented.[45] Arguably, however, the symbolist works of Debussy and Dukas had already pointed to a way forward—a way Messiaen would later follow.

Certainly, the avant-garde musical establishment of the time was antipathetic to almost all texted music, given its sullied associations with Nazi monumentalizing culture.[46] Pierre Boulez too agreed with his teacher's assessment of opera's decline in an excoriating and infamous interview in *Der Spiegel* in 1967, published with the "explosive" headline "Sprengt die Opernhäuser in die Luft" (Blow up the opera houses). While it is true that historically it had been European music drama that had often proved "to carry the burden of the New"—precisely because its texted music offered a means of access for audiences, even if the music was incomprehensible—in Messiaen's Paris it had even more often fallen to that other form of staged narrative—ballet—to fulfill this function.[47] From the early years of the century, in other words, from Stravinsky's *L'oiseau de feu* (1910), *Petrushka* (1911), and *Le sacre du printemps* (1913) onward, modernism's staged, embodied presence in Paris was primarily in the form of dance. After the two world wars, France arguably became even less an operatic culture; for many Parisians, film, theater, jazz, dance, literature, and experimental music were more important art forms.[48] In this context, Messiaen's venture into opera in the late 1970s is all the more surprising. Daniel Albright has written at length about how many of the multimedia modernist works for the stage were collaborations; not so *Saint François d'Assise*. This was to be Messiaen's solo *Gesamtkunstwerk*: like Wagner, he wrote both score and libretto and wanted to determine sets, costumes, lighting, casting, and even the placement of orchestra members. Given his quasi-synesthetic experience of color, he definitely wanted the staging to reflect the music's coloration. The opera's length, scale, and complexity, and even its subject matter, inevitably recall Wagner's own final work, *Parsifal*.[49]

Unlike Schoenberg, Stravinsky, Poulenc, Cocteau, and a host of other earlier modernists, Messiaen did not come back to his faith later in life; he never left it. His was a belief never shadowed by doubt. By contrast, Schoenberg's unfinished twelve-tone opera *Moses und Aron* (1932) has rightly been called "a profound meditation on faith and doubt, the difficulty of the language commensurate with the difficulty of the subject."[50] Messiaen's musical language, as we shall see, was no less (deliberately) difficult, and again for theological reasons.[51] The strange flowering of religious as well as spiritual music within modernism as a whole can also be seen in the work of Stravinsky after his reconversion in 1925. But there are significant differences between this and Messiaen's symbolist-inspired religious work. The composer of *Symphony of Psalms* (1930) and the oratorio *Oedipus Rex* (1927) rejected emotionality completely in the name of objectivity, something Messiaen could never have accepted. Where Stravinsky intentionally worked to omit from his compositions both "the psychological element and the notion of an intensely personal artistic expression," Messiaen (like the symbolists) insisted on both.[52] For him, what was most important was that his listeners be moved at once by his music's power and the text's Christian message: "For me that's the important thing. They're moved: that's what counts."[53] Where both Stravinsky pieces were composed to Latin texts, chosen (in the oratorio's case) deliberately as an estranging, dead language, Messiaen's libretto, like that of Dukas and Debussy (both of whom set plays by Maeterlinck), was in the vernacular French.[54]

Communication was central for this religious man who had seen it as his Christian duty to bring his faith into the concert hall—and now into the even more worldly opera house.[55] Arguably, one reason for agreeing to write an opera at all was the opportunity to compose an extended religious

work with texted music. He had always wanted his music to have a particular meaning—one he sought to assert directly by the titles he gave them
(e.g., *Vingt regards sur l'enfant-Jésus* or *Les couleurs de la cité céleste*) or the
prefaces he wrote for them. He had even created what he called a "com-
municable" musical language to translate particular letters of the alphabet
into notes of music.[56] Like Debussy, he believed that music, the most immaterial of the arts, came the closest to being able to express the inexpressible. But, unlike the symbolists, he was not completely satisfied by its kind
of communication, complaining that music "does not express anything directly. It may suggest, create a feeling, a state of mind, touch the subcon-
scious, expand the dream faculties, and these are its immense powers; however, it is not able to 'speak,' to inform with precision."[57] With the addition
of words, he might get closer to that precision.

The opera's libretto, to which this task fell, was compiled by Messiaen
himself from his own theological ruminations but also from early biographies of the saint, from the anonymous medieval *Fioretti* and the *Considerations on the Holy Stigmata*, from Saint Francis's own writings, as well as from
the Scriptures, Thomas à Kempis's *Imitation of Christ*, and the writings of
St. Thomas Aquinas. Not surprisingly, therefore, its diction is often liturgi-
cally tinged. But, like the symbolists, Messiaen eschewed the overly descriptive and realist in language despite his desire for precision, and he sought
instead a suggestive, evocative, metaphoric expression. To these he added
theological conundrums often worded in the libretto in a logically puzzling
manner, such as, "Dieu nous éblouit par excès de vérité. La musique nous
porte à Dieu par défaut de vérité." (God dazzles us with an excess of truth.
Music carries us to God by its lack of truth.)

What Messiaen did insist upon, however, was that the words of his text
be heard. The opera's simple vocal line is, in fact, separated musically from
the opulent orchestral sections: for perfect vocal intelligibility, he used unaccompanied or lightly supported declamation, recalling medieval psalm-
ody.[58] Like Debussy and Dukas before him but unlike some of his modernist
contemporaries—Boulez, Berio, and Ligeti come to mind—Messiaen refused
to submit the human voice or French prosody to distorting experimentation.[59] Using the same vivid and apt analogy that Vincent D'Indy had used
earlier about Debussy's opera, Paul Griffiths compared *Saint François* to a
medieval manuscript: the opera's sung sections are like the black readable
text, the orchestral parts are like the brilliant illumination.[60] Nonetheless,

Saint François d'Assise is not in the least medieval. Its resolutely modernist music is put to distinctly symbolist ends.

Saint François d'Assise: A Late Modernist/Symbolist Religious Opera?

This massive operatic work was composed for seven soloists, a chorus of 150, and an orchestra of 119. Its complex musical structure (as well as its subject matter, obviously) was chosen for its religious implications.[61] In fact, as Stefan Keym has convincingly argued, Messiaen created with it a new form of opera, one perfectly suited to his particular religious message. Arguably, this innovation was another reason for taking up the challenge to write a work for an art form he deemed moribund. But in the background are those symbolist operatic precursors—whose influence on the dramatic and textual aspects of the opera can readily be traced. Developing even further his compositional strategy of juxtaposing contrasting units or modules of sound, he created in each of the opera's eight tableaux a "huge musical mosaic" made up of vocal modules, instrumental modules, and instrumental birdsong imitations: "On the one hand, it allows the music to follow closely the narrative action; on the other hand, it provides the work with a purely musical, abstract architecture dominated by sharp contrasts that produce a strong sensuous impact on the listener."[62] From the Maeterlinck adaptations on, the symbolists too had sought not only to represent but also to produce deep-seated emotional and psychic states in their audience through dramatic and musical means that traditional operatic rhetoric or conventions could not express—or induce.[63]

In fact, it was the double impact of the music and the message on his audience that was Messiaen's goal in writing an opera about a well-known thirteenth-century saint, famous for his close relationship to nature (seen as God's creation), as well as for his receiving of the stigmata, the wounds of Christ. The composer-librettist selected scenes from the life of Saint Francis that he said demonstrated that "progress of grace" in his soul, omitting most of the biographical accounts of interpersonal conflicts or other distracting tensions—omitting, in short, the usual operatic plot staples, in a seeming antitheatrical move. Opera as a genre has usually specialized in stories about the darker passions, but not here—and not in symbolist opera, where external action is reduced in order to put the emphasis on atmosphere and on the evocation of inner psychic and emotional states. In Messiaen's late version

of symbolist opera, we watch as the miracle of Francis's sanctification occurs when he kisses (and thus cures) a leper; we follow him from the moment when he receives the stigmata in great pain as well as spiritual exalta-
tion to his final ecstatic death and welcome into heaven. As is the case in
symbolist opera, the intensity of these few actions both calls them to our
attention and heightens their impact and significance in emotional and
theological terms.[64]

Obviously, *Saint François d'Assise* does not offer your average musical
theatrical experience. Keym uses Wolfgang Ruf's distinction between the
"textual-dramatic" and the "sensual-theatrical" in drama to find a way to
describe Messiaen's peculiar opera.[65] In most Western musical theater, he
argues, everything involved serves the dramatic action; the music is meant
to intensify textually predetermined content. However, there is also another intense form of drama, here called sensual-theatrical, that focuses less
on the text and more on the audience's experience of a unique act of bodily
representation on stage. Here the music is an autonomous part of a multimedia experience. Keym's argument is that Messiaen's opera is a mix of
these two theatrical modes and owes its power to this very combination: as
a textual dramatic stage work, it uses music to represent the transcendent,
the emotional, and the nature-related aspects (birds) of the action. But the
music is not always part of the *dramatic* action and so often serves its own,
purely musical purposes as part of Messiaen's mosaic of sounds.

Yet, even these "purely musical purposes" have a religious intent. All of
Messiaen's considerable modernist experimentation with harmony and
rhythm had always been aimed at finding a musical means of representing
"the eternal coexisting with the temporal" and thereby making his audience
experience viscerally his Catholic version of the symbolist *au-delà*: the *divine
beyond*.[66] This is Messiaen's late take on that familiar modernist obsession
with time, about which so much had been written.[67] Marcel Proust, James
Joyce, Gertrude Stein, and many others had brought the experimentation
with "timeless Time" into narrative—the "veritable bastion of . . . chronological
time"; T. S. Eliot, Ezra Pound, and William Butler Yeats had turned to the past
to explore in their different technical and thematic ways the dynamic explosion of temporalities that the new century had provoked.[68] The psycholo-
gizing and the embodying of time in human experience—theorized by Bergson and others—were also part of this modernist challenge to the Western
sense of time.

Composers of French symbolist opera, including Debussy and Dukas, also took part in this challenge, working deliberately to blur their audience's sense of not only staged time but also musical time.[69] They attempted the latter specifically through experiments with harmony, defying the habitual forward motion in time implied by Western harmonic development. This could be bewildering to ears trained in that predominantly German tonal language that creates tensions and then resolves them harmonically—as Wagner famously took an entire opera to do in *Tristan und Isolde*. Listeners learn to desire resolution—and thus is born the musical representation of desire itself. When this is undercut, audiences are understandably confused. As the composer Richard Strauss said after seeing *Pelléas et Mélisande*, "But there's nothing in it. No music. It has nothing consecutive. No musical phrases, no development."[70] As noted earlier, the harmonies of Debussy, but also Satie in his different way, undermine that normalized sense of harmonic progression and create a music in which the harmonies are, instead, curiously static.[71] Debussy's use of the whole-tone scale further allows no attraction or tension between harmonic elements. It is these French modernist musical challenges that Messiaen would inherit and expand.

His characteristic harmonic language from early on had not been that of conventional key structures (while still recalling them) but, instead, that of his own version of modal technique that he called "modes of limited transposition" (of which Debussy's whole-tone scale is mode one).[72] These special scales, because of the internal symmetries, can be transposed only a limited number of times before their content repeats itself. These internal symmetries allow a kind of "invariance" that becomes the composer's musical symbol of constancy and immutability—that is, of eternity, the time of God. Taruskin explains, "Scales that reproduce themselves on transposition . . . are . . . devices that arrest the sort of progression on which musical 'development' (i.e., the sonorous illusion of directed motion) depends. Non-progressive structures are necessary to any music that wants to represent or symbolize the atemporal (i.e., the eternal) within an inexorably temporal medium."[73]

To this vertical harmonic dimension, Messiaen then adds the horizontal temporal equivalent, his "non-retrogradable rhythms" that "reproduce themselves in reverse"—again to create the sense of the divinely timeless in the humanly temporal: "That is the time-transcending truth that religion reveals through music, its handmaiden, in Messiaen's esthetic universe."[74] Messiaen had once argued that composers and musicians understand time even better than philosophers do, because they have the power to divide time.[75] But, if his late theoretical work, the *Traité de rythme, de couleur, et d'orni-thologie* (*Treatise on Rhythm, Color, and Ornithology*), is to be believed, Berg-son's theory of duration as a trait of human consciousness was central to the composer's use of (and belief in) duration as a tool to convince his listen-ers.[76] In dislocating our "forward-moving time sense," he could, as Griffiths argues, "offer new experiences of time: experiences of great slowness or great speed, experiences of time reversing itself or circulating in repetition, experiences of time disposed in the irregular impulses of changing time signatures and mixed values." Just as modernist visual artists sought new ways of experiencing space, so Messiaen offers new means for audiences to experience time in music.[77]

He firmly believed that music creates its own time that is not experi-enced as clock time. In this, he again meets the literary modernists from Stein to Joyce, Yeats to Eliot—who also sought a "sense of arrested time— aesthetic time"—but the motivation in this case was as religious as it was musical.[78] Frank Kermode's distinction between *chronos* and *kairos* is fitting to describe Messiaen's practice: in opposition to sequential time, he sought to create for his audience those moments where time takes on a totally dif-ferent, indeed theological, meaning. By *kairos*, Kermode means "a point in time filled with significance, charged with a meaning derived from its rela-tion to the end"; likewise, attempting to suspend chronological time in the name of the apocalyptic end of time, Messiaen sought to give his audience the sensuous, indeed, physiological experience of eternity.[79] He called this experience "éblouissement"—the sensory/sensual dazzlement of divine transcendence achieved by musical means.[80]

Saint François d'Assise is the culmination and indeed the summation of Messiaen's religious version of this modernist search for the technical means to suspend time in a resolutely temporal medium. Though, as an opera com-poser, Messiaen had to deal with a dramatic narrative staged in time, he worked to transcend it in complex ways, many of which recall the symbolist attempts to do the same. The eight tableaux are relatively static as scenic and sonic "pictures," and the effect has been compared to that of the "mon-umental stasis" of Dukas's symbolist *Ariane et Barbe-bleue*.[81] Like *Pelléas et Mélisande* before it and Kaija Saariaho's *L'amour de loin* after, as Joy H. Calico states in this volume, Messiaen's spiritual opera is one "whose dramatic sta-sis is calibrated by the psychological states of the characters rather than by the external action of more conventional plots." The libretto of *Saint Fran-*

çois is deliberately repetitive, both in terms of actions and words, and there is a kind of ritual stylization to the unfolding of the story. The tempi of the music are often (to some) unbearably slow, like the slow pulse of eternity. Time does indeed seem to stand still.[82]

The music's mosaic form presents the ears with strong juxtapositions and contrasts, instead of the traditional Western transitions and "organically evolving form."[83] The nonlinear, static effect of this form is the result of Messiaen's additive and discontinuous treatment of those various modules—instrumental, vocal, and birdsong, each with its own musical colors. The composer used the image of gothic stained glass windows to give a sense of the importance and role of color in his music, and as one critic has even suggested, "colour is indeed the key to much of Messiaen's musical thought, and it is this, rather than structural considerations which determine the nature of his harmonies and timbres."[84] His wife, Yvonne Loriod, recalled that he kept notebooks full of sound-colors at hand when composing.[85] Messiaen himself said he was inspired by the modernist paintings of Robert Delaunay, with their simultaneous contrasts through juxtapositions of different fields of color.[86] Where the symbolists deployed light and dark symbolic contrasts in their psychological dramas, Messiaen added color—both in the music and literalized on stage.[87]

In his opera, the composer would use whatever technical means he thought he needed to achieve the ultimately theological purpose of that symbolist-inspired *éblouissement*. For example, he turned to those very colorless—or, rather, grey and black shades—of serialist music to portray the dark horror of the stigmata scene, "resulting in an orchestral magma."[88] At the other end of the visceral effect scale, he used a triumphant C-major chord as Saint Francis moves into eternal life to signal (as it does for Haydn and others) transcendent light and joy.[89] He also created a sort of Wagnerian leitmotif structure, associating not only a birdsong but also a theme with each of his seven characters on stage. He even deployed his own invented instruments—the (lead pellet-filled) geophone, for one—or eerie-sounding ones like the electronic ondes Martenot in order to get the sound effects he wanted. Everything sonorous was musical material to this modernist composer.

Messiaen rightly called this opera "my densest work or at any rate a synthesis of my musical findings."[90] Christopher Dingle has called it his "compositional last will and testament."[91] It was also, however, something new and different. Among its innovations, according to the composer himself,

was "the superimposition of different tempos within a non-aleatory, organized chaos under the conductor's control."[92] Here what he was referring to
is the "Grand concert d'oiseaux" (Great concert of birds) of the sixth tableau, following the Franciscan's famous sermon to the birds. More than
forty birdsongs are orchestrated on more than seventy staves of music and
played together, but according to their own individual tempos. Messiaen
claimed to have learned this innovative superimposing of tempos from the
birds themselves, God's messengers on earth.[93] Again, it was his religion
that allowed for the creation of his particular modernist idiom.

In what he believed was the necessary reinvention of operatic form as a
whole, Messiaen once again used whatever he needed and in his own way
again managed to "make it new," in Pound's famous terms—leading to debates about what musical genre *Saint François d'Assise* really belongs to. For
some, its lack of action makes it more like oratorio; for others, the length
and the saintly subject matter align it more with mystery plays or even the
Catholic stations of the cross.[94] What Messiaen actually did was create a
new form, inspired by the symbolist turn inward and beyond. To find the
right shape for this new drama, like many modernists before him, Messiaen
turned to the ritualistic possibilities of what he called "the most powerful
theatrical expression in existence"—Japanese Noh drama.[95] The aurally and
dramatically static yet monumental opera he created is his late modernist
symbolist solution to what he saw as the crisis of the operatic genre.

Just as his French symbolist predecessors—from Baudelaire to Debussy—had looked to Wagner's radical late work either for inspiration or in
reaction, so Messiaen too (deliberately or unconsciously) once managed to
echo Wagner's last opera, a century later, in talking about his own technical
and theological position. In the first transformation scene of Wagner's *Parsifal*, time is said to become space and space-time; to these, Messiaen added
his color and temporal innovations—his own unique contributions to musical modernity. In his words, "Le temps est un espace, le son est une couleur,
l'espace est un complexe de temps superposés, les complexes des sons
existent simultanément, comme complexes de couleurs. Le musicien qui
pense, voit, entend, parle, au moyen de ces notions fondamentales, peut
dans une certaine mesure, s'approcher de l'au-delà." (Time is a space, sound
is a color, space is a complex of superimposed time, complexes of sounds
existing simultaneously, like complexes of colors. The musician who thinks,
sees, hears, speaks by means of these fundamental notions, can to a certain

degree, approach the beyond.)[96] No symbolist—early or late—could wish for more.

Notes

Our gratitude goes to a series of expert readers for both their critiques and support: Dan Welcher, Sherry Lee, Kim Canton, Helmut Reichenbächer, Katie Larson, Shirley Neuman, and Suddhaseel Sen.

1. Messiaen, *Music and Color* 27.

2. Ibid., 223.

3. Philippe Albèra makes an interesting point about this, Messiaen's midposition between the earlier and later modernists: "Placé entre deux générations fortes, et plutôt isolé, il a été, de l'une à l'autre, un médiateur éclairé, développant dans ses oeuvres des éléments essentials de la modernité du début du siècle, comme le chromatisme modal, l'harmonie-timbres, les nouvelles conceptions du rythme, les formes libres, qu'il a transmis à plusieurs générations de compositeurs, leur ouvrant des horizons insoupçonnés." (85; Placed between two strong generations, and rather isolated, he was an informed mediator between the two, developing in his works those essential elements of modernity at the start of the century, such as modal chromaticism, harmony-timbre, new concepts of rhythm, free forms, that he transmitted to several generations of composers, opening up for them unsuspected horizons.)

4. Frye 833.

5. Robichez 180–88; Berthier and Jerrety 198.

6. Samuel, "Messiaen à l'opéra" 19; Taruskin, *Oxford History* 2.

7. This nationalist drive argues against Michael Steinberg's postnational argument that operatic modernism, in particular, was "European, international, and emancipatory" (632). During the Second World War, the performances of Debussy's *Pelléas et Mélisande* at the Opéra-Comique were "an important manifestation of national identity and 'cultural resistance' during the Nazi occupation" (Weller 60). See also the introduction to this volume.

8. Griffiths, *Concise History* 13. For Wagner's influence on Debussy, see Goehr.

9. Taylor 87–89; Ross 45.

10. Harding 66.

11. Hill and Simeone 63.

12. Qtd. in Broad 5.

13. During the 1930s, Messiaen, who was already composing according to an original melodic and harmonic language using "modes of limited transposition," continued his already long exploration of rhythms, studying Greek metrics (and their survival in plain chant) and Indian *deçi-tâlas*, developing his own palindromic-shaped "nonretrogradable rhythms." For this composer rhythm was *not* regular (therefore,

jazz and military marches were not rhythmic) but was uneven, irregular, as were the rhythms of natural phenomena like waves or the wind.

14. Hill and Simeone 62.

15. Schoenberg 218.

16. Henze 41.

17. Qtd. in Ross 42.

18. This is not to say that some French composers were not influenced by or at least familiar with the works of Schoenberg, as Harding outlines. By age fourteen (in 1913), the young Francis Poulenc was playing Schoenberg on the piano (52); in the twenties, Arthur Honegger touted the then unfashionable Germans, including Schoenberg, to his French friends (49). In 1921, the composer and pianist Jean Wié-ner was organizing concerts of the music of Schoenberg, Anton Webern, and Stravinsky (82). We know that Messiaen himself had a copy of Schoenberg's early *Pierrot lunaire*. In 1922, Poulenc and Darius Milhaud went to Vienna and met Schoenberg, Webern, and Alban Berg (110).

19. Zagorsky 272.

20. Ross 387.

21. In 1978, Messiaen explained, "I have a class at the Conservatoire, and am surrounded by numbers of very young people. This has made me keep abreast of all techniques, languages and schools of thought, and I have been brought face to face with a quantity of schools and of different aesthetics" (qtd. in Nichols 20). His students agree completely about his aesthetic openness. See Boivin (98) and the testimony of both Iannis Xenakis and George Benjamin in Lesure and Samuel (223 and 224 respectively).

22. Messiaen, *Music and Color* 54.

23. Andrew Shenton explains this piece in more detail: "It separates four sound parameters and applies a generalized serial technique to each: it uses three 12-note groups (each consisting of the 12 chromatic notes in the octave) and ascribes 12 different types of attack, seven different dynamics, and 24 durations to the three 12-note groups. These groups are themselves divided into three different registers of the piano: high, medium, and low" (*Olivier Messiaen's System* 39).

24. Messiaen, *Music and Color* 80.

25. Pople 47.

26. Messiaen, *Music and Color* 168; "émouvant" qtd. in Cao 8.

27. *Olivier Messiaen: 1908-1992*, 194; Messiaen in Nichols 21.

28. Goehr 64.

29. Qtd. in Marti 233.

30. Franco Evangelisti, qtd. in Fox; see also Dingle, *The Life of Messiaen* 151-52.

31. Qtd. in Griffiths, *Concise History* 148.

32. Lipman 110.

33. Brindle 9.

34. As described in more detail by Lipman, Boulez's piece was written "following the preparation of matrix tables consisting of the numerical values of the original series of notes, its retrogrades and their inversions, and their transpositions. These tables were then used to determine all note durations, dynamics, and modes of attack, as well as to determine the order in which the note series themselves are used" (111).

35. Samuel, *Entretiens* 203.

36. Pople 46.

37. Qtd. in Hill and Simeone 226-27.

38. Albèra 91. Messiaen writes in his massive seven-volume theoretical study (published posthumously by his widow, Yvonne Loriod), *Traité de rythme, de couleur et d'ornithologie*, that "birds, as representatives of creation, unveil the elements of music in their song." He continues, "I have always thought that birds were great masters and that they had discovered everything: modes, neumes, rhythmics, melodies and timbres, and even collective improvisation" (qtd. in Fallon 130, 131). Fallon also points out that Messiaen not only went into the fields and forests but also listened to recordings of birdsongs from all over the world.

39. Qtd. in Moritz 8.

40. Childs 17.

41. Many modernist composers eschewed any thought of their audience. The independently wealthy Elliott Carter famously stated, "I decided for once to write a work very interesting to myself and to say to hell with the public and with the performers too" (qtd. in Ross 440). He could afford to do so, at least financially.

42. Van Maas 58.

43. As van Maas expresses the impact of the composer's belief, "In his definition of musical religious experience, Messiaen is more radical than any other composer before him; not only that, but by employing certain concepts that overcome the strict division between art and religion, he also explodes what had become an accepted notion since the nineteenth century, namely that these constitute two separate domains" (158).

44. In his words, "There are hardly more than about ten indisputable masterpieces. The rest can be divided into two categories: operas that are good theatre and bad music and those that are good music and bad theatre" (qtd. in Samuel, *Conversations* 208).

45. Marti 234. For a sense of the complexity of modernism's view of opera, see Canton's extended study of the role of opera among the Anglo-American modernist writers.

46. Salzman and Desi 9, 203.

47. Mitchell 30; Salzman and Desi 46.

48. Salzman and Desi 203.

49. What Messiaen's opera does *not* recall, in the least, is that other modernist

work about saints presented in a series of tableaux to which our title alludes: Gertrude Stein and Virgil Thomson's *Four Saints in Three Acts* (1927-33). In Messiaen's work, there is absolutely none of the Americans' irony or intellectual detachment, none of their playing with what has been called "Christian kitsch" (Albright 339), none of Thomson's "use of the simplest elements in our musical vernacular" (Thomson qtd. in Taruskin, *Oxford History* 598), and certainly none of the enigmatic "borderline-incomprehensible language" (Ross 151) of Stein's text. (See Cyrena N. Pondrom's chapter in this volume for more on the American opera's modernism and Stein's impact on later music.) In fact, Messiaen's words would be simple and deliberately set to be easily comprehensible: their religious message was crucial.

50. Ross 218.

51. In his typically astute and witty way, Taruskin writes of the intellectual difficulty—combined with sensuality—of Messiaen's writing: "Where ultimate truth is to be revealed, the senses must be overcome, the mind boggled" (*Oxford History* 242).

52. Salzman and Desi 47.

53. Qtd. in Nichols 21.

54. In fact, Stravinsky had Cocteau adapt the Oedipus story into French, which he then had translated into Latin, a "monumentalized" language, in order to avoid any risk of vulgarization (Ross 126).

55. Writing later of his intention in composing "Trois petites liturgies de la présence divine" to be played in the Salle du Conservatoire, not in a church setting, Messiaen asserted, "I intended to accomplish a liturgical act, that is to say, to bring a kind of Office, a kind of organized act of praise, into the concert hall" (qtd. in Kars 330).

56. See Shenton, *Olivier Messiaen's System*.

57. Qtd. in Shenton, *Olivier Messiaen's System*, 4.

58. Messiaen offered an excuse, of sorts, for the richness of the orchestral texture: "I've been told that my work is much too rich to describe a saint who was poor and didn't want to own anything. To this I say, indeed, he was extremely poor, he barely ate and only owned a single patched habit, but he was rich in sun, flowers, trees, birds, oceans, mountains. He was rich with everything that surrounded him. These are the most beautiful of riches" (*Music and Color* 211).

59. Fischer 61.

60. D'Indy qtd. in Goehr 68; Griffiths, "*Saint François*" 492.

61. Interestingly, the theme of Saint Francis was in the air, so to speak, in Paris earlier in the century as well: Charles Tournemire composed *Trilogie: Faust-Don Quichotte-Saint François d'Assise* (1916-29) and *Il poverello di Assisi* (1937-39); Gabriel Pierné wrote an oratorio called *Les fioretti di Saint François d'Assise* (1912) and later a work he called *Paysages franciscains* (1920); Robert Siohan's *La cantique du Frère Soleil* (1928) rounds out the list. See Hirsbrunner 192; and Keym, *Farbe* 45.

62. Keym, "The Art of the Most Intensive Contrast" 198, 205.

63. Weller 66.

64. Weller claims that "in symbolist art, the physical characteristics of what is represented are often *more* graphic for the spectator than in realist art—because they are treated selectively and in greater isolation than they would be within a fuller, and inevitably more cluttered, realist context. There is an intensity of focus on the important images that creates a sense of heightened perception and psychological response, without obliterating the manifest external qualities that have triggered them" (70).

65. Keym, *Farbe* 331-39.

66. Dingle, *The Life of Messiaen* 22.

67. See, for instance, Schleifer; Quinones; and chapter 1, "Modernity, Modernism and Time," in Armstrong.

68. Mitchell 74.

69. Weller 66-67.

70. Qtd. in Taruskin, *Oxford History* 95.

71. As Taruskin explains further, in Chabrier's and then Satie's work, the repeated hearing of chords that would otherwise require resolution weakens the "cadential imperative": "But not one of these intervals resolves according to traditional rules of voice leading. They are harmonically stable, making the music they inhabit harmonically static" (*Oxford History* 66).

72. As Camille Hill explains, "Each mode determines certain pitch-complexes that support the melodies, and each contains the tones of particular major triads, which make reference to major-minor tonality without evoking cadential patterns in any key" (157). Taruskin rightly points out that these modes are not his invention, but they are his systematization (*Oxford History* 231).

73. Taruskin, "Sacred Entertainments" 121.

74. Taruskin, *Oxford History* 235.

75. In Shenton, "Observations" 175.

76. Messiaen, *Traité* 1:21.

77. Griffiths, *Olivier Messiaen* 243.

78. Schleifer 6.

79. Kermode 47. For Messiaen, the Apocalypse was "extraordinary, extravagant, surrealistic and terrifying" (qtd. in Hill and Simeone 255).

80. Qtd. in Lesure and Samuel 34; see, for commentary, Keym, *Farbe* 29-32; Albèra 967; Mellers 222; van Maas 158. In a very symbolist definition of his own "musique colorée," Messiaen wrote of how it brought about this "éblouissement": "Touchant à la fois nos sens les plus nobles: l'ouïe et la vue, elle ébranle notre sensibilité, excite notre imagination, accroît notre intelligence, nous pousse à dépasser les concepts, à aborder ce qui est plus haut que le raisonnement et l'intuition, c'est-à-dire, la Foi." (qtd. in Lesure and Samuel 34; Touching all at once our most noble senses: hearing and sight, it unsettles our sensibility, excites our imagination, in-

creases our intelligence, pushes us beyond concepts, to reach what is higher than reasoning, or intuition, that is to say, Faith.)

81. Bruhn, *Messiaen's Interpretations* 167; Weller 64.

82. For the repetitive libretto, see Bossut. In a review of the premiere, Alan Rich wrote of the "spaced-out, meditative kind of music peculiarly Messiaen's own" as "agonizingly slow to outsiders, [but] . . . excruciatingly poignant to those with the patience to believe" (111).

83. Keym, "The Art of the Most Intensive Contrast" 189. Messiaen's former students described this aspect of his composition in curious terms: Boulez said that "he does not compose, he juxtaposes" and Stockhausen said his forms were like a tapeworm that could be cut in pieces without destroying the whole (both qtd. in Keym, "The Art of the Most Intensive Contrast" 190).

84. Johnson 184.

85. C. Hill 159.

86. Keym, *Farbe* 157.

87. Weller 69.

88. Smoje 16. In the composer's own words, "This super-serial passage gives you an idea of my feelings about serial music. I find it capable of expressing only fear, terror, and night" (Messiaen, *Music and Color* 241).

89. Keym, *Farbe*, 100–102. The key of A major would also come to be associated with the heavenly, especially the Angel (Bruhn, *Messiaen's Interpretations* 170). Albright briefly discusses other modern musicians' attempts to convey "heaven's immobility" with respect to Richard Strauss and Gabriel Fauré (313).

90. Quoted in Marti 229.

91. Dingle, *Messiaen's Final Works* 4.

92. Qtd. in Marti 229.

93. Messiaen also said of the role of birds in the opera: "Les oiseaux sont des personages musicaux essentials dans cette oeuvre, ils interviennent sans cesse, préviennent de l'arrivée des personages, les annoncent, ils les annoncent comme ils les accompagnent, ils peuvent aussi les interrompre." (qtd. in Couvignou 166; Birds are essential musical characters in this work, they intervene constantly, anticipate the arrival of characters, announce them, they announce them as they accompany them, they can also interrupt.)

94. The composer himself insisted that the movement of characters and the costuming were essential to the opera; it was not oratorio at all, in his eyes (Messiaen, *Music and Color* 248). He did not partake of the modernist post-Wagnerian antitheatricality described by Martin Puchner and explored in the introduction to this volume. See also Barish; Ackerman and Puchner.

95. Messiaen, *Music and Color* 100.

96. Qtd. in Penot 63.

Bibliography

Ackerman, Alan, and Martin Puchner, eds. *Against Theatre*. New York: Palgrave Macmillan, 2006.

Albèra, Philippe. "Le rythme repensé." *Olivier Messiaen: Le livre du centenaire*. Ed. Anik Lesure and Claude Samuel. Paris: Perpetuum mobile, 2008. 85-98.

Albright, Daniel. *Untwisting the Serpent: Modernism in Music, Literature and Other Arts*. Chicago: University of Chicago Press, 2000.

Armstrong, Tim. *Modernism*. Cambridge: Polity Press, 2005.

Arnault, Pascal and Nicolas Darbon. *Messiaen: Les sons impalpables du rêve*. Lillebonne: Millénaire III Éditions, 1999.

Barish, Jonas. *The Anti-Theatrical Prejudice*. Berkeley: University of California Press, 1985.

Berthier, Patrick, and Michel Jarrety. *Histoire de la France littéraire*. Vol. 3, *Modernités XIXᵉ-XXᵉ siècle*. Paris: Presses Universitaires de France, 2006.

Boivin, Jean. *La classe de Messiaen*. Paris: Christian Bourgois Éditeur, 1995.

Bossut, Annette. "Répétition et variation dans le livret *San François d'Assise* d'Olivier Messiaen." *Musica e immagine: Tra iconografia e mondo dell'opera*. Ed. Biancamaria Brumana and Galliano Ciliberti. Florence: L. S. Olschki, 1993. 233-42.

Boulez, Pierre. "Sprengt die Opernhäuser in die Luft." *Der Spiegel* 25 Sept. 1967. <http://www.spiegel.de/spiegel/print/d-46353389.html>.

Brindle, Reginald Smith. *The New Music: The Avant-Garde since 1945*. London: Oxford University Press, 1975.

Broad, Stephen. "Messiaen and Cocteau." *Olivier Messiaen: Music, Art and Literature*. Ed. Christopher Dingle and Nigel Simeone. Aldershot, UK: Ashgate Press, 2007. 1-12.

Bruhn, Siglind. *Messiaen's Contemplations of Covenant and Incarnation: Musical Symbols of Faith in the Two Great Piano Cycles of the 1940s*. Hillsdale, NY: Pendragon Press, 2007.

———. *Messiaen's Interpretations of Holiness and Trinity: Echoes of Medieval Theology in the Oratorio, Organ Meditations, and Opera*. Hillsdale, NY: Pendragon Press, 2008.

Canton, Kimberly Fairbrother. "The Operatic Imperative in Anglo-American Literary Modernism: Pound, Stein, and Woolf." Diss. University of Toronto, 2009.

Cao, Hélène. "Points de repère." *L'Avant-scène opéra, Saint François d'Assise* no. 223 (2004): 3-9.

Childs, Peter. *Modernism*. London: Routledge, 2000.

Cooke, Mervyn, ed. *The Cambridge Companion to Twentieth-Century Opera*. Cambridge: Cambridge University Press, 2005.

Couvignou, Lionel. "*Saint François d'Assise*." *Portrait(s) de Olivier Messiaen*. Ed. Catherine Massip. Paris: Bibliothèque nationale de France: 1996. 160-69.

Dingle, Christopher. *The Life of Messiaen*. Cambridge: Cambridge University Press, 2007.

————. *Messiaen's Final Works*. Aldershot: Ashgate, 2013.

Dingle, Christopher, and Nigel Simeone. *Olivier Messiaen: Music, Art and Literature*. Aldershot, UK: Ashgate Press, 2007.

Eliot, T. S. "Tradition and the Individual Talent." *The Sacred Wood: Essays on Poetry and Criticism*. 4th ed. London: Methuen, 1934.

Fallon, Robert. "Two Paths to Paradise: Reform in Messiaen's *Saint François d'Assise*." *Messiaen Studies*. Ed. Robert Sholl. Cambridge: Cambridge University Press, 2007. 206–31.

Fano, Michel. "Messiaen et l'opéra." *Olivier Messiaen: Le livre du centenaire*. Ed. Anik Lesure and Claude Samuel. Paris: Perpetuum mobile, 2008. 63–64.

Fischer, Michel. "Olivier Messiaen, *Saint François d'Assise (Scènes franciscaines)*: L'itinéraire musical d'un cheminement de la grâce." *Analyse musicale* 49 (Dec. 2003): 47–65.

Fox, Christopher. "The Darmstadt School." Accessed 20 Mar. 2010. <http://www.oxfordmusiconline.com>.

Frye, Northrop. "Symbol." *Encyclopedia of Poetry and Poetics*. Ed. Alexander Preminger. Princeton: Princeton University Press, 1965. 833.

Goehr, Lydia. "Radical Modernism and the Failure of Style: Philosophical Reflections on Maeterlinck-Debussy's *Pelléas et Mélisande*." *Representations* 74 (Spring 2001): 55–82.

Griffiths, Paul. *A Concise History of Modern Music from Debussy to Boulez*. London: Thames and Hudson, 1978.

————. *Olivier Messiaen and the Music of Time*. London: Faber and Faber, 1985.

————. "*Saint François d'Assise*." *The Messiaen Companion*. Ed. Peter Hill. 1994; rpt. London: Faber and Faber, 2008. 488–509.

Harding, James. *The Ox on the Roof: Scenes from the Musical Life in Paris in the Twenties*. London: MacDonald, 1972.

Henze, Hans Werner. *Music and Politics: Collected Writings 1953–81*. Trans. Peter Labanyi. London: Faber and Faber, 1982.

Hill, Camille Crunelle. "Saint Thomas Aquinas and the Theme of Truth in Messiaen's *Saint François d'Assise*." *Messiaen's Language of Mystical Love*. Ed. Siglind Bruhn. New York: Garland, 1998. 143–68.

Hill, Peter, ed. *The Messiaen Companion*. 1994; rpt. London: Faber and Faber, 2008.

Hill, Peter, and Nigel Simeone. *Messiaen*. New Haven: Yale University Press, 2005.

Hirsbrunner, Theo. *Olivier Messiaen: Leben und Werk*. Laaber: Laaber Verlag, 1988.

Johnson, Robert Sherlaw. *Messiaen*. London: Dent, 1989.

Kars, Père Jean-Rodolphe. "The Works of Olivier Messiaen and the Catholic Liturgy." *Olivier Messiaen: Music, Art and Literature*. Ed. Christopher Dingle and Nigel Simeone. Aldershot: Ashgate Press, 2007. 323–34

Kermode, Frank. *The Sense of an Ending: Studies in the Theory of Fiction with a New Epilogue*. 1996; rpt. Oxford: Oxford University Press, 2000.

Keym, Stefan. "'The Art of the Most Intensive Contrast': Olivier Messiaen's Mosaic Form up to Its Apotheosis in *Saint François d'Assise*. *Messiaen Studies*. Ed. Robert Sholl. Cambridge: Cambridge University Press, 2007. 188-205.

——. *Farbe und Zeit: Untersuchungen zur musiktheatralen Struktur und Semantik von Olivier Messiaens "Saint François d'Assise."* Hildesheim: Olms, 2002.

Lesure, Anik, and Claude Samuel, eds. *Olivier Messiaen: Le livre du centenaire*. Paris: Perpetuum mobile, 2008.

Lipman, Samuel. *Music after Modernism*. New York: Basic Books, 1979.

Marti, Jean-Christophe. "'It's a Secret Love': An Interview with Olivier Messiaen." Trans. Stewart Spencer. *Olivier Messiaen: 1908-1992*. Complete ed. Deutsche Grammophone liner notes. 229-37.

Mellers, Wilfrid. "Mysticism and Theology." *The Messiaen Companion*. Ed. Peter Hill. 1994; rpt. London: Faber and Faber, 2008. 220-33.

Messiaen, Olivier. *Music and Color: Conversations with Claude Samuel*. Trans. E. Thomas Glasow. Portland, OR: Amadeus Press, 1994.

——. *Traité de rythme, de couleur, et d'ornithologie*. 7 vols. Paris: A. Leduc, 1994-2002.

Mitchell, Donald. *The Language of Modern Music*. 1963; rpt. London: Faber and Faber, 1993.

Moritz, Reiner E. "'Music and Poetry Have Brought Me into Thy Presence': Observations on Olivier Messiaen's *Saint François d'Assise*. Liner notes to Opus Arte DVD, 2008. 8-11.

Nichols, Roger. "Messiaen at 70." *Music and Musicians* 27.4 (Dec. 1978): 20-23.

Olivier Messiaen: 1908-1992. Complete ed. Deutsche Grammophone liner notes.

Orchestre Symphonique de Montréal. *Olivier Messiaen: Saint François d'Assise*. Program book. Dec. 2008.

Penot, Jacques. "Olivier Messiaen Ornithologue." *Portrait(s) de Olivier Messiaen*. Ed. Catherine Massip. Paris: Bibliothèque nationale de France: 1996. 61-73.

Pople, Anthony. "Messiaen's Musical Language: An Introduction." *The Messiaen Companion*. Ed. Peter Hill. 1994; rpt. London: Faber and Faber, 2008. 15-50.

Puchner, Martin. *Stage Fright: Modernism, Anti-theatricality, and Drama*. Baltimore: Johns Hopkins University Press, 2002.

Quinones, Ricardo J. *Mapping Literary Modernism: Time and Development*. Princeton: Princeton University Press, 1985.

Rich, Alan. "Messiaen's Saintly Vision." *Newsweek* 12 Dec. 1983: 111-13.

Robichez, Jacques. *Le symbolisme au théâtre: Lugné-Poe et le débuts de l'Oeuvre*. Paris: L'Arche, 1957.

Ross, Alex. *The Rest Is Noise: Listening to the Twentieth Century*. New York: Picador, 2007.

Salzman, Eric, and Thomas Desi. *The New Music Theater: Seeing the Voice, Hearing the Body*. Oxford: Oxford University Press, 2008.

Samuel, Claude. *Conversations with Olivier Messiaen*. Trans. Felix Aprahamian. London: Stainer and Bell, 1976.

———. *Entretiens avec Olivier Messiaen*. Paris: Pierre Belfond, 1967.

———. "Messiaen à l'opéra." L'Orchestre Symphonique de Montréal. *Olivier Messiaen: Saint François d'Assise*. Program book. Dec. 2008. 19-22.

Schleifer, Ronald. *Modernism and Time: The Logic of Abundance in Literature, Science, and Culture, 1990-1930*. Cambridge: Cambridge University Press, 2000.

Schoenberg, Arnold. *Style and Idea*. Ed. Leonard Stein. Berkeley: University of California Press, 1975.

Shenton, Andrew. "Observations on Time in Olivier Messiaen's *Traité.*" *Olivier Messiaen: Music, Art and Literature*. Ed. Christopher Dingle and Nigel Simeone. Aldershot, UK: Ashgate Press, 2007. 173-90.

———. *Olivier Messiaen's System of Signs: Notes towards Understanding His Music*. Aldershot, UK: Ashgate Press, 2008.

Smoje, Dujka. Preamble. Orchestre Symphonique de Montréal. Program book. Dec. 2008. 15-18.

Steinberg, Michael P. "The Politics and Aesthetics of Operatic Modernism." *Journal of Interdisciplinary History* 36.4 (2006): 629-48.

Taruskin, Richard. *The Oxford History of Western Music*. Vol. 4. New York: Oxford University Press, 2005.

———. "Sacred Entertainments." *Cambridge Opera Journal* 15.2 (2003): 109-26.

Taylor, Timothy. *Beyond Exoticism: Western Music and the World*. Durham, NC: Duke University Press, 2007.

Van Maas, Sander. *The Reinvention of Religious Music: Olivier Messiaen's Breakthrough toward the Beyond*. New York: Fordham University Press, 2009.

Weller, Philip. "Symbolist Opera: Trials, Triumphs, Tributaries." *The Cambridge Companion to Twentieth-Century Opera*. Ed. Mervyn Cooke. Cambridge: Cambridge University Press, 2005. 60-84.

Zagorsky, Marcus. "Material and History in the Aesthetics of 'Serielle Musik.'" *Journal of the Royal Musical Association* 34.2 (2009): 271-317.

12 Saariaho's *L'Amour de Loin*
Modernist Opera
in the Twenty-First Century

Joy H. Calico

Kaija Saariaho's first opera, *L'amour de loin* (2000), is one of the most criti-cally acclaimed and commercially successful new operas of the twenty-first century. Its Salzburg premiere was well received, as were stagings of the same production in Paris (2001), Santa Fe (2002), and Helsinki (2004). The true test for any new opera is the number of subsequent interpretations it receives, however, and by that measure *L'amour de loin* has far exceeded reasonable expectations. New productions in Bern, Darmstadt, Bergen, Linz, Amsterdam, and Quebec City (the latter slated for the Metropolitan Opera stage in New York City in the 2016-17 season); concert performances in Brussels, London, Beirut, Strasbourg, Berlin, Tokyo, Trondheim, and Paris; and a version in English translation by the English National Opera, given the Cirque du Soleil treatment by stage director Daniele Finzi Pasca, all attest to sustained audience appeal. This is an extraordinary run for a new opera, and particularly one in a modernist idiom. As such, it challenges the tenacious postmodern shibboleth that to be modernist is to be atonal (and hence unpopular), as well as its corollary that to be postmodern is to be diatonic (and hence popular). Taking David Metzer's model as my frame-work, I argue that *L'amour de loin* is evidence that late modernism offers an idiom for opera in the twenty-first century that is musically complex, emo-tionally expressive, and broadly accessible.

Late Modernism

I begin by situating this analysis within the current discourse on musical modernisms. In the first decade of the new century, scholars have shown renewed interest in such questions, paying particular attention to music composed in the late twentieth century and beyond. Literary scholar Mar-jorie Perloff, who discerned crucial links between experimental poetry writ-

ten since 2000 and modernist poetry written a century earlier, catalyzed
this inquiry. The challenge issued in the final sentence of her monograph
has proved irresistible: "Ours may well be the moment when the lessons of
early modernism are finally being learned."[1] Increasingly, scholars turn their
attention to "analyzing the connections between recent music and the founding principles of modernism."[2]

   To contextualize modernist connections across the past century, however, one must confront what came to pass in the interim: postmodernism.
The word itself, replete with a prefix that declares the death of the root, is
an apt indication of the public relations difficulties that have plagued musical modernism, particularly since World War II. Björn Heile notes that it is
"hard to dispel the suspicion that for many musicologists the attraction of
postmodernism lay primarily in its seeming to offer an intellectual cover for
anti-modernist sentiment: all of a sudden the familiar, basically conservative, resentment against modernism sounds fashionable, up to date and
even ideologically progressive."[3] Indeed, Andrew Timms's dissection of the
discourse finds that the shrewd equation of musical modernism with atonality has served antimodernists well because it reduces the entire range of
modernist styles and processes to just one: serialism—more specifically,
total serialism as it emanated from Darmstadt after World War II. It is no
accident that this particular manifestation of modernism is also the one that
has proved least popular with audiences and the one whose prestige and
vast institutional support also bred resentment among musicians. "Modernism" easily became shorthand "for music that many will habitually avoid,
find unappealing, and wish on only their worst enemies."[4]

   The status of "modernism = atonality" as an article of postmodern faith
meant that modernism in any manifestation that does not fit the cliché of
"elitist, ugly music taken to intellectual extremes that appeals to deluded
cognoscenti" can produce a kind of cognitive dissonance.[5] This equivalence
is sufficiently common that some critics struggle to reconcile the appeal of
L'amour de loin with its composer's credentials: "The consonant nature of
the opera's harmonies and the beauty and intelligibility of its melodies further suggest that L'amour de loin is not a purely modernist opera, despite the
composer's background in the Central-European avant garde."[6] Consonance
and melody are then taken as evidence of postmodern aesthetic grafted on to
modernist technique. This rhetorical maneuver negates the possibility that
modernism could include such features and resolves the cognitive dissonance
with the reassurance that postmodernism has, in fact, carried the day.

Advocates of modernist music have mounted a counteroffensive, beginning with a critique of postmodernism. Some contend that, as in the field of
literature, postmodern music's brief heyday has already passed; others dismiss the notion of a division between postmodernism and modernism entirely.[7] Many argue that pronouncements of postmodernism's ascendance
and modernism's attendant demise were both premature and greatly exaggerated from the start. Sufficient hindsight permits a general consensus that
there was some sort of turning point around 1980, but it was not a turn in
which postmodernism simply killed off modernism. Instead, these scholars
describe other, concurrent developments that perpetuated or reinvigorated
the modernist music project, described variously as "transformed modernism" (Alastair Williams), "second modernism" (Claus-Steffen Mahnkopf),
"critical modernism" (Björn Heile), and "late modernism" (David Metzer).[8]
The turn may not have represented the dominant art-music trend, but its
red thread can be traced in works written since 1980 by composers whose
modernist credentials were never in question, such as Luigi Nono, Helmut
Lachenmann, and György Ligeti.[9] That red thread emerges in the new century as one particularly vibrant compositional option among the many cur-
rently in use. It would seem that musical modernism is not dead after all.

Metzer presents a persuasive, nuanced argument to support his claim
that we are witness to a period of late modernism that began around 1980.
A brief summary of his approach is necessary at this point. In his view, narra-
tives of modernism premised solely upon innovation are insufficient, because
the late modernist reorientation around 1980 abandoned some approaches
from the 1950s and 1960s while continuing to use others. Instead, he offers
an account based on *lines of inquiry* and advocates thinking about pieces according to the ways in which composers pursue these lines therein. He focuses on inquiries into *compositional states* and *the act of expression*. The
former (inquiries into compositional states) "involves the shaping of the
musical language in a work so as to emulate a specific ideal." He investigates
inquiries into four ideal states in late modernist music—purity, silence, the
fragmentary, and the flux of sound—and interprets these as providing "new
ways of conceiving and organizing pieces" after "the decline of serialism and
other systematic methods." As to the latter (inquiries into the act of expression), Metzer finds that the consistent presence of "prominent, graspable
means of expression, evocations of subjectivity, modes of direct communication, and forceful gestures" distinguishes late modernist works from their
immediate predecessors.[10]

The paradigmatic narrative of musical modernism as predicated upon innovation has an analog in general accounts of aesthetic modernism that privilege speed. Conventional understanding links technology to the aesthetic modernism of literature, film, philosophy, and the visual arts through the valorization of unprecedented speed, emphasizing "the exhilarating effects of velocity, acceleration, shock, and ongoing mobility."[11] Speed's triumph of time over space is less evident in accounts of musical modernism, even those that are teleological and technologically oriented, but much as Metzer dismisses innovation as constitutive of modernism, Lutz Koepnick discards its corollary speed as an essential component of modernism. Instead, Koepnick locates a kernel of what he calls slow modernism, a modernist aesthetic of slowness, even in the work of the Italian futurists. He calls for "recognizing important strains within aesthetic modernism" from its earliest origins that did not necessarily denigrate slowness as "anti-modern, nostalgic, and anti-aesthetic."[12] Unlike Odo Marquard's compensatory slowness, however, which holds that the pace of modern life has outstripped the human capacity to keep up and advises that individuals withdraw and retreat to natural and biological rhythms instead, Koepnick's slow modernism is not reactionary.[13] It is one in a plurality of modernisms, not an alternative to them, and its hallmark is not duration so much as a distinctive experiential quality: "Rather than seeing the present as a dialectical stage of asynchronous oppositions and negativity, modernist slowness approaches the now—without necessarily abiding critical awareness—as an open meeting ground of various streams of time, a space too complete in its temporal layering simply to be negated as a whole, a site at which neither past nor future existed in the singular and a traditional dialectician's concept of totality no longer appeared quite applicable."[14] Those who have heard and seen L'amour de loin may find this an apt description of that experience.

Two more themes of modernist discourse warrant mention in this context. The first concerns the nature of the relationship between opera and modernism. Timms notes that opera "played a vital role in the birth of musical modernity" a century ago, yet the genre is "barely mentioned" in accounts of modernism.[15] Conversely, a recent study of opera in the twentieth-century does not foreground opera's role as midwife to modernism, either.[16] In other words, Erwartung, Wozzeck, Pelléas et Mélisande, and Bluebeard's Castle (A kékszakállú herceg vára) are landmarks in the history of opera and in the history of musical modernism, yet the notion that opera may be a genre uniquely well suited to this idiom has remained largely unexplored until the present volume. I would argue that a symbiotic relationship between opera and modernism is still generative and constitutive of each. From the compositional perspective, it is significant that Metzer traces the initial modernist inquiry into expression to two operas, *Erwartung* and *Oedipus Rex*, and sees a late modernist exemplar in Lachenmann's *Das Mädchen mit den Schwefelhölzern*.[17] From the historiographical perspective, recent literature on early modernism has staked a strong claim for the role of opera with the reconsideration of works by Franz Schreker (Adrian Daub, Stephen Downes, Peter Franklin), Erich Korngold (Franklin), and Giacomo Puccini (Alexandra Wilson, Arman Schwartz, Ellen Lockhart), lending credence to Timms's position that more than one musical style can reside under that rubric.[18] Saariaho continues this work on the symbiotic relationship between the opera genre and modernist idioms in *L'amour de loin*.

The other recurring theme of modernist discourse that warrants mention in the present context is gender. The significance of misogyny in modernist literature, and in the discourses cultivated by many male modernist composers, has been well established by scholars such as Susan McClary, Catherine Parsons Smith, and Georgina Born.[19] Ellie Hisama argues that, unlike literature, the materials and procedures of musical modernism are not inherently sexist, yet there is no denying that the number of prominent composers who are women remains quite small, whether the subperiod is early, middle, or late modernism, and despite the advances in women's rights during the same period.[20] Certainly the demographic of the institutions in which Saariaho received her training skewed overwhelmingly male. When asked about her residency at IRCAM, or Institut de Recherche et Coordination Acoustique/Musique (Institute for Music/Acoustic Research and Coordination), her experience seems to bear out Born's observations about its gendered environment: "It was a crazy thing to do. First to go into this man's profession, and then to stick my head into that place, where at that time, ten to fifteen years ago, there were really no women at all, except for the secretaries."[21] She told another interviewer that "if one is a woman, composer, and, in addition, working with the computers, it is, for many, a shocking combination."[22] Very few new operas are staged by major opera companies each year and fewer still appear poised to enter the canon, enjoying subsequent new productions at other houses; *L'amour de loin* is the only opera among that elite group that was composed by a woman. The woman-as-modernist-composer theme remains central in much of the literature on Saariaho, but it is not the focus of the present study.[23]

The Late Modernist Inquiry into the Flux of Sound

As Metzer notes, late modernism perpetuates some aspects of post–World War II modernism, and Saariaho received extensive training in those idioms. Her education as a composer began on the cusp of the aesthetic turn of late modernism. She studied with Paavo Heininen at the Sibelius Academy in her hometown of Helsinki from 1976 to 1980. Heininen had built a reputation as the leading serialist composer in Finland, and Saariaho's tutelage coincided with his transition into postserialism. In 1977, together with Esa-Pekka Salonen, Magnus Lindberg, and other young Finnish composers, she founded Korvat auki! (Ears Open!). The group promoted the performance and analysis of contemporary music to "counteract the conservative nationalistic tropes" of the Finnish art-music scene, which was dominated by Sibelius and his followers.[24] She studied postserial techniques with Ferneyhough at the Freiburg Musikhochschule but changed trajectory after she took a course in computer music at IRCAM in Paris in 1982. IRCAM was founded by Pierre Boulez, a fixture at Darmstadt and standard-bearer of post–World War II modernism, to promote technology in acoustic and musical research. Its state-of-the-art equipment draws composers, sound technicians, and psychoacoustic scientists from all over the world. There, and at the studio of Radio France's Groupe de Recherches Musicales, Saariaho learned various techniques for computer-assisted composition, working with tape, and using live electronics.

IRCAM became the official French face of post–World War II modernism. Aspects of spectralism, if not officially acknowledged as such, infiltrated IRCAM's aesthetic discourse once Hugues Dufourt, Gérard Grisey, and Tristan Murail were invited to work there, following their success with Groupe de l'Itinéraire. They put forth this compositional approach as an alternative to serialism, and Saariaho embraced it as such; she has incorporated aspects of spectral practice into her work ever since. Simply put, computer software is used to analyze the overtones of sounds as well as human perception of them, and then those acoustic properties, or sound spectra, become the basis for composition. Sounds may then be subjected to computer-generated manipulation and transformation. In essence, she replaces the narrow parameters of "consonance and dissonance" with the far "broader spectrum of tone and noise."[25] She became keenly interested in the timbral possibilities of mixed music (the combination of live performers and electronics), and this development is evident in important works from the 1980s. *Verblendungen* (1982-84) for tape and orchestra was followed by *Lichtbogen* (1986) for nine musicians and live electronics "entirely created through processing of amplified instruments."[26] Over time she came to prefer the latter configuration. She does not always incorporate electronics into her scores, but "analyzing sound phenomena as the basis for creating harmony" remains fundamental to her compositional process.[27]

Spectralist music does not necessarily make for easy listening. In his description of Grisey's iconic *Les espaces acoustiques* Alex Ross notes that "forbiddingly thick, ultradissonant textures" are punctuated by "arresting moments of simplification, as quasi-tonal harmonies rush to the fore"—and yet, somehow, "spectralism is often just a step or two removed from the singing and shimmering textures of Debussy and Ravel."[28] Ross is not the only one to hear a link between spectralism and early modernist—often French—music. Metzer treats the emergence of spectralism around 1980 as a manifestation of late modernism because it continues one of the original modernist lines of inquiry, that into the flux of sound. This inquiry "began with the unprecedented emphasis placed on timbre in the works of Debussy and the Second Viennese School" and was further pursued by Edgard Varèse, John Cage, and György Ligeti.[29] Jann Pasler sees spectralism as "part of a cumulative development" in French music since impressionism, one more concerned with explorations of timbre, process, and their perception than with pitch and rhythm.[30] Indeed, in an interview Saariaho gave while completing *L'amour de loin* in 1999, she described her instrumentation practices in language frequently associated with impressionism. When working out instrumentation for specific timbres, she conceives of colors in "degrees of luminosity" and in association with "a certain atmosphere."[31]

As Metzer has noted, Saariaho's inquiry into sonic flux determines all aspects of a composition.[32] This includes a focus on process, which lends itself to aesthetic slowness, as sounds are gradually transformed over extended periods according to the spectralist concept of interpolation. She determines the outer poles of sound between two fixed points in time and uses an algorithm to generate materials for a smooth transition from one point to the other across that duration. Another catalyst for the spectralists' focus on "gradually evolving process" instead of "sudden contrasts and abrupt juxtapositions" was the music of a composer with whom the Finnish Saariaho was already very familiar: Jean Sibelius. His music is replete with "a bold and experimental attitude towards time, timbre, musical texture and form."[33] Post-World War II modernism had no more use for Sibelius than it did for Puccini. His recuperation into the discourse of late modernism suggests that Metzer's lines of inquiry provide a productive approach for reconsidering the earliest antecedents.

Opera and the Late Modernist Inquiry into the Act of Expression

With significant exceptions such as Luigi Dallapiccola, Hans Werner Henze, and Luigi Nono, postwar serialists generally did not place a premium on the opera genre or on inquiry into the act of expression. Politically speaking, this orientation reflects the reification of Cold War divisions. As a favorite genre of party ideologues in the Soviet bloc, opera was frequently called into service to model the social virtues and musical conservatism mandated by socialist realism. By contrast, Western Europe provided generous state funding for numerous institutions, like the International Music Institute Darmstadt and IRCAM, that supported the most advanced compositional techniques, and opera was not a medium that easily lent itself to that agenda. Neglect of opera in those quarters was also indicative of priorities in lines of inquiry. Opera is a genre traditionally known for its capacity for emotional expression and direct communication, so it is not surprising that Metzer traced the initial modernist inquiry into the act of expression to *Erwartung* and *Oedipus Rex*. However—and bearing in mind that crude stereotypes of all post-World War II modernist music as cerebral and sterile are overly simplistic—it seems fair to say that most serialist music in the 1950s and 1960s was not *primarily* concerned with expression.[34] In sum, Saariaho's training in post-World War II modernist compositional technique, spectralism (whose proponents did not compose opera, either), and electronic music is hardly the conventional recipe for a successful opera composer.

Indeed, until she saw Peter Sellars's production of Messiaen's *Saint François d'Assise* in 1992, Saariaho maintained she would never compose an opera. That she would have an affinity for the music of a modernist who had taught Gérard Grisey and Tristan Murail, and whose music is frequently described as prespectralist, is hardly unexpected. She credits Sellars's staging, however, with convincing her that opera was a viable genre for her process-driven and timbre-oriented idiom, as well as for the subtle type of story line to which that idiom is so well suited. This is why *L'amour de loin* is frequently grouped with *Saint François d'Assise* and *Pelléas et Mélisande* to comprise a body of spiritual operas whose dramatic stasis is calibrated by the psychological states of the characters rather than by the external action of more conventional plots.[35]

Myriad combinations of three solo human voices, chorus, thirty different orchestral instruments, and live electronics attest to her inquiry into the flux of sound, but most important in the context of opera and late modernism is the fact that she shapes these sounds into explicitly communicative gestures. This feature emerged forcefully and consistently in her music after the encounter with Sellars's production of Messiaen's opera at Salzburg, and Saariaho has said that everything she composed between 1993 and 2000 was directly related to the *L'amour* opera project.[36] Among these are *Oltra mar* (1999) for choir and orchestra, some of which was incorporated directly in *L'amour de loin*; *Lonh* for soprano and electronics (1996); and *Château de l'âme* for soprano and orchestra (1996). The song cycles were written for Dawn Upshaw, the soprano who had sung the role of the angel in *St. François d'Assise* and for whom Saariaho subsequently composed the role of Clémence in *L'amour de loin*. The pieces written in preparation for the opera are all characterized by recurring motives and distinct melodies that emerge from and recede into her characteristically dense soundscapes with far greater consistency and prominence than in earlier works.[37] These features, together with the stage and the human voice, are the essence of traditional operatic material. Their combination imbues opera with its capacity for direct expression. Motives delineate characters and their development, melody is a vehicle for emotion, staging gives characters three-dimensional form, and the human voice provides at least the impression of unmediated access (although opera houses frequently boost vocal power with discreet sound enhancement systems, the presence of which may remain undisclosed). Saariaho's exploration of the act of expression culminated in *L'amour de loin*, a return to the genre in which that line of modernist inquiry had originated nearly a century earlier.

L'Amour de Loin

L'amour de loin demonstrates the pursuit of two lines of inquiry characteristic of late modernism: investigation into the possibilities of sound, via combination and manipulation of human voices, orchestral instruments, and live electronics; and experimentation with "more directly expressive idioms," via recurring musical gestures, distinct melodies, and the staged component of the opera genre.[38] An introduction to the opera is followed by an analysis of the ways in which Saariaho pursues these lines of inquiry in the score. I conclude with a brief discussion of Sellars's staging.

L'amour de loin was the first collaborative project among Saariaho, American stage director Peter Sellars, and French Lebanese author Amin Maalouf. This team went on to produce the grand opera *Adriana mater* (2005) and the oratorio *La passion de Simone*; Saariaho and Maalouf wrote the monodrama *Emelie* (2009) together as well. *L'amour de loin* is based upon the *vida* of twelfth-century French troubadour Jaufré Rudel, prince of Blaye, who is said to have been inspired to go on crusade by tales of the beautiful Countess Clémence in Tripoli. According to legend, he became ill en route and died in her arms as soon as he arrived. In the opera there is a third character, known only as Le Pèlerin (the pilgrim), who bears witness and acts as catalyst and intermediary. Jaufré first learns of Clémence from the pilgrim; when the pilgrim returns to Tripoli, she performs for Clémence one of the love songs Jaufré wrote for her; the pilgrim takes Jaufré on the ill-fated sea voyage to Tripoli.

Maalouf's five-act libretto incorporates original texts from the twelfth-century sources. The historical Jaufré's *vida* provides the skeleton for the libretto, and passages from the love songs he wrote for his "amor de lonh"— the woman he loved from afar but met only at his death—appear throughout "in the form of quotations, references, [and] thematic elaboration."[39] The troubadour's language is lofty and complex, and he often seems to speak in riddles, while Clémence's language evolves from the vain musings of a restless young woman to the transcendence befitting a poet's muse when, in the final scene, her thwarted desire for human love is redirected into an ecstatic spiritual love—although whether the object of that love is God or her dead beloved is not clear. The text, written in both French and Occitan, is highly stylized, chaste, and spiritual, in keeping with the courtly love tradition of troubadour songs. Maalouf incorporates references to four of Jaufré's lyrics into the libretto. They are concentrated in act 1, scene 1, presumably to establish the troubadour's character, although they infuse the other acts as well.[40] Scholars have interpreted the libretto as intertextual, drawing on literature of the Crusades, biblical scripture, mystic Persian love poetry, and the opera tradition.[41]

Saariaho's score contains an extraordinary wealth of material, some of it derived from the same twelfth-century sources. Musical fragments of Jaufré's troubadour song "Lanquan li jorn" provided initial inspiration, and the composer "exploits the potentials of the old melody from within her own

Figure 12.1. Basic chord of *L'amour du loin*

spectral idiom."[42] The harmonic foundation is modal, and it is established in the first eight measures of the opera's overture (B♭, C#, D, E, F, F#, G, B). The fluctuation between B♭-B may allude to the notational inconsistencies and ambiguities typical of *musica ficta*, but there is no doubt about the opera's fundamental tone: B♭ "stretches as a gigantic pedal tone throughout the five acts of the opera."[43] In her compositional notes Saariaho identifies the chord above, which contains the opening sonority from the overture above, as the "basic chord" of the entire opera (fig. 12.1). The significance of this chord can hardly be overstated. Jaufré and Clémence are each characterized by a set of distinctive sonorities derived from the basic chord, while the musical material for Le Pélerin adapts to each of their worlds: when she is with Jaufré, her music is inflected by his soundscape; when she is with Clémence, she "speaks" the musical language of the distant beloved. Almost all of the live electronic cues are filtered through one of these chords.[44] The nearly continuous presence of some iteration of that sonority throughout the opera facilitates the experience of aesthetic slowness as well.

The central trichord of the sonority above (D-E-F) is also the essential motivic idea in the melody of "Lanquan li jorn," and that melody in turn is the basis of the troubadour song in the opera. Its lyrics contain the essence of the story: the simultaneous joy and misery of yearning for a distant love. The song is first heard in act 2, when the pilgrim tells Clémence about the troubadour who loves her from afar, and she sings for her, in French, stanzas 2, 5, and 7 from one of the songs Jaufré wrote about her ("Jamais d'amour je ne jouirai" [Never shall I delight in love]).[45] When Clémence thinks the pilgrim has gone, she sings an elaborate version of stanza 2 to herself in Occitan ("Ja mais d'amor no'm gauzirai"), and while walking alone in act 3, scene 2, she sings ornamented versions of stanzas 5 and 7 ("Ben tenc la Seignor" [I hold faith with our Lord]). These are filled with vocal glissandi and extended melismas in an extremely high tessitura. Together with the Occitanian language, these musical features accentuate the exotic allure of the distant beloved in Tripoli, who lives at the farthest end of the Mediterranean in what is now Lebanon. The pilgrim performs a version of the troubadour song for Clémence, who then sings it for herself, but Jaufré himself does not sing it (although some of his text in act 1 is derived from stanza 5, and the words of the song she sings in his dream in act 4 are derived from stanza 3).[46]

The solo vocal lines, always foregrounded and often lyrical, and the B♭ tonic anchor are the most self-consciously operatic elements of the work. This diatonic material is buoyed by a dense harmonic texture of microtones that often shades into pure sound color and in which Saariaho exploits the entire continuum of the sound/noise axis. The distinction is largely one of clarity, meaning that "the far points of sound include sonorities with little acoustical or textural interference, things like 'the ringing of a bell or a human singing in the Western tradition,'" while "noise includes rough, unstable sonorities" ranging from strings playing *sul ponticello* to very dense textures.[47] The opera is scored for large wind section (including alto flute, piccolo, English horn, bass clarinet, and contrabassoon) and full complement of brass, harp, piano, percussion, strings, and electronics. The constant and gradual fluctuation of nonvocal timbre, pitch, and dynamics is achieved through conventional instrumentation (four-part divisi of the first violins, for example), extended techniques, and live electronics. Sound technicians manipulate the instrumental sounds through reverberation, harmonization, filtering, and amplification during performance, and adapt them to fit the acoustics of a particular space.[48] The electronic element is so thoroughly integrated into the soundscape, and so thoroughly grounded in the basic chord, that the listener may be unaware of its presence. Nevertheless its presence allows Saariaho to pursue the line of inquiry into the flux of sound beyond what is possible without electronic means, from the diaphanous to the densely layered. One critic described the orchestral writing as running the gamut "from the luminous to the shattering"; another savored the "luminous washes of iridescent color" and noted that, despite the fact that "the score cannot be called tonal, its harmonic language hits the ear as hypnotically consonant."[49]

This is not merely sound exploration for exploration's sake, however; Saariaho deploys these elements in the service of her inquiry into the act of expression. Each character is distinguished not only by sonorities derived from the basic chord but by consistent, recurring musical features. The character of Jaufré is sung by a baritone. His vocal lines are extrapolated from his historical period so that his melodies tend to move in stepwise motion within a relatively narrow range, and he is frequently accompanied by harps and open fourths and fifths. Clémence's voice, in contrast, is very high, and her music is virtuosic: large leaps, rising scales, glissandi, and ornamentation across a wide range are the sonic emblems of her ethereal Otherness, her great distance from the poet and her exoticism. The role of the pilgrim is sung by a female mezzo soprano whose vocal range and sonorities mediate between those of the lovers just as her actions do, and whose "presence is announced by descending scales, played in turns by piccolo and three other flutes."[50] Characterization through melodic gesture, harmonization, and instrumentation is standard operatic technique, and Saariaho exploits the communicative properties of these conventions. In combination with prominent lyrical melodies and a constant timbral undulation along the sound/noise axis, they constitute an expressive idiom calibrated for maximum immediacy.

Metzer isolates one particularly effective moment in act 4, scene 3, in which Jaufré is en route to Tripoli and is overcome by anxiety and then sorrow at the prospect of coming face to face with the object of his idealized affections.[51] This emotional crisis precipitates his fatal illness. The aria "Je devrais être l'homme le plus heureux au monde" (I ought to be the happiest man in the world) is identified in the libretto as a *complainte*, a medieval poetic genre that Saariaho adapts musically to a modern lament. She builds the lament out of three melodic phrases that the troubadour repeats obsessively, "all built around dyads a fifth apart, with each of the pairs being presented in a melodic sequence made up largely of semitones and tritones."[52] Repetition is an emblem of the lament. The connotations are the same as those in Dido's "When I Am Laid in Earth" from Purcell's *Dido and Aeneas*, in which the relentless reiteration of the strict ground bass pattern descending chromatically through the interval of a fourth signals both infinite sorrow and inexorable movement toward its deadly conclusion. Also familiar from seventeenth- and eighteenth-century opera is the poetic simile in which a storm acts as metaphor for the emotional turmoil of the character. In this scene the lament is framed by a storm at sea. The orchestral prelude to act 4, "Mer Indigo," is derived from her *Oltra mar* (1999), a fine piece of seafaring program music, and the storm returns at the end of the act. The ebb and flow of waves and the churning danger beneath is portrayed in gestures opera-goers will recognize from Benjamin Britten's *Peter Grimes* and particularly Richard Wagner's *Tristan und Isolde*. Musically they are quite different, but Wagner's opera is also a romanticized medieval tale of ill-fated lovers that takes a definitive turn at sea. There are parallels in the finales of each opera as well; Isolde's "Liebestod" apotheosis is mirrored by Clémence's "Si tu t'appelles Amour" (If you are called Love). Saariaho draws upon familiar operatic topoi in these scenes as part of the inquiry into the act of expression. Allusions to canonical laments and sea scenes create a richer, multivalent experience for the audience.

Given the collaborative nature of *L'amour de loin* and his role in its inception, Sellars's production warrants at least a brief mention. The stasis—one could say the aesthetic slowness—that drew Saariaho to his staging of Messiaen's *St. François d'Assise* and convinced her that opera was an appropriate medium for her particular late modernist idiom is also a feature of his concept for *L'amour de loin*. Working with designer George Tsypin, he devised a bare stage framed by a tower downstage on each side. Jaufré was ensconced on the edge stage right and Clémence stage left. They were separated by a body of water that covered the entire stage between them. In the Santa Fe Opera production, the upstage wall was completely removed so that the audience could see the desert sky behind and, in the distance, the lights of Los Alamos. The evening breeze occasionally ruffled the surface of the water. The lovers moved up and down the stairs in their towers and occasionally descended to touch the water, but each appeared trapped on the edge of the stage in his or her edifice—a stark contrast to the vast free space of ocean that stretched all the way to the horizon behind them. The pilgrim glided back and forth between them in a boat, moving at a smooth, glacial pace. Stylized, repetitive gestures unified the visual field. The most powerful moment onstage occurred during Clémence's apotheosis. She lay flat on her back in the shallow water while she sang, gesturing away from her body so that her hand motions read vertically to the audience. Her voice trailed off, as did the rest of the soundscape, and the lights faded to black. Silence.

The fact that *L'amour de loin* was the first opera of the twenty-first century to garner both popular and critical acclaim, and that it has continued to do so for over a decade, bodes well for the future of late modernism on the opera stage. Saariaho's work is evidence that pursuing the modernist line of inquiry into the possibilities of sound need not alienate her audience, while exploiting the traditional expressive vocabulary associated with the opera genre need not compromise a modernist idiom. At the same time, slow modernism offers another means of understanding the experience of attending, and attending to, a performance of this opera, linking it to a significant if less vaunted strand of early modernist aesthetics. For this audience member, *L'amour de loin* fully manifests "slowness's aesthetic pursuit of being contemporary to one's present in all its potentiality."[53]

Notes

I am grateful to Eric Drott for reading this manuscript and making many insightful suggestions for its improvement, and to Heidy Zimmermann for granting access to the uncatalogued Kaija Saariaho Collection at the Paul Sacher Foundation.

1. Perloff 200. Perloff qtd. in Heile 1-3. David Metzer (1) quotes Perloff in the introduction to his book as well.

2. Heile 3.

3. Heile 1.

4. Timms 18.

5. Metzer 29.

6. Iitti.

7. Heile 1-2. See also Metzer's conclusion to *Musical Modernism* (238-47).

8. Williams 523; Mahnkopf, Cox, and Schurig; Heile 5; Metzer 3. Metzer discusses Williams and Mahnkopf on pages 1-3.

9. Analyses by Mahnkopf, Cox, and Schurig; and Metzer are representative.

10. Metzer 8, 12, 11, 19.

11. Koepnick 15.

12. Ibid. 19.

13. Ibid. 35.

14. Ibid. 42.

15. Timms 23.

16. Cooke.

17. Metzer 20-21, 15.

18. Daub; Downes; Franklin, "Wer weiss, Vater"; Franklin, "Style, Structure, and Taste"; and Franklin, *Reclaiming Late-Romantic Music*; Wilson; Schwartz; Lockhart.

19. McClary; Smith; Born.

20. Hisama.

21. See her interview with Beyer, "Kaija Saariaho: Colour, Timbre and Harmony" (314).

22. Cited in Moisala, *Kaija Saariaho* 14.

23. See especially Moisala, "Gender Negotiation of the Composer Kaija Saariaho in Finland"; and Moisala, *Kaija Saariaho*. The annual meeting of the American Musicological Society in Louisville in November 2015 included a special session called "Women Composing Modern Opera," in which Saariaho's work featured prominently. The composer was present and participated in the discussion.

24. Moisala, *Kaija Saariaho* 7.

25. O'Callaghan 1. For a primer on spectralism, see Fineberg 1-5.

26. O'Callaghan.

27. Moisala, *Kaija Saariaho* 13.

28. Ross 573-74.

29. Metzer 7.

30. Pasler 82. Regarding the politics of spectralism, see Drott.

31. Beyer 308.

32. Metzer investigates Saariaho's use of sonic flux in a detailed analysis of *Du cristal* and . . . *à la fumée* (1990) in *Musical Modernism* 182-95.

33. Anderson 197. Anderson does not mention Saariaho in this context.

34. Metzer notes that "much more work needs to be done before we can appreciate the range of expressive positions" in serial and aleatoric music of this period (19).

35. Moisala, *Kaija Saariaho* 100.

36. Beyer 309.

37. Moisala, *Kaija Saariaho* 92.

38. Metzer 20.

39. Neytcheva 215. The volume contains three other essays about *L'amour de loin* as well. See also Oberhuber.

40. Neytcheva 234. Lyrics from the following songs appear in act 1, scene 1: "Belhs m'es l'estiu" (I love summer), "No sap chanter qui so non di" (He cannot sing), "Quan lo rossinhols el follos" (When the nightingale in the leaves), and "Lanquan li jorn" (When the days are long in May). Lyrics from the first song also appear in act 4. "Lanquan li jorn" is discussed below.

41. Liisamaija Hautsalo cited in Moisala, *Kaija Saariaho* 97.

42. Neytcheva 221.

43. Ibid.

44. The "basic chord" and the chords for each character are identified as such in a file with sketches for *L'amour de loin* (Kaija Saariaho Collection). The cues for live electronics are in the next folder. The collection at the Paul Sacher Foundation is not yet catalogued, and I am grateful to Heidy Zimmermann for permission to consult these documents.

45. The original libretto and a parallel English translation are available online at www.tripoli-city.org/amour/.

46. Neytcheva 234.
47. Saariaho qtd. in Metzer 185.
48. For details regarding the equipment requirements for the live electronics, see the publisher's websi•: http://www.chesternovello.com/default.aspx?TabId=2432& State_3041=2&WorkId_3041=11937#.
49. Shirley Fleming's remark, originally from MusicalAmerica.com, 31 July 2002, is reproduced on the publisher's website (http://www.chesternovello.com/default.as px?TabId=2432&State_3041=2&WorkId_3041=11937#); Ellison.
50. Moisala, *Kaija Saariaho* 98.
51. Metzer 163-67.
52. Ibid. 164.
53. Koepnick 30.

Bibliography

Anderson, Julian. "Sibelius and Contemporary Music." *The Cambridge Companion to Sibelius*. Ed. Daniel M. Grimley. Cambridge: Cambridge University Press, 2004. 196-216.

Beyer, Anders. "Kaija Saariaho: Colour, Timbre and Harmony." *The Voice of Music: Conversations with Composers of our Time*. Ed. and Trans. Anders Beyer and Jean Christensen. Aldershot, UK: Ashgate, 2000. 301-321.

Born, Georgina. *Rationalizing Culture: IRCAM, Boulez, and the Institutionalization of the Musical Avant-Garde*. Berkeley: University of California Press, 1995.

Cooke, Mervyn, ed. *The Cambridge Companion to Twentieth-Century Opera*. Cambridge: Cambridge University Press, 2005.

Daub, Adrian. "Adorno's Schreker: Charting the Self-Dissolution of the Distant Sound." *Cambridge Opera Journal* 18.3 (2006): 247-71.

Downes, Stephen. *Music and Decadence in European Modernism: The Case of Central and Eastern Europe*. Cambridge: Cambridge University Press, 2010.

Drott, Eric. "Spectralism, Politics and the Post-Industrial Imagination." *The Modernist Legacy: Essays on New Music*. Ed. Björn Heile. Burlington, VT: Ashgate, 2009. 39-60.

Ellison, Cori. "When Lady and Troubador Become One." *New York Times* 21 July 2002. <http://www.nytimes.com/2002/07/21/arts/music-when-lady-and-trouba dour-become-one.html?src=pm>.

Fineberg, Joshua. "Spectral Music." *Contemporary Music Review* 19.2 (2000): 1-5.

Franklin, Peter. "Modernism's Distanced Sound: A British Approach to Schreker and Others." *Art and Ideology in European Opera: Essays in Honour of Julian Rushton*. Ed. Rachel Cowgill, David Cooper, and Clive Brown. Woodbridge, UK: Boydell, 2010. 351-61.

———. *Reclaiming Late-Romantic Music: Singing Devils and Distant Sounds*. Berkeley: University of California Press, 2014.

———. "Style, Structure and Taste: Three Aspects of the Problem of Franz Schreker." *Proceedings of the Royal Musical Association* 109 (1982-1983): 134-46.

———. " 'Wer weiss, Vater, ob das nicht Engel sind?' Reflections on the Pre-Fascist Discourse of Degeneracy in Schreker's *Die Gezeichneten*." *Music, Theatre and Politics in Germany: 1848 to the Third Reich*. Ed. Nikolas Bacht. Aldershot, UK: Ashgate, 2006. 173-83.

Heile, Björn. "New Music and the Modernist Legacy." *The Modernist Legacy: Essays on New Music*. Ed. Björn Heile. Burlington, VT: Ashgate, 2009. 1-12.

Hisama, Ellie. *Gendering Musical Modernism: The Music of Ruth Crawford, Marion Bauer, and Miriam Gideon*. New York: Cambridge University Press, 2006.

Iitti, Sanna. "*L'Amour de Loin*: Kaija Saariaho's First Opera." *Journal of the IAWM* (2002). <http://iawm.org/stef/articles_html/Iitti_saariaho.html>.

Koepnick, Lutz. *On Slowness: Toward an Aesthetics of the Contemporary*. New York: Columbia University Press, 2014.

Lockhart, Ellen. "Photo-Opera: *La fanciulla del West* and the Staging Souvenir." *Cambridge Opera Journal* 23.3 (2011): 145-66.

Maalouf, Amin. *L'Amour de Loin / Love from Afar*. <http://www.tripoli-city.org/amour/index.html>.

Mahnkopf, Claus-Steffen, Frank Cox, and Wolfram Schurig, eds. *Facets of the Second Modernity*. Hofheim: Wolke Verlag, 2008.

McClary, Susan. "Terminal Prestige: The Case of Avant-Garde Music Composition." *Cultural Critique* 12 (Spring 1989): 57-81.

Metzer, David. *Musical Modernism at the Turn of the Twenty-First Century*. Cambridge: Cambridge University Press, 2009.

Moisala, Pirkko. "Gender Negotiation of the Composer Kaija Saariaho in Finland: The Woman Composer as Nomadic Subject." *Music and Gender*. Ed. Pirkko Moisala and Beverley Diamond. Urbana: University of Illinois Press, 2000. 166-88.

———. *Kaija Saariaho*. Women Composers Series 1. Urbana: University of Illinois Press, 2009.

Neytcheva, Svetlana. "Reading the Imaginary: Kaija Saariaho's Opera *L'Amour de Loin*." *Musiktheater der Gegenwart: Text und Komposition, Rezeption und Kanonbildung*. Ed. Jürgen Kühnel, Ulrich Müller, and Oswsald Panagl. Anif: Verlag Mueller-Speiser, 2008. 211-235.

Oberhuber, Andrea. " 'Ja mais d'amor no-m jauziray / Si no-m jau d'est'amour de lonh: Höfisches Liebeskonzept und Liebsdiskurs am Beispiel von Jaufré Rudel und seiner Reaktualisierung in Amin Maaloufs Libretto zu *L'amour de loin*." *Oper in Kontext: Musiktheater bei den Salzburger Festspielen*. Ed. Bettina Huter. Innsbruck: Studien Verlag, 2003. 53-68.

O'Callaghan, James. "Gesture Transformation through Electronics in the Music of Kaija Saariaho." <http://www.ems-network.org/IMG/pdf_EMS10_OCallaghan_Eigenfeldt.pdf>.

Pasler, Jann. *Writing through Music: Essays on Music, Culture, and Politics*. Oxford: Oxford University Press, 2008.

Perloff, Marjorie. *21st-Century Modernism: The "New" Poetics*. Malden, MA: Blackwell, 2002.

Ross, Alex. *The Rest Is Noise*. New York: Farrar, Straus and Giroux, 2007.

Saariaho, Kaija. *L'amour de loin*. Santa Fe Opera. Program. 2002.

Schwartz, Arman. "Puccini, in the Distance." *Cambridge Opera Journal* 23.3 (2011): 167–89.

Smith, Catherine Parsons. "'A Distinguishing Virility': Feminism and Modernism in American Art Music." *Cecilia Reclaimed: Feminist Perspectives on Gender and Music*. Ed. Susan C. Cook and Judy Tsou. Urbana: University of Illinois Press, 1994. 90–106.

Timms, Andrew. "Modernism's Moment of Plentitude." *The Modernist Legacy: Essays on New Music*. Ed. Björn Heile. Burlington, VT: Ashgate, 2009. 13–24.

Williams, Alastair. "Ageing of the New: The Museum of Musical Modernism." *The Cambridge History of Twentieth-Century Music*. Ed. Nicholas Cook and Anthony Pople. Cambridge: Cambridge University Press, 2004. 506–38.

Wilson, Alexandra. *The Puccini Problem: Opera, Nationalism and Modernity*. Cambridge: Cambridge University Press, 2007.

Contributors

DANIEL ALBRIGHT was the Ernest Bernbaum Professor of Literature at Harvard University, specializing in the relation of modernism to music and the other arts. Among his many books are *Putting Modernism Together: Literature, Music, and Painting, 1872–1927* (Johns Hopkins University Press, 2015), *Panaesthetics: On the Unity and Diversity of the Arts* (Yale University Press, 2014), *Modernism and Music: An Anthology of Sources* (University of Chicago Press, 2004), *Beckett and Aesthetics* (Cambridge University Press, 2003), *Berlioz's Semi-Operas* (University of Rochester Press, 2001), *Untwisting the Serpent* (University of Chicago Press, 2000), *Quantum Poetics* (Cambridge University Press, 1997), *W. B. Yeats: The Poems,* ed. (Everyman's Library, 1990), *Stravinsky: The Music-Box and the Nightingale* (Gordon and Breach, 1989), *Tennyson: The Muses' Tug-of-War* (University of Virginia Press, 1986), and *Representation and the Imagination: Beckett, Kafka, Nabokov, Schoenberg* (University of Chicago Press, 1981). He also served as general editor of *Border Crossings: Modernism in Music, Literature, and the Visual Arts,* a series of volumes of new essays in comparative arts, published by Garland Publishing.

RICHARD BEGAM, professor of English at the University of Wisconsin-Madison, has published articles on modern and postcolonial literature, Irish literature, and literary theory. He is the author of *Samuel Beckett and the End of Modernity* (Stanford University Press, 1996) and coauthor with James Soderholm of *Platonic Occasions: Dialogues on Literature, Art and Culture* (Stockholm University Press, 2015). He is coeditor of three collections of essays: *Modernism and Colonialism: British and Irish Literature, 1899–1939* (Duke University Press, 2007), *Text and Meaning: Literary Discourse and Beyond* (Düsseldorf University Press, 2011), and *Modernism, Postcolonialism and Globalism: Anglophone Literature, 1950 to the Present* (Oxford University Press, forthcoming 2017).

JOY H. CALICO is professor of musicology at Vanderbilt University. She is the author of *Arnold Schoenberg's "A Survivor from Warsaw" in Postwar Europe* (University of California Press, 2014) and *Brecht at the Opera* (University of California Press, 2008). Her articles have appeared in such journals as *New German Critique, Cambridge Opera Journal, Musical Quarterly*, and *Opera Quarterly*. She is editor in chief of *JAMS (Journal of the American Musicological Society)*.

BRYAN GILLIAM is the Bass Professor in Humanities at Duke University. He has published widely on late nineteenth- and early twentieth-century German and Austrian music, specializing in German opera, fin-de-siècle Vienna, film music, and Wagner, Bruckner, Strauss, and Weill. Among his many books are *Rounding Wagner's Mountain: Richard Strauss and Modern German Opera* (Cambridge University Press, 2014), *Music, Image, Gesture* (Duke University Press, 2005), *The Life of Richard Strauss* (Cambridge University Press, 1999), *Music and Performance during the Weimar Republic* (Cambridge University Press, 1994), *Richard Strauss and His World* (Princeton University Press, 1992), and *Richard Strauss: New Perspectives on the Composer and His Work* (Duke University Press, 1992).

LINDA HUTCHEON is university professor emerita of English and comparative literature at the University of Toronto. Her most recent books include *A Theory of Adaptation* (Routledge, 2006), as well as *Bodily Charm: Living Opera* (University of Nebraska Press, 2000), *Opera: The Art of Dying* (Harvard University Press, 2004), and *Four Last Songs: Aging and Creativity in Verdi, Strauss, Messiaen, and Britten* (University of Chicago Press, 2015), all coauthored with Michael Hutcheon. She has been the recipient of numerous fellowships and awards, and she has served as the president of the Modern Language Association.

MICHAEL HUTCHEON is a physician and coauthor of three books on opera with Linda Hutcheon.

DEREK KATZ is associate professor of music history at the University of California, Santa Barbara. He is the author of *Janáček beyond the Borders* (University of Rochester Press, 2009) and has written about Czech music for American and European academic journals. He frequently lectures for the San Francisco Opera Guild.

HERBERT LINDENBERGER is the Avalon Foundation Professor of the Humanities Emeritus at Stanford University. Among his numerous books are *Opera: The Extravagant Art* (Cornell University Press, 1984), *Opera in History: From Monteverdi to Cage* (Stanford University Press, 1998), and *Situating Opera: Period, Genre, Reception* (Cambridge University Press, 2010), which discusses opera of the last four hundred years in a variety of contexts, including the social, historical, and aesthetic. His most recent book is *Aesthetics of Discomfort: Conversations on Disquieting Art* (University of Michigan Press, 2016), coauthored with Frederick Aldama.

BERNADETTE MEYLER is the Carl and Sheila Spaeth Professor of Law at Stanford University. Prior to joining the Stanford Law School faculty, she was a professor of law and English at Cornell University and served as the inaugural Mellon/LAPA Fellow in Law and Humanities at Princeton in 2009-10. Her essays on law, culture, and theory have appeared in the *Stanford Law Review*, *Yale Journal of Law and Humanities*, *Theory and Event*, and *diacritics*, among other journals. Her coedited volume, *New Directions in Law and Literature*, is forthcoming from Oxford University Press.

KLÁRA MÓRICZ is the Joseph E. and Grace W. Valentine Professor of Music at Amherst College. Coeditor of *Journal of Musicology* from 2009 to 2016, she is the author of *Jewish Identities: Nationalism, Racism, and Utopianism in Twentieth-Century Music* (University of California Press, 2008), coeditor of *Funeral Games in Honor of Arthur Lourié* (Oxford University Press, 2014), and editor of the forthcoming second volume of the *Béla Bartók Complete Critical Edition*.

IRENE MORRA is reader in English literature at Cardiff University. She is the author of *Twentieth-Century British Authors and the Rise of Opera in Britain* (Ashgate, 2007), *Britishness, Popular Music, and National Identity: The Making of Modern Britain* (Routledge, 2013), and *Modern Verse Drama: Nation, Art, and Modernity* (Methuen, 2016). She is also editor of the forthcoming *The New Elizabethan Age: Nation, Culture, and Society after WW II* (I. B. Tauris, 2016). Her essays on British opera, drama, and fiction have appeared in such journals as *Modern Drama* and *Contemporary Theatre Review*.

CYRENA N. PONDROM is professor emerita of English at the University of Wisconsin–Madison. She is the author of *The Road from Paris* (Cambridge University Press, 1974; reissued 2010) and the introduction and annotations to Gertrude Stein's *Geography and Plays* (University of Wisconsin Press, 1993). She has published numerous articles on Modern British and American literature, especially modern poetics and the avant-garde.

MATTHEW WILSON SMITH is associate professor of German studies and theater and performance studies at Stanford University. He is the author of *The Total Work of Art: From Bayreuth to Cyberspace* (Routledge, 2007) and the editor of *George Büchner: The Major Works* (Norton critical edition, 2012). He has edited special issues of *Opera Quarterly* and *Modern Drama* and has published widely on theater, film, opera, and digital media.

Index

Page numbers in *italics* refer to figures.

Molière, 133
Monsieur Croche antidilettante (Debussy), 90
Monteverdi, Claudio, 81, 276, 281
Morris, Mark, 264n65
Moses und Aron (Schoenberg), 8, 9, 18, 155,
    177, 208, 323; central conflict in, 210,
    213-17, 222; climactic confrontation
    in, 217-18; on compromise between
    abstractionism and pictorialism, 222;
    commentaries on, 221-22; conclusion
    of, 220-21, 222; engagement of, with
    Wagner, 223, 227-32, 239-40n74; ideal-
    ism and pragmatism in, 220; invoking
    discourse against degenerate art, 219-20;
    modernism of, 206, 209; motivation for,
    224; music of, 206; musical silence in, 219,
    220, 222; *Parsifal* linked with, 220-21;
    Platonic philosophy in, 212-13; pre-
    occupied with representation, 209;
    questioning nature of theatricality,
    283; representational literalism in, 227;
    score of, *228, 230, 232*; serialism in, 214;
    staging of, 219; text of, 206; twelve-tone
    composition of, 222-23; *Vorstellung* in,
    212-16
Mother of Us All, The (Stein and Thomson), 244
Mozart, Wolfgang Amadeus, 2-3, 133, 276,
    281
Munch, Edvard, 280
Munich Artists' Theater, 193
Murail, Tristan, 346, 348
music: capturing physicality, 42; centrality
    of, for Wagner, 33; cosmopolitan
    modernism in, 188; ethical content of,
    279; history and, 167, 168-69, 171;
    improvisational composition of, 252;
    internalization of, 54; mathematical
    composition of, 252; minimalism in, 16,
    18, 244, 247; modernism and, 15-16,
    196-97, 316-22, 342-45; philosophy and,
    150; pictorialism in, 217; reception of,
    159; representation and, 211; serving
    drama, 37, 38; space associated with, 131;
    superiority of, 37; time and, 267-70
Mussorgsky, Modest, 297, 298
Mustafa, Domenico, 97

Nabokov, Vladimir, 74
narrative cycle, 280

national culture, redefining, 294
national identity, music and, 121
nationalism, 7, 13
national opera, 293, 296
national poetry, 306
National Socialism. *See* Nazi regime
national theater, 306
National Theater (Prague), 192-93, 196, 198,
    200-201
naturalism, 16, 232
naturalist theater, 50
Nazi regime, 9, 13; art condemned by, 207;
    assault of, on antirepresentationalism,
    224-25; *Blut und Boden* ideology of, 227;
    doctrinal and aesthetic purity of, 219;
    identifying modernism with Judaism, 18;
    on Jewish influence on music, 224-25;
    misappropriation of Nietzsche, 236n32;
    philosophers favored by, 212; purging
    Jews from musical positions, 208
Neale, J. E., 301
Nejedlý, Zdeněk, 197, 198, 199
neoclassicism, 7, 20, 271-75, 283-84
neonationalism, 103
Neue Musik (the New Music), 134, 135, 143
Neue Sachlichkeit (the New Objectivity),
    134, 135, 143, 177
Neues Deutsches Theater (Prague), 196
New Criticism, 5
new Elizabethan era, 302, 303, 305, 306, 307
Newman, Ernest, 299
Newmarch, Rosa, 202
New Modernist Studies, 4-5, 6, 7
new music, function of, 171
New Music, 226
New Musicology, 5-6, 129
New School (New York), 251
Nezval, Vítězslav, 189-90, 195, 199, 200, 201
Nichols, Roger, 83
Nietzsche, Friedrich, 1-2, 10, 37-38, 210,
    211, 213, 222; anti-Platonic stance of,
    236-37n38; Nazis' misappropriation of,
    236n32; on perception and reality, 211;
    phenomenological thinking of, 235n30;
    on Schopenhauer, 57n5; theatricality and,
    38, 54; on Wagner, 40, 44, 54, 211-12;
    writings of, 38, 40
Nijinsky, Vaslav, 3
Nocturnes (Debussy), 86, 88, 97